How Did Britain Come to This?
A century of systemic failures of governance

Gwyn Bevan

Press

Published by
LSE Press
10 Portugal Street
London WC2A 2HD
press.lse.ac.uk

Text © Gwyn Bevan, 2023

First published 2023

Cover design by Glen Wilkins, glenwilkins.com

Print and digital versions typeset by Siliconchips Services Ltd.

ISBN (Paperback): 978-1-911712-10-7
ISBN (PDF): 978-1-911712-11-4
ISBN (EPUB): 978-1-911712-12-1
ISBN (Mobi): 978-1-911712-13-8

DOI: https://doi.org/10.31389/lsepress.hdb

The full text of this book has been peer-reviewed to ensure high academic standards. For our full publishing ethics policies, see https://press.lse.ac.uk

Suggested citation:
Bevan, Gwyn (2023) *How Did Britain Come to This? A century of systemic failures of governance,* London: LSE Press.
https://doi.org/10.31389/lsepress.hdb License: CC BY-NC

To read the free, open access version of this book online, visit https://doi.org/10.31389/lsepress.hdb or scan this QR code with your mobile device:

For Gillian

Every system is perfectly designed to get the results it gets.

Paul Batalden[1]

[1] Conway, Earl and Batalden, Paul (2015) 'Like Magic? ("Every system is perfectly designed...")', *Institute for Healthcare Improvement*, blogpost. 21 August.
http://www.ihi.org/communities/blogs/origin-of-every-system-is -perfectly-designed-quote

Contents

Extended contents

List of figures

About the author

Gwyn Bevan is emeritus professor of policy analysis in, and a former head of, the Department of Management at the London School of Economics and Political Science. He is an affiliate professor in the Istituto di Management of the Scuola Superiore Sant'Anna, Pisa. He has served on advisory committees to the Inspectorate of Police and Fire Services in England and Wales, the Education Commission of the Rockefeller Foundation on research in developing countries; and governments in England on allocating resources for healthcare and public health, the reform of publicly financed legal services, and funding research into overseas aid. He was director of the Office for Healthcare Performance at the Commission for Health Improvement (2001 to 2004), which was responsible for inspections of quality of care in the NHS in England and Wales.

Preface

How Did Britain Come to This? This book aims to show that it is because, in Paul Batalden's haunting phrase, 'every system is perfectly designed to get the results it gets'. The book begins by showing how systems of governance were perfectly designed to result in scandals when the NHS was still revered, at Bristol Royal Infirmary in the 1980s and 1990s, and at Mid Staffordshire NHS Foundation Trust in the 2000s. Douglass North describes institutions as setting 'the rules of the game'. The book looks at how systems of governance developed under four different rules of the game in Britain. First, the UK's version of the minimal state in the 1920s and 1930s nurtured the growth of William Beveridge's five giant evils of Want, Idleness, Squalor, Disease and Ignorance. Second came the planned state as developed under Clement Attlee's Labour government, which tackled Beveridge's five giant evils but ran into problems in the 1970s, in council housing, running public services, high government borrowing, inflation and unemployment ('stagflation'). The Attlee settlement was largely dismantled by Margaret Thatcher's Conservative governments from 1979 to 1991. The Thatcher settlement of neoliberalism began by developing the third institution of the marketised state. That still applies to education, has been abandoned for the NHS after three failed attempts, and morphed into the fourth institution, the financialised state, in which 'only money matters'. The dysfunctional consequences of this apotheosis of neoliberalism include: the demise of successful private corporations; the Global Financial Crisis of 2008; unaffordable housing; and failures in government outsourcing and privatisation. Its structured inequalities in opportunities and incomes mean that a small minority live in a plutonomy of luxury watches, super yachts and private jets, and nearly 30 per cent of British children live in poverty, with many of their families having to choose between eating and heating in the winter.

There was once a hope that Covid-19 would, like the Second World War, create a window of opportunity for a new political settlement. The final chapter shows that Covid-19 exposed systemic weaknesses in the UK's preparedness for, and responses to, the pandemic, and that without the interventions of a courageous few there would have been even greater catastrophic outcomes. And, as the UK emerged from the shadow of Covid-19 in 2022, instead of a new political settlement, we had three prime ministers. An afterword argues that we need to move on from the settlement based on neoliberalism and indicates what an alternative would look like.

Acknowledgements

I am indebted to my grounding in mathematics from inspirational teaching in the sixth form of Manchester Grammar School and as an undergraduate at Oriel College, Oxford. This book draws on what I learnt from working for the National Coal Board, HM Treasury, London Economics and the Commission for Health Improvement; and the University of Warwick, the London School of Economics and Political Science, and medical schools of St Thomas' Hospital and the University of Bristol. I have been at LSE since 1997, where I have had the privilege of learning from our students, and teaching and research with Mara Airoldi, Simon Bastow, Timothy Besley, Christine Cope, Barbara Fasolo, Christopher Hood, Alec Morton and James Valverde. One aim of this book is to give readers a feel of what it is like to be graduate students at LSE. My obsession with improving public services has benefited so much from discussions with Michael Barber, Julian Le Grand, Rudolf Klein, Nicholas Mays, Adam Oliver and Rodney Scott, and from spending time at the University of Toronto, with Steini Brown and Carolyn Tuohy; at Dartmouth College, with David Goodman and Jack Wennberg; at Scuola Sant'Anna of Pisa, with Sabina Nuti and Milena Vainieri and those in MeSLab; and at Oxford's Blavatnik School of Government with Thomas Elston and the GoLab research team.

Michael Lewis tells great stories in diagnosing the systemic failures of the Global Financial Crisis and the US's response to Covid-19. His explanation of why academic papers are so impenetrable is that they are written so as to ward off anticipated attacks by other academics. The extent to which I have avoided that fate is due to invaluable critical feedback from Tom Gash at the start, and Jonathan Lane and Huw Bevan on early drafts of the book. My aim has been to write to help you, the reader, contribute to the debate about how we can make a better future. The book's structure and argument have benefited from editing by Patrick Dunleavy and Alice Park. I have had great support from Lucy Lambe and Ellie Potts at LSE Press. I am grateful for comments by three anonymous referees. Individual chapters have benefited from comments from, or discussions with, James Alt, Nicholas Barr, Simon Bastow, Oliver Bevan, Saul Estrin, Charles Goodhart, Keith Sisson and Yuxi Zhan. The references show how much I owe to books by Nick Timmins and Peter Hennessy, the great chroniclers of post-war Britain; to journalists at the *Financial Times* for helping me understand the impacts of financialisation; and the researchers of the House of Commons Library. My greatest debt is to my wife, Gillian Forrest, who began working in the NHS when it was the envy of the world. As a child psychiatrist, her multidisciplinary team at the Park Hospital for children in Oxford was able to heal children with severe psychiatric illnesses. She has experienced with dismay the loss of that capability in the NHS, wonders what happens to those children now, and has understood why I needed to write this book.

1. Why governance matters – analysing systemic failures in the NHS

> It may seem a strange principle to enunciate as the very first require-
> ment in a hospital that it should do the sick no harm.
>
> <div align="center">Florence Nightingale (1863) <i>Notes of Hospitals</i>[1]</div>

I begin this book with two devastating case studies of harm wrought within the English National Health Service (NHS). Pressure from courageous whistleblowers over the tragic death of a toddler at the Bristol Royal Infirmary in 1995, and a mother at Mid Staffordshire NHS Foundation Trust in 2007, eventually resulted in official public inquiries. These two cases identified different systemic failings in governance as the root causes of scandalously poor care at each hospital and why patients died who would have lived if they had gone elsewhere. They exemplify Paul Batalden's observation that 'every system is perfectly designed to get the results it gets'.[2] The analysis of the two case studies shows that details matter if we are to understand systemic failures of governance. Although much of the book is grounded in the government of Britain, I also try to follow Alfred Marshall's invaluable advice to scholars, 'always to remember the one in many and the many in one'. So, the book's central subject is the challenge of governing well. Focusing first on the NHS demonstrates why it is so hard for governments to ensure that public services are of uniformly high quality. As I write, the NHS is struggling to remain an iconic legacy of the Attlee settlement, established by Labour governments from 1945 to 1951. That settlement set a central frame for post-war British politics until 1979. The subsequent radical changes in governance of the NHS, based on the idea of markets, are symbolic of the reach of the Thatcher settlement, which was established by her Conservative governments from 1979 to 1991.

The chapter has four sections. The first is about how the scandal at Bristol continued, in the 1980s, under the Attlee settlement, and the 1990s, in the 'internal market' of the Thatcher settlement. The second section is about how Blair's New Labour government aimed to fix the failures of self-regulation

How to cite this book chapter:

Bevan, Gwyn (2023) *How Did Britain Come to This? A century of systemic failures of governance*, London: LSE Press, pp. 1–20.
https://doi.org/10.31389/lsepress.hdb.a License: CC BY-NC

by the medical profession by requiring NHS organisations to implement systems of clinical governance and holding them to account with an independent inspectorate. The third section is about the grand strategy of the Blair government to remedy limitations of governance by targets and the 'internal market' with an attempt to make a regulated market work. That resulted in the scandal at Mid Staffordshire. The fourth section illustrates a recurring theme of this book: the failures of experiments with markets that developed for services under the Thatcher settlement. These services have characteristics that cause markets to fail (healthcare is the exemplar – see Chapter 8), and the UK lacks the institutions that could make them work. The final section outlines the structure of the argument in the rest of the book.

1.1 The Bristol babies' scandal

Mandy Evans remembers her son Joshua Loveday as being well and full of life for his first real Christmas in 1994 when he was 18 months old.[3] But there was a shadow hanging over those precious days: Joshua had a congenital heart defect, and would survive only if he had a successful switch operation. This major open-heart surgery transposes the great arteries through which blood flows to and from the heart.[4] Now only two or three babies die in 100 operations, and one has complications (such as brain damage). Back then, typically about 10 in 100 died.[5] But Joshua's operation was scheduled for 12 January 1995 in the Bristol Royal Infirmary, which *Private Eye* had called, in 1992, 'the killing fields' and 'the departure lounge'.[6] Dr Stephen Bolsin was the source of that information.[7] He had been appointed at Bristol in 1988 as a consultant anaesthetist, having worked at two specialist centres for paediatric cardiac surgery in London (the Brompton and Great Ormond Street hospitals).

Bolsin was deeply troubled about how much longer surgery took at Bristol because that increased the risk of bad outcomes.[8] From 1990, he courageously persisted in raising concerns over the evidence he had of the poor outcomes at Bristol, despite being under pressure not to do so. He had raised that problem with the trust's chief executive, Dr John Roylance; the professor of cardiac surgery at Bristol, Gianni Angelini; and the trust's medical director, Mr James Wisheart, who did the paediatric cardiac surgery with Mr Janardan Dhasmana.[9] On 19 July 1994, Dr Peter Doyle, the senior medical officer in the Department of Health, came to a meeting at Bristol. Bolsin went with him in a cab back to the station and gave him an envelope with data relating to his concerns. Doyle 'did not read it and put it away in a filing cabinet without further scrutiny', but he did seek reassurances from Professor Angelini and Dr Roylance.[10]

On 6 January 1995, Gianni Angelini tried to persuade Wisheart that it would be unwise for Dhasmana to proceed with Joshua's operation. Angelini discussed this with Roylance and Doyle, and put his views in writing.[11] On 11 January, at 5.30 pm, there was an extraordinary meeting of nine people involved in paediatric cardiac surgery, to discuss whether that operation ought to go ahead. Wisheart did not disclose to those at the meeting that this was opposed by Angelini.[12] Nor that Dr Roylance had in mind commissioning an independent review of their service.[13] The outcome was the decision that Dhasmana would proceed with the operation. Bolsin was the only one who disagreed. He contacted Doyle to let him know that a switch operation was scheduled for the next day.[14] That evening, Doyle telephoned Roylance, expressing worries about the operation going ahead. Roylance said that, 'although he was a doctor, he could not intervene over the clinical judgement of the doctors directly involved'.[15] At 11pm, as Joshua's parents were going to bed, there was a knock at the door: they were required to sign the consent form for the operation. 'Mr Dhasmana said Joshua had an 80% chance of survival. They were reassured, signed the consent form and went to bed.'[16]

Stephen Bolsin wanted to tell Joshua's mother and father, who were staying at the hospital that night, to take Joshua away, but realised that, if he had done so, he would have been struck off the medical register. When his wife, Maggie, then volunteered to do so, he told her that would result in her being struck off the nurses' register. In 1996, Bolsin left Bristol for Geelong Hospital, near Melbourne, Australia – he was advised that he would not be appointable in Britain.[17] (Sixteen years later, in 2013, the Royal College of Anaesthetists awarded Professor Steven Bolsin the RCA Medal for promoting safety in anaesthesia that acknowledged his vital actions at Bristol, which he hoped would 'help people to stand up and speak out when they need to'.[18])

On the morning of 12 January, when the surgical staff tried to wheel Joshua away, Mandy Evans clung on to the trolley and was weeping hysterically as the hospital staff pulled her away. As they did so, she remembers 'being transfixed by the expression on the face of one of hospital staff. It wasn't blank, it was like fear. If I read it now, he was saying to me, "What are you doing? Take him away."'[19] The surgery lasted eight hours. Mr Dhasmana had to redo the switch operation. One of Joshua's coronary arteries was severed. At 7.30pm, Joshua's parents were told that he had died on the operating table.[20] When Dr Doyle was told of Joshua's death, he wrote to Dr Roylance, saying 'it would be extremely inadvisable to undertake any further neonatal or infant cardiac surgery'.[21]

In June 1998, the General Medical Council (GMC) found James Wisheart, Dr John Roylance and Janardan Dhasmana guilty of serious professional misconduct. Wisheart was criticised for not letting Dhasmana know that Angelini opposed the operation on Joshua, Roylance for not intervening, and Dhasmana for not stopping paediatric cardiac surgery before the operation on Joshua Loveday. Wisheart and Roylance were struck off the medical register; Dhasmana was allowed to remain on the register subject to a three-year ban on doing paediatric cardiac surgery.[22] Sir Robert Francis, the defence lawyer for John Roylance at the GMC hearings, had been so sickened by its punitive atmosphere that it had made him feel like emigrating.[23] Professor Martin Elliott, an expert paediatric cardiac surgeon, was at the GMC hearings and was also distressed by 'the daily humiliation of the surgeons'. He was also troubled by 'the lack of criticism of wider system issues'. He argued that others at Bristol were equally culpable:

> It takes a remarkable amount of confidence to operate on a child, and one does the procedure within a team that is watching every aspect of your work and performance.

> Sometimes, when the outcome of a procedure has been poor and a child has suffered, it can be very difficult to operate the next day. I have felt this and I have relied on those around me to 'get me back on the horse'. ... The surgeons may have held the knife in the operating room, but the cardiologists had the right and perhaps the responsibility to refer patients elsewhere, to a centre where results for such cases were known to be good. Just because the consent form is signed by the surgeon, it does not mean that they alone bear the responsibility for the outcome. I understand that, as a surgeon, one should have the insight and strength to be able to recognise that one should not be doing certain operations, but just as one may need moral support to get back on the horse, one may need as much or perhaps even more to be forced off it ... and that is most effectively done by one's immediate colleagues and line management.[24]

At the GMC hearings, parents of babies who had died brought floral tributes, and those of children who were brain damaged or who had learning difficulties as a result of operations following surgery at Bristol displayed a board with 160 names. They pressed for a public inquiry, which began in October 1998. Its report (the Kennedy Report) was published in 2001.[25] Its expert statistical analysis estimated that, between '1988 and 1994, the mortality rate at Bristol was roughly double that elsewhere in five of seven years', and between 1991 and 1995 there had been about 30 excess deaths (as compared with other centres).[26] The Kennedy Report argued that:

> whatever the temptation to focus on the actions of individuals and to seek to blame someone when things go wrong, it is important to pay attention to the systems in which those individuals find themselves.[27]

So, how were the systems of governance in the 1980s and 1990s designed to enable Bristol to continue to deliver scandalously poor outcomes for paediatric cardiac surgery?

Good outcomes from paediatric cardiac surgery are more likely when concentrated in specialist centres that do high volumes of cases. That is why, in 1984, the Department of Health decided that paediatric cardiac surgery be

recognised as a supra-regional service for earmarked funding in a few desig-
nated centres governed by the Supra-Regional Service Advisory Group. Officials from the department, of whom Dr Peter Doyle was one, were key to the
running of that Advisory Group. It was chaired by a chairman of a regional
health authority; its members were doctors and NHS managers.[28] The Kennedy Report describes their choice of Bristol, as a centre for paediatric cardiac
surgery, as 'something of a mystery' because 'problems about the adequacy of
care were built into Bristol from the start'.[29] Care was delivered across two separate sites, there was a shortage of paediatric cardiologists, and the part-time
paediatric cardiac surgeons did low numbers of operations.[30] The justification
for choosing Bristol as a centre, rather than expanding the capacity of Southampton or Birmingham, seems to have been its convenience for parents living
in the South West and Wales.[31] In 1991, Martin Elliott decided against moving
to Bristol because he found its arrangements to be 'inefficient, archaic, inhib-
itory to progress and potentially dangerous'.[32] In 1992, when the low numbers
of cases at the Bristol Royal Infirmary continued, the Advisory Group decided
against its de-designation because 'it would be difficult if not invidious to [do
that] on the basis of surgical expertise'.[33]

The leading psychologist Daniel Kahneman describes how the way we make
decisions depends on how we frame our choices. And that, when we decide,
we focus on the regret we imagine that we would feel afterwards, having made
that choice, when outcomes are known.[34] In healthcare, typically, the choices
are framed for us. The Kennedy Report points out that 'if it had been put to
parents that by travelling 80 miles further up a motorway, the chances of survival of their child could well be doubled (or more) the parents would have
probably opted for elsewhere'.[35] *Eighty miles?* If the choice were framed in that
way, then most of us would willingly go to the end of the world. For Mandy
Evans, the regret she experiences at the thought that had Joshua had his operation elsewhere, he could have survived, at times made her physically ill.[36] For
Joshua's father, Bert Loveday, the choice was framed for him as either agreeing
to the operation, to give his son a high chance of survival, or let him die. He
was unable to cope with having signed the consent form for Joshua's operation. He became progressively more depressed and disoriented, participated
in an armed robbery, gave himself up, got three years, and hanged himself in
his cell. By 2000, three other 'Bristol parents' had died by suicide.[37]

In 1991, the Thatcher government aimed to introduce financial incentives to improve hospital performance in the NHS through competition. In
this 'internal market', the NHS was reorganised into a 'purchaser'/'provider'
split: local health authorities stopped running local hospitals and became
'purchasers' of hospital services, and NHS hospitals became self-governing NHS trusts (see Chapter 8). The 'purchasers' were supposed to contract
selectively between hospitals competing on price and quality in a system in
which 'money followed the patient'.[38] There was, however, a lack of comparative information on prices and virtually none on outcomes.[39] And, as the
Blair government argued, in *The NHS Plan* of 2000, purchasers were deterred

from moving a contract for an obviously poor service away from a local trust because the resultant loss of income could destabilise the trust financially and undermine its capacity to deliver other services, such as accident and emergency services, where people want to go to their local hospital.[40] Paediatric cardiac surgery was, exceptionally, where the 'internal market' ought to have worked. The Advisory Group became the 'purchaser' and had data on costs and outcomes (mortality rates). Parents would have been willing to travel to a centre with better outcomes. But nothing changed. The Advisory Group relied on individual units to ensure a satisfactory service and lacked 'the machinery' (a spreadsheet?) to analyse mortality data.[41]

1.2 If Bristol was the problem, was clinical governance the answer?

Tony Blair's government, elected in 1997, sought to ensure that there was not another 'Bristol' in the NHS. They established the Commission for Health Improvement (CHI) in 1999 to inspect the implementation of clinical governance by NHS organisations in England and Wales. The CHI's rolling programme of clinical governance reviews assessed how effectively NHS organisations had implemented systems to assure and improve quality of care.[42] I worked for the CHI, as the director of the Office for Information on Health Care Performance, and was responsible for the analyses for our clinical governance reviews. From inspecting all acute trusts in England and Wales, we developed five golden rules:

1. *Judgement not standards.* We did not use standards because none were available from the Department of Health when we began. And we were concerned that doing so would lead to trusts responding by ticking boxes. The CHI's review manager organised the inspections for our review team, which included active clinicians and a member of the public, who were trained to exercise their judgement on what was, and was not, acceptable.
2. *Routinely collected data are inadequate.* Because the statistical data that were routinely available were so limited in scope (mainly mortality rates), our analyses were mainly of textual material: reports by external bodies, internal reports, minutes of meetings, and reports from the CHI's staff of feedback from local people reported to our publicly organised sessions. The CHI's analysts explored with each trust the issues that emerged in an interactive dialogue and prepared a report for our review team prior to their visit.
3. *Visits.* The week's visit by our review team was the focus of our inspections. They interviewed staff and met the trust board to investigate issues identified from the CHI's analyses. They experienced

the atmosphere at the trust and its likely impact on the quality of care. These visits provided ample opportunity for whistleblowers to relate their concerns, in confidence, to members of our review team.

4. *Self-assessments by trusts are unreliable.* We found that the trusts we had most heavily criticised for their weak clinical governance were in pathological denial about their problems.

5. *It is essential to inspect all general acute hospitals.* We found that quality varied greatly within the same general acute hospital, which had typically at least one dysfunctional clinical team. The challenge in organising inspections so that they are 'targeted and proportionate' is within hospitals – *not* choosing which hospitals to inspect.[43]

The 2001 Kennedy Report diagnosed institutional arrangements as the root cause of the Bristol scandal: there was confusion about which organisation was responsible for assuring and monitoring the quality of care. The report pointed out that in this confusion, the health, welfare and indeed lives of children were at stake in an administrative game of 'pass the parcel'.[44] My recurrent thought experiment at the CHI was to ask: 'If we'd done a clinical governance review of the Bristol Royal Infirmary in the 1990s would we have discovered what was wrong?' I knew we would not have been able to have done that from our analyses of routinely available statistical data at the hospital level: 30 excess deaths over five years is too small a number to be spotted. We would only have found out what was wrong from the serendipitous elements of the CHI's visits: reports to the CHI's staff at publicly organised sessions where parents and local GPs would have been able to voice their concerns in confidence. Plus, the week's visit by the CHI's review team offered safe opportunities for whistleblowing by any staff members who were troubled by poor quality of care and bad outcomes.

1.3 Mid Staffordshire – from clinical governance to market and regulatory failure

In 2002, the Blair government developed a grand strategy that aimed to improve patient care in another competitive market. The role of the Department of Health changed from being responsible for running the NHS to developing a competitive market for publicly financed hospital care. NHS patients could choose to go for elective care between NHS hospitals and thousands of hospitals and clinics in the independent sector. In 2004, the government reorganised regulation of quality of care in the NHS and independent sector:

- It abolished the CHI, and also the National Care Standards Commission for the independent providers of health and social care (17 days after it had just begun).[45]

- A new Commission for Healthcare Audit and Inspection, which became the Healthcare Commission (HCC), was established to regulate the quality of healthcare in the NHS and the independent sector.[46] (The HCC was later abolished in 2009 and replaced seven years later by the Care Quality Commission (CQC), spanning both the NHS/ health and social care sectors in England, a role that it still has.[47])
- The government also established an organisation called Monitor to regulate NHS foundation trusts – a set of high-performing NHS trusts that had 'earned autonomy' to be freed from bureaucratic control by the Department of Health.[48] (Monitor became part of a wider body, NHS Improvement, in April 2016.[49])

In this new system, the Healthcare Commission assessed quality of care in annual health checks. These rated the Mid Staffordshire NHS Foundation Trust as 'fair' for 2005–06[50] and 2006–07, when it was praised for being one of the four '*most improved acute and specialist trusts*' (emphasis added).[51] In 2007, Julie Bailey was outraged at 'the gross negligence and cruelty in the treatment of her 86-year-old mother, Bella, at Stafford hospital in the eight weeks before she died'.[52] Julie Bailey became the whistleblower whose determination, and organisation of the pressure group 'Cure the NHS', led to a public inquiry into Mid Staffordshire NHS Foundation Trust.[53] (In 2013, *The Guardian* described the consequences: her mother's grave was vandalised and she moved into hiding after being subjected to threats and abuse.[54])

The report of the public inquiry into Mid Staffordshire NHS Foundation Trust, chaired by Sir Robert Francis, began by stating that: 'Between 2005 and 2008 conditions of appalling care were able to flourish in the main hospital serving the people of Stafford and its surrounding area.' These included patients being left in excrement in soiled bed clothes for lengthy periods, assisted neither in their feeding (when they could not eat without help) nor in their toileting (despite persistent requests for help); treated by staff with what appeared to be callous indifference; and denied privacy and dignity, even in death.[55] Over that period there were estimated to be 500 excess deaths.[56]

The Francis Report was scathing in its criticisms of Monitor and HCC. Monitor approved the application from the board of the Mid Staffordshire General Hospital NHS Trust to become a foundation trust in its 'elaborate, resource-consuming process'.[57] That process:

> failed to achieve what should have been its primary objective – ensuring that the only organisations authorised were those with the ability and capacity to deliver services compliant with minimum standards on a consistent and sustainable basis.[58]

Although HCC was 'the first organisation out of the plethora with relevant responsibilities to identify serious cause for concern, and to take the action which led to the full exposure of the scandal', it had 'failed to prevent or detect over three-quarters of its lifetime what has been described as the biggest scandal in NHS history'.[59] Unlike at Bristol, that public inquiry had no need of expert statistical analysis because the appalling care at Mid Staffordshire was so glaringly obvious.

The Francis Report identified four key themes as explaining the chronic problems at the trust:

- The trust board leadership between 2006 and 2009 was characterised by lack of experience, great self-confidence, a focus on financial issues and on obtaining foundation trust (FT) status. It aimed only to meet targets and lacked insight into the impact of their decisions on patient care. The non-executive leadership remained aloof from serious operational concerns even when they had obvious strategic significance and the potential for causing risk to patients.
- The clinical executive leadership lacked, or did not raise, a strong professional voice on the board. The medical professional staff remained largely disengaged from management throughout the period and did not pursue their concerns effectively or persistently.
- There was a culture of tolerance of poor practice. The significance of concerning mortality figures or of patient complaints were constantly denied, and top managers operated in isolation with a lack of openness.
- The focus on achieving financial targets led to staffing cuts made without any adequate assessment of the effect on patients. Once it was appreciated that there was a shortage of nursing staff, ineffective steps were taken to address it. Serious concerns about accident and emergency (A&E) care were not addressed. Issues of poor clinical governance were not remedied.[60]

Florence Nightingale would have been appalled at the way hospital staff at Mid Staffordshire would do the sick harm, on an industrial scale, day in day out, for years. But, as the Francis Report observes, that record was hidden in plain sight from 'a plethora of agencies, scrutiny groups, commissioners, regulators and professional bodies'.[61] The system was so dysfunctional because its key players failed in their roles, did not understand what each was supposed to do, and failed to collaborate.

- The local 'purchasers' were so incapable at monitoring quality that 'it is not in the least surprising that, in spite of the rhetoric of quality, one of the worst examples of bad quality service delivery imaginable was not detected by this system'.[62] They took so long subsequently to address issues because of the obstacles to moving contracts identified by *The NHS Plan* in 2000.[63] In addition, the wide local media coverage of the

scandal at Mid Staffordshire had no impact on the numbers of patents 'choosing' to go there.[64]
- HCC relied on local organisations to check the veracity of trusts' self-assessments of the quality of their services, and Monitor to raise concerns over quality of care. But these organisations assumed that quality of care was being assessed by HCC and Monitor, and they detected Mid Staffordshire's self-assessments were wrong only after HCC's investigation.[65]
- HCC lacked financial expertise and Monitor lacked clinical expertise. Each worked quite independently of the other. So together they proved to be incapable of recognising that the severe reductions in costs and staff numbers by the board at Mid Staffordshire would impact on its safety and quality of care.[66]

So, how did such an incoherent and inadequate regulatory system ever come about? And why did the Blair government decide on their grand strategy in 2002? What did it get right and wrong? And what went so awry in its implementation?

1.4 Diagnosing the causes of systemic failures in governance of the NHS

Julian Le Grand described governance based on trust and altruism as one of the founding principles of the welfare state, as developed by the Attlee government from 1945 to 1951:

> Professionals, such as doctors and teachers were assumed to be motivated primarily by their professional ethic, and hence to be concerned only with the interests of the people they were serving. Politicians, civil servants, state bureaucrats, and managers were supposed accurately to divine social and individual needs in the areas concerned, to be motivated to meet those needs and hence operate services that did the best possible job from the resources available.[67]

Le Grand argued that the Attlee settlement assumed that *all* who worked in the NHS were 'knights' who were dedicated to healing and caring for patients and could be blindly trusted to act ethically and professionally. Any such lingering belief was shattered in 1998, which Kamran Abbasi described as an '*Annus horribilis*' for the medical profession. His leader in the *British Medical Journal*, titled 'Butchers and gropers', was about the:

> Horror stories of medical incompetence, arrogance, and libidinousness have filled newspapers; broadsheets and tabloids have been

united in their condemnation of a profession unable to regulate itself except when it's too late.[68]

The Bristol scandal was just one horror story.

Le Grand also argued that in the Attlee settlement those in government and professionals could treat the recipients of their services as mere 'pawns' (for example, in the decision to locate paediatric cardiac surgery at Bristol and its consequences). The scandals at Bristol and Mid Staffordshire illustrate a classic problem of effective governance: the external agencies of government can be captured by the producers, for example, deciding against the de-designation of Bristol on the basis of surgical expertise.[69] (The way Julie Bailey, the whistleblower at Mid Staffordshire, was treated shows the intensity of this producer capture.) These scandals also show the problems of trying to govern healthcare by markets. In 1997, the Blair government abandoned the idea of hospital competition for the NHS and returned to governance by trust and altruism.[70] So, although the government set targets for reducing waiting lists, when hospitals failed to meet targets, they were rewarded with extra funding to do so. That, by assuming all were 'knights', created perverse incentives.[71]

In the midst of an acute 'winter crisis' in the NHS, in 1999/2000, Clive Smee, the chief economist of the Department of Health, was reading drafts of an OECD report. It described the NHS as underfunded, with outdated hospitals, poor clinical outcomes and long waiting times.[72] On Sunday, 16 January 2000, when interviewed on the television programme *Breakfast with Frost* – 'the most expensive breakfast in British history' – Tony Blair pledged the government to raising the percentage of GDP that the UK spent on healthcare to the European average.[73] This pledge was made without consulting his infuriated Chancellor of the Exchequer, Gordon Brown.[74] Figure 1.1 shows what that meant with a rapid increase in funding up to 2010. It also shows how the NHS was then subjected to no increase as a percentage of GDP for the next decade (2010 to 2020).

To justify the increased funding of the NHS, the Prime Minister's Delivery Unit (PMDU) held the Department of Health to account for transforming NHS waiting times. The PMDU, established in 2000, was led by Michael Barber to tackle 'awful' performance in the NHS, schools, transport and crime.[75] It set increasingly demanding targets to reduce the maximum wait for NHS patients for elective surgery, from 18 months in 2001, to 18 weeks in 2009.[76]

To ensure that the PMDU's demanding targets were met, the Department of Health's *The NHS Plan* of 2000 outlined what became a new regime of 'star ratings' (see Chapter 8).[77] Consequently, hospital waiting times were transformed in England (but not in the devolved countries of the UK).[78] Those at the heart of the Blair government recognised, however, that top-down targets could improve NHS performance from 'awful' to 'adequate' only; and the public wanted a service that was 'good' or 'great'.[79] Hence the government's later grand strategy, in 2002, was to move from governance by targets to a second attempt at an NHS quasi-market, which entailed radical changes to regulation of quality.

Figure 1.1: NHS spend as a per cent of the UK's GDP, from 1960 to 2019

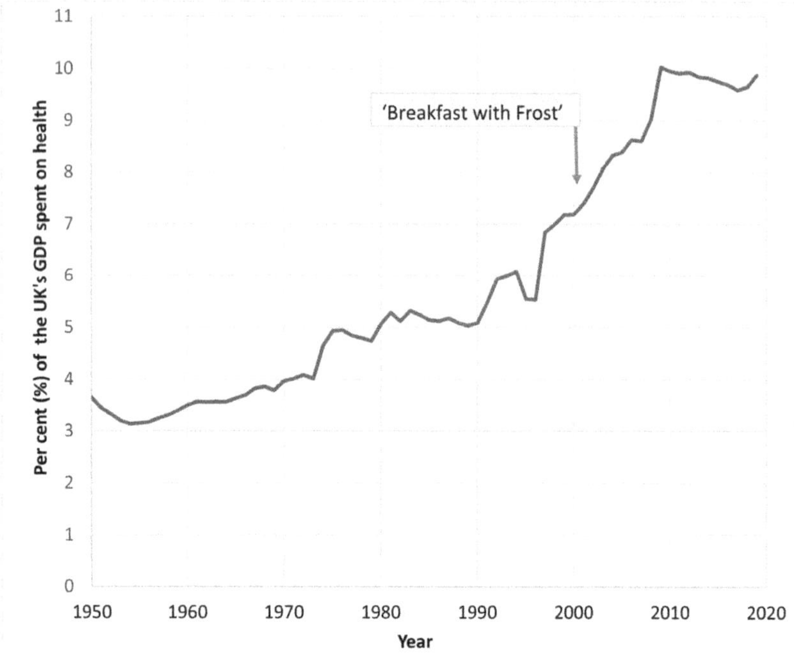

Source: Office of Health Economics and OECD.[80]

The Commission for Health Improvement was an oxymoron: a supposedly 'independent' body subject to direction by the secretary of state for health. In my experience, officials in the Department of Health ceded power to bodies like the CHI as willingly a leech gives up sucking blood. So, they would have felt unhappy that the government's grand strategy had proposed establishing, as the CHI's successor, 'a new tough independent healthcare regulator/inspectorate covering both the NHS and the private sector, with a new Chief Inspector of Healthcare' – one not appointed by ministers and reporting annually to Parliament.[81] It did not happen. The Francis Report emphasised that the HCC's board was subject to being 'hired and fired by the Secretary of State' and described its system of regulation as one which it was 'given to run' (emphasis added) by the Department of Health.[82] The department's abiding priorities were finance and hospital waiting times. That is what the Kennedy Report found in the 1980s and 1990s.[83] And, in 2000, for the regime of star ratings for hospitals, the Department of Health initially proposed that it would be driven by performance on waiting times and finance only. However, on this occasion the CHI was able to persuade ministers to incorporate assessments from its earlier inspections: otherwise, another Bristol could have become a 'high-performing' three-star trust.[84] The Francis Report points out that the HCC's inspections were based on a generic set of core standards 'formulated not by the regulator but by the government, thereby inhibiting the engagement with the standards of those working in the system and therefore the effectiveness of the regulator.'[85]

The Department of Health required the HCC to develop a 'targeted and proportionate' system of inspections on a 'level playing field' for the NHS and independent sectors. The HCC correctly decided it could not organise its inspections of the thousands of organisations in the independent health and social care sector based on visits, but that did not entail doing likewise for the 156 general acute NHS trusts in England.[86] The HCC wrongly framed its regulatory task in terms of the relative *numbers* of organisations in the two sectors (dominated by the independent sector). But expenditure on private healthcare was about 7 per cent of NHS expenditure and it was concentrated on general and elective surgery.[87] A 'targeted and proportionate' system ought to have taken into account the far greater scale and complexity of care provided by the NHS. That is where the risk of failings in quality of care are highest and harder to identify from routinely available data. Instead, however, for NHS trusts, the HCC abandoned a rolling programme of visits for 'inspections' based only on the Department of Health's core standards, and analyses of the basic data that were routinely available, and self-assessments.[88] The way that the Department of Health framed the HCC's regulatory task proved to be quite incapable of detecting the pathologies of governance by targets, which the CHI had found in visits by its review teams.[89]

My second thought experiment is this: what would have happened if the CHI had continued its rolling programme of visits and inspected the Mid Staffordshire trust in 2006? The CHI's inspection of Mid Staffordshire in 2002 highlighted shortages of nurses, the poor quality of its clinical data, and that the board had prioritised improving its financial position and performance on waiting times over the quality of patient care.[90] Hence an inspection by the CHI in 2006 would have begun by looking for improvements in each of those problem areas. If the trust had claimed that its high mortality rates were a consequence of the poor quality of its clinical data, that would have raised *two* red flags. The publicly organised sessions arranged by our review manager also would have offered the same opportunity for the public to report episodes of truly appalling care, as found by the HCC's investigation in 2008.[91] So, if the Blair government had established as the CHI's successor 'a new tough independent healthcare regulator/inspectorate' that had followed the CHI's golden rules in framing regulation to be 'targeted and proportionate', would that have prevented the scandal at Mid Staffordshire?

1.5 The structure of this book – political settlements and their fault lines

Every system of governance, once established, will have some weaknesses – some key areas where things can go wrong or be badly handled. A concern for any state is inequality across geographical areas, the multiple factors that may tend to make geography destiny for people depending on where they live. In Chapter 2, I take a long view at some fundamental geographical fault lines in Europe, beginning with how the Black Death in mediaeval times created a fault line between East and West Europe and Northern and Southern Italy, leading on to enduring centuries of inequalities between regions, and later to many of the failures of communism. Then, focusing down within the UK, and looking much more recently, the chapter also describes how Oldham (where I grew up) and Oxford (near where I now live) have grown apart over my lifetime.

The next two chapters explain the two major political settlements of post-war Britain, of Clement Attlee's Labour and Margaret Thatcher's Conservative governments. I look at how they created long-run systems of governance that went on to produce different outcomes for those living in Oldham and Oxford. Both settlements were important in establishing different set of *institutions*, defined by Douglass North as 'the rules of the game' that shape how people interact as members of organisations in social, political or economic settings.[92] This book focuses on how public institutions shaped systems of governance. The rules of the game of the Attlee settlement covered in Chapter 3 centred on institutions of central planning designed to tackle William Beveridge's five giant evils – 'Want, Disease, Ignorance, Idleness and Squalor'. Chapter 4 describes how, by the 1970s, those institutions were failing and justified the shift to a different set of rules of the game of the Thatcher settlement, which Chapter 5 shows were based on the ideology of neoliberalism. Chapter 6 uses the institutional economics of transaction costs, developed by Oliver Williamson, to examine the pros and cons of using markets in privatisation and outsourcing, and the consequences of financialisaton of those markets and housing. Chapter 7 deploys the economics of transaction costs to examine the marketisation of our schools and universities. Margaret Thatcher famously used to assert TINA – There Is No Alternative – to her neoliberal policies. Chapters 6 and 7 suggest that now there has to be. Chapter 8 is about why markets fail in healthcare and effective alternative systems of governance to steer healthcare in the 'iron triangle' of the objectives of cost control, equity and high performance. Chapter 9 compares systems of governance in England and Germany in response to the Covid-19 pandemic. It examines why Germany had a substantially lower mortality rate in the 'opening game' (before effective vaccines were available) and England was more successful in the 'middle game' (after vaccines became available). This chapter shows again the importance of authoritative independent bodies and courageous individuals. The Afterword looks towards a new political settlement to tackle our five giant evils from 40 years of neoliberalism: Want is even more acute, and we are troubled by systems that result in Insecurity, Ill-health, Miseducation and Despair.

Endnotes

SSH here means 'Secretary of State for Health'.

[1] Nightingale, Florence (1863) *Notes of hospitals* (third edition), UK: Longman, p.iii.
https://archive.org/details/notesonhospital01nighgoog/page/n10/mode/2up

[2] Conway, Earl and Batalden, Paul (2015) 'Like magic? ("Every system is perfectly designed…")', Institute for Healthcare Improvement, blogpost. 21 August. https://perma.cc/9L6P-DL35

[3] *BBC News* (1998) 'Our rights were ignored', 8 June.
https://perma.cc/QMP3-ECQH

[4] British Heart Foundation (2008) *Understanding your child's heart. Transposition of the great arteries.*

[5] *BBC News*, 'Our rights were ignored'.

[6] *BBC News* (1999) 'Ward known as "departure lounge"', 19 October.
https://perma.cc/DB9D-TGNH

[7] 1000 Lives Improvement (2012) 'Phil Hammond – Working for Private Eye'. YouTube, 31 May.
https://www.youtube.com/watch?v=D5pVM1qSbDc

[8] Secretary of State for Health (SSH) (2001) *Learning from Bristol – Report of the public inquiry into children's heart surgery at the Bristol Royal Infirmary* (The Kennedy Report), CM 5207(1), UK: The Stationery Office, pp.44, 136. https://webarchive.nationalarchives.gov.uk/ukgwa/20090811143758/http://www.bristol-inquiry.org.uk/index.htm; and A Change of Direction (2017) *Interview with Stephen Bolsin (subtitled eng)* [Video]. YouTube, 12 October.
https://www.youtube.com/watch?v=2yzYOAQy6Bg

[9] SSH, *Learning from Bristol*, pp.137–49.

[10] SSH, *Learning from Bristol*, pp.157–58; and *BBC News* (n.d.) 'How the scandal developed'. https://perma.cc/D2DU-K4B2

[11] SSH, *Learning from Bristol*, p.149.

[12] Dyer, Clare (1998) 'Bristol doctors found guilty of serious professional misconduct', *BMJ*, vol. 316, p.1924.
https://doi.org/10.1136/bmj.316.7149.1924a

[13] SSH, *Learning from Bristol*, p.169.

[14] SSH, *Learning from Bristol*, p.149.

[15] *BBC News* (1999) 'Uncovering the Bristol scandal', 15 March.
https://perma.cc/T87M-77T8

[16] *BBC News*, 'Our rights were ignored'.

[17] The Whistleblower Interview Project (2018) *Stephen Bolsin* [Video], YouTube, 6 March. https://www.youtube.com/watch?v=XXHcLDWTuFA&t=1s

[18] *BBC News* (2013) 'Bristol babies whistleblower Steven Bolsin given college award', 23 October. https://perma.cc/BZ5V-F669

[19] Ellen, Barbara (2000) 'I saw fear on the nurse's face', *The Guardian*, 30 September. https://perma.cc/F65G-56XB

[20] *BBC News*, 'Our rights were ignored'.

[21] SSH, *Learning from Bristol*, p.150.

[22] Dyer, Clare, 'Bristol doctors found guilty of serious professional misconduct'.

[23] Elliott, Martin (2015) *The Bristol scandal and its consequences: Politics, rationalisation and the use and abuse of information.* Gresham Lecture, 18 February. https://www.gresham.ac.uk/lectures-and-events/the-bristol-scandal -and-its-consequences-politics-rationalisation-and-the-use

[24] Elliot, Martin, *The Bristol scandal and its consequences.*

[25] Ballinger, Alex (2017) 'Lessons have not been learned from Bristol heart babies scandal 20 years on, says lawyer', *Bristol Post*, 10 August. https://perma.cc/NH8F-Y93R

[26] SSH, *Learning from Bristol*, p.4.

[27] SSH, *Learning from Bristol*, p.258.

[28] Hansard (9 March 1988) HL Deb, vol. 494 cc791-2WA. https://api.parliament.uk/historic-hansard/written-answers/1988/mar /09/nhs-supra-regional-services

[29] SSH, *Learning from Bristol*, p.226.

[30] SSH, *Learning from Bristol*, p.44.

[31] SSH, *Learning from Bristol*, p.227.

[32] Elliot, Martin, *The Bristol scandal and its consequences.*

[33] SSH, *Learning from Bristol*, p.188.

[34] Kahneman, Daniel (2011) *Thinking, fast and slow*, US: Farrar, Strauss and Giroux, Chapter 34, 'Frames and reality', pp.383–74; and Chapter 26 'Prospect theory', pp.278–88.

[35] SSH, *Learning from Bristol*, p.227.

[36] Ellen, Barbara, 'I saw fear on the nurse's face'.

[37] Ellen, Barbara, 'I saw fear on the nurse's face'.

[38] Secretaries of State for Health, Wales, Northern Ireland and Scotland (1989) 'Funding hospital services', in *Working for Patients*. Cm 555, UK: The Stationery Office, Chapter 4, pp.30–38.

[39] Tuohy, Carolyn (1999) *Accidental logics*, UK: Oxford University Press, pp.170–71.

[40] Secretary of State for Health (2000) *The NHS plan*. Cm 4818-I, UK: The Stationery Office.

[41] SSH, *Learning from Bristol*, p.188.

[42] SSH (1997) *The new NHS: modern, dependable*, Cm 3807, UK: The Stationery Office; Department of Health (1998) *A first class service: quality in the new NHS*, UK: Department of Health.

[43] Bevan, Gwyn and Cornwell, Jocelyn (2006) 'Structure and logic of regulation and governance of quality of health care: Was OFSTED a model for the Commission for Health Improvement?' *Health Economics, Policy and Law*, vol, 1, no. 4, p.357. https://doi.org/10.1017/S1744133106005020

[44] SSH, *Learning from Bristol*, p.6.

[45] SSH (2002) *Delivering the NHS Plan*. Cm 5503, UK: The Stationery Office, p.38.

[46] SSH, *Delivering the NHS Plan*, pp.38–39.

[47] Healthcare Commission (n.d.) 'Healthcare Commission website'. https://www.gov.uk/government/organisations/healthcare-commission

[48] Health and Social Care (Community Health and Standards) Act 2003. https://www.legislation.gov.uk/ukpga/2003/43/section/2/enacted

[49] Department of Health and Social Care (n.d.) Monitor. https://www.gov.uk/government/organisations/monitor

[50] Healthcare Commission (2006) *The annual health check: Assessing and rating the NHS. NHS performance ratings 2005/2006*, UK: Health Care Commission.

[51] Healthcare Commission (2007) *The annual health check 2006/2007. A national overview of the performance of NHS trusts in England*, UK: Health Care Commission, p.33.

[52] Adams, Tim (2013) 'Mid Staffs whistleblower Julie Bailey: "I don't go out here on my own any more"', *The Guardian*, 26 October. https://perma.cc/R3SN-GBHH

[53] Cure the NHS (n.d.) *Cure the NHS*. http://www.curethenhs.co.uk; Secretary of State for Health (SSH) (2013) *Report of the Mid Staffordshire NHS Foundation Trust Public Inquiry*, UK: The Stationery Office, p.9.

https://assets.publishing.service.gov.uk/government/uploads/system
/uploads/attachment_data/file/279124/0947.pdf

[54] Adams, Tim, 'Mid Staffs whistleblower Julie Bailey: "I don't go out here on my own any more"'.

[55] SSH, *Report of the Mid Staffordshire NHS Foundation Trust Public Inquiry*, p.7.

[56] Weinberg, Isobel (2013) 'The Mid Staffs scandal'. *BMJ*, vol. 346, f941. https://doi.org/10.1136/sbmj.f941

[57] SSH, *Report of the Mid Staffordshire NHS Foundation Trust Public Inquiry*, p.7.

[58] SSH, *Report of the Mid Staffordshire NHS Foundation Trust Public Inquiry*, p.53.

[59] SSH, *Report of the Mid Staffordshire NHS Foundation Trust Public Inquiry*, p.54.

[60] SSH (2010) *Independent Inquiry into care provided by Mid Staffordshire NHS Foundation Trust January 2005 – March 2009*, volume I (chaired by Robert Francis QC), p.139. https://assets.publishing.service.gov.uk/government/uploads/system /uploads/attachment_data/file/279109/0375_i.pdf

[61] SSH, *Report of the Mid Staffordshire NHS Foundation Trust Public Inquiry*, p.9.

[62] SSH, *Report of the Mid Staffordshire NHS Foundation Trust Public Inquiry*, p.48.

[63] SSH, *Report of the Mid Staffordshire NHS Foundation Trust Public Inquiry*, p.49.

[64] Laverty, Anthony; Smith, Peter; Pape, Utz; Mears, Alex; Wachter, Robert; and Millett, Christopher (2012) 'High-profile investigations into hospital safety problems in England did not prompt patients to switch providers', *Health Affairs*, vol. 31, no. 3, pp.593–601. https://doi.org/10.1377/hlthaff.2011.0810

[65] Colin Thomé, David (2009) *Mid Staffordshire NHS Foundation Trust: A review of lessons learnt for commissioners and performance managers following the Healthcare Commission Investigation*, UK: Department of Health; House of Commons Health Committee (2009) *Patient safety*, Sixth Report of Session 2008–09, vol. I. HC 151-I, UK: The Stationery Office, p.23. https://www.londoncouncils.gov.uk/node/7595

[66] SSH, *Report of the Mid Staffordshire NHS Foundation Trust Public Inquiry*, p.53.

[67] Le Grand, Julian (2003) *Motivation, agency and public policy: Of knights and knaves, pawns and queens*, UK: Oxford University Press, p.5. https://doi.org/10.1093/0199266999.001.0001

[68] Abbasi, Kamran (1998) 'Butchers and gropers', *BMJ*, vol. 317, no. 7172, p.1599. https://doi.org/10.1136/bmj.317.7172.1599b

[69] Le Grand, Julian, *Motivation, agency and public policy*, pp.13–14.

[70] SSH, *The new NHS: modern, dependable*, pp.10–11.

[71] *BBC News* (1998) 'Dobson pledges cash to tackle waiting lists', 18 May. https://perma.cc/HFK7-PKFQ; SSH, *The NHS plan*, p.28.

[72] Organisation for Economic Co-operation and Development (OECD) (2000) *OECD Economic Surveys 2000*. France: OECD.

[73] Smee, Clive (2005) *Speaking truth to power: Two decades of analysis in the Department of Health*, UK: Radcliffe Press, pp.24–25; Riddell, Mary (2000) 'He had the courage to speak out', *New Statesman*, 24 January. https://perma.cc/W6Y9-A8N2

[74] Smee, Clive, *Speaking truth to power*, pp.24–25.

[75] Barber, Michael (2008) *Instruction to deliver: Fighting to transform Britain's public services*, UK: Politicos.

[76] Bevan, Gwyn and Wilson, Deborah (2013) 'Does "naming and shaming" work for schools and hospitals? Lessons from natural experiments following devolution in England and Wales', *Public Money and Management*, vol. 33, no. 4, p.249. https://doi.org/10.1080/09540962.2013.799801; Bevan, Gwyn; Karanikolos, Marina; Exley, Josephine; Nolte, Ellen; Connolly, Sheelah; and Mays, Nicholas (2014) *The four health systems of the United Kingdom: How do they compare?* UK: Health Foundation, p.78. https://www.health.org.uk/publications/the-four-health-systems-of-the -united-kingdom-how-do-they-compare

[77] SSH, *The NHS plan*, p.28.

[78] Connolly, Sheelah; Bevan, Gwyn; and Mays, Nicholas (2010) *Funding and performance of healthcare systems in the four countries of the UK before and after devolution*, UK: The Nuffield Trust, pp.56–57, 93–95. https://researchonline.lshtm.ac.uk/id/eprint/3827/1/funding_and_perfor mance_of_healthcare_systems_in_the_four_countries_report_full.pdf

[79] Barber, Michael, *Instruction to deliver*, p.335.

[80] For 1950 to 1969: Office of Health Economics (1995) *Compendium of health statistics*, 9th edition, and (1997) *Compendium of health statistics*, 10th edition, UK: Office of Health Economics. For 1970 to 2019: OECD (2020) *Health expenditure and financing*. Paris: OECD. https://stats.oecd.org/Index.aspx?DataSetCode=SHA#

[81] SSH (2002) *Delivering the NHS Plan*, UK: HMSO, p.6.

[82] SSH, *Report of the Mid Staffordshire NHS Foundation Trust Public Inquiry*, p.54.

[83] SSH, *Learning from Bristol*, p.186.

[84] Bevan, Gwyn and Cornwell, Jocelyn, 'Structure and logic of regulation and governance of quality of health care'.

[85] SSH, *Report of the Mid Staffordshire NHS Foundation Trust Public Inquiry*, p.54.

[86] Commission for Health Improvement (2003) *NHS Performance Ratings, Acute Trusts, Specialist Trusts, Ambulance Trusts*, UK: Commission for Health Improvement, p.10.

[87] Propper, Carol (1989) 'An econometric analysis of the demand for private health insurance in England and Wales', *Applied Economics*, vol. 21, no. 6, pp.777–92. https://doi.org/10.1080/758520273

[88] SSH, *Report of the Mid Staffordshire NHS Foundation Trust Public Inquiry*, p.54.

[89] Bevan, Gwyn and Hood, Christopher (2006) 'What's measured is what matters: Targets and gaming in the English public health care system', *Public Administration*, vol. 84, no. 3, pp.517–38. https://doi.org/10.1111/j.1467-9299.2006.00600.x; Bevan, Gwyn and Hamblin, Richard (2009) 'Hitting and missing targets by ambulance services for emergency calls: Effects of different systems of performance measurement within the UK', *Journal of the Royal Statistical Society: Series A (Statistics in Society)*, vol. 172, no. 1, pp.161–90. https://doi.org/10.1111/j.1467-985X.2008.00557.x

[90] Commission for Health Improvement (2002) *Report of a clinical governance review at Mid Staffordshire General NHS Trust*, UK: The Stationery Office.

[91] Healthcare Commission (2009) *Investigation into Mid Staffordshire NHS Foundation Trust*. London: Healthcare Commission, https://cdn.ps.emap.com/wp-content/uploads/sites/3/2009/06/Investigation_into_Mid_Staffordshire_NHS_Foundation_Trust.pdf. p.36.

[92] North, Douglass (1990) *Institutions, institutional change and economic performance*, UK: Cambridge University Press, pp.3–10. https://doi.org/10.1017/CBO9780511808678

2. Economic and geographical fault lines

The UK had and has a more unbalanced economy than almost all our immediate biggest competitors in Europe and more unbalanced than pretty much every major developed country … For too many people geography turns out to be destiny.

Boris Johnson (15 July 2021)[1]

The modern study of institutions can help explain how geographical fault lines developed in Europe and the UK. The first section in this chapter examines the impacts of the Black Death on feudal societies. These were based on a social contract in which peasants supplied labour to their landlords, who reciprocated by maintaining law and order and giving the peasants protection. Feudalism is an exemplar of what Daron Acemoglu and James Robinson call an 'extractive society': corrupt and designed to extract benefits for a small ruling elite, who obstruct developments that might threaten their privileged position.[2] Acemoglu and Robinson argue that an extractive society explains *Why Nations Fail*, and will continue to do so, until a critical juncture offers a window of opportunity for radical change. The different consequences of the critical juncture of the Black Death in the 14th century resulted in geographical fault lines that have persisted to this day. That ended feudalism in much of Europe (in England there was the peasants' revolt of 1381) but not in Russia and Southern Italy. The second section briefly considers how Russia moved from feudalism to communism without developing the institutions necessary for a market economy: property rights and an independent legal, fiscal and justice system. That is why, after the fall of communism, its institution of authoritarian corruption enabled oligarchs to benefit from the privatisation of state assets, which has resulted in another kind of extractive society.[3] The third section is about how the regions of Southern Italy remain relatively poor as they moved from feudalism to a polity with strong organised crime and corruption. The fourth section shows how the institutions of Soviet planning and a market economy created fault lines between East and West Germany after the Second World War. The final two sections contrast the development of fault lines in the UK's centralised state with the economic transformation

How to cite this book chapter:

Bevan, Gwyn (2023) *How Did Britain Come to This? A century of systemic failures of governance*, London: LSE Press, pp. 21–52.
https://doi.org/10.31389/lsepress.hdb.b License: CC BY-NC

of East Germany, after unification, in Germany's federal constitution; and describe the entrenched divisions visible in the UK, exemplified by what has happened to Oxford and Oldham.

2.1 A mediaeval pandemic and the divergence of inclusive and extractive societies in Europe

The Black Death in the 14th century was the deadliest global pandemic in human history. In his book *Doom*, Niall Ferguson estimates that, across Europe, 30 per cent to 60 per cent of the population died.[4] In the first wave of 1348–49 alone, it reduced England's population by about a third.[5] There was a second wave in 1361–62, a third in 1369 and a fourth in 1375.[6]

By the time of the Black Death, the feudal social contract in much of Western Europe had evolved so that peasants were paid by the landlord for working his land. After the plague, landlords in England tried through legislation to freeze the price of labour at pre-plague levels. King Edward III's Statute of Labourers 1351 targeted restrictions on migration and was directed:

> against the malice of servants who were idle or unwilling to serve after the pestilence without taking outrageous wages … that such servants, both men and women, should be obliged to serve in return for the salaries and wages which were customary (in those places where they ought to serve) during the twentieth year of the present King's reign (1346–47) or five or six years previously … Servants are not to depart from the vill[age]s in which they live during the winter to serve elsewhere in the summer if they can find work in their own vills at the wages mentioned above; saving that the people of the counties of Stafford, Lancaster and Derby and those of the Craven, the Marches of Wales and Scotland and elsewhere may come and go in other counties during August and then return safely, as they have been accustomed to do before this time. Those who refuse to take such an oath, or to fulfil what they have undertaken shall be put in stocks for three days or more by the said the lords, stewards, bailiffs and constables of the vills or sent to the nearest gaol, there to remain until they are willing to submit to justice. For this purpose stocks are to be constructed in every vill between now and Whitsunday.[7]

This Statute of Labourers brought out so clearly the problems of restricting migration by recognising that exceptions were necessary. (As they were in the UK after Brexit for butchers, bricklayers, welders, fishmongers, bakers, horticultural workers, childminders, nursery nurses, health professionals, senior care workers and nursing assistants.[8]) The statute also pioneered a national incomes policy, which John Hicks pointed out was as problematic then as, later, in the 20th century.[9] In setting prices, the 1351 Statute was highly specific in fixing different upper limits for rates of pay for threshing (60 per cent higher for threshing a quarter of wheat or rye than for a quarter of barley, beans or oats). But it experienced the same problems of measurement of shoes as central planners in the Soviet Union seven centuries later: the statute required that shoemakers 'shall not sell boots, shoes or anything else connected with their mystery otherwise than they did in the said twentieth year'.[10]

Although the Statute of Labourers 1351 was revised and re-enacted over the following 30 years, according to nearly all contemporary accounts, all this legislative activity was futile.[11] One source observed that:

> The labourers were so arrogant and hostile that they took no notice of the king's mandate; and if anyone wanted to employ them, he was obliged to give them whatever he asked, and either lose his fruits and crops, or satisfy at will the labourers' greed and arrogance.[12]

The landlords faced what is known as a collective action problem. As Hatcher explains, although they as a body

> supported the enactment of labour legislation they lacked the solidarity necessary to ensure its successful enforcement. In default each employer's own best interests were served by securing enough labour to perform the work which he needed to be done, and this involved competing with other employers by offering higher wages and more allowances.[13]

The pandemic's impact shattered feudal society in much of Western Europe. But, in Russia, serfs were still owned by their landlords in a social contract that required them to work for their landlords on some days and were free to work for themselves on others. If serfs sought to escape their feudal ties and become free men after the plague, they were remorselessly and brutally hunted down by their landlords. The nobility's success in this endeavour entrenched feudalism in a second serfdom. Hicks describes the path dependent outcomes of the critical juncture of the Black Death that shaped the future of much Eastern Europe:

> The decline in population, which was the occasion for this parting of the ways, was itself a transitory phenomenon; in a couple of generations, or a little longer, it had probably been made up. But the habits and the social institutions which had grown up as a reaction to it were not easily eradicated. Prussia (now part of modern Poland and Russia) and Poland and Russia remained for centuries in the grip of a nobility of landlords, extracting what revenue they could

from poor peasants whom they kept dependent on them; defending as their lifeline an oppressive system which they were unwilling to reform for fear that the whole house of cards they had built would fall on their heads.[14]

2.2 From serfdom to a maximal state

Bo Rothstein is one of the world's leading scholars on corruption.[15] If you ask him what helps a country end corruption, he replies, 'Lose a major war.' The defeat of the Russian army in the Crimean War (1853 to 1856) was a critical juncture that was followed by the 'abolition of serfdom in 1861'. Thomas Piketty points out that this failed, however, because of Russia's weak institutional arrangements.[16] Serfdom only came to an end with the Bolshevik revolution after the critical junctures of the failures of its army and economy in the First World War.[17]

Karl Marx had predicted that the development of a communist society was an inevitable outcome of the class struggle in capitalist societies of the 19th century, in which the alienation of the working class in producing surplus value for the owners of capital would inexorably lead to a crisis.[18] Paradoxically, however, it was in Russia's feudal society that the Soviet model of communism was established. For Lenin, Trotsky and Stalin the kulaks were incompatible with that model.[19] They were the richest 5 per cent of peasants, who could afford a square meal every day from owning a few horses, cows and smallholdings. Only 1 per cent were in a position to exploit more than one labourer.[20] Kulaks were 'publicly reviled as a menace and bloodsucker, perhaps taxed heavily, and always conscious of appearing a menace in the eyes of at least some men in the Kremlin'.[21] There was a great debate, in the 1920s, between communist leaders over their coexistence with communism.[22] Under Stalin's brutal 'dekulakisation', the 'worst kind' of kulaks were sent to concentration camps; others were deported from where they had lived; and those who were allowed to remain were given the worst kind of land.[23] What followed from the programme of collectivisation of agriculture in Ukraine, between 1931 and 1934, was Holodomor – derived from the Ukrainian words for hunger (*holod*) and extermination (*mor*). Nearly four million people died.[24]

The brutal Stalinist system of centralised planning and direction in the maximal state succeeded in moving Russia, within a generation, from a feudal agrarian economy to a primitive industrial society. Gary Gerstle argues that now we forget how 'powerful and prestigious a movement communism once was'.[25] He points out that in the 1930s, whilst chaotic market mechanisms caused production to plummet in the United States and the rest of the Western capitalist world, under intelligent government planning it had soared in the Soviet Union.[26] Edward Luce in the *Financial Times* observed that 'the year before FDR [Franklin Delano Roosevelt] was elected, 100,000 Americans applied for jobs in the Soviet Union'.[27] In the US, Gerstle argues that the threat of communism explains why, under FDR's 'New Deal', workers enjoyed high wages as the outcome of the compromise between capital and labour.[28] In Britain, in 1956, Anthony Crosland argued for a different future for socialism from the pervasive influence of Marxist analysis on the British Labour Movement in the 1930s.[29]

In 1957, Russia inaugurated the space age with the launch of Sputnik 1.[30] In 1961, the Communist Party of the Soviet Union under Nikita Khrushchev produced what Archie Brown describes as both 'the last authoritative document to take entirely seriously the building of a communist society' and 'a remarkable combination of self-delusion, wishful thinking and, utopianism'.[31] It declared that, by 1970, 'they would have surpassed the United States in production per head of population'.[32] Yoram Gorlizki and Oleg Khlevniuk focus on Riazan, a medium-sized agricultural region 200 kilometres south-east of Moscow, which was the model that would show how the Soviet Union could achieve a great breakthrough in agriculture to match that of Stalin's industrialisation in early 1930s.[33] Alec Nove (alongside many others) predicted in 1961, however, that the Soviet system, of the maximal state running the whole economy by centralised planning, would fail because it would prove to be incapable of handling the complex information requirements of running a modern economy.[34] That was the criticism of central planning that Friedrich von Hayek made in 1945.[35] A fundamental problem of running the economy based on targets was that it resulted in gaming on an industrial scale.

Because central targets could not capture quality, they were often set by weight, which created endemic problems over the quality of consumer goods.[36] For a manager, the consequences of missing the tonnage target under Stalin was, at best, a trip for a short and brutal lifetime in Siberia. So, there were strong incentives *not* to experiment with technological innovations that might have reduced costs and improved quality, because this would interrupt production and put the tonnage target at risk.[37] It is said that when managers did experiment, this was in ways to make the goods they produced heavier. So, if in-year monitoring showed that they might miss their tonnage target, they could switch to heavier means of production. This system was designed to result in shortages, a lack of innovation, heavy goods of poor quality, and baths without bathplugs – the notorious complaint of visitors to the USSR. These failings have been described in many accounts and are summed up in the famous *Krokodil* cartoon of a nail factory cartoon satirising how increasing the weights of products helped to meet quantitative Soviet production targets (Figure 2.1). In the 1960s Khrushchev's unrealistically ambitious targets for agriculture resulted in those who honestly reported their actual performance being 'branded as laggards and publicly humiliated'.[38] Hence gaming became pervasive. The discovery of the scale and pervasiveness of fraudulent reporting of meeting targets in Riazan:

> delivered a death blow to the idea that a dictator in Moscow could bring about a great leap forward with the aid of substate dictators in the regions … it showed that Khrushchev's most vaunted achievements were in fact based on a tissue of lies.[39]

Figure 2.1: The Krokodil nail factory cartoon

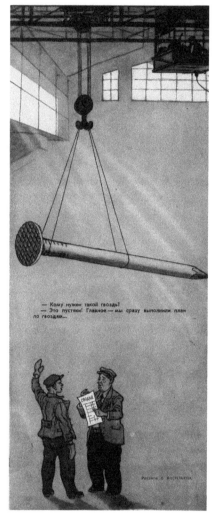

Worker: 'Who on earth needs a nail like this?'

Manager: 'Ah who cares? The most important thing is that we've immediately fulfilled our nail quota'.

Source: Крокодил [Krokodil].[40]

2.3 Governance and corruption effects in Western Europe

Nicholas Charron at the Quality of Government Institute, Gothenburg, has led research in developing and mapping a European Quality of Government Index (EQI) for regions in Europe.[41] The EQI is based on samples of residents of each region answering questions in surveys about three public services (healthcare, education and law enforcement) across four dimensions (corruption, bribery, equity of access, and public services quality). In 2015, Bo Rothstein described the variation in EQI within European countries as greatest in

Italy. The best of Italy's northern regions was comparable with Denmark, but the worst southern regions compared most with African countries.[42] Figure 2.2 shows the most recent data, for 2017. Comparing Italy with the UK, the EQI

Figure 2.2: Map of the European Quality of Government Index scores at regional level, in 2017

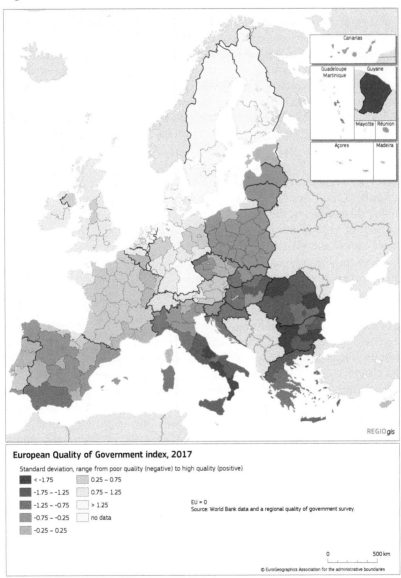

European Quality of Government index, 2017

Standard deviation, range from poor quality (negative) to high quality (positive)

■ < -1.75	▨ 0.25 – 0.75
■ -1.75 – -1.25	▨ 0.75 – 1.25
■ -1.25 – -0.75	▢ > 1.25
▨ -0.75 – -0.25	▨ no data
▨ -0.25 – 0.25	

EU = 0
Source: World Bank data and a regional quality of government survey.

0   500 km

© EuroGeographics Association for the administrative boundaries

Source: European Commission.[43]
Notes: The average score for the EU as a whole is set to zero. The dark orange to red shading indicates increasing negative scores, below the EU average. The lighter oranges scores show regions with positive numbers, above the EU average.

score for the best region in Italy was lower than for the worst region in the UK. The worst scores are for Italy's southern regions.

Robert Putnam et al sought to explain the marked differences they found, in 1974, in the capabilities of regional governments in the north and south of Italy after regional devolution.[44] Figure 2.3 gives a map of Renaissance Italy, whose fragmented condition persisted in many different permutations right through to the country's national unification (led by Piedmont, situated in the country's far north-west) in 1861. In the north of Italy, the powerful city medi-aeval republics created strong social capital with 'an ethic of civic involvement social responsibility, and mutual assistance among equals'.[45] These civic virtues survived the fall of those republics, despite a growth in inequality, exploita-tion and factional conflict. That is why, centuries later in the 1870s, various communal institutions developed in the north (such as 'agrarian associations, mutual aid societies, chambers of commerce, and savings banks') that proved crucial for fostering rapid modern capitalist development.[46]

However, Italy's southern regions were governed by the autocratic regimes of foreign kings (the Hapsburgs and the Bourbons) from 1504 until 1860. Their feudal-like regimes maintained the primacy of vertical ties of dependence and exploitation by 'promoting mutual distrust and conflict among their subjects, destroying ties of solidarity in order to maintain the primacy of vertical ties of dependence and exploitation'.[47] The absence of social capital and civic virtues in the south resulted in weak institutions, which in turn 'strengthened the family, the clientage and *Mafiosi* positions'. There are two causes of regional inequalities in modern Italy. First, the south-ern regions' low social capital. Second, the culture of *omertà*, which requires men to avenge offences without the help of authorities and avoid contact with the police – to do that brings a loss of respect and threats.[48] That sustains organised crime and undermines effective government in its three poorest regions, which are, in order of their declining poverty, Campania, Sicily and Calabria.

The Sicilian Mafia is well known from the *Godfather* films and the *Montal-bano* television series – the last episode of *The Young Montalbano* ends with the actual assassination via car bomb of prosecuting magistrate Giovani Fal-cone by the Mafia on 23 May 1992. On 19 July 1992, his friend and fellow magistrate Paolo Borsellino was also assassinated by the Mafia with another car bomb. Both had taken on the Mafia with great success and dauntless cour-age knowing full well that they were on Mafia hit lists for assassination. In January 2023, Italian investigators captured the 60-year-old Messina Denaro at a clinic in Palermo, Sicily's capital. He had helped 'orchestrate the devas-tating 1992 car bombings in Palermo that killed Giovanni Falcone and Paolo Borsellino'.[49]

Miles Johnson, Rome correspondent of the *Financial Times*, explains how the subsequent success of the Italian state in taking on the Mafia created a market opportunity for the 'Ndrangheta, based in Calabria, to take over Latin

Figure 2.3: Map of Renaissance Italy, 1350 to 1600

Source: Wikimedia Commons (User: Shadowxfox; User: Enok), available under a Creative Commons Attribution-Share Alike Licence (CC BY-SA 3.0).[50]

American drug cartels. The power and reach of the 'Ndrangheta in Calabria was uncovered by an investigation by the *Financial Times*.[51] In one case they detailed, a financial bond became, in fact, a financial spin-off from organised crime that exploited the grieving families of those who die in the hospital of the Calabrian city of Lamezia Terme. Here, a funeral company had through intimidation gained access to the hospital's central medical records and so knew before a father did that his son was going to die and so was able to make him an offer to bury his son that he could not refuse. Johnson explains how the 'Ndrangheta has financialised its organised crime:

From 2015 to 2018, hundreds of millions of euros of invoices signed off by officials in Calabria's cash-strapped municipal health authorities were purchased by intermediaries. These middlemen bought the unpaid invoices from suppliers at a steep discount because they were, in effect, guaranteed by the Italian state. They were then sold on to specialist financial companies, who merged them into pools of assets and sold investor bonds backed by the unpaid bills.[52]

Johnson cites a US diplomatic cable of 2008 that observed that, 'if it were not part of Italy, Calabria would be a failed state.'[53] He singles out the public prosecutor Nicola Gratteri, who was born in Calabria and lived there almost his entire life, for his bravery in taking on the 'Ndrangheta: 'Gratteri has been under permanent police protection since 1989 and is unable to leave his office in Catanzaro without a bodyguard.'[54] The BBC reported that, in November 2021, Gratteri's 30-year campaign against local corruption resulted in sentencing 70 members of the 'Ndrangheta in 'maxi trials' that took place behind closed doors in a specially converted courtroom in Lamezia Terme. In addition, 'over the next two years, 355 alleged mobsters and corrupt officials will face court for their involvement with Italy's richest and most powerful organised crime group.'[55]

Roberto Saviano's book *Gomorrah* describes the grip of another notorious branch of Italian financialised organised crime, the Camorra in Campania (capital Naples).[56] He also lives under constant threat of assassination. His book *Zero Zero Zero* (2016) describes how organised crime relies on the City of London and Wall Street to launder money from cocaine.[57] Jennifer Shasky Calvery gave an estimate to the US Congress in 2012 of the scale of transnational organised crime when she was chief of the Asset Forfeiture and Money Laundering Section of the Department of Justice: $1.6 trillion was laundered through the global financial system; about $600 billion was related to transnational organised crime.[58] London has been described as the money laundering capital of the world by *The Times* (2014), the *New York Times* (2021) and the *Financial Times* (2022).[59]

2.4 Social capital, governance and innovation

In the 1949 film *The Third Man*, which has been consistently voted one of the greatest British films ever made, Harry Lime (played by Orson Welles) observed this paradox:

You know what the fellow said – in Italy, for 30 years under the Borgias, they had warfare, terror, murder and bloodshed, but they produced Michelangelo, Leonardo da Vinci and the Renaissance. In Switzerland, they had brotherly love; they had five hundred years of democracy and peace – and what did that produce? The cuckoo clock.[60]

In *Germany, Memories of a Nation* Neil McGregor points out that, whilst Harry Lime was right about the extraordinary creativity of the Italian Renaissance under the Borgias, he was almost certainly wrong in crediting Switzerland with the invention of the cuckoo clock. He suggests that the sounds we associate with Germany might be a Bach cantata, a Beethoven symphony, a Wagner opera, or the crowd's roar as its football team used to beat England. But he would add another sound: that 'of metal on metal, the hum and thrum of skilled engineering'.[61] McGregor explains that this dates back to the 14th century, when workshops of skilled metalworkers developed. They led the world in the production of clocks and watches; complex scientific instruments (requiring a mix of mathematics, science and creative industry); production of the first internal combustion engines (in the 1880s); and the first working motor cars by Daimler-Benz. The crisis of the 1930s resulted in a combination of mass unemployment and hyperinflation, which impoverished its middle class and meant they could not afford to buy cars.

So, although our image of modern Germany is of a dominant automobile industry, its development was stalled in the 1930s, when it was reduced to producing small numbers of fine limousines for plutocrats. Hitler aimed to rectify that. He asked Ferdinand Porsche to design a cheap, sturdy people's car (Volkswagen) that could be left outside in the street at night (hence designed to be air-cooled). The prototype of his VW Beetle was produced just before the outbreak of the Second World War in 1938.[62] After the end of the Second World War, the Soviet system was rigorously applied within the eastern sector of the divided Germany. Thus it created the basis for a remarkable 'natural experiment'. From 1945 to 1989 the Soviet bloc East Germany and the Western capitalist Federal Republic shared much the same well-established traditions of skilled engineering and manufacturing. Each had to cope with the devastation of losing the Second World War.

After the war, over 20 million VW Beetles were produced, first in West Germany and later in 13 other countries. It has been described as the 'first global car in terms of popularity, affordability and presence' and is famous for its 'impeccable quality and durability'.[63] German cars produced by Volkswagen, Audi, BMW, Porsche and Mercedes symbolise the German reputation for skilled engineering and high quality in mass production. In East Germany, the Audi factory in Zwickau was 'sequestered by the occupying Soviet Army, dismantled, then reconstituted as part of the state-owned automobile VEB'.[64] That factory produced the Trabant, which was East Germany's rival to the Beetle. It first rolled (or was it pushed?) off the production line nearly 20 years after the first Beetle prototype. The Trabant is a strong contender for being one of the worst cars made in the second half of the 20th century. Its distinctive features included:

- No fuel pump: fuel reached the carburettor by gravity, which required the Trabant to be designed with its fuel tank above the engine. In accidents this brought the added excitement of a serious risk of fire.

- No fuel gauge: a dipstick had to be inserted into the tank to determine how much fuel remained.
- No indicators for turning.
- A two-stroke engine that was highly polluting. The driver had to fill the tank and shake it to mix gasoline with oil.
- The 'acceleration of the Trabant' was an excellent example of an oxymoron.[65]

The 'consumers' of East Germany who wanted to buy a new Trabant had to pay more than a year's average income and, if you lived a long way from Berlin, wait up to 13 years (Berliners might have to wait for 10 years only), or pay double that for a second-hand Trabant.[66] It is fitting that the abiding image of the Trabant is as the means of escape from East to West Germany after the demolition of the Berlin Wall in November 1989.

2.5 The institutions of capitalism in the UK and Germany

Although in the 1920s and 1930s the British suffered mass unemployment (see Chapter 3), unlike in Germany, the British middle class could afford to buy motor cars from various manufacturers: Humber, Austin, Hillman, Morris, Riley, Rover, Singer, Standard, Sunbeam, Triumph and Wolsey. The British were the first to put the VW Beetle into mass production in Germany after the end of the War – for their forces of occupation. British car manufacturers decided against its production: the Beetle did not meet 'the fundamental requirements of a motor car' and was 'quite unattractive to the average buyer'[67] (an error of judgement comparable to that of the record company that turned down the Beatles in 1962[68]). In the UK, a succession of mergers failed to remedy key structural problems that resulted in the successive production of badly designed cars of poor quality by the top firm: the British Motor Corporation, from 1952 to 1968; British Leyland from 1968 to 1986; and the Rover Group from 1986 to 2005.[69] The car industry that exists in Britain today is completely managed under foreign owners committed to designing and manufacturing high-quality cars. If we were to think of how to characterise car industries as movies after the end of the Second World War, that for West Germany would be a feelgood movie, that for East Germany a B movie in monochrome, and that for Britain would be *Carry On Making Motor Cars*.

So central planning in East Germany and the market in the UK failed to produce cars of the quality of West Germany. Why did the market work in West Germany and fail in the UK? In 1996, the *Economic Journal* published three articles by British economists that had aimed to 'explore the causes of the poor British industrial performance over the period since 1960, with a particular focus on the significance of deindustrialisation and the role of policy in the relative decline'.[70] A commentary by Barry Eichengreen argued that they had failed to diagnose the root cause, which was that Britain's institutional arrangements had not changed from those that had enabled its early industrialisation.[71] In Germany and France, defeat in the Second World War had created windows of opportunity for institutional renewal that was missing in Britain:

> The inheritance of undersized firms, an impersonal financial system, and a fragmented structure of industrial relations remained. The dominance of the stock market encouraged managers to think in terms of short horizons and heightened their sensitivity to financial-market conditions; long-term investment was thereby made difficult. The fragmentation of the union movement made it impossible to secure agreements to moderate wages and coordinate the changes in work rules necessary to justify the adoption of new technologies. Lack of cooperation between unions, employers' associations and government made it infeasible to adopt a German-style system of apprenticeship training.[72]

So the UK's banking system specialised in the provision of trade credit rather than industrial finance; its industrial structure was dominated by atomistic, single-plant firms and a system of fragmented, craft-based unionism. What Britain had required were networks of investment banks lending to large enterprises that challenged unions in implementing the technologies of modern mass production. But, Eichengreen concluded, those changes would need to develop in concert, which would not happen under Britain's market institutions.[73]

Bernard Rieger explains the four key developments in Germany that explain its success.[74] These and the institutional differences from Britain and Germany were:

1. *Government*: after the Second World War West Germany took the vital step of recreating its apprenticeship system (for over 300 trades) to develop a highly skilled workforce in future capable of manufacturing goods of the highest quality. This linked to a system of secondary education with different academic and technical schools (*gymnasiums* and *technische hochschule*).
2. *Quality*: Volkswagen focused remorselessly on improving quality, even when demand for Beetles outstripped their capacity to produce them. By contrast, as discussed in Chapter 5, the dysfunctional consequences of financialisation for the UK's economy means senior executives are driven to focusing on making profits and maximising shareholder value.
3. *Institutions*: German industries are governed in ways where their workers are recognised as stakeholders in companies. In addition, German banks financed firms with patient capital, rather than the UK pattern of acute pressure from financial markets for quick returns.
4. *Identity*: the focus on production quality was central to a mission to redefine the identity of what it meant to be German. From 1955, when Volkswagen started to export more cars than they sold at home, they

saw their mission as exporting much more than a commodity. It was about the meaning and identity of being German. Bernard Rieger observed 'there being something psychological about this German pinning of success to the maintenance of high quality' and 'the reha- bilitation of the label "made in Germany", to symbolise high-quality engineering and manufacturing'. (At that time, it would have been unthinkable for Volkswagen to design the 'diesel dupe' for exports to the US, which was discovered in 2015. This device switched the engine into a sort of safety mode when operating under the controlled laboratory conditions used for tests. Here the engine ran below nor- mal power performance and seemed to meet regulatory standards. But, once on the road, the engines switched out of this test mode and it emerged that they then emitted nitrogen oxide pollutants up to 40 times above what was allowed in the US.[75])

Figure 2.4: Regions in European countries with lower GDP per capita than former East Germany in 2017

Source: Data from Eurostat.[76]
Notes: Map shows regional data for UK, Italy, Germany and other European countries.

After 45 years of communism, Maddison estimated that, in 1991, GDP per capita in in East Germany was 28 per cent of that in West Germany (5,400 and 19,400, respectively, in US$).[77] In comparison, in the UK, after deindustrialisation in 1994, GDP per capita in the poorest region was 50 per cent of the richest region (£7,000 in West Wales and the Valleys and £14,000 in London).[78] The fall of communism was a critical juncture that resulted in a Rebuilding the East (Aufbau Ost) programme in Germany. The government spent €1.7 trillion, over 25 years, on infrastructure projects in a 'modern equivalent to the Marshall plan'.[79] This included modernisation of railway lines and rolling stock and building a new network of *Autobahnen*. Volkswagen reconfigured the former Trabant works and Opel, Porsche and BMW now each have a presence in the former East.[80] The result has been the eroding of the fault lines between East and West Germany.

In the UK and the US, the fall of communism enabled the rise of neoliberalism, which has deepened fault lines in these countries. Gerstle argues that, as 'there seemed to be no challenge to the capitalist way of organising economic life', there was no need to continue to pay workers high wages.[81] With the collapse of communism, Margaret Thatcher was able to argue in the 1980s that 'There Is No Alternative (TINA)' to the neoliberal reforms she implemented. Figure 2.4 uses Eurostat data to compare the per capita GDP in the regions of the former East Germany with other regions across Europe and the UK as a whole. Every region shaded red had a lower per capita GDP than the eastern Germany regions (shaded blue). Eastern Germany outperformed not only all regions in the other former Soviet bloc countries to the east but also all of Greece, almost all of Spain and Portugal, a swathe of Southern Italy, much of France and large parts of the UK.

In 2019, Eurostat data show that the mean GDP per capita (in Euros) in the former *Laender* of East Germany had increased to over 70 per cent of the former regions of the West (€28,000 and €38,000).[82] Figure 2.5 uses Eurostat data and data from the Office for National Statistics in the UK.[83] The richest and poorest regions or cities (with GDP per capita in €s in parentheses) in the UK, Italy and western and eastern Germany were:

- UK: Inner London – West (€195,000) and Tees Valley and Durham (€23,000);
- Italy: Bolzano (€49,000) and Calabria (€18,000);
- West Germany: Hamburg (€61,000) and Lüneburg (€27,000);
- East Germany: Leipzig (£31,800) and Mecklenburg-Vorpommern (€27,000).

The mean GDP per capita of the UK's richest region was eight times that of its poorest, compared with less than three times in Italy and West and East Germany. This is not due to Inner London – West having a small population: its 1.2 million is comparable with Hamburg (1.9 million) and more than twice that of Bolzano (0.5 million). The regions of East Germany were richer in

Figure 2.5: GDP per capita in 2019 in euros for the UK, Italy, the former West Germany regions, and the former East Germany regions

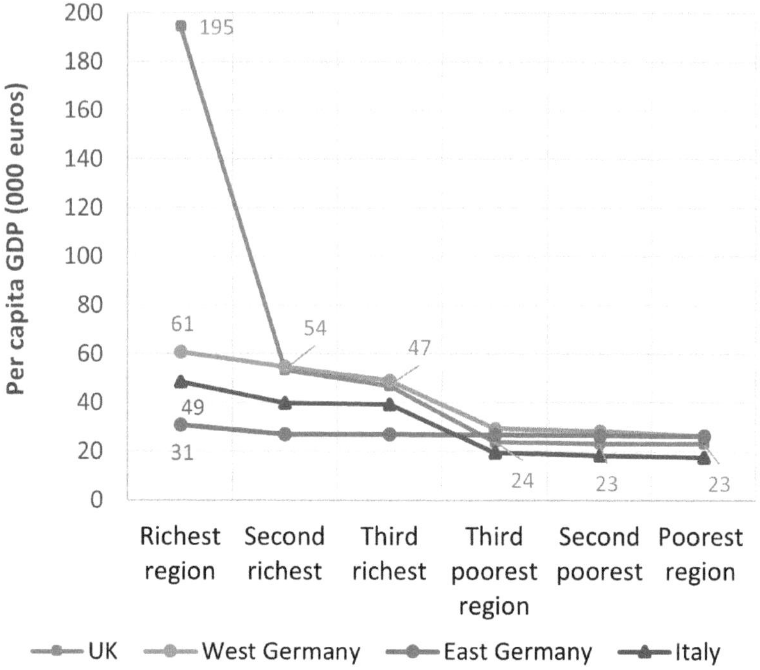

Source: Eurostat and the Office for National Statistics in the UK.[84]

2019 than the three poorest regions in Britain. Italy's three poorest regions are those impeded by varieties of organised crime: Campania, Sicily and Calabria.

Luke Raikes argues that systems of governance and finance were vital to the economic transformation of the *Laender* of East Germany, and are serious handicaps for tackling the UK's structural inequalities.[85] In Germany, the federal government works with its 16 *Laender*, the different political parties collaborate, and the *Laender* work cooperatively and learn from each other in their federal laboratory. Figures 2.4 and Figure 2.5 show that the UK's systems of governance and finance have created fault lines comparable with those of 45 years by communism in East Germany and organised crime in Southern Italy. To illuminate this conundrum, I want to explore the contrasting post-1945 histories of a town and a city in England: Oldham, where I was brought up, and Oxford, near to which I now live.

2.6 Oldham and Oxford: divergent development in the UK

When he was serving as ambassador to India in the early 1970s, former Senator Daniel Moynihan was asked what Bombay (now Mumbai) needed to do to become a great global city. He replied, 'Build a world-class university and wait 200 years.'[86] When I went by train to Oxford station, in 1965, Oxford had one small ancient but exclusive university. The signs on the station platforms said, 'Welcome to Oxford – the home of Pressed Steel Fisher.' The car industry at Cowley, which was only a few miles from the heart of the university, belonged in another world. Oxford undergraduates at that time enjoyed a grant for living expenses and paid no tuition fees, while they enjoyed the privileges of weekly hour-long tutorials, with at most a few other students, from outstanding individual scholars. I found its beauty was breath-taking.

Over the years since, Oxford has enjoyed a virtuous circle in which success breeds success. The university's academic excellence has attracted outstanding researchers who won the research grants that came to generate its main source of income (over £600 million per year).[87] In turn, these grants attracted more outstanding researchers, who further enhanced its academic excellence. In 1992, Oxford Polytechnic became Oxford Brookes University and the old and new universities together have about 24,000 full-time students each year. Knowledge-based businesses have been thriving and the economy has been growing nearly twice as fast as the national average.[88] The city has become a major hub for biotech, publishing and high-tech engineering. An investment firm, Top Tier, cites the city as being the originator of four 'unicorns' – the name given to start-ups worth more than US$1 billion.[89]

Average salaries in Oxford have been among the highest in the UK and two-thirds of workers are in managerial and professional occupations.[90] So many residents commute to London that a second railway station, Oxford Parkway, was opened in 2015, operated by a different company on a different train route. On a good day, the journey time to London (over 50 miles away) is about an hour from its stations. Oxford's worldwide academic reputation means that it is an attractive location for its 18 independent schools, with about 14,000 pupils. Oxford's mediaeval buildings mean that it also has a thriving tourist industry, which attracts 7 million tourists who spend nearly a billion pounds and come to visit its art galleries, and go to its theatres, concerts and cinemas.[91]

Oldham's mid-Victorian heyday, with its smokestacks and thriving industries, epitomised the northern saying that 'where there's muck there's brass'. My memories of Oldham, in the 1950s and 1960s, are of a bustling town full of vitality with people who were warm, welcoming, friendly and hospitable. From its Repertory Theatre, many actors went on to starring roles in *Coronation Street*.[92] In 1978, it became Oldham's Coliseum and Minnie Driver and Ralph Fiennes performed there. Oldham's grand town hall was recently restored, having stood empty and decaying for over 30 years – as frontage for a cinema. A letter in *The Guardian* told of a man, in the 1950s, asking a ticket officer in Delhi in India for a train to Oldham. He was asked: 'Do you want Oldham Mumps, Oldham Werneth, Oldham Clegg Street, or Oldham Guide Bridge, sir?'[93] In 2009, Oldham 'probably achieved the distinction of being the largest town in Britain without a train service'.[94] Its landmark railway bridge was removed to make way for the Metrolink tram service across Greater Manchester, which opened in 2012. The nine-mile journey from Oldham to Manchester now takes much longer by tram – over 40 minutes.

In January 2023, Sebastian Payne gave a grim description of Oldham. It has lost shops, restaurants and three of its police stations. It has scores that are high for reported crime and low for trusting neighbourhoods and social fabric. He quotes the locals saying that taking a tram to Manchester means venturing into an empty and threatening carriage, so 'You take your life into your hands for a £3.60 return' and 'There is not a chance you walk round Oldham town centre on your own'.[95] In November 2022, the Arts Council of England decided to stop funding the Oldham Coliseum Theatre from its National Portfolio, so performances ended there after the funding ended in April 2023.[96] A leader in *The Guardian* points out that every £1 of public money spent on a local theatre generates £8 for its local economy.[97] University Campus Oldham, which opened in May 2005, offers degrees that are validated by a number of universities. It has 10,000 full-time and part-time students on higher education courses.[98] Oldham's three independent schools have about 1,000 pupils.[99]

What has happened to Oxford and Oldham is emblematic of the way that deepening fault lines became established following deindustrialisation in Britain (and in so many other countries). Daniel Markovits describes deindustrialisation and financialisation of economies producing the divide, based on university education, between those with 'gloomy' and 'glossy' jobs.[100] 'Gloomy' jobs are concentrated in the large areas of England, Wales and Scotland that remain scarred by the collapse of their dominant industries, especially manufacturing, mining, steel and shipping. These are the blighted communities that have been left behind in Britain and voted for Brexit.[101] Deborah Mattinson has used focus groups to understand why Labour's 'red wall' of previously safe working-class seats voted for Brexit and crumbled to the Boris Johnson's populist Conservative message in the 2019 general election. She points out that Brexit was the symptom; the cause was that those who live in places like Oldham feel that they have been failed by successive governments in the living standards they experience and the prospects for their children.[102]

Figure 2.6, from the Johnson government's 2022 'Levelling Up' White Paper, maps key indicators showing the areas that are left behind in the UK. This is based on local authorities in the bottom quartile for level 3+ equivalent skills in the adult population, gross value added (GVA) per hour worked, median gross weekly pay and healthy life expectancy. It shows the extraordinary persistence of the fault line that runs from the Severn to the Wash. Those with 'gloomy' and 'glossy' jobs tend to live north and south of that line. There are pockets of acute deprivation in the North East, Greater Manchester and South

Figure 2.6: Which places in the UK are most left behind?

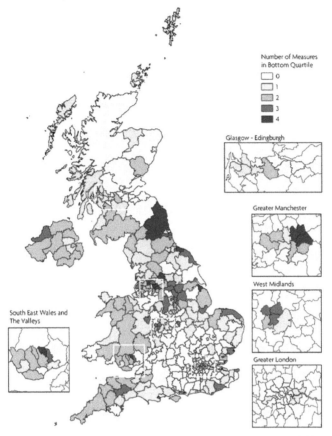

Source: Secretary of State for Levelling Up, Housing and Communities. Available under Crown copyright, published under the Open Government Licence 3.0.[103]
Notes: Shows local authorities in the bottom quartile for level 3+ equivalent skills in the adult population, GVA per hour worked, median gross weekly pay and healthy life expectancy.

East Wales and the Valleys. The map also shows that the South West has been left behind too.

The obvious inference from this analysis is that we would expect those with 'glossy' jobs in Oxford would enjoy much higher levels of life satisfaction than those with 'gloomy' jobs in in Oldham. Markovits argues, however, that financialisation makes lives difficult for both. And Figure 2.7 shows little difference in various measures of life satisfaction.

In April 2022, the median gross weekly earnings for full-time employees were £720 in Oxford and 24 per cent higher than in Oldham (£580).[104] Figure 2.8, also from the Levelling Up White Paper, maps the ratio of house prices to residence-based earnings for local authority districts in England and

Figure 2.7: Residents' view of wellbeing in Oldham and Oxford are very similar (in 2021–22)

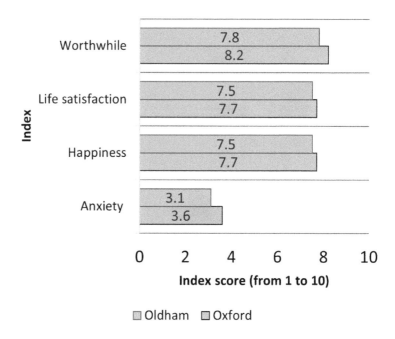

Source: Office of National Statistics and *Daily Mail*.[105]

Wales for 2020, which were in the range from 3 to 7 for Oldham, but in the range from 10 to 14 for Oxford.[106] In 2020–21, there were shocking numbers of children living in poverty (after housing costs) – 26 per cent in Oxford and 40 per cent in Oldham (and doubtless even higher in its most deprived areas).[107] Oxford's housing crisis is a consequence of the financialisation of private house building and the decline in the supply of social housing in the UK (see Chapter 5). The local governments of Oxfordshire are trapped on a hamster wheel. They are rightly under pressure from central government to do something about Oxford's acute housing shortage. But giving planning permission to private developers to build thousands of new homes means that most are affordable only to those who commute to London (and pay the costs in time and rail fares). It does little for those on middle and low incomes. The lack of social housing means that those who cannot afford a mortgage are faced with private rents that reflect the high prices of property relative to earnings.

The house price differential means that nurses and teachers who could afford to live in Oldham would struggle to do so in Oxford. The main acute hospitals in Oxford and Oldham are the John Radcliffe and the Royal Oldham, respectively. In 2023, the Care Quality Commission's 'overall assessment' was

Figure 2.8: Ratio of house prices to residence-based earnings across local authority districts in England and Wales, in 2020

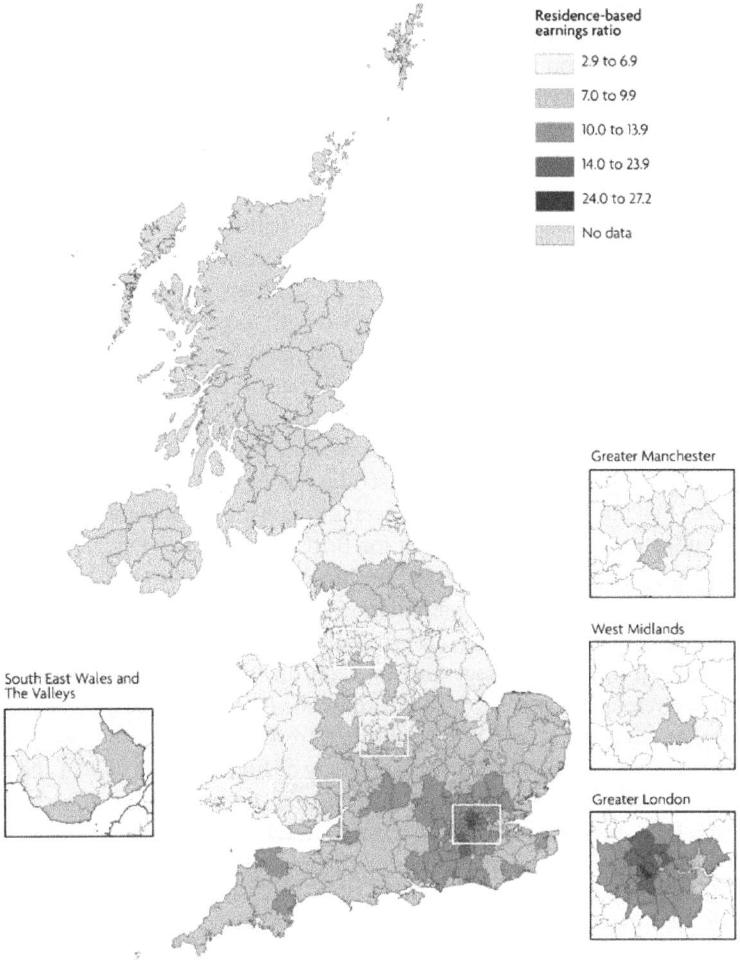

Residence-based
earnings ratio

- 2.9 to 6.9
- 7.0 to 9.9
- 10.0 to 13.9
- 14.0 to 23.9
- 24.0 to 27.2
- No data

Greater Manchester

West Midlands

South East Wales and
The Valleys

Greater London

Source: Secretary of State for Levelling Up, Housing and Communities. Available under Crown copyright, published under the Open Government Licence 3.0.[108]

that each required improvement.[109] The Education Policy Institute (EPI) has developed its contextual measure of performance, which aims to measure the impact of school quality, rather than the characteristics of school admissions.[110] It was used to rank the performance of 236 academy chains and local authorities in 2017 at the key stage 2 (for pupils aged seven to 11): Oxfordshire was ranked 129th and Oldham 195th.[111] The EPI reported that the average grades for English and maths at GCSE in 2020 in Oldham and Oxford were 4.34 and 5.02. But 33 per cent of Oldham's pupils were 'disadvantaged' (that is, eligible for free school meals over the past six years), which was more than twice that in Oxford (15 per cent). The pupils who were disadvantaged in Oldham achieved grades closer to the national average for non-disadvantaged students than in Oxford: the attainment gaps were 1.45 and 1.53.[112]

For government to change Britain for the better we need a better rallying call than the Johnson government's meretricious and (as it turns out) short-lived promise of 'levelling up'. One informed commentator observed that 'It's hard to think of a more stupid phrase' and it has been banned by the government in a 'mercy killing'.[113]

For Oldham, a town whose community has been blighted by deindustrial-isation, there are no 'quick win' strategies that within a generation could create employment opportunities that come close to those of Oxford. For example, what would be the impact of enabling University Campus Oldham to be upgraded to full university status, combined with reopening Oldham's railway line? A useful comparator here is Bolton, which is also in Greater Manchester. It has a railway station (with about 50 trains a day to Manchester, with the 15-mile journey taking around 20 minutes) and a new university, Bolton Institute, whose leadership delivered signal achievements. The institute gained the right to award taught undergraduate degrees in 1992 and research degrees in 1996. By 2004 it had won full university status. In the Complete University Guide's university league tables for British universities for 2023, Bolton was ranked '1st for student satisfaction in the North West since 2019'.[114] (By contrast, LSE was ranked 56th nationally in that year.[115]) But, in the wider rankings across multiple 'excellence' criteria, Bolton was ranked 124th. Cambridge, Oxford, LSE, Imperial College and UCL (all in the south-east UK's 'golden triangle') were in the top 10.[116] The Institute for Fiscal Studies (IFS) estimates of average earnings at age 29 by graduates from higher educational institutions ranged from £22,000, for the University of Bolton, to £60,000 at the top (for LSE).[117] (These estimates are at 2018 prices, and cover those in sustained employment, including dropouts, excluding self-employment income and people at the extremes at the 1st and 99th percentiles.) These factors suggest that there is no prospect of Bolton becoming a world-class university within a generation. And, even with its new university and a railway station, 24 per cent of Bolton's 177 small areas were included in the 10 per cent most deprived in Britain (as measured in the 2011 Index of Multiple Deprivation), compared with 30 per cent in Oldham and 1 per cent in Oxford.[118]

In 2001, Oldham was one of the towns that featured in national news for riots. These were investigated by the Community Cohesion Review Team, which was chaired by Ted Cantle. Their report gave a salutary warning to national and local governments:

> Unfortunately, the programmes devised to tackle the needs of many disadvantaged and disaffected groups, whilst being well intentioned and sometimes inspirational, often seemed to institution-alise the problems. The plethora of initiatives and programmes, with their baffling array of outcomes, boundaries, timescales and other conditions, seemed to ensure divisiveness and a perception

of unfairness in virtually every section of the communities we visited.[119]

The population of East Germany in 1990 was similar to the total of four English regions that have been most 'left behind' (the South West, North West, Yorkshire and the Humber, and the North East), plus Wales.[120] Spending there on the same scale as in the former East Germany would mean committing £7 billion a year from now until 2047, which is about 1 per cent of the UK's GDP. Even given the current anaemic prospects of the British economy, that ought to be manageable. But history and institutions also matter. What worked so well in Germany was partly rooted in its constitution, designed by the Allies after the Second World War and imposed on a defeated (and subsequently grateful) nation.[121] As later chapters make clear, the British history of undermining local government goes back to 1945–51, resulting in a heavily centralised state.

In 2017, the government identified the development of local industrial strategies (LISs) as a key commitment of its national industrial strategy. In 2018, the government established the Industry Strategy Council (ISC) to provide impartial and expert evaluation of their progress. In July 2020, Anna Romaniuk et al produced a report on the policymaking processes behind LISs for the ISC. They highlighted England's systemic weaknesses in tackling its endemic and acute problem of low productivity. England lacks local capability, co-production by local and central government, and coordination across central government.[122] The ISC's last annual report, published in April 2021, identified 'Levelling Up' as the government's most important mission. It argued that sustained local growth in places like Oldham requires investment in the local capacity and capability to develop and implement local strategies that cover infrastructure, skills, sectors, education and culture.[123] The ISC was abolished in March 2021.[124]

In April 2022, the government published its Levelling Up White Paper (see Figures 2.6 and 2.8).[125] Although it emphasised the importance of devolving power, its constant refrain was that 'the UK government will' (a phrase repeated nearly 200 times). There was no exploration of how to make devolution work more effectively with the governments in Scotland and Wales. That would have entailed collaboration between different political parties that was so vital in Germany. Nor did the White Paper identify the important changes needed to create opportunities in the areas that have been 'left behind'. The massive challenge for future governments is not 'levelling up' but enabling different kinds of prosperity in different places from effective devolution.

Conclusions

The causes of major geographical fault lines and inequalities found elsewhere in Europe – the institutions of feudalism, communism, or organised crime – cannot explain the different geographical fault lines that have developed in the UK. But weak regional social capital and the state-centralism of the UK compared with post-war Germany seem to have played a role. Chapter 1 also showed how different systems of centralised/professionalised governance in the NHS were perfectly designed to enable the scandals at the Bristol Royal Infirmary Mid Staffordshire NHS Foundation Trust. In the next chapter I show in detail how the way British systems of governance have developed in ways that cause both the UK's current governance malaise and its deep-set territorial fault lines, starting with the history and ideas that shaped Britain's pre-war institutions and created the agenda tackled by the Attlee settlement.

Endnotes

[1] Prime Minister's Office, 10 Downing Street (2021) *The Prime Minister's levelling up speech: 15 July 2021*, UK Government: Government Reform, 15 July.
https://www.gov.uk/government/speeches/the-prime-ministers-levelling-up-speech-15-july-2021

[2] Acemoglu, Daron and Robinson, James (2012) *Why nations fail: The origins of power, prosperity and poverty*, UK: Profile.

[3] Intriligator, Michael; Wedel, Janine; and Lee, Catherine (2006) 'What Russia can learn from China in its transition to a market economy', in Verweij, Marco and Thompson, Michael (eds) *Clumsy solutions for a complex world*, UK: Palgrave Macmillan, pp.105–31.
https://link.springer.com/content/pdf/10.1057/9780230624887_5.pdf?pdf=inline%20link

[4] Ferguson, Niall (2021) *Doom: The politics of catastrophe*, UK: Penguin, p.131.

[5] Dobson, R.B. (ed.) (1970) *The peasants' revolt of 1381*, UK: Macmillan, p.59.

[6] Ferguson, Niall, *Doom: The politics of catastrophe*, p.131.

[7] Dobson, R.B., *The peasants' revolt of 1381*, pp.64–65.

[8] Migration Advisory Committee (2020) *Migration Advisory Committee reviews shortage occupation lists*, UK: Migration Advisory Committee.
https://www.gov.uk/government/news/migration-advisory-committee-reviews-shortage-occupation-lists

[9] Hicks, John (1969) *A theory of economic history*, UK: Oxford University Press. p.112.

[10] Dobson, R.B., *The peasants' revolt of 1381*, p.66.

[11] Dobson, R.B., *The peasants' revolt of 1381*, p.69.

[12] Dobson, R.B., *The peasants' revolt of 1381*, p.62.

[13] Hatcher, John (1994) 'England in the aftermath of the Black Death', *Past & Present*, vol. 144, p.19. https://doi.org/10.1093/past/144.1.3

[14] Hicks, John, *A theory of economic history*, p.113.

[15] Rothstein, Bo (2021) *Controlling corruption: The social contract approach*, US: Oxford University Press. https://doi.org/10.1093/oso/9780192894908.001.0001

[16] Piketty, Thomas (2020) *Capital and ideology*, US: Harvard University Press, p.251. https://doi.org/10.4159/9780674245075

[17] Nove, Alec (1972) 'War, revolution and revolutionaries', in *An economic history of the USSR*, UK: Penguin, Chapter 2, pp.20–36.

[18] Marx, Karl (2004) 'The transformation of surplus value into capital', in *Capital* (Volume 1), translated by Ben Fowkes, UK: Penguin, pp.723–60.

[19] Nove, Alec, *An economic history of the USSR*, p.98.

[20] Nove, Alec, *An economic history of the USSR*, p.98.

[21] Nove, Alec, *An economic history of the USSR*, p.103.

[22] Nove, Alec, *An economic history of the USSR*, pp.109–25.

[23] Nove, Alec, *An economic history of the USSR*, p.157.

[24] Applebaum, Anne (2022) 'Holodomor', in *Encyclopedia Britannica*. https://perma.cc/RP5H-ZM6Y

[25] Gerstle, Gary (2022) *The rise and fall of the neoliberal order: America and the world in the free market era*, UK: Oxford University Press, p.29. https://doi.org/10.1093/oso/9780197519646.001.0001

[26] Gerstle, Gary, *The rise and fall of the neoliberal order*, p.32.

[27] Luce, Edward (2020) 'Will America tear itself apart? The Supreme Court, 2020 elections and a looming constitutional crisis', *Financial Times*, 15 October. https://perma.cc/QZ9X-7BNC

[28] Gerstle, Gary, *The rise and fall of the neoliberal order*, pp.23–24.

[29] Crosland, Anthony (1963) *The future of socialism*, US: Schocken, p.1.

[30] Brown, Archie (2010) *The rise and fall of communism*, UK: Vintage, p.260.

[31] Brown, Archie, *The rise and fall of communism*, p.256.

[32] Brown, Archie, *The rise and fall of communism*, p.256.

[33] Gorlizki, Yoram and Khlevniuk, Oleg (2020) *Substate dictatorship: Networks, loyalty, and institutional change in the Soviet Union*, US: Yale University Press, p.197. https://www.jstor.org/stable/j.ctv14rmq50.11

34 Nove, Alec (1961) *The Soviet economy*, UK: George Allen and Unwin, p.295.

35 Von Hayek, Friedrich (1945) 'The use of knowledge in society', *The American Economic Review*, vol. 35, no. 4, pp.518–30. https://www.jstor.org/stable/1809376

36 Kornai, Janos (1959) *Overcentralization in economic administration: A critical analysis based on experience in Hungarian light industry*, UK: Oxford University Press; Dobb, Maurice (1970) *Socialist planning: Some problems*, UK: Lawrence and Wishart.

37 Berliner, Joseph (1988) 'Bureaucratic conservatism and creativity in the Soviet economy', in *Soviet industry from Stalin to Gorbachev: Essays on management and innovation*, UK: Edward Elgar, Chapter 8, pp.188–211; Nove, Alec, *An economic history of the USSR*, p.309.

38 Gorlizki, Yoram and Khlevniuk, Oleg, *Substate dictatorship*, p.217.

39 Gorlizki, Yoram and Khlevniuk, Oleg, *Substate dictatorship*, p.225.

40 Vasilyeva, E. (1954) 'The Nail Factory' [cartoon]. *Крокодил [Krokodil]*, No 5, p.5. https://croco.uno/year/1954

41 Charron, Nicholas; Lapuente, Victor; and Annoni, Paola (2019) ' Measuring quality of government in EU regions across space and time', *Papers in Regional Science*, vol. 98, no. 5, pp.1925–53. https://doi.org/10.1111/pirs.12437

42 Rothstein, Bo (2015) *The Quality of Government Institute: Report for the first ten years of a research programme at University of Gothenburg*. https://www.gu.se/en/research/the-quality-of-government-institute

43 Dijkstra, Lewis (ed.) (2017) *My region, My Europe, our future. The 7th cohesion report*, p.10. Belgium: European Commission, copyright European Union. Reuse authorised under European Decision 2011/833/EU (OJ L 330, 14.12.2011, pp.30, 39). https://ec.europa.eu/regional_policy/information-sources/publications/reports/2017/7th-report-on-economic-social-and-territorial-cohesion_en

44 Putnam, Robert; Leonardi, Robert; and Nanetti, Rafaella (1992) *Making democracy work: Civic traditions in modern Italy*, US: Princeton University Press, p.18. https://doi.org/10.1515/9781400820740

45 Putnam, Robert et al, *Making democracy work*, p.135.

46 Putnam, Robert et al, *Making democracy work*, p.145.

47 Putnam, Robert et al, *Making democracy work*, p.136.

48 Travaglino, Giovanni; Abrams, Dominic; and De Moura, Georgina (2016) 'Men of honor don't talk: The relationship between masculine honor and social activism against criminal organizations in Italy',

Political Psychology, vol. 37, no. 2, pp.183–99.
https://doi.org/10.1111/pops.12226

[49] Kazmin, Amy and Ricozzi, Giuliana (2023) 'Messina Denaro's arrest saps strength of the Sicilian Mafia', *Financial Times*, 18 January. https://perma.cc/32TL-573N

[50] Wikimedia Commons (User: Shadowxfox; User: Enok) (2012) 'Map of Italy in 1494'. https://commons.wikimedia.org/wiki/File:Italy_1494.svg

[51] Johnson, Miles (2020) 'How the Mafia infiltrated Italy's hospitals and laundered the profits globally', *Financial Times*, 9 July. https://perma.cc/DHZ5-H9JC

[52] Johnson, Miles, 'How the Mafia infiltrated Italy's hospitals'.

[53] Wikileaks (2008, 2 December) 'Can Calabria be saved?' *Public Library of US Diplomacy*. https://perma.cc/FFK5-Q3F6

[54] BBC iPlayer (2023) *Italy's Crusader: Man vs Mafia*, 13 January. https://www.bbc.co.uk/iplayer/episode/p0dw2zm8/italys-crusader-man -vs-mafia

[55] *BBC News* (2021) 'Italian Mafia: 'Ndrangheta members convicted as Italy begins huge trial', 7 November. https://perma.cc/EW9D-PS2H

[56] Saviano, Roberto (2006) *Gomorrah*, UK: Pan Macmillan.

[57] Saviano, Roberto (2016) 'Operation money laundering', in his *Zero Zero Zero*, UK: Penguin, Chapter 11, pp.253–69.

[58] Saviano, Roberto, *Zero Zero Zero*, p.262.

[59] Wilson, Harry (2014) 'London is "money laundering capital"', *The Times*, 2 September. https://perma.cc/M95U-F8FN; Shaxson, Nicholas (2021) 'The City of London is hiding the world's stolen money', *New York Times*, 11 October. https://perma.cc/X2S7-UK6E; Kuper, Simon (2022) 'Who are the Londoners enabling the Russian elite?' *Financial Times* 3 March. https://perma.cc/X85Q-RTBM; *Financial Times* (2022, 22 April) *How London became the dirty money capital of the world | FT Film* [Video]. https://www.youtube.com/watch?v=gyk12Wf_TeQ.

[60] Gray, John (2012) 'A point of view: Are tyrants good for art?' *BBC News*, 10 August. https://perma.cc/J39N-FH92

[61] MacGregor, Neil (2014) *Germany: Memories of a nation*, UK: Penguin, p.335.

[62] MacGregor, Neil, *Germany: Memories of a nation*, pp.347–48.

[63] Herbez, Vukasin (2018) '100 years of automobiles: 20 most important cars of the 20th century'. *Motor Junkie*, 25 June. https://perma.cc/T3M5-SNYW

[64] Rubin, Eli (2009) 'The Trabant: Consumption, Eigen-Sinn, and movement', *History Workshop Journal*, vol. 68, no. 1, p.30.

[65] DeMuro, Doug (2016) *The Trabant was an awful car made by communists* [Video], 9 November. https://www.youtube.com/watch?v=No1-4GsQa-g; Miltimore, Jon (2019) 'The worst car ever: A brief history of the Trabant', *FEE Stories*, 6 November. https://perma.cc/CM38-ETEH

[66] Rubin, Eli, 'The Trabant: Consumption, Eigen-Sinn, and movement', p.35.

[67] MacGregor, Neil, *Germany: Memories of a nation*, p.348.

[68] Viner, Brian (2012) 'The man who rejected the Beatles', *The Independent*, 12 February. https://perma.cc/3S5T-UEXH

[69] Turner, Graham (1969) 'The car makers', in *Business in Britain*, UK: Eyre & Spotiswoode, pp.378–97.

[70] Dixon, Huw (1996) 'Deindustrialisation and Britain's Industrial Performance Since 1960', *The Economic Journal*, vol. 106, no. 434, pp.170–71. https://doi.org/10.2307/2234940

[71] Eichengreen, Barry (1996) 'Explaining Britain's economic performance: a critical note', *The Economic Journal*, vol. 106, no. 434, pp.213–18.

[72] Eichengreen, Barry, 'Explaining Britain's economic performance', p.217.

[73] Eichengreen, Barry, 'Explaining Britain's economic performance', p.217.

[74] Rieger, Bernard (2013) *The people's car: A global history of the Volkswagen*, US: Harvard University Press. Quoted in *Germany: Memories of a nation*, p.351.

[75] Hotten, Russell (2015) 'Volkswagen: The scandal explained'. *BBC News*, 10 December. https://perma.cc/48D4-QH6X

[76] European Commission (2019) 'Regional GDP per capita ranged from 31 per cent to 626 per cent of the EU average in 2017', *Eurostat News Release* 34/2019, 26 February. https://perma.cc/5TJZ-YJ54

[77] Maddison, Angus (2006) *The world economy*. France: Organisation for Economic Co-operation and Development (OECD), p.178. http://dx.doi.org/10.1787/486663055853

[78] Office for National Statistics (2000) *Regional Trends, No. 35, 2000 Edition*. https://webarchive.nationalarchives.gov.uk/ukgwa/20160129145432 /http://www.ons.gov.uk/ons/rel/regional-trends/regional-trends/no--35 --2000-edition/index.html

[79] 'Deutsche Einheit hat fast zwei Billionen Euro gekostet' (2014) *Franfurter Allegemeine*, 4 May. https://perma.cc/X6RX-5FR2; Kampfner, John (2020) *Why the Germans do it better: Notes from a grown-up country*, UK: Atlantic, p.87.

[80] Kampfner, John, *Why the Germans do it better*, p.87.

[81] Gerstle, Gary, *The rise and fall of the neoliberal order*, p.146.

[82] Eurostat (2022) *GDP per capita in PPS*.
https://ec.europa.eu/eurostat/databrowser/view/tec00114/default/table?lang=en

[83] Office for National Statistics (2022) *Regional economic activity by gross domestic product, UK: 1998 to 2020*.
https://www.ons.gov.uk/economy/grossdomesticproductgdp/bulletins/regionaleconomicactivitybygrossdomesticproductuk/1998to2020

[84] Eurostat (2023) *Gross domestic product (GDP) at current market prices by NUTS 3*. https://ec.europa.eu/eurostat/databrowser/view/NAMA_10R_3GDP/default/table?lang=en&category=reg.reg_eco10.reg_eco10gdp; Office for National Statistics (2022) *Regional economic activity by gross domestic product, UK: 1998 to 2020*.
https://www.ons.gov.uk/economy/grossdomesticproductgdp/bulletins/regionaleconomicactivitybygrossdomesticproductuk/1998to2020

[85] Raikes, Luke (2022) *Levelling up? Lessons from Germany*, UK: Fabian Society. https://fabians.org.uk/publication/levelling-up/

[86] UPP Foundation (undated) *Truly civic: Strengthening the connection between universities and their places*, p.18. https://perma.cc/8KB9-JVE8

[87] University of Oxford (n.d.) 'Finance and funding'. *University of Oxford*. https://perma.cc/P4SF-GE9S

[88] Williams, Maire (2016) *Fast growth cities*, UK: Centre for Cities, p.4. https://perma.cc/NQ83-KP47

[89] Top Tier (2019). *The UK's golden triangle*, UK: Top Tier, 5 September. https://perma.cc/SK6R-DZE5

[90] Office for National Statistics (2023) *Nomis, labour market profile Oxford*. https://perma.cc/2727-ZTGS

[91] Oxford City Council (2020) *Economic statistics: Quick facts*. https://perma.cc/XSX6-N8HT

[92] Oldham Coliseum Theatre (2023) 'History'. https://perma.cc/Y6CR-63XR

[93] Wells, Martin (2022) 'On track from Oldham Mumps to Delhi', *The Guardian*, 12 August. https://perma.cc/ES46-MXGZ

[94] Price, Bevan and Wright, Paul (2017) 'Station name: Oldham Mumps'. *Disused Stations*. https://perma.cc/6EDG-JLXD

[95] Payne, Sebastian (2023) 'Quickest way to level up is to stop the yobs', *The Times*, 26 January. https://perma.cc/K3Y6-YUNJ

[96] Oldham Coliseum Theatre (2023) 'Oldham Coliseum Theatre website'. https://perma.cc/KC4W-6HCH

[97] Editorial (2022) 'The Guardian view on cuts in theatre funding: a threat to playwriting', *The Guardian*, 9 December. https://perma.cc/5YL9-Y47L

[98] University Campus Oldham (2023) 'Study near – to go far… Prospectus 2023/24'. https://perma.cc/X6Z2-BDCS

[99] Independent Schools Council (n.d.) 'Independent Schools Council website'. https://www.isc.co.uk

[100] Markovits, Daniel (2019) *The meritocracy trap*, UK: Penguin.

[101] Cooper, Luke and Cooper, Christabel (2020) '"Get Brexit done": The new political divides of England and Wales at the 2019 election', *The Political Quarterly*, vol. 91, no. 4, pp.751–61. https://doi.org/10.1111/1467-923X.12918

[102] Mattinson, Deborah (2020) *Beyond the red wall: Why Labour lost, how the Conservatives won and what will happen next?* UK: Biteback.

[103] Secretary of State for Levelling Up, Housing and Communities (2022) *Levelling up the United Kingdom*, Figure 1.13, p.18. https://assets.publishing.service.gov.uk/government/uploads/system/uploads/attachment_data/file/1052708/Levelling_up_the_UK_white _paper.pdf

[104] Office for National Statistics (2022) *Employee earnings in the UK: 2022.* https://www.ons.gov.uk/employmentandlabourmarket/peopleinwork /earningsandworkinghours/bulletins/annualsurveyofhoursandearnings /2022

[105] Office for National Statistics (2022) *Measures of national well-being dashboard: Quality of life in the UK.* https://www.ons.gov.uk/peoplepop ulationandcommunity/wellbeing/articles/measuresofnationalwellbeing dashboardqualityoflifeintheuk/2022-08-12; Brown, Tom (2022) 'Colchester is the UNHAPPIEST place in Britain with Redditch, Norwich, Tunbridge Wells and Lambeth trailing behind, new ONS data reveals… so where does YOUR area rank in the UK's misery league?' *Daily Mail*, 4 December. https://perma.cc/Q3TR-3CQW

[106] Secretary of State for Levelling Up, *Levelling up the United Kingdom*, p.73.

[107] End Child Poverty (2023) 'Child poverty in your area'. https://endchildpoverty.org.uk/child-poverty/

[108] Secretary of State for Levelling Up, *Levelling up the United Kingdom*, Figure 1.48, p.73. https://assets.publishing.service.gov.uk/government /uploads/system/uploads/attachment_data/file/1052708/Levelling_up _the_UK_white_paper.pdf

[109] Care Quality Commission (2023) 'Royal Oldham Hospital'. https://perma.cc/ZU7M-97NB; Care Quality Commission (2023) 'John Radcliffe Hospital'. https://perma.cc/472Z-FK39

[110] Andrews, John (2018) *School performance in academy chains and local authorities – 2017*, UK: Education Policy Institute, p.6. https://epi.org.uk/publications-and-research/performance-academy -local-authorities-2017/

[111] Andrews, John, *School performance in academy chains and local authorities – 2017*, pp.60, 63.

[112] https://epi.org.uk/education-gap-data/

[113] Scott, Geraldine (2023) 'Levelling up is so 2019… Rishi Sunak's Tories are now gauging up', *The Times*, 18 January. https://perma.cc/C8MQ-RWU6

[114] Complete University Guide (2023) 'University of Bolton'. https://perma.cc/6EYE-DRAV

[115] Complete University Guide (2023) 'London School of Economics and Political Science'. https://perma.cc/UNV7-TH6M

[116] Complete University Guide (2023) 'University league tables 2023'. https://perma.cc/6L3H-L7DE

[117] Belfield, Chris; Britton, Jack; Buscha, Franz; Dearden, Lorraine; Dickson, Matt; van der Erve, Laura; Sibieta, Luke; Vignoles, Anna; Walker, Ian; and Zhu, Yu (2018) *The impact of undergraduate degrees on early-career earnings*, UK: Institute for Fiscal Studies. https://assets.publishing.service.gov.uk/government/uploads/system /uploads/attachment_data/file/759278/The_impact_of_undergraduate _degrees_on_early-career_earnings.pdf

[118] Ministry of Housing, Communities and Local Government (2019) *The English indices of deprivation 2019*, UK: Ministry of Housing, Communities and Local Government. https://assets.publishing.service.gov.uk/government/uploads/system /uploads/attachment_data/file/835115/IoD2019_Statistical_Release.pdf

[119] The Community Cohesion Review Team (Chair Ted Cantle) (2001) *Community cohesion: A report of the Independent Review Team*, UK: Home Office, p.10. https://tedcantle.co.uk/pdf/communitycohesion%20cantlereport.pdf

[120] World Population Review (2023) 'Germany'. https://perma.cc/QUJ4-WCPA; and Census 2021 (2022) 'Population Estimates'. *Office for National Statistics.* https://www.ons.gov.uk/peoplepopulationandcommunity/populationand migration/populationestimates

[121] Kampfner, John, *Why the Germans do it better*, pp.5–6.

[122] Romaniuk, Anna; Osborne, Catherine; Rainsford, Emily; and Taylor, Abigail (2020) *Understanding the policy-making processes behind local growth strategies in England*, UK: Industrial Strategy Council, pp.6–7. https://industrialstrategycouncil.org/understanding-policy-making -processes-behind-local-growth-strategiesengland

[123] Industrial Strategy Council (2021) *Annual report*, UK: Industrial Strategy Council. https://industrialstrategycouncil.org/sites/default/files/attachments /ISC%20Annual%20Report%202021.pdf

[124] Haldane, Andy (2021) 'UK industrial strategy is dead, long may it live', *Financial Times*, 23 March. https://perma.cc/28PV-DWVR

[125] Secretary of State for Levelling Up, Housing and Communities, *Levelling Up the United Kingdom*.

3. The interwar period and the Attlee settlement

The plan for social security is put forward as part of a general programme of social policy. It is one part only of an attack on five giant evils: upon the physical Want with which it is directly concerned, upon Disease which often causes that Want and brings many other troubles in its train, upon Ignorance which no democracy can afford amongst its citizens, upon Squalor which arises mainly from the haphazard distribution of industry and population, and upon Idleness which destroys wealth and corrupts men whether they are well fed or not, when they are idle.

William Beveridge (1942)[1]

A political 'settlement' results in major resets of a country's systems of governance that create radical changes in how its economy and society work. Britain is famous for its distinctive institutional continuity. Only two fundamental 'settlements' have occurred in modern Britain. The first was wrought by Labour governments led by Clement Attlee from 1944 to 1951 and the second by Conservative governments led by Margaret Thatcher, from 1979 to 1992 (covered in Chapter 5). In each case, an impressive avalanche of changes was pushed through in a few years, which were directed at problems that had accumulated over previous decades.

For the Attlee settlement, the problems of the interwar period were caused by the British version of the minimal state, based on largely unfettered capitalist logics. In this chapter, I begin by setting out the background and tracing the influence of interwar problems on the wartime refounding of a policy consensus. The middle section describes how key foundations of that consensus were developed under the wartime coalition government of Conservative and Labour ministers. The prime minister, Winston Churchill, concentrated on the war effort and foreign policy, and his deputy, Clement Attlee, on domestic policy. The final section shows how Labour's programme of reforms followed policies agreed by the coalition government to tackle three of Beveridge's

How to cite this book chapter:

Bevan, Gwyn (2023) *How Did Britain Come to This? A century of systemic failures of governance*, London: LSE Press, pp. 53–89.
https://doi.org/10.31389/lsepress.hdb.c License: CC BY-NC

five giant evils: Want, Ignorance and Idleness. Aneurin Bevan, as minister of health, made radical changes in tackling Disease and Squalor.

3.1 The roots of the problems – Britain before 1939

At 8am on Tuesday, 14 October 1913, an explosion at the colliery in the mining village of Senghenydd, near Caerphilly, killed 439 miners and a rescuer.[2] The following Sunday its chapels were bereft of men. Aneurin Bevan, who became the MP for Ebbw Vale and minister of health in the Attlee government, would have been working down another colliery near Senghenydd on the day of the explosion. He would have been aged 16 – he left his elementary school before his 14th birthday.[3] The inquiry into that worst ever mining disaster in Britain found the company and its management to have been negligent. They were fined £34 in total.[4] Taking account of inflation to current prices seems a poor way of accounting for how this must have seemed so flagrantly unjust to the close-knit mining communities of Senghenydd and the South Wales coalfield.

Another way of assessing the meaning of the fine of £34 is to compare it with the compensation made 80 years before, when Britain legislated for the abolition of slavery. If you were to think the issue here was the problem of fairly compensating slaves for their years of living death, you would be sadly mistaken. Indeed, what 'freedom' meant for many slaves was being forced to sign contracts and endure semi-forced labour for long periods.[5] Thomas Piketty describes how the fundamental purpose of proprietarian ideology is to justify absolute protection to private property.[6] The stumbling block in winning support for the legislation to abolish slavery was agreeing 'fair' compensation to British slave owners (dramatised by Juliet Wilks Romero in the play *The Whip*[7]). Piketty reports that, in 1833, British slave owners were paid compensation of £25 per slave (about £50 in 1913 money).[8] That debt was so vast that the Treasury finalised payment only in 2015.[9] It seemed that the lives of 440 Welsh miners in 1913 were valued less than the compensation to a slaveowner for freeing one slave in 1833.

For the first half of the 20th century the coal industry was fundamental to the British economy. It was the primary source of energy, and second only to agriculture in numbers employed, value of output, and capital invested. Richard Tawney pointed that that the typical annual death toll in 1920 was over 1,000 miners a year – equivalent to an infantry battalion at full strength in the First World War.[10] That war ended on 11 November 1918 with the Armistice. Later that month, the prime minister, David Lloyd George, made the famous promise:

> To make Britain a fit country for heroes to live in … to make victory the motive power to link the old land up in such measure that it will be nearer the sunshine than ever before, and that at any rate it will lift those who have been living in the dark places to a plateau where they will get the rays of the sun.[11]

After the end of the First World War, economist John Maynard Keynes (pictured in Figure 3.1) worked on financial agreements that were integral to the Peace Treaty of Versailles: the reparations to be made by Germany and settlements of debts between the Allies. Although he was only 25 years old, he was HM Treasury's official representative and deputy for the Chancellor of the Exchequer on the Supreme Economic Council. Bertrand Russell, one the foremost philosophers of the 20th century, described Keynes's intellect as 'the sharpest and clearest I have ever known'.[12] Keynes combined his towering analytic intellect with intuitive thinking. He was the leading public intellectual of his generation who comfortably bestrode the worlds of academia, Whitehall, international diplomacy, and the writers and artists in Bloomsbury. In June 1919, Keynes and the German foreign minister, Count Brockdorff-Rantzau, objected so strongly to the Peace Treaty of Versailles that each resigned. In December 1919, Keynes published *The Economic Consequences of the Peace*.[13] He quoted with approval from the Count's speech that 'those who sign this Treaty will sign the death sentence of many millions of German men, women and children'.[14] For the Allies, Keynes foresaw their heroes returning to 'an inefficient, unemployed, disorganized Europe … torn by internal strife and international hate, fighting, starving, pillaging, and lying'.[15]

The failings of the coal industry powerfully illustrate Eichengreen's argument cited in Chapter 2: that Britain's institutions in the 20th century were

Figure 3.1: John Maynard Keynes by Gwen Raverat (*c*.1908)

Source: National Portrait Gallery, London. Available under the National Portrait Gallery Academic Licence.[16]

still those that had enabled its early industrialisation. They lacked networks of investment banks lending to large enterprises that challenged unions in implementing the technologies of modern mass production.[17] The British coal industry's incapability of meeting the demands of the First World War resulted in the government taking control. In 1919, the majority report of the Sankey Royal Commission of 1919–20 recommended that control continue by nationalisation, but the government returned it to private ownership.[18]

In 1925, the pound sterling re-entered the gold standard. Keynes criticised the decision by the Chancellor of the Exchequer, Winston Churchill, to enter at too high a rate of exchange for sterling. He argued that the first of *The Economic Consequences of Mr Churchill* was the proposal by the colliery owners to reduce the wages of miners:

> Like other victims of economic transition in past times, the miners are to be offered the choice between starvation and submission, the fruits of their submission to accrue to the benefit of other classes … On grounds of social justice, no case can be made out for reducing the wages of the miners. They are the victims of the economic Juggernaut.[19]

The government subsidised the industry to prevent reductions in miners' wages whilst another Royal Commission considered the future of the coal industry.[20]

In 1926, this Samuel Commission recommended that the mine owners invested in mechanisation and concentrated production in large efficient mines, but recognised that would not happen without government being empowered to bring that about by buying out private mineral rights. The government failed to act. When the subsidy ran out on 1 May 1926, the mine owners required miners to earn 20 per cent less than in 1914 (in real terms).[21] They went on strike. Support from other unions in the General Strike lasted for nine days only. The mine owners' strategy resulted in the defeat of the miners' strike after six months; financial losses; no revival in exports; and reduction by a third of the 1.2 million employed in 1920 by 1938.[22]

3.2 The problem of unemployment

For the British heroes who returned from the war, and failed to find jobs, their relief from poverty was still governed by the Poor Law Act of 1834. That view was shaped by Nassau Senior, a member of the Royal Commission on the Poor Law 1834 and the first Drummond professor of political economy at Oxford. He used the market to determine the level of payment for welfare: the principle of 'less eligibility', which meant that it must be lower than the meanest form of employment. That principle was based on the assumption that the reason people are unemployed is because they refuse to accept what the market had to offer for their labour.[23] The Commission's report posed this rhetorical question: what motive has the man to seek employment when he 'knows that his income will be increased by nothing other than an increase in his family ... and has no reference to his skill, honesty or diligence?'[24] Poor relief of paupers was made conditional on admission to the workhouse, which entailed stigmatisation and humiliation. Workhouses were strictly regulated to disarm the unemployed 'of their main weapon – the plea of impending starvation' by ensuring 'that no one need perish from want'.[25]

In his evidence to the Royal Commission that reviewed the Poor Law 1909, J.S. Davy, the permanent head of the Poor Law Division, stated his firm belief that an unemployed man 'must suffer for the general good of the body politic'.[26] And the principal concern in evidence from working men and women (some of whom had been inmates of workhouses and recipients of outdoor relief) was the failure of the Poor Law to weed out (what we would call) 'scroungers'.[27] The Royal Commission's Majority Report found the Poor Law principles of 1834 to be 'both sound and *humane*' (emphasis added).[28] The Minority Report called for radical change:

> The mere keeping of people from starving – which is essentially what the Poor Law sets out to do – may have been useful in averting a social revolution; it cannot, in the twentieth century, be regarded as any adequate fulfilment of a social duty.[29]

No change was made to the Poor Law until the 1920 Unemployment Insurance Act, which introduced insurance for practically all manual workers.[30] This change was blamed by an influential French economist, Jaques Rueff, in 1925, for 'the underlying cause of unemployment which has been so cruelly inflicted on England since 1920'.[31] Figure 3.2 shows that unemployment soared in the Great Depression and only returned to earlier levels just before the war. The National Economies Act 1931, which followed the report of Sir George May's Committee on national expenditure, targeted expenditure on unemployment benefit, which had increased from £12 million in 1928 to £128 million in 1931.[32] Those who had been claiming unemployment benefit for a period of 26 weeks were subjected to the humiliation of the means test.[33] Libby Purves describes how that required family income to be taken into account:

> You had to prove just how poor you were, in intimate domestic detail. It imposed form-filling, impertinent questions, and regular, shamingly visible, visits from investigators licensed to peer into your cooking-pots, rule that one chair per person was enough, and order you to sell your spare blankets.[34]

Aneurin Bevan, the MP for Ebbw Vale, speaking in the House of Commons, described the means test as designed 'to make whole communities of paupers'.[35]

Figure 3.2: UK unemployment rate (%), 1919 to 1939

Source: Bank of England.[36]

Unemployment was concentrated in the coal, cotton, wool, shipbuilding and iron and steel industries of Wales, Yorkshire, Lancashire, Tyneside and central Scotland.[37] But the Midlands and the South East of England prospered from growth in house building and the electrical engineering and motor industries.[38] Figure 3.3 shows the dramatic geographical variations across Britain in unemployment: from 30 per cent below the average to over 170 per cent above. Nick Timmins points out that when unemployment was only 3 per cent and 7 per cent in High Wycombe and Deptford it was 67 per cent in Jarrow (near Newcastle).[39] 'Red Ellen' Wilkinson, the Labour MP for Jarrow who became minister for education in the Attlee government, described life there: 'No one had a job except a few railwaymen, officials, the workers in the co-operative stores, and a few workmen who went out of the town'.[40] She had gone from a working-class family to elementary school in Manchester, won a scholarship to the selective Ardwick Higher Elementary Grade school and on to the University of Manchester.[41] In 1936, she led the 'Jarrow crusade' of 200 who marched to London, where she presented a petition to Parliament 'demanding that a steel works be built to bring back jobs to their town'.[42]

In 1944, in the Employment White Paper, the Treasury agreed to a summary of the 'Treasury view' of the 1920s and 1930s, namely that the British economy was a self-regulating system so that:

> every trade depression would bring its own corrective, since prices *and wages* would fall, the fall in prices would bring about

an increase in demand, and employment would thus be restored (emphasis added).[43]

That was why governments did practically nothing about unemployment. The 'Treasury view' endowed the market economy with magical healing powers. It would revitalise the mining communities, after cuts in wages and job losses. And, even after the UK government cut feet off their feet by setting too high an exchange rate for sterling, the magic of the market would make them grow again.

In 1936, Keynes published *The General Theory of Interest, Employment and Money*.[44] This described the struggle to free his thinking from classical economics that justified the 'Treasury view' that the market will operate as a self-regulating system. That microeconomic theory requires that there are so many buyers and sellers that the decisions of any one of them has no effect. Keynes developed the new field of macroeconomics by focusing on analysis of aggregates. In 1925 he argued that driving down wages throughout the coal industry and cutting public expenditure would reduce aggregate demand. In a self-regulating market economy, this would result in sustained unemployment, as in the 1930s, when national unemployment was 10 per cent on average. But real income per capita increased by over 20 per cent (see Figure 3.4).

Figure 3.3: Relative unemployment rates in Britain in local areas as a percentage (%) of the national average, for 1927–31 and 1931–36

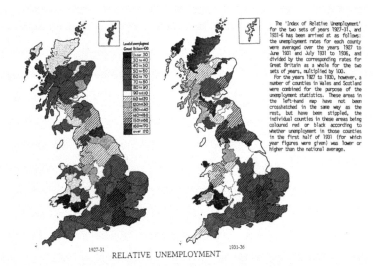

RELATIVE UNEMPLOYMENT

Source: Official Publications Library/Ministry of Labour.[45]
Notes: An index of relative unemployment compares the average unemployment in each county for the two five-year periods with the national average and shows it as a percentage running from 30 to 99 per cent (local unemployment is better than the national average) and upwards from 100 per cent (local unemployment is worse than the national average).

Keynes identified three criteria that applied to classical economics of his day, which also apply to the neoliberal economics of the Thatcher settlement:

1. It produced austere unpalatable conclusions that are counterintuitive from a vast consistent logical structure.
2. It explained why economic progress requires policies that are socially unjust and cruel because more palatable alternatives could provide short-term relief only and worse outcomes in the long run.
3. It justified unbridled capitalism.[46]

Keynes was a member of the Macmillan Committee, appointed to advise the government on how to respond to the global slump of 1929 following the Wall Street Crash.[47] There he argued that history showed that 'for centuries there has existed intense social resistance to any matters of reduction in the level of money incomes' and when last tried in England in the 1820s and 1830s it had brought the country to the 'verge of revolution'.[48] He invited five economists to produce 'an agreed diagnosis of our current problems and a reasoned list of remedies', chiefly that the government ought to increase public expenditure and run a deficit.

Lionel Robbins disagreed. He had just been appointed by William Beveridge, the director of LSE, to its chair of political economy. Robbins was then aged 31 – the youngest professor in the country.[49] Forty years later, his autobiography expressed 'deep regret' that, 'although I was acting in good faith and with a strong sense of social obligation, I should have opposed what might have mitigated the economic distress of those days' in 'the greatest mistake of my professional career'.[50] He had 'become the slave of theoretical constructions' of the Austrian School of Economics of Ludwig von Mises and Friedrich von Hayek.[51] Robbins described his position 'as invalid as denying blankets and stimulants to a drunk who has fallen into an icy pond, on the ground that his original trouble was overheating'.[52] That perfectly describes the Treasury view of the 1920s and 1930s. When, in 1931, Friedrich von Hayek outlined the complex mathematics of the Austrian School of Economics at a seminar in Cambridge, these brilliant economists were left bewildered. After a long silence, this exchange took place:

Richard Kahn: 'Is it your view that if I went out tomorrow and bought a new overcoat that would increase unemployment?'

Friedrich von Hayek: 'Yes ... but it would take a very long mathematical argument to explain why.'[53]

3.3 The economic freeze of healthcare, education and housing

The global slump of 1919 to 1921 reduced real income per capita by 20 per cent. That was three times larger than in the global slump that followed the

Wall Street Crash of 1929. Figure 3.4 gives post-war statistics for Britain for real income and public expenditure per capita (indexed to 1919 = 100 at 2013 prices), showing the near-continuous stagnation in both measures. Figure 3.2 shows that unemployment increased to 10 per cent in 1921, and over 15 per cent in 1932. These slumps created budget deficits. Although there had been shifts within classical economics since 1776 from Adam Smith's vehement opposition to governments incurring debts and running deficits, in the 1920s and 1930s, the British Treasury was as adamant as Smith that the government ought to aim to balance the budget each year.[54]

Although from 1918 various policies were recommended that could have 'made Britain a fit country for heroes', over time government policies were blighted by the hold of the 'Treasury view' on successive governments. Thus they nurtured the growth of William Beveridge's five giant evils, quoted at the start of this chapter. Unemployment and the principle of less eligibility resulted in Idleness and Want; and the remorseless drive for economies in public spending for Disease, Ignorance and Squalor.

In tackling Disease, the Majority Report of the 1909 Royal Commission on the Poor Law recognised that: 'to the extent to which we can eliminate or diminish sickness among the poor, we shall eliminate or diminish one half of the causes of pauperism'. But it ridiculed 'those enthusiasts who contemplate unfettered and uninterrupted and unintermittent medical control,

Figure 3.4: UK real GDP per capita and public expenditure per capita in the interwar period (1919 = 100)

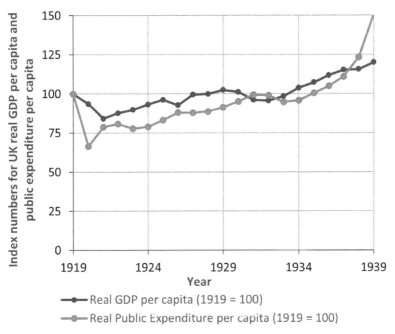

Source: Bank of England.[55]

supervision and treatment of every human being from the cradle to the grave.[56] The Minority Report called for 'a unified medical service', freeing public infirmaries from the grip of the Poor Law and moving them to local government. However, it did not advocate 'the gratuitous provision of medical treatment to all applicants'.[57]

The 1911 National Insurance Act introduced health insurance for workmen only (up to an income limit), for access to a general practitioner (GP) only (chosen from a panel), and excluded their dependants. Otherwise, GPs charged fees and bought and sold their practices on a commercial basis. Reports from the 1926 Royal Commission on National Health Insurance recommended extending coverage for healthcare, but subsequent governments made no changes.[58] Before developments in effective therapies and control of infections in the 20th century, hospitals were places best avoided. These beneficial developments increased their costs, so consequently access largely depended on ability to pay. That resulted in Julian Tudor Hart's 'inverse care law': the quality and quantity of care were distributed geographically in an inverse relationship to need.[59]

In addition to the Poor Law infirmaries there was an unregulated chaotic mix of voluntary and cottage hospitals. Voluntary hospitals included the elite London teaching hospitals (for example, Guy's, St Thomas' and St Bartholomew's[60]) and far too many small special hospitals of poor quality.[61] Specialists were subject to training and regulation under the oversight of the Royal Colleges. There was, however, no training of GPs.[62] They provided medical and surgical care in cottage hospitals and were too often scandalously incompetent.[63]

In 1919, the newly established Ministry of Health commissioned Lord Dawson of Penn (who was 'the most admired and respected doctor of his generation') to chair a committee to consider reform.[64] His report a year later recommended radical change. GPs should work in health centres with strong links to a general hospital, which should in turn be linked to a teaching hospital with a medical school (see Figure 3.5).[65] The only change the government made, however, was a piecemeal transfer of the Poor Law infirmaries to local authorities. How councils developed their hospitals varied a lot from place to place.[66] The surveys for the Beveridge Report of 1942 found that only for medical services did 'Britain's achievements fall seriously short of what has been accomplished elsewhere'.[67]

In tackling Ignorance, the 1918 Education Act raised the school leaving age from 12 to 14, abolished all fees in state elementary schools and widened the provision of school medical inspections, nursery schools, and special needs education.[68] But then, in 1921, Liberal PM David Lloyd George set up a high-powered committee of businessmen to make draconian cuts in public expenditure. The committee was chaired by Sir Eric Geddes, a dynamic businessman and minister who had achieved worldly success despite having been required to leave most of the high fee-paying 'public schools' he had attended.[69] The 'Geddes axe' resulted in cutting (current) public expenditure by about 25 per cent between 1920 and 1925,[70] and on schools by 36 per cent.[71]

Figure 3.5: The organisation of health services recommended by the Dawson Report in 1920

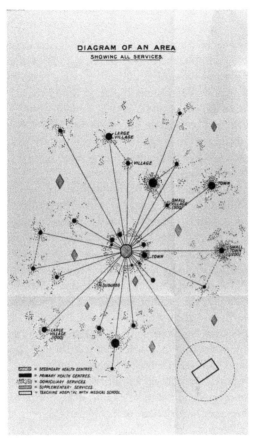

The school starting age was raised from five to six, the pupil/teacher ratio increased, and teachers were paid less.[73]

The Board of Education was responsible for oversight of schools in England. Its Consultative Committee produced two reports that called for radical change. The first was the Hadow Report of 1926, which recommended replacing the elementary schools with a system of primary and secondary schools and raising the school leaving age from 14 to 15.[74] In 1931, the May Committee was charged with making draconian cuts in public expenditure. In the 1938 preface to Tawney's classic text on *Equality* he quoted from the 1931 report of the May Committee:

> Since the standard of education, elementary and secondary, that is being given to a child of poor parents, is already in very many cases

superior to that which the middle-class parent is providing for his own child, we feel that it is time to pause in this policy of expansion.[75]

The second key report, the Spens Report in 1938, recommended the abolition of elementary schools, the raising of the school leaving age to 16, and the development of three types of secondary school of equal parity: grammar, modern and technical.[76] When Richard Austen Butler (RAB) was appointed as head of the Board of Education in 1941 he lamented the 'economic freeze' that meant so little had been done on any of this. For the vast majority of children, their only education to age 14 was in elementary schools blighted by poverty and stigmatised by inferiority – only a small minority went to grammar schools as the route to the professions.[77]

Tackling Squalor also stalled after the initial post-war impetus. In 1918, the government appointed the Welsh architect and Liberal MP Sir John Tudor Walters to chair a committee that set standards for development of public authority houses.[78] These ought to be spacious, in areas with low density, with a good social mix, use waste heat from power stations, and be developed with public transport to avoid social isolation.[79] The report also recommended selective demolition and rehabilitation of existing older houses, and not wholesale clearance.[80] Yet, after only three years, the programme of building new houses to the Tudor Walter standards was suspended. Only 50,000 of the 700,000 new houses that were estimated to be needed had been completed.[81] Later, in the 1920s, of the million houses that were built, half were bought by the middle class and half were rented by the working class.[82]

In 1940, the Report of the Royal Commission on the Distribution of the Urban Population recommended that: 'a Central Authority national in scope and character is required', with as one of its objectives:

> encouragement of a reasonable balance of industrial development as far as possible throughout the various divisions or regions of Great Britain, coupled with appropriate diversification of industry in each division or region of the country.[83]

That year Thomas Sharp published his best-selling book, *Town Planning*.[84] He had gone from a mining village in Durham to elementary and grammar schools, and on to become a lecturer at Durham University. His book identified three failings in planning between the wars. First, people were unable to live close to where they were educated, worked and enjoyed recreation. Second, the unemployed in the vulnerable areas and regions were unable to move to new jobs because of the lack of houses that they could rent. Third, there were such social barriers between different classes that 'one half of England has only the vaguest idea of how the other half lives'.[85] He captured what the Beveridge Report meant by Squalor:

The distressed areas of South Wales, County Durham, Cumberland, Lancashire and the Scottish Highlands would be a shameful blot on any civilised country, let alone a country that professes to lead the civilised world. For fifteen years and more in places like Rhondda, Jarrow and Bishops Auckland hundreds of thousands of Englishmen [sic] have been eating their heart out in squalid dole-supported unemployment spent among fouled landscapes and filthy slum-built towns with hardly a had lifted to help them. And all the while the new industries they require have been piling up in prosperous places in the Midlands and the South; and our governments have done practically nothing.[86]

3.4 Foundations laid by the wartime coalition government

Under the coalition government of Conservative and Labour ministers, the two key figures who laid the foundations of what became the Attlee settlement were Liberals: William Beveridge and Maynard Keynes. The Beveridge Report is remembered not for its herculean endeavour in reshaping social security but for the passage quoted as epigraph to this chapter that identified his five giant evils. Maynard Keynes is remembered for his influence on committing post-war governments to a policy of maintaining high levels of employment.

William Beveridge (pictured in Figure 3.6) was one of the 'great and the good' – indeed, in his own estimation, one of the best. In 1919, at the age of 39, he was one of the youngest ever to reach the top rank of permanent secretary in the civil service. He was knighted and moved to be the greatest director of LSE in its first century.[87] In 1925, he was appointed as a member of the Samuel Commission on the coal industry.[88] Lionel Robbins remembered Beveridge as an unhappy workaholic, and an autocratic director of LSE with an unjustified belief in his superiority over all its faculty.[89] In her biography of Beveridge, Jose Harris recounts so many sources of misery in his personal life that we can understand why he was such a difficult man.[90] Come the Second World War, he struggled to join the academics flooding into Whitehall. He added to the difficulty of placing a former permanent secretary by treating Clement Attlee, the deputy prime minister, as if he were still a junior lecturer at LSE.[91]

Beveridge lasted a year before he got under the skin of Ernest Bevin in his Ministry of Labour and was made an offer he could not refuse. In June 1941 he was banished to Whitehall's equivalent of hard labour in Siberia, to chair a committee of officials from seven government departments, with these arid terms of reference:

> To undertake, with special reference to the interrelation of the schemes, a survey of the existing national schemes of social insurance and allied services, including workmen's compensation and to make recommendations.[92]

Figure 3.6: William Beveridge and his report (first draft)

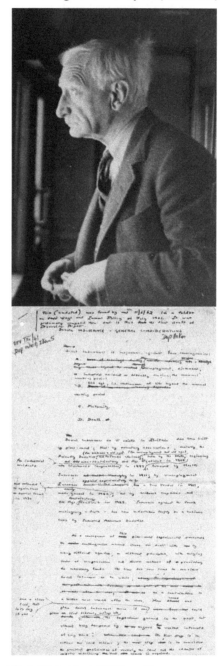

Sources: Both images from LSE Archives, LSE Library.[93]
Notes: William Beveridge in 1947 and his manuscript, 'Social insurance – general consid-erations manuscript memo', with note that this document was found by him on 11 June 1952, and that it was presumably composed in July 1941 and is thus the first draft of the Beveridge Report.

Beveridge accepted this brief with bitter tears of disappointment.[94] When he was in his sixties he married his cousin, Janet (Jessy) Mair, after her husband had died. This 'bossy, self-centred, histrionic' woman had attached herself to Beveridge like a limpet in his working and personal life from 1915.[95] She saved his report from merely taking space in filing cabinets. Her advice was that he ought to concentrate on three main policy objectives: 'prevention rather than care', 'education of those not yet accustomed to clean careful ways of life' and 'plotting the future as a gradual millennium taking step after step, but not flinching on ultimate goals'.[96]

The Beveridge Report was published in December 1942 and became a bestseller. As ever, timing was crucial. In June 1941, Hitler had attacked the Soviet Union.[97] In November 1942, the British Eighth Army had defeated Rommel in North Africa. Churchill ordered the ringing of church bells (which had previously been silent in the war) to celebrate that victory, and famously declared 'Now is not the end. It is not even the beginning of the end. But it is perhaps the end of the beginning.'[98] Anticipating victory, Beveridge completely ignored his restrictive terms of reference. He set out two general principles. First:

> Now, when war is abolishing landmarks of every kind, is the oppor-
> tunity for using experience in a clear field. A revolutionary moment
> in the world's history is a time for revolutions, not for patching.

Second, he called for a comprehensive policy of social progress to tackle his five giant evils.[99]

Beveridge was required, by the alarmed Chancellor of the Exchequer, to make clear in his report that he lacked official support. His report stated that as he alone was responsible, 'every recommendation and every word stands or falls on its merits and its argument'.[100] The coalition government heavily promoted the Beveridge Report for propaganda purposes abroad.[101] But, at home, the government adopted one of Cornford's impressive list of classic delaying tactics.[102] This is the principle of unripe time: 'People should not do at the present moment what they think is right at that moment, because the moment at which they think it will be right has not yet arrived.'[103]

Keynes had undermined the principle of less eligibility as the solution to the problems of unemployment. Beveridge showed that the 'abolition of want just before this war was easily within the economic resources of the community: want was a needless scandal due to not taking the trouble to prevent it'.[104] (The expenditure on unemployment relief of £128 million in 1931 was 0.4 per cent of the UK's GDP.[105]) Beveridge criticised the means test for penalising 'the duty and pleasure of thrift'.[106] He recognised the danger of allowing benefit payments for the unemployed to equal or exceed earnings in work. But he argued that:

> It is not likely that allowances for children … will … lead parents who do not desire children for gain … Children's allowances should be regarded both as a help to parents in meeting their responsibilities, and as an acceptance of new responsibilities by the community.[107]

So, he proposed a scale that increased payments according to the number of children in a family. Iain Duncan Smith, the later (failed) leader of the Conservative Party and architect of Universal Credit, saw things very differently, which is why since 2017 it has been the case that:

> If you're already claiming Universal Credit, have responsibility for 2 children and you then give birth to a new child, you won't get an additional amount of Universal Credit for that new child, unless special circumstances apply.[108]

In 2023, Reader et al showed that this inhumane policy has failed in its primary objective to drive people into work based on the economics of less eligibility.[109] Beveridge proposed:

> a flat rate of benefit irrespective of the amount of earnings that had been lost, for a flat contribution … designed to be high enough by itself to provide subsistence and prevent want in all normal circumstances; and will last as long as the unemployment lasts … without a means test.[110]

It was designed to make the difference between earnings in work and on benefit as large as possible and thus encourage people to seek work.[111] Beveridge had seen voluntary insurance through friendly societies as an integral feature of his *Plan for Social Security*. He described them as 'organisations for brotherly aid in misfortune and channels for the spirit of voluntary service as well as being agencies for mutual insurance and personal saving'.[112] In February 1943 the government announced that the approved status of friendly societies would be abolished and that aspect of their work would be transferred to a Ministry of National Insurance. In 1948, Beveridge identified that as the only element of his recommended plan for social security that that had not become law.[113]

Keynes was enthusiastic about Beveridge's system of state-run insurance from the cradle to the grave and convinced the government, prior to publication of the report, that it could be financed by employers, the taxpayer and employees.[114] The coalition government aimed to develop policies for Beveridge's other four 'giant evils'. For Beveridge the greatest of these was Idleness. He stated that delivering income security for the unemployed was:

> so inadequate a provision for human happiness that to put it forward by itself as a sole or principal measure of reconstruction hardly

seems worth doing. It should be accompanied by an announced determination to use the powers of the State to whatever extent may prove necessary to ensure for all, not indeed absolute continuity of work, but a reasonable chance of productive employment.[115]

The 1944 White Paper *Employment Policy* began: 'The Government accepts that one of their primary aims and responsibilities is the maintenance of a high and stable level of employment.'[116] It dismissed the older 'Treasury view' that a self-regulating market would deliver full employment:

> Experience has shown however, that under modern conditions this process of self-recovery, if effective at all, is likely to be extremely prolonged and accompanied by widespread distress, particularly in a complex modern society like our own.[117]

Arguments over the policies of the White Paper were chiefly between two sets of officials – not ministers. The team of brilliant academics in the Cabinet Office, led by Lionel Robbins, sought to develop economic policies to deliver a full employment level after the war – Keynes's 'general' theory had been directed at a slump. The fundamental change was from aiming to balance the budget over a year to across an economic cycle: running a surplus in a boom and a deficit in a recession.[118] The Treasury could not agree to planning a deficit in a slump.[119]

There was agreement on the need to diversify the economies of areas that were dependant on a single industry, for example shipbuilding in Scotland, coal and iron in South Wales, and cotton in Lancashire. During the war, when the government had directed men and materials into the depressed areas, that had showed the benefits of locating employment where workers lived.[120] The White Paper identified two future macroeconomic threats. First, from overvaluation of the pound sterling in international rates of exchange. That threat was nullified by agreement at the 1944 Bretton Woods conference, where Keynes played a vital role in persuading 44 countries to agree to the system of fixed rates of exchange.[121] Second, if there were full employment after the war, that brought the potential threat of inflation, to which no solution was proposed.

On education, in 1941 the Conservative minister RA Butler outlined to Churchill the need for major reform of state schools. Churchill invoked the principle of unripe time, which Butler decided to ignore. He went ahead with a White Paper on education in 1943 and the bill that became the 1944 Education Act.[122] Butler's achievements were extraordinary. He reached an agreement with the churches on their schools. He reduced the number of local authorities administering schools (from 400 to 146 larger areas in England). He replaced the Board of Education with a full Ministry of Education in Whitehall. He abolished elementary schools and established instead state primary and secondary schools.[123] The Butler Act enabled the development of nursery education, various types of secondary schools (which had been recommended by the 1938 Spens Report), new vocational education, and raising the school leaving age to 15 and 16.

Sir Cyril Norwood chaired a committee that, in 1943, made recommendations on the curricula and examinations for state secondary schools. The Norwood Report began with a quote from Plato's laws – *in Greek*. In Plato's republic, those with the power of command are made of mingled gold, the auxiliaries of silver, husbandsmen of brass and craftsmen of iron.[124] Sir Toby Weaver, who became deputy secretary in the Department of Education when Anthony Crosland and Margaret Thatcher were secretaries of state, caricatured the Norwood Report as creating a modification of Plato's republic for state secondary education.[125] 'Golden' children, having demonstrated that they were capable of abstract thinking by passing the 11-plus exam, would go to grammar schools. 'Silver' children would go to technical schools. 'Iron' children would go to 'secondary modern schools'.[126]

Butler had gone to preparatory and public schools in England and on to Cambridge University. Norwood had been to an elite public school and Oxford University and been head of Harrow School and an Oxford college. Norwood's achievements were all the greater given his lowly origins. His father had been the sole teacher and head of a rural grammar school in Lancashire – these were malodorous, 'ugly and dingy to a degree which not even a photograph could faithfully represent'.[127] He later resigned and took to drink. In 1939 and 1940, Cyril Norwood had written articles, in *The Spectator*, arguing for an end to England's two separate school systems in which that of the 'public schools' was counted to be so superior.[128]

On healthcare, the Beveridge Report had recommended:

> a health service providing full preventive and curative treatment of every kind to every citizen without exceptions, without a remuneration limit, and without an economic barrier at any point to delay response to it.[129]

The government actuary estimated that a national health service would cost £170 million.[130] That would be (at current prices) about 5 per cent of its current costs. The actuary made the spectacularly erroneous assumption that there would be no increase in costs for 20 years, because there would be 'some development of the service, and as a consequence of this development a reduction in the number of cases requiring it'.[131] In 1942, representatives of the different branches of the medical profession agreed the Report of the Medical Planning Commission, which recommended a system of healthcare like the Dawson Report of 1920. The 1942 report also recommended unimpeded access to all medical services for all.[132] But, in trying to implement these recommendations, the coalition government made concessions to the vested interests of the medical profession and the existing voluntary hospitals. The consequence was that its 1944 White Paper, *A National Health Service*, was 'long, diffuse and confusing'.[133] Henry Willink, the minister for health in the short-lived Conservative caretaker government prior to the 1945 election, made further concessions. His draft of another White Paper was deemed so inadequate that it was not published. For Charles Webster, the official historian of the NHS, the objective of implementing Beveridge's recommendation for healthcare in Britain 'was no nearer realization in 1945 than in 1942'.[134]

Finally, on housing, Peter Malpass points out that the officials in the Ministry of Health, who were then also responsible for housing, were content with their policy of the 1930s:

> Private sector output of houses had boomed, affordable home ownership had become a realistic aspiration for a third of the population, and the local authorities had begun to make inroads into the problems of slum clearance and relief of overcrowding.[135]

The ministry's ambition, which featured in the 1945 White Paper on housing, was that:

> Every family who so desires should be able to live in a separate dwelling possessing all the amenities necessary to family life in the fullest sense, and special provision must be made for old people and single women.[136]

When officials and ministers worked on targets for new house building to meet the expected shortage of houses after the war, their mantra was to rely on local authorities for the first two years and then private enterprise in the long term.[137]

3.5 The post-war Attlee settlement

The Labour Party won a landslide victory in the 1945 general election. Peter Hennessy described its promise that this time:

> Never again would there be a war, never again would the British people be housed in slums, living off a meagre diet thanks to low wages or no wages at all; never again would mass unemployment blight the lives of millions, never again would natural abilities remain dormant in the absence of educational stimulus.[138]

The new prime minister, Clement Attlee, lacked charisma compared with Winston Churchill and the 'big beasts' of his own cabinet: Herbert Morrison, the deputy prime minister; Ernest Bevin, the foreign secretary; and Aneurin Bevan, the minister of health. Yet Attlee exercised calm authority over them. He had a formidable reputation for being a ruthless 'butcher' of cabinet ministers who were 'not up to the job'. He offered this account of the mismatch between how other viewed him and his achievements:

> Few thought he was even a starter,
> There were many who thought themselves smarter,
> But he ended PM,
> CH and OM,
> An earl and a knight of the garter.[139]

On *the economy*, the linchpin of the Attlee settlement was delivering the commitment of the 1944 Employment White Paper to 'a high and stable level of employment', as compared with the 1930s and 1920s.[140] Figure 3.7 shows that for the first three decades of the post-war period UK unemployment levels were much lower than those in the interwar period (under governments of both the main parties), with only a slight and gradual growth before the 1970s. That is strong evidence that there is no need for the economics of the Poor Law, which used the principle of less eligibility to encourage people to seek work, provided (of course) that they can find jobs near where they live.

'Keynesian economics' was listed by Denis Healey (the Chancellor of the Exchequer 1974–79) as one of the reasons why the economies of Europe enjoyed strong and sustained economic growth from 1945.[141] But it was practised under benign conditions (quite unlike those of the 1930s). European

Figure 3.7: UK unemployment in the first 31 post-war years (1946–76) compared with the 20 interwar years (1919–39)

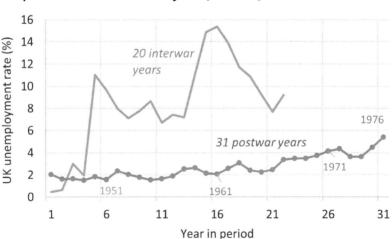

Source: Bank of England.[142]

Figure 3.8: UK real GDP per capita and public expenditure in the post-war period (1946–76)

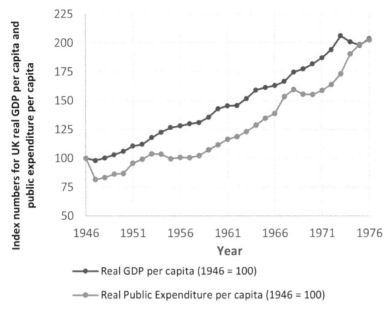

Source: Bank of England.[143]

governments were committed to free trade. There were fixed exchange rates (under the Bretton Woods regime). Energy (including oil) was cheap. Figure 3.8 shows that both real GDP and public expenditure (indexed to 1945 = 100) per capita increased for *les trente glorieuses* (30 glorious years), as they were termed in Europe. The near-continuous increases shown here form a strong contrast with the stagnation in both indices for almost all the interwar period (see Figure 3.4).

For Aneurin Bevan, the coalition government's 1944 Employment White Paper posed an existential threat to the Labour Party: 'This Party believes in public ownership of industry because it thinks that only in that way can society be progressively and intelligently organised.'[144] Bevan aimed for a major advance in state control by 'nationalising the commanding heights of the economy'.[145] Although that had been the aim of the Soviet Union in 1921, Alec Nove points out that this meant a *retreat*: from the error of attempting total nationalisation of manufacturing, and towards the targeting of banking, foreign trade and large-scale industry only.[146] Except for the case of steel, the Labour government's programme of nationalisation was uncontroversial.

Liberal and Conservative governments had worked out how to run industries as public corporations; Conservative governments had nationalised broadcasting, the generation of electricity, and overseas airways; and Conservative-dominated investigating committees recommended nationalisation for the Bank of England, gas, and coal.[147] Shleifer pointed out, in 1998, that leading economists in the 1940s were so concerned about inequities or potential market failure across a wide range of sectors that they recommended nationalisation as the remedy.[148] These sectors included: rail, the utilities, land, mineral deposits, telephone service, insurance, the motor car, iron and steel, and chemical industries.[149] The parlous states of the coal and rail industries were indictments of the failures of private enterprise.[150] They exemplified Eichengreen's analysis of the weaknesses in Britain's institutional arrangements.[151] Nationalisation was more efficient than for local government to continue to run the utilities (water, gas and electricity).[152]

As other European countries had been devastated, the UK government had an opportunity to begin sustained development to diversify the economies of its vulnerable areas. It made a start with great success, halving unemployment in areas where this had been over 20 per cent in 1937. But this policy was abandoned after only two years.[153] The nationalised industries then offered a way of maintaining employment in the vulnerable areas by subsidising their loss-making units. The government's programme of nationalisation included the Bank of England, gas, electricity, coal, iron and steel, British Road Services and British Waterways.[154] However, each had headquarters in London and different regional geographies. If the Attlee government had developed a new regional tier of government, that could have provided a consistent regional geography for the nationalised enterprises.

On social security, for those still unemployed, Jim Griffiths, minister for national insurance in the Attlee government, was responsible for the legislation of the scheme that Beveridge had proposed. Timmins describes Griffiths as one of the unsung heroes of the Attlee government.[155] He was responsible for the introduction of the payment of family allowances in early 1946, the passage of the 1946 National Insurance Act (which created a comprehensive system of social security) and the passage of the 1948 Industrial Injuries Act.[156] He had 'all the Welsh eloquence of Bevan without the egotism'.[157] Griffiths created a new department, which combined the work of six government departments and over 6,000 approved friendly societies, and 1,000 social security offices, so no one would have to travel more than five miles.[158] On the 80th anniversary of the Beveridge Report, Gavin Kelly and Nick Pearce describe Beveridge as a 'highly successful "policy entrepreneur"', noting that 'the architecture of the key National Insurance, National Assistance and Family Allowances Acts of the late 1940s was recognisably Beveridgean'.[159] They point out, however, that:

> the attempt to ground social security so squarely on Beveridge's version of the contributory principle was ultimately a failure. Poverty alleviation demanded greater means-testing, on the one hand, while the parsimonious level of benefits secured by flat rate contribution resulted in inadequate income insurance and attempts to build up earnings-related provision, on the other. The British welfare state consequently embodies a blend of principles: residual fragments of entitlement in return for contribution, means-tested alleviation

of need, and provision of flat rate benefits and universal services financed through general taxation.[160]

Modernising healthcare was the second crucial area that came to define the Attlee settlement. In 1945, Clement Attlee appointed Aneurin Bevan as minister of health. He was then aged 43 and the youngest member of his cabinet. The British Medical Association (BMA) vehemently objected to Bevan's proposals to create a national health service. A former secretary of the BMA described Bevan's National Health Service Bill of 1946 in their journal as 'uncommonly like the first step, and a big one, towards National Socialism as practised in Germany'.[161] Lord Moran, the patrician president of the Royal College of Physicians, played a vital role in handling the BMA's opposition. He enabled Bevan to negotiate the political settlement that created and shaped our NHS.[162] Bevan brought within the NHS the elite members of the medical profession, GPs, local government and voluntary hospitals. He abolished the sale of practices by general practitioners and established the Medical Practices Committee to direct new positions away from 'over-doctored areas'.[163]

The compromises made by this socialist firebrand included: granting teaching hospitals independent status from the regional structure for other hospitals; allowing hospital consultants to practise privately on pay beds in NHS hospitals; creating a system of distinction awards for hospital consultants in which they decided who merited increased salaries; and allowing general practitioners to be independent contractors.[164] He later declared that he won support from doctors because he 'stuffed their mouths with gold'.[165] That now looks to have been a bargain. The collateral damage of the politics of the creation of the NHS was widening the separation between general practice and hospital medicine, and leaving community health services in local government.[166]

Herbert Morrison, Attlee's deputy prime minister, argued unavailingly against moving hospitals out of local government into a new NHS:

> It is possible to argue that almost every local government function, taken by itself, could be administered more efficiently in the technical sense under a national system, but, if we wish local government to thrive – as a school of political and democratic education as well as a method of administration, we must consider the general effect on local government of each particular proposal. It would be disastrous if we allowed local government to languish by whittling away its most constructive and interesting functions.[167]

The NHS offered a model of Bevan's vision of a democratic socialist society: public ownership and ministerial accountability. Its lack of local accountability means that ministers who followed have rued the promise attributed to Bevan that 'If a bedpan falls in Tredegar, it should echo in the palace of

Westminster'. Timmins notes that if the Labour government had implemented its original policy of reorganising local government into regions, then, as Bevan recognised, the largest local councils could have taken over the running of hospitals.[168] But Bevan was not built to compromise on his commitment to a 'free' NHS. In 1951, he resigned as a minister, objecting to the breach of his commitment to a 'free' NHS when the Labour government decided to introduce charges for teeth and spectacles.[169]

On housing, Aneurin Bevan, as minister of health, was also responsible for tackling the acute housing crisis. Much of the existing stock of houses had been destroyed or was of poor quality; there was a dramatic increase in demand with the post-war baby boom; and the UK faced acute shortages of supply of skilled labour and materials. Before the war, housing development had met the needs of those with higher incomes, spoiled the country by private ribbon development, and built council houses of poor quality.[170] In October 1945, Bevan set out a radically different direction for his housing policy, although the government did not implement its manifesto commitment to establish a Ministry of Housing and Planning.[171]

Bevan aimed to begin with local authorities building council houses of high quality to rent by those on lower incomes.[172] He stood firm against arguments within the government for greater pluralism in the role of housing associations and a return to private ownership once wartime shortages were over.[173] In his socialist utopian dream, 'council housing should become a universally provided service like the NHS' as 'council houses would be built in a range of sizes to suit every income and heathy social mix and dispel the stigma of living in council accommodation'.[174] The principle of 'socialised medicine for all' works because it makes sense as an insurance policy: from each according to ability to pay with care provided on the basis of need (see Chapter 8). It is hard to conceive of a 'socialised housing for all' having the same appeal. From the 1970s onwards, council housing degenerated into the ghettoes that Bevan and Sharp had sought to avoid recreating. And people living in council housing in economically vulnerable areas and regions also found it hard to move to jobs elsewhere, as detailed in Chapter 4.

On education, change was more conservative. In 1942, at Labour Party Conference, a vote was passed favouring comprehensive education.[175] Clyde Chitty emphasises that the 1944 Education Act (Butler Act) did not prescribe how the system of secondary schools would develop. Indeed, 20 years after it was enacted, no change was required to this legislation for the change to create comprehensive schools.[176] In 1945, Clement Attlee appointed 'Red Ellen' Wilkinson, who had led the Jarrow crusade, as minister for education responsible for the implementation of the Butler Act. As minister, she ensured that the government raised the school leaving age to 15, implemented policies of free school milk and free school meals, brought in smaller classes, and funded extensive school building.[177] She remembered having been frustrated by teachers who set a slow pace for the huge classes at her elementary school and treated the intelligent few as a nuisance.[178] She favoured selection and the development of grammar and secondary modern schools.[179] She failed to overcome the commitment of her officials to the narrow and undemanding curriculum proposed for secondary modern schools by the Norwood Report.[180] She was seriously ill with chronic bronchitis and asthma and died in February 1947. Her successor, George Tomlinson, also favoured selection. The outcomes were three principal types of secondary schools in England and Wales: 'public', grammar, secondary modern (and not technical).

Wilkinson missed the opportunity in 1945 to end the social divisiveness that Tawney and Norwood saw as a fundamental flaw in the English school system.[181] 'Golden' children went to the elite 'public' schools – the nine 'Clarendon schools': Charterhouse, Eton, Harrow, Merchant Taylor's, Rugby, Shrewsbury, St Paul's, Westminster and Winchester College. (These were the 'certain colleges and schools' included in the Report of the Royal Commission chaired by the Earl of Clarendon that reported on schools in 1864.[182]) A study by Reeves et al, *in 2017*, found that that the alumni of the nine 'Clarendon schools' were '94 times more likely to reach the British elite than are those who attended any other school'. They accounted for 36 of the 54 prime ministers elected to office in the UK.[183] Simon Kuper points out that most went to Eton and Oxford.[184]

'Silver' children went to grammar schools. Within this group the direct grant grammar schools creamed off the most able pupils within their catchment area. They charged fees and received a grant direct from the government in return for free places for local children winning scholarships. State grammar schools were for the 20 per cent who passed the 11-plus exam. There is a popular perception that the grammar schools offered the opportunity for 'silver' children to become 'golden'. These were the remarkable achievements of, for example, Dennis Potter, Joan Bakewell, Melvyn Bragg and Peter Hennessy. But, as Lynsey Hanley points out, their blazing success blinds us to the more common fate for children from working-class families. They typically left before going on to the sixth form and spent their lives in low-paid, routine clerical jobs.[185] And Hanley cites the findings of the study by Brian Jackson and Dennis Marsden, who found that grammar schools rarely provided the ladder for 'bright' children from the working class but largely selected those who were already well placed to gain from the education they offered.[186]

'Iron' children were the 75 per cent publicly labelled as 'failures' at age 11 who went to secondary modern schools. The Spens Report of 1938, Butler in 1944 and Wilkinson in 1945 had emphasised the importance of parity of esteem between the different types of state secondary schools. But ministry officials were keen to avoid diluting standards in selective education sector (for those pupils who went to grammar and technical schools).[187] Consequently, the secondary modern schools had a third of the spend per pupil of the state grammar schools.[188] After the war, boys aged 13 did not go down mines or work in factories. But what did they gain from leaving a secondary modern school at age 15 without any qualifications? (The only exam they could take was designed for the grammar schools: the General Certificate of

Education set by the university examining boards.) The Spens Report had called for an end to elementary schools and the development of technical schools. The last elementary school was closed in 1964.[189] By 1958, only 4 per cent of children went to technical schools.[190] Neither nursery nor vocational education as envisaged by Butler was developed.

Conclusions: Attlee's legacy

The Attlee settlement was an eclectic mix of pragmatic policies directed at tackling the problems of the 1930s. Beveridge and Keynes were both Liberals. Keynes had dismissed state socialism as 'little better than a dusty survival of a plan to meet a problem of 50 years ago, based on a misunderstanding of what someone said a hundred years ago'.[191] Nationalisation was a continuity of Liberal and Conservative policies. Aneurin Bevan compromised in creating the NHS, which is the last institution standing of the Attlee settlement. On education, Butler before 1945 was a Conservative, and later 'Red Ellen' Wilkinson ignored Norwood's call to end the exclusive benefits offered by England's public schools and the vote at a Labour Party Conference for introducing comprehensive education.

With hindsight there were three crucial missed opportunities. First, the failure to diversify industries in the industrial regions and areas that are now 'left behind', resulting in a mismatch between the availability of good jobs and affordable housing. Second was the failure in secondary schools to develop technical education and blunt the socially divisiveness from the entitlements granted to those going to 'public schools'. Third, Labour only accentuated the process of centralisation of government and concentration of the best jobs in London. Yet the Attlee government achieved so much in times of such turmoil at home and abroad. It had to ride through trying economic circumstances from pressure by the US to pay back the loan that had financed the Second World War.[192] Its impact is eloquently summarised by Peter Hennessy:

> Britain had never, and still hasn't, experienced a progressive phase to match 1945–51. [In] 1951 Britain, certainly compared to the Britain of 1931, or *any* previous decade, was a kinder, gentler and far better place to be born, to grow up, to live, love, work and even to die. (emphasis in original)[193]

Endnotes

[1]   Beveridge, William (1942) *Social insurance and allied services*, UK: HMSO, p.170.
      https://archive.org/details/in.ernet.dli.2015.275849/page/n7/mode/2up

[2] Paxman, Jeremy (2021) *Black gold: The history of how coal made Britain*, UK: HarperCollins, p.152; Carradice, Phil (2011) *The Senghenydd pit disaster*. https://perma.cc/H7BT-UFHS

[3] Paxman, Jeremy, *Black gold*, p.23.

[4] Paxman, Jeremy, *Black gold*, p.154.

[5] Piketty, Thomas (2020) *Capital and ideology*, US: Harvard University Press, p.208.

[6] Piketty, Thomas, *Capital and ideology*, p.154.

[7] Royal Shakespeare Company (2020) *The Whip*. https://perma.cc/YUS5-H3QD

[8] Piketty, Thomas, *Capital and ideology*, p.208.

[9] Olusoga, David (2018) 'The Treasury's tweet shows slavery is still misunderstood', *The Guardian*, 12 February. https://perma.cc/RVR5-J4RE

[10] Tawney, Richard (1920) 'The British coal industry and the question of nationalization', *The Quarterly Journal of Economics*, vol. 35, no. 1, p.65. https://doi.org/10.2307/1883570

[11] The Newsroom (2007) 'The speech: David Lloyd George, 23 November, 1918', *The Scotsman*, 23 November 2007. https://perma.cc/JXE9-XFSB

[12] Russell, Bertrand (1967) *The autobiography of Bertrand Russell*, UK: George Allen and Unwin, p.72.

[13] Keynes, John Maynard (1919/2017) *The economic consequences of the peace*, UK: Routledge. https://www.econlib.org/library/YPDBooks/Keynes/kynsCP.html

[14] Keynes, John Maynard, *The economic consequences of the peace*, p.90.

[15] Keynes, John Maynard, *The economic consequences of the peace*, p.97.

[16] Raverat, Gwen (*c*.1908) *John Maynard Keynes, Baron Keynes* [painting]. National Portrait Gallery, London. https://www.npg.org.uk/collections/search/portrait/mw03627/John-Maynard-Keynes-Baron-Keynes

[17] Eichengreen, Barry (1996) 'Explaining Britain's economic performance: a critical note', *The Economic Journal*, vol. 106, no. 434, pp.213–18. https://doi.org/10.2307/2234944

[18] Tawney, Richard, 'The British coal industry and the question of nationalization'.

[19] Keynes, John Maynard (1925) *The economic consequences of Mr. Churchill*, UK: Hogarth Press, p.23.

https://books.google.co.uk/books?hl=en&lr=&id=euArAAAAMAAJ&oi=
fnd&pg=PA5&dq=the+economic+consequences+of+mr+churchill&ots=sI
_VzFewmP&sig=wPMI3MQKrgBA--qJrgLupztlOy0#v=onepage&q=the%
20economic%20consequences%20of%20mr%20churchill&f=false

[20] Hewes, Amy (1926) 'The Task of the English Coal Commission', *Journal of Political Economy*, vol. 34, no. 1, pp.1–12.
https://doi.org/10.1086/253735

[21] Labour Research Department (1926) *The coal crisis: Facts from the Samuel Commission*, UK: Labour Research Department, p.59.
https://books.google.com/books?id=oN4wAAAAIAAJ&printsec=front cover&source=gbs_ViewAPI#v=onepage&q&f=false

[22] *BBC News* (2011) 'What was the General Strike of 1926?'
https://perma.cc/LQ5Z-9TWU; Simons, Richard B. (1953) 'The British coal industry-A failure of private enterprise', *The Historian*, vol. 16, no. 1, pp.11, 13. https://doi.org/10.1111/j.1540-6563.1953.tb00150.x

[23] Bowley, Marion (1937) 'The Poor Law problem', in Bowley, Marion, *Nassau Senior and classical economics*, UK: George Allen & Unwin, pp.282–334.

[24] Watkin, Brian (1975) *Documents on health and social services. 1834 to the present day*, UK: Methuen, p.6.

[25] Watkin, Brian, *Documents on health and social services*, p.7.

[26] Watkin, Brian, *Documents on health and social services*, p.17.

[27] Harris, Jose (2009) 'The Webbs and Beveridge', in, *From the workhouse to welfare*, UK: Fabian Society, p.63.
https://fabians.org.uk/publication/from-workhouse-to-welfare/

[28] Watkin, Brian, *Documents on health and social services*, p.21.

[29] Watkin, Brian, *Documents on health and social services*, p.27.

[30] Witmer, Helen Leland (1931) 'Some effects of the English Unemployment Insurance Acts on the number of unemployed relieved under the Poor Law', *The Quarterly Journal of Economics*, vol. 45, no. 2, pp.262–88.
https://doi.org/10.2307/1885475

[31] Skidelsky, Robert (1992) *John Maynard Keynes: The economist as saviour, 1920–1937* (vol. 2), UK: Macmillan, p.347.

[32] McKibbin, Ross (1975) 'The economic policy of the second Labour government 1929–1931', *Past & Present*, vol. 68, no. 1, pp.95–123.
https://doi.org/10.1093/past/68.1.95

[33] Ward, Stephanie (2008) 'The means test and the unemployed in South Wales and the north-east of England, 1931–1939', *Labour History Review*, vol. 73, no. 1, p.114. https://doi.org/10.1179/174581808X279136

[34] Purves, Libby (2008) 'There is nothing mean about a means test' 17 November, *The Times*, cited in Marsh, Sue (2011) '1930s means test'. *Diary of a Benefit Scrounger*. https://perma.cc/2A4U-WV9F

[35] Foot, Michael (1962) *Aneurin Bevan: A biography; volume One: 1897–1945*, UK: MacGibbon & Kee, p.160.

[36] Bank of England (2016) *A millennium of macroeconomic data*. https://www.bankofengland.co.uk/statistics/research-datasets

[37] Addison, Paul (1975) *The road to 1945: British politics and the Second World War* (revised edition), UK: Johnathan Cape, p.30.

[38] Foot, Michael, *Aneurin Bevan: A Biography; Volume One*, p.26.

[39] Timmins, Nicholas (2017) *The five giants: A biography of the welfare state* (3rd paperback edition), UK: HarperCollins Publishers, p.29.

[40] Timmins, Nicholas, *The five giants*, p.29.

[41] Timmins, Nicholas, *The five giants*, pp.151–52; Women's History Network (2011) 'Women's History Month: "Red Ellen", Ellen Wilkinson 1891–1947', 7 March. https://perma.cc/V28X-DPHE; Hitchens, Peter (2022) *A revolution betrayed: How egalitarians wrecked the British education system*, UK: Bloomsbury, p.53.

[42] Collette, Christine (2011) The Jarrow Crusade. *BBC*. https://perma.cc/49UP-NR4Y

[43] Minister for Reconstruction (1944) *Employment policy*, UK: HMSO, Cmd 6527, p.16. You can see Margaret Thatcher's annotated copy at https://perma.cc/2BP6-Q6LU

[44] Keynes, John Maynard (1973) *The general theory of interest, employment and money*, UK: Macmillan.

[45] Official Publications Library/Ministry of Labour (1937) Index of Relative Unemployment. London, UK. As cited in Candler, Andrew James (1988) *The re-making of a working class: Migration from the South Wales coalfield to the new industry areas of the Midlands c1920–1940*. [Doctoral dissertation, University of Wales, College of Cardiff] EThOS, inside cover (noted in Appendix 6). https://ethos.bl.uk/OrderDetails.do?uin=uk.bl.ethos.329622

[46] Keynes, John Maynard, *The general theory of interest, employment and money*, pp.32–33.

[47] Skidelsky, Robert, *John Maynard Keynes*, p.364.

[48] Skidelsky, Robert, *John Maynard Keynes*, p.347.

[49] Wapshott, Nicholas (2011) *Keynes Hayek: The clash that defined modern economics*, UK: WW Norton & Company, p.47.

[50] Robbins, Lionel (1971) *Autobiography of an economist*, UK: Macmillan, pp.155, 152.

[51] Robbins, Lionel, *Autobiography of an economist*, p.153.

[52] Robbins, Lionel, *Autobiography of an economist*, p.154.

[53] Wapshott, Nicholas (2011) *Keynes Hayek: The clash that defined modern economics*, UK: WW Norton & Company, p.71.

[54] Burkhead, Jesse (1954) 'The balanced budget', *The Quarterly Journal of Economics*, vol. 68, no. 2, pp.191–216. https://doi.org/10.2307/1884446; Peden, George C. (1993) 'The road to and from Gairloch: Lloyd George, unemployment, inflation, and the "Treasury View" in 1921', *Twentieth Century British History*, vol. 4, no. 3, pp.224–49. https://doi.org/10.1093/tcbh/4.3.224; Peden, George C. (2003) 'British Treasury responses to the Keynesian revolution, 1925–1939', *Annals of the Society for the History of Economic Thought*, vol. 44, pp, 31–44. https://doi.org/10.11498/jshet1963.44.31

[55] Bank of England (2016) *A millennium of macroeconomic data.* https://www.bankofengland.co.uk/statistics/research-datasets

[56] Watkin, Brian, *Documents on health and social services*, p.20.

[57] *The Minority Report of the Poor Law Commission 1909*, p.293. https://wellcomecollection.org/works/qyhjfw7n

[58] The National Archives (n.d.) 'National Health Insurance: National Health Insurance Act 1911'. https://www.nationalarchives.gov.uk/cabinetpapers/themes/national-health-insurance.htm

[59] Hart, Julian Tudor (1971) 'The inverse care law'. *The Lancet*, vol. 297, no. 7696, pp.405–12. https://doi.org/10.1016/S0140-6736(71)92410-X

[60] Abel-Smith, Brian (1964) *The hospitals 1800–1948*, UK: Heinemann, pp.384–85.

[61] Abel-Smith, Brian, *The hospitals*, pp.22–31, 156–64, 170–71, 408.

[62] Stevens, Rosemary (2009) *Medical practice in modern England: The impact of specialization and state medicine*, US: Transaction Publishers, p.57.

[63] Abel-Smith, Brian, *The hospitals*, pp.102–03, 138, 409–10.

[64] Ramsay, Rolland (1994) 'A king, a doctor, and a convenient death', *BMJ*, vol. 308, p.1445. https://doi.org/10.1136/bmj.308.6941.1445

[65] Ministry of Health (1920) *Interim report on the future provision of medical and allied services 1920* (Lord Dawson of Penn), Cmd. 693 UK: HMSO. https://perma.cc/CE3V-79NH

[66] Robbins, Lionel, *The hospitals*, pp.382–83.

67 Beveridge, William, *Social insurance and allied services*, p.5.

68 Education Act 1918, c. 39.
    https://www.legislation.gov.uk/ukpga/Geo5/8-9/39/enacted?view=plain

69 Barber, Michael (2020) *Ten characters who shaped a school system.
    1870–2020: 150 Years of Universal Education in England*, UK: Foundation
    for Education Development, p.11. https://perma.cc/45KF-BDEK

70 Hood, Christopher; Emmerson, Carl; and Dixon, Ruth (2009) *Public
    spending in hard times*, ESRC Public Services Programme. https://perma
    .cc/K4FE-3J8Q; Geddes Committee (Committee on National Expenditure)
    https://www.nationalarchives.gov.uk/education/resources/twenties
    -britain-part-one/geddes-axe/

71 Barber, Michael, *Ten characters who shaped a school system*, p.12.

72 Consultative Council on Medical and Allied Services (Ministry of Health,
    Great Britain) (1950) *The Dawson report on the future provision of medical
    and allied services 1920: An interim report to the Minister of Health*. King
    Edward's Hospital Fund for London (original work published 1920).
    https://archive.kingsfund.org.uk/concern/published_works
    /000018795?locale=en#?cv=10&xywh=-2827,-269,7228,2289

73 Barber, Michael, *Ten characters who shaped a school system*, p.12.

74 Board of Education (1926) *Report of the Consultative Committee on the
    Education of the Adolescent* (The Hadow Report), UK: HMSO.
    http://www.educationengland.org.uk/documents/hadow1926/hadow
    1926.html#02

75 Tawney, Richard (1952) *Equality*, UK: George Allen and Unwin.
    https://archive.org/details/in.ernet.dli.2015.275419/page/n3/mode/2up

76 Board of Education (1938) *Report of the Consultative Committee on
    Secondary Education with Special Reference to Grammar Schools and
    Technical High Schools*, UK: HMSO. https://perma.cc/JZ7J-HAX2

77 Butler, Richard (1973) *The art of the possible*, UK: Harmondsworth, p.90.

78 Stilwell, Martin (2017) *Housing the returning soldiers 'homes fit for
    heroes'*. https://perma.cc/PD28-QTTE

79 Report of the Local Government Board (1918) *Report of the committee
    appointed by the president of the Local Government Board and Secretary
    for Scotland to consider questions of building construction in connection
    with the provision of dwellings for the working classes in England and
    Wales, and Scotland and report upon methods of securing economy and
    despatch in the provision of such dwellings*. Cd 9191, UK: HMSO.
    https://books.google.com/books?id=0Hw3AQAAMAAJ&printsec=front
    cover#v=onepage&q&f=false

[80] Powell, Christopher (1974) 'Fifty years of progress', *Built Environment*, vol. 3, no. 10, pp.532–35. https://www.jstor.org/stable/44398033

[81] Powell, Christopher, 'Fifty years of progress', pp.532, 534.

[82] Addison, Paul, *The road to 1945*, p.33.

[83] *Report of the Royal Commission on the Distribution of the Urban Population*, UK: HMSO, pp.201–2. https://perma.cc/4SZG-SEEJ

[84] Sharp, Thomas (1940) *Town planning*, UK: Pelican, p.88.

[85] Sharp, Thomas, *Town planning*, p.74.

[86] Sharp, Thomas, *Town planning*, pp.142–43.

[87] Dahrendorf, Ralf (1995) *LSE. A history of the London School of Economics and Political Science*, UK: Oxford University Press, p.327. https://doi.org/10.1093/acprof:oso/9780198202400.001.0001

[88] Anonymous (1925) 'British commission to investigate coal; government names board, aided by experts, to recommend ways of improving industry', *The New York Times*, 4 September. https://timesmachine.nytimes.com/timesmachine/1925/09/04/99985452 .html?pageNumber=23

[89] Robbins, Lionel, *Autobiography of an economist*, pp.135–42.

[90] Harris, Jose (1997) 'Prologue', in *William Beveridge: A biography*, UK: Oxford University Press, pp.7–8. https://doi.org/10.1093/acprof:oso/9780198206859.003.0002

[91] Harris, Jose, *William Beveridge*, p.365.

[92] Beveridge, William, *Social insurance and allied services*, p.2.

[93] Both images LSE Library Archives. Photograph of William Beveridge, Ref: Beveridge/9A/36/13, Report note, Ref: Beveridge/9A/41/1 No known copyright restrictions. Available from: https://www.flickr.com/photos/lselibrary/albums/72157622776229992

[94] Harris, Jose, *William Beveridge*, p.363.

[95] Harris, Jose, *William Beveridge*, p.23.

[96] Harris, Jose, *William Beveridge*, p.375.

[97] Timmins, Nicholas, *The five giants*, p.37.

[98] Timmins, Nicholas, *The five giants*, p.42.

[99] Beveridge, William, *Social insurance and allied services*, p.6.

[100] Beveridge, William, *Social insurance and allied services*, p.3.

[101] Addison, Paul, *The road to 1945*, p.220.

102 Addison, Paul, *The road to 1945*, p.224.

103 Cornford, F.M. (1908) *Microcosmographia academica*, UK: Bowes and Bowes, p.10. https://www.maths.ed.ac.uk/~v1ranick/baked/micro.pdf

104 Beveridge, William, *Social insurance and allied services*, p.166.

105 McKibbin, Ross (1975) 'The economic policy of the second Labour Government 1929–1931', *Past & Present*, vol. 68, p.112. https://www.jstor.org/stable/650274; Bank of England A millennium of macroeconomic data https://www.bankofengland.co.uk/statistics/research-datasets

106 Beveridge, William, *Social insurance and allied services*, p.12.

107 Beveridge, William, *Social insurance and allied services*, p.154.

108 Department for Work and Pensions (2017) 'Universal Credit: Support for a maximum of 2 children: Information for claimants', updated 27 January 2021. https://www.gov.uk/guidance/universal-credit-and-families-with-more-than-2-children-information-for-claimants

109 Reader, Mary; Andersen, Kate; Patrick, Ruth; Reeves, Aaron; and Stewart, Kitty (2023) *Making work pay? The labour market effects of capping child benefits in larger families*, UK: Centre for Analysis of Social Exclusion, LSE. https://sticerd.lse.ac.uk/CASE/_NEW/PUBLICATIONS/abstract/?index=10186

110 Roman Styran (2016, 16 April) 'Sir William Beveridge explains his proposals for a Welfare State – 2 December 1942' [Video]. YouTube. https://www.youtube.com/watch?v=EEDuNz6w9Gw. This is from the transcript published in Beveridge, William (1943) *Pillars of security and other war-time essays and addresses*, UK: George Allen & Unwin, p.54.

111 Timmins, Nicholas, *The five giants*, pp.58–59.

112 Beveridge, William (1948) *Voluntary action. A report on methods of social advance*, UK: George Allen & Unwin, p.62. Cited in Weinbren, Daniel (2011) '"Organisations for brotherly aid in misfortune": Beveridge and the friendly societies', in Oppenheimer, Melanie and Deakin, Nicholas (2010) (eds) *Beveridge and voluntary action in Britain and the wider British world*, UK: Manchester University Press, pp.51–65. https://hdl.handle.net/1959.11/9277

113 Weinbren, Daniel, 'Organisations for brotherly aid in misfortune'.

114 Harris, Jose *William Beveridge*, pp.399–404. Beveridge explains how the scheme will be financed in *Pillars of security and other war-time essays and addresses*, pp.121–25.

115 Beveridge, William, *Social insurance and allied services*, p.163.

[116] Minister for Reconstruction, *Employment policy*, p.3.

[117] Minister for Reconstruction, *Employment policy*, p.16.

[118] Hennessy, Peter (1993) *Never again: Britain 1945–51*, UK: Vintage, p.187.

[119] Hennessy, Peter, *Never again*, pp.186–89.

[120] Hennessy, Peter, *Never again*, p.210.

[121] Skidelsky, Robert (2001) *John Maynard Keynes: Fighting for Britain, 1937–46*. vol. 3, US: Viking, pp.337–60.

[122] Butler, Richard (1944) *Education Act 1944*, UK: HMSO. https://www.legislation.gov.uk/ukpga/Geo6/7-8/31/contents/enacted

[123] Timmins, Nicholas, *The five giants*, pp.92–93.

[124] Jowett, Benjamin (Translator) (1970) *The dialogues of Plato. Volume 4 The republic*, UK: Sphere Books, p.186.

[125] Norwood, Sir Cyril (Chair) (1943). *Report of the Committee of the Secondary School Examinations Council appointed by the President of the Board of Education in 1941*, UK: HMSO, p.15. http://www.educationengland.org.uk/documents/norwood/norwood 1943.html

[126] Timmins, Nicholas, *The five giants*, pp.87–88.

[127] McCulloch, Gary (2006) 'Cyril Norwood and the English tradition of education', *Oxford Review of Education*, vol. 32, no. 1, p.61. https://doi.org/10.1080/03054980500496460

[128] Timmins, Nicholas, *The five giants*, p.75.

[129] Beveridge, William, *Social insurance and allied services*, p.162.

[130] Beveridge, William, *Social insurance and allied services*, p.104.

[131] Beveridge, William, *Social insurance and allied services*, p.105.

[132] Eckstein, Harry (1963) 'The genesis of the National Health Service', *Current History*, vol. 45, no. 263, pp.6–51. https://www.jstor.org/stable/45310948

[133] Webster, Charles (1998) *The National Health Service: A political history*, UK: Oxford University Press.

[134] Webster, Charles, *The National Health Service*, p.11.

[135] Malpass, Peter (2003) 'The wobbly pillar? Housing and the British postwar welfare state', *Journal of Social Policy*, vol. 32, no. 4, pp.594–95. https://doi.org/10.1017/S0047279403007177

[136] Malpass, Peter, 'The wobbly pillar?' p.595.

[137] Malpass, Peter, 'The wobbly pillar?' p.598.

[138] Hennessy, Peter, *Never again*, p.2.

[139] Harris, Kenneth (1984) *Attlee*, UK: Weidenfeld and Nicolson, p.545. CH (Companions of Honour) and OM (Order of Merit) are awarded by the sovereign for distinction and limited to 65 and 24 living recipients, respectively.

[140] Minister for Reconstruction, *Employment policy*, p.3.

[141] Healey, Denis (1979) 'Oil, money and recession', *Foreign Affairs*, vol. 58, no. 2, pp.217–30. https://doi.org/10.2307/20040412

[142] Bank of England (2016) *A millennium of macroeconomic data*. https://www.bankofengland.co.uk/statistics/research-datasets

[143] Bank of England (2016) *A millennium of macroeconomic data*.

[144] Campbell, John (1997) *Nye Bevan*, UK: Richard Cohen Books, p.130.

[145] Hennessy, Peter, *Never again*, p.184.

[146] Nove, Alec (1989) *The soviet economy*, UK: George Allen and Unwin, p.75.

[147] Eckstein, Harry (1958) *The English Health Service*, US: Harvard University Press. Cited in Addison, Paul, *The road to 1945*, p.277.

[148] Shleifer, Andrei (1998) 'State versus private ownership', *Journal of Economic Perspectives*, vol. 12, no. 4, p.133. https://doi.org/10.1257/jep.12.4.133

[149] Lewis, Arthur (1949) *The principles of economic planning*, UK: George Allen & Unwin Ltd, p.101; Meade, James (1948) *Planning and the price mechanism: the liberal socialist solution*, UK: George Allen & Unwin Ltd, p.67; Simons, Henry (1934) 'A positive program for laissez-faire', in *Economic policy for a free society*, US: University Press of Chicago, p.51.

[150] Wolmar, Christian (2022) *British Rail: A new history*, UK: Michael Joseph; Simons, Richard B. (1953) 'The British Coal Industry-A Failure of Private Enterprise', *The Historian*, vol. 16, no. 1, p.15. https://doi.org/10.1111/j.1540-6563.1953.tb00150.x

[151] Eichengreen, Barry, 'Explaining Britain's economic performance'.

[152] Hennessy, Peter, *Never again*, pp.205–06.

[153] Hennessy, Peter, *Never again*, p.211.

[154] Tookey, Mark (2000) 'The "commanding heights": Nationalisation and the 1940s Attlee government', Chapter Two, pp.49–86, in *The Labour party and nationalisation from Attlee to Wilson, 1945–1968: Beyond the commanding heights*, UK: Durham theses, Durham University. http://etheses.dur.ac.uk/4522/

[155] Timmins, Nicholas, *The five giants*, p.134.

[156] Jones, John (2008) 'Griffiths, James (Jeremiah) (1890–1975), Labour politician and cabinet minister', *Dictionary of Welsh Biography*. https://perma.cc/NQ33-R9VV

[157] Timmins, Nicholas, *The five giants*, p.134.

[158] Timmins, Nicholas, *The five giants*, p.138.

[159] Kelly, Gavin and Pearce, Nick (2021) 'Beveridge at eighty: Learning the right lessons', *The Political Quarterly*, vol. 94, no. 1, pp.5, 4. https://doi.org/10.1111/1467-923X.13227.

[160] Kelly, Gavin and Pearce, Nick, 'Beveridge at Eighty', p.5.

[161] Hennessy, Peter, *Never again*, p.141.

[162] Foot, Michael (1975) *Aneurin Bevan: Volume two: 1945-1960*, UK: Paladin, pp.196–98.

[163] Foot, Michael, *Aneurin Bevan: Volume two: 1945-1960*, p.135.

[164] Webster, Charles, *The National Health Service*, pp.19–28.

[165] Webster, Charles (1991) *Bevan on the NHS*, UK: Wellcome Unit for the History of Medicine, p.220.

[166] Honigsbaum, Frank (1979) *The division in British medicine: A history of the separation of general practice from hospital care, 1911–1968*, US: St Martin's Press.

[167] Hennessy, Peter, *Never again*, p.139.

[168] Timmins, Nicholas, *The five giants*, p.116.

[169] Foot, Michael (1975) 'The Clash 1950–51', in *Aneurin Bevan: Volume two: 1945-1960*, UK: Paladin, Chapter 8, pp.280–346.

[170] Campbell, John, *Nye Bevan*, p.157.

[171] Malpass, Peter, 'The wobbly pillar?' p.603.

[172] House of Commons Debates, 17 October 1945, vol. 414, col. 1222. Cited in Malpass, 'The wobbly pillar?' pp.601–02.

[173] Campbell, John, *Nye Bevan*, pp.157–58.

[174] Campbell, John, *Nye Bevan*, pp.157–58.

[175] Hitchens, Peter, *A revolution betrayed*, pp.56, 59.

[176] Chitty, Clyde (2004) *Education policy in Britain*, UK: Palgrave, p.20.

[177] Barber, Michael, *Ten characters who shaped a school system*, p.17.

[178] Timmins, Nicholas, *The five giants*, pp.151–52.

[179] Hitchens, Peter, *A revolution betrayed*, pp.56, 59.

180 Timmins, Nicholas, *The five giants*, p.152.

181 Timmins, Nicholas, *The five giants*, pp.86, 95.

182 Clarendon, Lord (1864) *Report of Her Majesty's Commissioners Appointed to Inquire into the Revenues and Management of Certain Colleges and Schools and the Studies Pursued and the Instruction Given Therein* (The Clarendon Report), UK: George Edward Eyre and William Spottiswoode. https://books.google.com/books?id=rYNLAAAAcAAJ&pg=PR1& source=gbs_selected_pages&cad=2#v=onepage&q&f=false

183 Reeves, Aaron; Friedman, Sam; Rahal, Charles; and Flemmen, Magne (2017) 'The decline and persistence of the old boy: Private schools and elite recruitment 1897 to 2016', *American Sociological Review*, vol. 82, no. 6, pp.1139–66. https://doi.org/10.1177/0003122417735742

184 Kuper, Simon (2022) *Chums: How a tiny caste of Oxford Tories took over the UK*, UK: Profile.

185 Hanley, Lynsey (2016) *Respectable: The experience of class*, UK: Penguin, p.139.

186 Hanley, Lynsey, *Respectable*, p.52.

187 Timmins, Nicholas, *The five giants*, p.152.

188 Barnett, Correlli (1986) *The audit of war: The illusion & reality of Britain as a great nation*. Macmillan, Cited in Timmins, Nicholas *The five giants*, p.100.

189 Chitty, Clyde, *Education policy in Britain*, p.21.

190 Chitty, Clyde, *Education policy in Britain*, p.25.

191 Wapshott, Nicholas, *Keynes Hayek*, p.36.

192 Foot, Michael, *Aneurin Bevan: Volume two: 1945-1960*, pp.47–56.

193 Hennessy, Peter, *Never again*, p.454.

4. The Attlee settlement's failures: stagflation, slums in the sky and educational geography

> The gap between the incomes of the richest and those of the poorest in Britain reached its narrowest point in 1979 … But the unfortunate effect of narrowing inequality in the 1970s was to make everyone feel as though they'd never had it so bad. British people saw no reason to celebrate their egalitarianism, when the apparent cost over the course of the decade had been endless industrial action, government spending cuts, high inflation, rising unemployment, scary punk rockers and National Front Rallies. In some small way a socialist society had been achieved in Britain; it's just that people seemed to find it a dreadful place in which to live.
>
> Lynsey Hanley (2017)[1]

The Attlee government's eclectic mix of pragmatic policies built on proposals for the wartime coalition government by individuals from across the political spectrum. It was designed to tackle the problems of the 1930s – Beveridge's five giant evils. After Labour's 1951 defeat, the succession of Conservative governments to 1964 and from 1970 to 1974 governed within the Attlee settlement. They aimed to maintain the 'welfare state' but favoured limits on public spending and shifting the balance of the economy more to the private sector. This chapter looks at where the post-war settlement ran into three problems for which the neoliberalism of the later Thatcher settlement seemed to promise solutions. First, the linchpin of the Attlee settlement was that the state could steer the economy to deliver a high and stable level of employment. In the mid-1970s that linchpin fractured. Second, significant problems emerged with some post-war public housing. And, third, weaknesses in the post-war systems of public education and its attempted reform also became apparent.

How to cite this book chapter:

Bevan, Gwyn (2023) *How Did Britain Come to This? A century of systemic failures of governance*, London: LSE Press, pp. 91–108.
https://doi.org/10.31389/lsepress.hdb.d License: CC BY-NC

4.1 Stagflation and the failure to control public expenditure

In the UK the three post-war decades of high and stable levels of employment were still marked in economic policy terms by recurrent crises from deficits on the balance of payments. There were currency crises in 1956, because of the Suez crisis debacle, and in 1967, when a major devaluation was forced on the Labour government by money market pressure. In 1976, in the system of floating exchange rates, high government borrowing again resulted in a run on the value of sterling. Britain's Labour Chancellor Dennis Healey was forced to make a humbling submission to the International Monetary Fund (IMF) for external financial support. For some commentators the episode:

> discredited the whole postwar economic consensus of demand management, and fiscal and monetary policy fine-tuning. It powerfully reinforced the case Margaret Thatcher's radical Conservatives had been making about the failure of the Keynesian consensus, laid the groundwork for her election victory in 1979 and the dominance for a decade or more of the ideas she and her American ally Ronald Reagan espoused of free markets and fiscal restraint.[2]

Nearly half a century later, in September 2022, the 'minibudget' put forward by the Tory Chancellor of the Exchequer Kwasi Kwarteng in the short-lived (49 days) Liz Truss premiership triggered a similar sharply adverse bond market reaction, a 'biting attack' by the IMF on government budgeting, which was compared to the Healey crisis.[3]

However, a former permanent secretary to the Treasury, Nicholas McPherson, reads history differently. He recalls that when he joined the Treasury in 1985 senior officials still shuddered, not at the humiliating outcome of the 1976 IMF loan but at mention of Anthony Barber. As the Conservative Chancellor of the Exchequer in the early 1970s, Barber had sought to unleash Britain's growth potential through unfunded tax cuts and easy credit (like Kwarteng in 2022). There was a brief soar in output,

> before hitting a wall of high inflation, industrial unrest and an oil crisis … His boom was seen as triggering the series of policy errors that led inexorably to Britain's emergency loan from the IMF in 1976.[4]

The economist Milton Friedman, who laid key foundations of the neoliberal revolution in economics (see Chapter 5), diagnosed two systemic problems with 'Keynesian economics'.[5] The first was its incapability to control inflation from feedback between workers demanding increases in pay to cover costs of increases in prices, as was strongly triggered by the Barber boom.[6] The annual rate of inflation increased from 7 per cent in 1973 to 23 per cent in 1975 (see Figure 4.1) and in combination with unemployment produced 'stagflation'. The second problem was that of 'long and variable lags' between the government decision to intervene and its impact on the economy.[7] By the time a government's decision to reduce demand in a boom had taken effect it could exacerbate a recession. This was compounded in the UK by the Treasury's system of 'volume control' of public expenditure, which was based on historic constant prices.[8] So, government expenditure in March 1973 was supposed to be controlled against a budget set at prices prevailing in November 1970! In January 1974, members of the Expenditure Committee of the House of Commons were perplexed by how the Treasury could 'fine-tune' the economy with cuts of £300 million in 1972–73 (Anthony Barber's attempt to reduce the demand he had stimulated) when the Treasury only knew, nine months after that financial year had ended, that expenditure turned out to be £900 million less than the budget.[9]

The UK had a third problem. In principle, the Treasury's forecasts of economic growth were intended to constrain the growth in public expenditure. But, in practice, the Treasury was required to make forecasts of economic growth to finance what the cabinet had collectively agreed would be total levels of public expenditure. The Treasury's forecast for economic growth published in 1976 required 'almost an economic miracle'.[10] That is why George Osborne's initiative, when Chancellor of the Exchequer in 2010, to require the government's budget to be assessed by the independent, authoritative Office for Budgetary Responsibility (OBR) was a vital strengthening of the UK's

Figure 4.1: Annual percentage (%) increases in the UK Consumer Price Index (CPI), 1970 to 2000

Source: Bank of England.[11]

institutional arrangements.[12] (This requirement was notoriously ignored by Prime Minister Liz Truss and Chancellor Kwarteng when announcing their catastrophic 'minibudget' of September 2022.[13]) From 1972–73 to 1974–75, although there were 'shortfalls' of 'actual' spending in each year against budget plans, the percentage financed by borrowing increased to a peak of 14 per cent in 1975 (see Figure 4.2) from overoptimistic projections of economic growth.[14] The Treasury's forecasts of the borrowing requirement were £2 billion too low for 1974–75 and £2 billion too high for 1976–77. The then Chancellor, Dennis Healey, later observed that, if the 1976 forecast had been correct, the government would have avoided the humiliation of asking the IMF for a loan, but 'none of the independent forecasters had a better record'.[15] J.K. Galbraith famously observed that, as a general rule, 'the only purpose of economic forecasting is to give astrology a good name'.[16]

4.2 Public housing and 'slums in the sky'

If you ask estate agents what the three most important determinants are of the price of a house or flat, they will tell you that they are location, location

Figure 4.2: The percentage share (%) of UK public expenditure financed by borrowing, 1970 to 1990

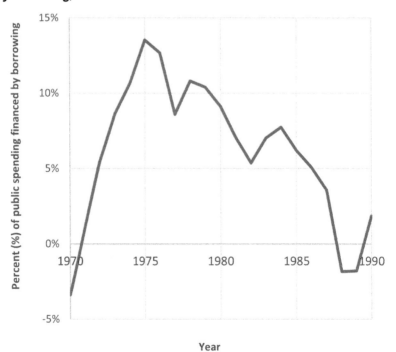

Source: Bank of England.[17]

and location. It determines access to work, education, shops, services and recreation. In responding to the acute shortage of housing in 1945, Aneurin Bevan prioritised building council houses of lasting quality (see Chapter 3).[18] This approach had also been tried just after the First World War, when 50,000 council houses had been built to the exacting Tudor Walters standards; they were more spacious than many privately owned suburban homes and in attractive cottage estates.[19] But, as Lynsey Hanley points out, they were poorly located: 'far from their extended network of friends and relatives and lacking good public transport, churches, pubs and community halls'.[20] The problematic implication of developing a good social mix of housing is that this requires those who can afford to buy their own houses to subsidise the building of council houses for others in more desirable locations.

Even though more than a million new houses were built by the time of the 1951 general election, there was still an acute post-war housing shortage.[21] The Conservative Party was elected in 1951 with a manifesto promise to double the total number built in a year to 300,000. Figure 4.3 shows that Harold Macmillan, the minister of the newly created Ministry of Housing, delivered that promise in 1954. He did so by reducing their size.[22] By boosting home ownership he aimed to develop a 'property-owning (Conservative voting) democracy'.[23] Figure 4.4 shows that he halved the percentage of new houses built by local authorities and trebled that by private builders. (Under the Conservative government, from 1993, local authorities accounted for at most 1 per cent of completions.)

The Labour Party next won a general election in 1964. The prime minister, Harold Wilson, appointed Richard Crossman as the minister of housing and local government. He was a fellow of an Oxford college, an 'unashamed intellectual' who could not 'understand the motivations and thoughts of those

Figure 4.3: Total new housing completions in England, 1946 to 2020

Source: Office for National Statistics.[24]

Figure 4.4: The percentage mix of public, social and private housing in new completions, 1946 to 2020

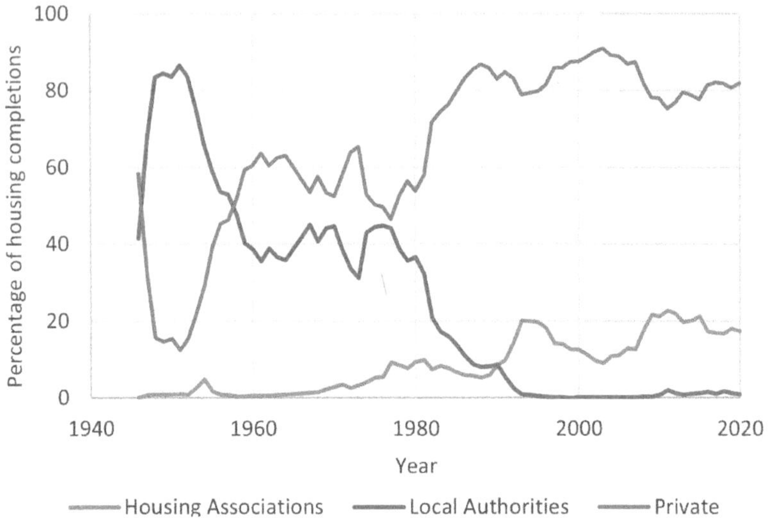

Source: Office for National Statistics.[25]

who were not like him'.[26] He explained how his 1965 White Paper trashed Bevan's housing policy:

> It is a new thing for a Labour Government to admit that owner-occupation is a normal and natural way for people who live and that living in a council house is an exception to that rule.[27]

He had introduced tax relief on mortgage repayments in 1964.[28] The White Paper continued the tax relief policy and introduced exemption from the new capital gains tax for higher-rate taxpayers, access to low interest loans and 100 per cent mortgages.[29] Wilson chaired its discussion by the cabinet, which took eight minutes.[30]

In his 1978 doctoral thesis Patrick Dunleavy explained that there were three sets of reasons why local authorities developed council estates of high-rise blocks at scale.[31] First, to avoid urban sprawl, preserve rural areas close to the cities (particularly green belts), and provide more open space. Second, to make space for other uses of land: farming, schools, decongested industrial zones and improved transport systems. Third, architects favoured high-density residential development because of advances in construction technology as exemplified by Le Corbusier's Unite d'Habitation in Marseilles, which was built in the 1950s. Alexi Marmot describes how Unite followed Corbusier's design principles. Its structure was supported by reinforced concrete stilts (the pilotis), which enabled its lively facades and ground plan to be freely designed. All had a sculptural grand quality. Its windows were long strips of ribbon that flooded the interiors with light. There were garden terraces on the roof and six types of attractive sound-proof dwellings (330 in total) with private facades and patios. Its community of 1,600 was a city in microcosm. It was expensive to build and keep running smoothly 'to landscape and maintain the grounds, to operate lifts, to run the clubs, kindergartens and sports facilities.'[32]

James Stirling described Alton West, in the Roehampton estate in Wimbledon, as the first built example of Le Corbusier's 'City in the Park'. Alexi Marmot highlights what got lost in translation to Alton West, which had five identical blocks, each of 75 identical two-bedroom dwellings. They lacked privacy, light and sound proofing, shops, kindergarten and easy access to recreation. With 300 residents only, they were on too small a scale to create a community.[33]

In early December 1964, Crossman wrote in his diary that he had 'decided to give Birmingham a huge area of housing in the green belt at Water Orton'. Although the Chelmsley Wood council estate was nine miles from the city,[34] the view of the *Birmingham Post* was that, for those who lived there, the city would feel 'a million life years away'.[35] The journalist Lynsey Hanley lived on the Chelmsley Wood council estate and saw Alton West as one of the best of England's council tower blocks.[36] Her experience of the phrase 'council estate' is 'a sort of psycho-social bruise: everyone winces when they hear it'.[37] Crosland described 'the whiff of welfare, subsidisation, of huge uniform estates and generally of second-class citizenship' where the council 'decides what repairs will be done, what pets may be kept, what colour the door may be painted'.[38] The Former Labour MP Frank Field had, in 1975, when Director of the Child Poverty Action Group, passionately denounced the feudal attitude of councils to their tenants who were treated as 'council serfs'[39]. In 2018, he summarised his argument for radical reform:

> the best council housing almost never became available for reallocation, as tenants stayed put and children inherited tenancy rights. … My plan was to sell dear, with the whole of a working-class family clubbing together to acquire an asset and, crucially, for councils to use all those monies to rebuild and repair stock. The Wilson and Callaghan governments undertook reviews of this idea but civil servants thought the plan unworkable…. After Labour refused to act, Mrs Thatcher came along and turned the idea on its head: sold cheaply, cut taxes, and the rest is history.[40]

In many urban areas, as the council estates were built for those who were in extreme housing need, the tower blocks became 'slums in the sky'.[41] Professor Anne Power found that, in many of the poorest outer areas in the UK, surrounding cities such as Birmingham, Liverpool, Glasgow and Strathclyde, and in Europe and most American cities:

> governments subsidised mass housing in large, monolithic, poorly designed blocks that tore apart social networks and often failed, through brutalist design, to foster new links … without adequate

funding for the transport connections that would make them work … a sense of isolation, poverty and powerlessness dominates.[42]

In Britain, the overriding principle in the design and construction of council blocks has been to cut costs to the bone. And, if really necessary, into the bone even if that put lives at risk: a gas explosion led to the destruction of the Ronan Point tower block in 1968 (Figure 4.5).[43] Some lessons drawn then were later 'unlearnt'. In 2017, 72 people were killed, and many more injured, in an uncontrollable fire at Grenfell Tower, which had been clad in the cheapest, non-fire-proof materials.[44] That tower block was owned by Kensington Council, by far the richest area of the UK (see Chapter 2).

Figure 4.5: Effects of the explosion at Ronan Point tower block on 16 May 1968

Source: Derek Voller. Available under a Creative Commons Attribution-ShareAlike Licence (CC BY-SA 2.0).[45]

In 1978, Dunleavy considered that the ideological effects of the high-rise/mass housing era of council housing 'may prove to have been some of the most important and enduring legacies'.[46] In 1980, Margaret Thatcher's government introduced the right to buy scheme for tenants of council houses. This allowed council tenants discounts for purchasing the home they had rented.[47] Sales occurred differentially within the most attractive council house stocks, especially of family houses in more desirable estates, and less so in flats. The new law also stripped local authorities of the power to invest in replacing the stock they lost. The percentages of new housing completions built by councils fell from nearly 40 per cent in 1980 to 1 per cent by 1993 (see Chapter 5).

4.3 Schools, universities and educational geography

In 1956, Crosland described the school system in Britain, which was developed by the Attlee government, as 'the most divisive, unjust and wasteful of all aspects of social inequality'.[48] A 1953 report of a House of Commons Select Committee found that secondary modern schools lacked teachers and adequate buildings – some were 'no better than slums'.[49] Grammar schools disproportionately benefited children from the middle class. In 1965, Wilson appointed Crosland as secretary of state for education and science. He had four missions. First, 'to destroy every f***ing grammar school in England ... And Wales. And Northern Ireland'.[50] Second, to ensure no fall in standards from the move to comprehensive schools.[51] Third, to ensure that removing grammar schools did not 'increase the *disparity* of esteem within the system as a whole' by 'leaving the public schools still holding their present commanding position' (emphasis in original).[52] Fourth, to develop a substantial sector of higher education by developing colleges under local authorities 'away from our snobbish, caste-ridden hierarchical obsession with university status'.[53]

Crosland had specified demanding requirements for the new comprehensive schools: 'an exceptional calibre of headmaster ... high-quality staff for sixth form teaching ... buildings of an adequate scale or scope' and catchment areas with populations 'drawn to straddle of neighbourhoods of different social standing'. And that these requirements had to be satisfied before closing down grammar schools to avoid 'a decline in educational standards and discredit the whole *experiment*' (emphasis added).[54]

In 1970, a new comprehensive school, designed for an intake of 1,000 pupils, opened on the Chelmsley Wood estate. When Lynsey Hanley went there, in 1987, it looked as if it were 50 years old. Its buildings were 'like half-abandoned husks'. It struggled to operate on just over half its original budget. The 600 students who went there felt they had no alternative, and 'had been condemned to a dump' that was 'a secondary modern in all but name'.[55] Its teachers made clear that they believed that their pupils 'just don't want to learn'.[56] Hanley explains that to become well-educated meant becoming middle class, which meant rejecting the working-class values of their parents and community.[57] George Akerlof and Rachel Kranton, who developed the concept of the

economics of identity, show how that explains why for so many young people the economic returns from education are a weak incentive because they
undermine their sense of identity.[58]

Hanley contrasted her peers' low expectations with those of middle-class
children, who are expected, and under pressure, to do well.[59] If the 11-plus
exam had continued, she would probably have gone to a grammar school (if
her parents could have afforded to buy the uniform) and there would have
been no 'wall in her head' that made it so difficult for her to realise her potential.[60] She recognises that, if she had gone to one of Birmingham's great King
Edward VI grammar schools, that 'might have made a difference to my education, but only *mine*' (emphasis in original).[61] Farquharson, McNally and Tahir
cite evidence showing that 'countries that have weakened selectivity have
found higher levels of average achievement'.[62] An OECD report found that:

> Students' performance is influenced by their personal characteris-
> tics, but also by those of their schoolmates … The concentration of
> low achievers usually has negative consequences on student perfor-
> mance, and this is especially the case for students who are them-
> selves low achievers. By contrast, high-ability students are usually
> less sensitive than their low-achieving peers to the composition of
> their classes.[63]

The Attlee settlement was based on the belief that the way to run the public
services was to trust professionals as 'knights' (see Chapter 1).[64] An occasional
visit by the collegial Her Majesty's Inspectors (HMIs) of schools also preserved the 'secret garden' of the teaching profession. Governance by the Inner
London Education Authority in the 1970s was based on the principle that
'you appoint a good headteacher, and then he [sic] runs the show'.[65] And what
a show that turned out to be at one of its junior schools, William Tyndale. In
the autumn term of 1974, the school day was divided into sets of one-hour
periods that alternated between the basic skills of language and mathematics
and open sessions. These offered children a free choice from (for example)
swimming, cookery, woodwork, watching television and playing games.[66]
Annie Walker, a part-time remedial reading teacher at the school, objected
to these changes because they neglected educational basics and denied pupils
the opportunity for academic progress. She organised a protest with a manifesto and involved parents, who criticised the radical teachers at public meetings in the summer of 1974.[67] The Auld Inquiry into William Tyndale was
told that its education consisted of playing in the classroom or the playground
and that 'lessons hardly existed'. As one of its unfortunate pupils so eloquently
put it 'You don't get learned nothing at this school'.[68] In 1976, in response to a
perceived 'crisis' in schools, in a famous speech at Ruskin College in Oxford,
the Labour prime minister James Callaghan called for a 'great debate' on education.[69] One explanation for that 'crisis' is the revolt by middle-class parents

over their loss of access of their children to the privileged education provided by grammar schools. Over time, however, the system of comprehensive schools has largely replaced the selection of pupils by exams with a selection by class and house price.[70]

The problem with the Attlee settlement was that its systems of governance of public services had no remedy to failures like that of the William Tyndale school (and the scandal at the Bristol Royal Infirmary – see Chapter 1). In 1992, the old HMI inspections were replaced in the 'reign of terror' of the Office for Standards in Education (OFSTED). Christopher Hood et al found that 67 of the 3,600 secondary school OFSTED inspected from 1993 to 1997 were deemed to be 'failing'.[71] One was Hackney Downs, despite it having 'expenditure per pupil higher than some of the most exclusive public schools in this country'.[72] Michael Barber was a member of the committee (the 'hit squad') who decided that Hackney Downs ought to be closed as soon as possible. Its best results for GCSEs were in Turkish, which the school did not teach. In a maths class for 16-year-olds, several were 'unable to say how many pence there were in £1.86'. Barber attributed its failings to 'a culture of excuses and low expectations' blamed on 'the high poverty of many of the students' families'.[73] The lack of corrective action by local governments that allowed the failings between William Tyndale and Hackney Downs to continue unchecked in the glare of their media notoriety may have explained why the model of the Thatcher settlement of a 'quasi-market' in which parents chose schools and 'money followed the pupil' was so appealing (see Chapter 7).

On his second area of action, in 1965 Crosland established a Public Schools Commission to recommend the best way of integrating Britain's elite independent schools with the state-financed school system.[74] But, Nicholas Hillman explains, this was wanted by neither his ministerial colleagues nor his officials, nor the public schools, nor local authorities.[75] Hillman's verdict, in 2010, was that:

> Labour's attempt in the 1960s to make public schools less dependent on parental income, less academically selective, more integrated with the maintained sector, more responsive to boarding need and less socially divisive all failed: school fees continued to rise; the public school sector became more selective as the state sector became less selective; there was no big increase in the links between the maintained and independent sectors; it became no easier for people from lower incomes to board at public schools; and former public school pupils, though small in number, continued to dominate access to the leading universities and continued to be disproportionately represented at the top of key professions.[76]

There is, however, a substantial body of evidence that what we inherit largely determines our educational achievement and the impact of our schools is relatively minor. This is the principal finding of the 2018 study by Kaili Rimfeld et al of the 6,000 twin pairs in the UK-representative Twins Early Development Study sample.[77] Freddie be Boer put it more bluntly based on studies in the US: 'in thousands of years of education humanity has discovered no replicable and reliable means of taking kids from one educational percentile and raising them up into another'.[78] He argued that what matters is '*relative learning* – performance in a spectrum or hierarchy of ability that shows skills in comparison to those of other people' (emphasis in original).

On his last priority Crosland followed a previous government initiative to raise the status of technical education by creating a new sector in higher education. That is easier to change than the much larger school system, but changing schools is a precondition for increasing the number of students qualified by ability and attainment to benefit from higher technical education. In 1965, Crosland established 30 'polytechnics', governed by local authorities.[79] In 1966, the 10 colleges of advanced technology (CATs), which had been established in 1956, became universities.[80] In 1992, the polytechnics became autonomous universities.[81]

In his 1976 book *Social Limits to Growth* Fred Hirsch argued that there are two types of goods.[82] Non-positional goods are those where what matters is just your own consumption. For instance, if a government were to implement a policy so the majority of people rather than just a rich minority can afford to buy the food they need to live on a healthy diet, then the value of food for the best-off minority would not be impaired. But a good education is a 'positional good', one whose intrinsic value depends on its scarcity. The expansion of university education, as recommended by the 1963 Robbins Report on Higher Education, was implemented under subsequent governments.[83] Hirsch, who was then at the University of Warwick, argued that this changed the hurdle set by employers for having access to 'glossy' top jobs from simply having a degree to having an Oxbridge degree and access to their elite network.[84]

Education has been one reason why geography remained destiny in Britain into the 2020s. At the macro scale, Britain's best universities were, and still are, concentrated in the golden triangle of Oxford, Cambridge and London. At the micro scale, access to good state schools depends on where you live and so whether you can take advantage of the changes in Oxbridge admissions policies. The *Sunday Times* reported on 30 October 2022 that, between 2017 and 2022, the state school intake at Cambridge increased from 63 to 73 per cent, and at Oxford from 58 to 68 per cent.[85] The education system illustrates what Julian Le Grand found about the welfare state, which was that, even though this obviously benefited the poor as compared with what had gone before, across healthcare, social services, education and transport 'almost all public expenditure benefits the better off to a greater extent than the poor'.[86] A report by the Institute for Fiscal Studies found that:

Young people from better-off families – and especially those who attended private school – enjoy much higher financial rewards from completing a degree than their peers from disadvantaged backgrounds, even holding constant attainment during school and at university as well as subject and institution.[87]

When interviewing for an undergraduate place at Cambridge University, current Conservative MP (and briefly Chancellor or the Exchequer in 2022 during the short-lived government of Liz Truss) Kwasi Kwarteng, having been to Eton, complimented the fellow interviewing him at Trinity College Cambridge, for whom this had been his first interview: 'Oh, don't worry, sir, you did fine.'[88] Lynsey Hanley harbours bitter memories of the humiliation to which she was subjected at her interview at Christ's College Cambridge, which came to a premature end.[89] Hanley argues that:

> The further up the social ladder you are, the more external influences are set up to favour you and your kind so that to the extent that privilege becomes invisible and so weightless that – literally – you don't know how lucky you are. At the other end of the social scale, there is an acute sense of how little social trust or esteem is placed in you as an individual, a feeling that is absorbed in low self confidence.[90]

Conclusions

The Attlee settlement aimed to tackle the problems of the 1930s: Beveridge's five giant evils of Want, Disease, Ignorance, Squalor and Idleness. Markets had delivered unacceptable levels of unemployment and failed in industries (for example, coal and the railways). Previous government policies of austerity had resulted in poverty for the unemployed, and inequalities in access to decent housing, good education and healthcare. Under the Attlee settlement, by the end of the 1970s, the UK was more equitable than before (or since). But the economy suffered from high inflation, unemployment and debt; the weakening of market arrangements resulted in nationalised industries favouring the interests of the producers, as did public services. Margaret Thatcher terminated the Attlee settlement at the 1979 general election, when her governments promised to tackle the problem of inflation, reduce government debt, and develop markets to remedy the failures of government – a saga of neoliberalism's advance. That is the subject of the next chapter.

Endnotes

[1] Hanley, Lynsey (2017) *Estates an intimate history*, UK: Granta, pp.132–33.

2 Baker, Gerard (2022) 'Market chaos points to a new political era', *The Times*, 29 September. https://perma.cc/A969-KSB3

3 Giles, Chris (2022) 'Is Britain now in a full-blown economic crisis?' *Financial Times*, 27 September. https://perma.cc/2Q8F-QVLT; Sherman, Natalie and Espiner, Tom (2022) 'IMF openly criticises UK government tax plans', *BBC News*, 28 September. https://perma.cc/27UW-UVFK

4 Macpherson, Nicholas (2022) 'Outlier Britain needs a credible economic plan in a hurry', *Financial Times*, 30 September. https://perma.cc/4YLA-Y84N

5 Krugman, Paul (1994) *Peddling prosperity: Economic sense and nonsense in the age of diminished expectations*, UK: WW Norton & Company, pp.43–47.

6 The National Archives (n.d.) *1960s and 1970s radicalisation*. https://www.nationalarchives.gov.uk/cabinetpapers/alevelstudies /1960-radicalisation.htm

7 Krugman, Paul, *Peddling prosperity*, pp.43–47.

8 Bevan, Gwyn (1980) 'Cash limits', *Fiscal Studies*, vol. 1, no. 4, pp.26–43. https://doi.org/10.1111/j.1475-5890.1980.tb00450.x

9 Expenditure Committee (1973–74). *Public expenditure to 1977–78* (Cmnd 5519). *Public expenditure and the balance of resources*, UK: HMSO. https://perma.cc/2PDA-L6JK

10 *Fourth Report from the Expenditure Committee* (1975–76), UK: HMSO.

11 Bank of England (2016) *A millennium of macroeconomic data*. https://www.bankofengland.co.uk/statistics/research-datasets

12 Office for Budget Responsibility (2023) 'International Engagement'. https://perma.cc/PBN3-P3BY

13 Cavendish, Camilla (2022) 'This was a railroading, electioneering mini-Budget', *Financial Times*, 23 September. https://perma.cc/Y3GV-DAAW

14 *Second Report from the Expenditure Committee (1977–78)*, UK: HMSO.

15 Healey, Denis (1989) *The time of my life*. Michael Joseph, pp.380–81, quoted in Goodman, Geoffrey (2003) *From Bevan to Blair: Fifty years' reporting from the political front line*, Pluto Press, pp.166–67.

16 Corder, Matthew and Weale, Martin (2012) 'Uncertain uncertainty', *British Actuarial Journal*, vol. 17, no. 3, pp.542–61.

17 Bank of England, *A millennium of macroeconomic data*.

18 Campbell, John (1997) *Nye Bevan: A biography*, UK: Richard Cohen Books, p.156.

[19] Powell, Christopher (1974) 'Fifty years of progress', *Built Environment*, vol. 3, no. 10, pp.532–35. https://www.jstor.org/stable/44398033

[20] Hanley, Lynsey, *Estates*, p.66.

[21] Timmins, Nicholas (2017) *The five giants: A biography of the welfare state*. (3rd paperback edition), UK: HarperCollins, p.148.

[22] Timmins, Nicholas, *The five giants*, p.182.

[23] Hanley, Lynsey, *Estates*, pp.89–91.

[24] Office for National Statistics (2022) *House building, UK: permanent dwellings started and completed* https://www.ons.gov.uk/peoplepopulationandcommunity/housing /datasets/ukhousebuildingpermanentdwellingsstartedandcompleted

[25] Office for National Statistics (2022) *House building, UK*.

[26] Burchell, Andrew and Purton, Marie-Astrid (2012) 'About Richard Crossman – a short biography', Warwick University Library: Modern Records Centre. https://warwick.ac.uk/services/library/mrc/archives_online/digital /crossman/urss/bio/

[27] Crossman, Richard (1975) *The diaries of a cabinet minister, vol. 1, minister of housing 1964–66*, UK: Hamish Hamilton and Jonathan Cape, p.383.

[28] Timmins, Nicholas, *The five giants*, p.232.

[29] Timmins, Nicholas, *The five giants*, p.233.

[30] Crossman, Richard, *The diaries of a cabinet minister*, pp.382–83.

[31] Dunleavy, Patrick (1978) *The politics of high rise housing in Britain: Local communities tackle mass housing*, D-Phil thesis, UK: University of Oxford, p.87. http://eprints.lse.ac.uk/82066 (note: Dunleavy is editor in chief of LSE Press).

[32] Marmot, Alexi (1981) 'The legacy of Le Corbusier and high-rise housing', *Built Environment*, vol. 7, no. 2, pp.82–95, 93. https://www.jstor.org/stable/23288674

[33] Marmot, Alexi, 'The legacy of Le Corbusier and high-rise housing', pp.88–91.

[34] Crossman, Richard, *The diaries of a cabinet minister, vol. 1*, p.87.

[35] Hanley, Lynsey, *Estates*, p.16.

[36] Hanley, Lynsey, *Estates*, p.102.

[37] Hanley, Lynsey, *Estates*, p.ix.

[38] Timmins, Nicholas, *The five giants*, p.364.

[39] Field, Frank (1975) *Do we need council houses?*, UK: Catholic Housing Aid Society.

[40] Field, Frank (2018) 'Council Housing', *The Times*, 3 September. https://frankfield.co.uk/news/Council-Housing

[41] *Economist* (2005) 'Slums in the sky', 29 September. https://www.economist .com/britain/2005/09/29/slums-in-the-sky; Hanley, Lynsey, 'Slums in the Sky', in *Estates*, Chapter 3, pp.97–147.

[42] Power, Anne (2012) 'Social inequality, disadvantaged neighbourhoods and transport deprivation: An assessment of the historical influence of housing policies', *Journal of Transport Geography*, vol. 21, p.42. https://doi.org/10.1016/j.jtrangeo.2012.01.016

[43] Cook, Chris (2018) 'Ronan Point: a fifty-year building safety problem', *BBC News*, 15 June. https://perma.cc/8B37-QRAH

[44] *BBC News* 'Grenfell Tower: What happened' (2019), 29 October. https://perma.cc/MM3C-WJV8

[45] Voller, Derek (1968) 'Tower block collapse. Canning Town'. https://www.geograph.org.uk/photo/2540469

[46] Dunleavy, Patrick, *The politics of high rise housing in Britain*, p.451.

[47] Davies, Aled (2013) '"Right to buy": The development of a Conservative housing policy, 1945-1980', *Contemporary British History*, vol. 27, no. 3, pp.421–44. https://doi.org/10.1080/13619462.2013.824660

[48] Crosland, Anthony (1967) *The future of socialism*, US: Schocken, p.188.

[49] *Eighth Report from the Select Committee on Estimates* (Session 1952–53), UK: HMSO, pp.vii, ix. Cited in Crosland, Anthony, *The future of socialism*, p.190.

[50] Kogan, Maurice (2006) 'Anthony Crosland: intellectual and politician', *Oxford Review of Education*, vol. 32, no. 1, p.78. https://doi.org/10.1080/03054980500496452

[51] Crosland, Anthony 'Comprehensive schools in practice', in Crosland, Anthony, *The future of socialism*, pp.201–04.

[52] Crosland, Anthony, *The future of socialism*, p.205.

[53] Timmins, Nicholas, *The five giants*, p.244.

[54] Crosland, Anthony, *The future of socialism*, p.205.

[55] Hanley, Lynsey (2016) *Respectable: The experience of class*, UK: Penguin. p. 88.

[56] Hanley, Lynsey, *Respectable,* p.49.

[57] Hanley, Lynsey, *Respectable* p.100.

[58] Akerlof, George and Kranton, Rachel (2010) 'Identity and the economics of education', in *Identity economics*, UK: Princeton University Press, pp.61–80. https://doi.org/10.1515/9781400834181

[59] Hanley, Lynsey, *Respectable*, p.49.

[60] Hanley, Lynsey, 'The Wall in the Head', in *Respectable*, pp.148–84.

[61] Hanley, Lynsey, *Respectable*, p.150.

[62] Farquharson, Christine; McNally, Sandra; and Tahir, Imran (2022) *Education inequalities*, UK: IFS Deaton Review of Inequalities, p.42. https://ifs.org.uk/inequality/wp-content/uploads/2022/08/Education-inequalities.pdf

[63] OECD (2019) *Balancing school choice and equity: An international perspective based on PISA*. France: OECD, p.46. https://www.oecd.org/publications/balancing-school-choice-and-equity-2592c974-en.htm

[64] Le Grand, Julian (2003) *Motivation, agency, and public policy: Of knights and knaves, pawns and queens*, UK: Oxford University Press, p.5. https://doi.org/10.1093/0199266999.001.0001

[65] Davis, John (2002) 'The Inner London Education Authority and the William Tyndale Junior School affair', *Oxford Review of Education*, vol. 28, no. 2–3, pp.275–98. https://doi.org/10.1080/03054980220143423

[66] Davis, John, 'The Inner London Education Authority', p.284.

[67] Davis, John, 'The Inner London Education Authority', p.275.

[68] Davis, John, 'The Inner London Education Authority', p.286.

[69] Chitty, Clyde (2004) *Education policy in Britain*, UK: Palgrave, pp.40–45.

[70] Adonis, Andrew and Pollard, Stephen (1997) *A class act: the myth of Britain's classless society*, UK: Hamish Hamilton, p.55.

[71] Hood, Christopher; James, Oliver; Jones, George; Scott, Colin; and Travers, Tony (1999) 'From secret garden to reign of terror? The regulation of state schools in England', in *Regulation inside government: Waste watchers, quality police, and sleazebusters*, UK: Oxford University Press, pp.139–61. https://doi.org/10.1093/0198280998.001.0001

[72] Hanley, Lynsey, *Estates*, p.545.

[73] Barber, Michael (2008) *Instruction to deliver: Fighting to transform Britain's public services*, UK: Politicos, p.25.

[74] Hillman, Nicholas (2010) 'The Public Schools Commission: "Impractical, expensive and harmful to children"?' *Contemporary British History*, vol. 24, no. 4, pp.511–31. https://doi.org/10.1080/13619462.2010.518413

[75] Hillman, Nicholas, 'The Public Schools Commission', pp.514–15.

[76] Hillman, Nicholas, 'The Public Schools Commission', p.526.

[77] Rimfeld, Kaili; Malanchini, Margherita; Krapohl, Eva; Hannigan, Laurie; Dale, Philip; and Plomin, Robert (2018) 'The stability of educational achievement across school years is largely explained by genetic factors', *NPJ Science of Learning*, vol. 3, no. 1, pp.1–10. https://doi.org/10.1038/s41539-018-0030-0

[78] DeBoer, Freddie (2022) 'Education doesn't work 2.05'. *Substack.* https://freddiedeboer.substack.com/p/education-doesnt-work-20

[79] Hirsch, Fred (2005) *Social limits to growth*, UK: Routledge, pp.243–45.

[80] Hanley, Lynsey, *Estates*, pp.200–03.

[81] Timmins, Nicholas, *The five giants*, pp.482–83.

[82] Hirsch, Fred, *Social limits to growth*.

[83] *Report of the Committee appointed by the Prime Minister under the Chairmanship of Lord Robbins* (1963),UK: HMSO. https://perma.cc/K55H-Y3V2

[84] Hirsch, Fred, *Social limits to growth*, p.49.

[85] Griffiths, Sian (2022) 'Oxbridge leaders urge 95 per cent intake from state schools'. *Sunday Times*, 30 October. https://perma.cc/RU22-J537

[86] Timmins, Nicholas, *The five giants*, p.485.

[87] Farquharson, Christine et al, *Education inequalities*, p.80.

[88] Pochin, Courtney (2022) 'Kwasi Kwarteng's bold comment to tutor after Cambridge University interview'. *The Mirror.* https://perma.cc/U74D-XHBU

[89] Hanley, Lynsey, *Respectable*, pp.128–29.

[90] Hanley, Lynsey, *Respectable*, p.xi.

5. Neoliberalism and the new Thatcher settlement

Contemplation of an optimal system may suggest ways of improving the system, it may provide techniques of analysis that would otherwise have been missed and, in certain special cases, it may go far to providing a solution. But in general its influence has been pernicious. It has directed economists' attention away from the main question, which is how alternative arrangements will actually work in practice. It has led economists to derive conclusions for economic policy from a study of an abstract model of a market situation.

Ronald Coase[1]

The Attlee settlement developed out of a post-war consensus across the three main political parties. In stark contrast, Margaret Thatcher aimed to impose a new, neoliberal ideological settlement. She did not, however, make that apparent on Friday, 4 May 1979, when, standing on the threshold of 10 Downing Street after winning the 1979 election, she offered a healing government for Britain:

I would just like to remember some words of St. Francis of Assisi which I think are really just particularly apt at the moment … Where there is discord, may we bring harmony. Where there is error, may we bring truth. Where there is doubt, may we bring faith. And where there is despair, may we bring hope.[2]

This prayer in fact dates from seven centuries after St Francis of Assisi had died. It was published, in 1912, in a small spiritual French magazine (called *La Clochette – The Little Bell*).[3] Two years after Thatcher had promised to bring harmony and hope, her policies had so devastated parts of Britain that there were street riots – in London (Brixton) and Liverpool (Toxteth). Later, her catastrophic flagship reform of local government finance, the poll tax in 1990, also resulted in riots in Trafalgar Square.[4]

How to cite this book chapter:

Bevan, Gwyn (2023) *How Did Britain Come to This? A century of systemic failures of governance*, London: LSE Press, pp. 109–138.
https://doi.org/10.31389/lsepress.hdb.e License: CC BY-NC

The Conservatives' election campaign in 1979 was helped by the aggressive advertising of Saatchi and Saatchi – then the hottest advertising company in Britain. Figure 5.1 shows its most memorable poster, 'Labour isn't working'. It vividly captured the failure of Labour government of 1974 to 1979 as the first since 1945 to fail to deliver on the commitment of the 1944 Employment White Paper to 'a high and stable level of employment'. [5] There had been a troubling uptick in unemployment (from around 5 per cent to nearly 7 per cent in 1979). Yet Figure 5.2 demonstrates that the new Conservative government then converted this slippage into a post-war record level of unemployment: the

Figure 5.1: Conservative campaign poster for the 1979 general election

Source: Poster produced by Saatchi & Saatchi for The Conservative Party.[6]

Figure 5.2: UK unemployment (%), 1946–2015

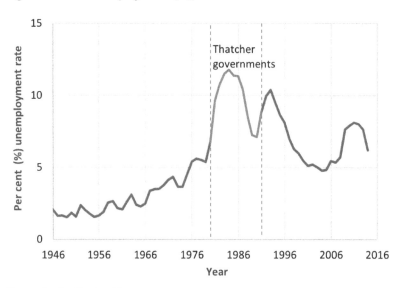

Source: Bank of England.[7]

percentage of the workforce unemployed increased dramatically to nearly 12 per cent in 1983, and it was not until 1996 that it again fell below 7 per cent.

So, why did the Thatcher government go on to win elections in 1983 and 1987? Her answer was TINA: There Is No Alternative. Alwyn Turner explains that this stance applied to both the lack of serious competition from potential rivals in the Conservative Party and a divided opposition.[8] A ferocious left–right internecine row within the Labour Party resulted in a substantial group of MPs and voters moving to the new Social Democratic Party.[9] As a result, Margaret Thatcher remained prime minister from 1979 until 1991, when she lost the support of Conservative MPs and members of her cabinet. Her three successive Conservative governments developed the Thatcher settlement further by rolling back the role of the state and replacing state activities with markets. As markets later morphed through successive waves of financialisation, the eventual result was the Global Financial Crisis of 2008, which hit the UK especially hard. I focus here on four of the Thatcher settlement's distinctive impacts:

- subjecting the economy to reforms inspired by neoliberal ideology, especially 'monetarist' economics;
- requiring industries to focus on increasing profits and shareholder value;
- deregulating finance; and
- enabling tenants to buy council houses, thus ushering in the near-complete financialisation of the housing market.

Carolyn Tuohy argues that the consequence of a political settlement is an 'accidental logic' that shapes how policy develops.[10] In this chapter I give an account of how the 'accidental logics' of neoliberalism played out at a macro-level in its systems of governance based on 'monetarism' and financialisation.

5.1 The ideology of neoliberalism

Friedrich von Hayek's *The Road to Serfdom* was published in 1944.[11] According to the Margaret Thatcher foundation, this

> became part of her enduring outlook. In fact one can argue that few books influenced her more deeply at any point in her life … she found herself exposed to one of the most effective and courageous political works ever written, a head-on assault against socialism, the fashionable cause of the day, an armed doctrine at the height of its power … She absorbed deeply Hayek's idea that you cannot compromise with socialism, even in mild social democratic forms, because by degrees socialism tends always to totalitarian outcomes, regardless of the intentions, professed or real, of its proponents.[12]

Two years younger than Aneurin Bevan, von Hayek was the diametrical opposite of his vision of democratic socialism in Britain. Bevan had left school before he was 14 and witnessed the suffering of the mining communities caused by unemployment and the 'means test' in the 1930s. Von Hayek had studied at the University of Vienna and experienced hyperinflation that destroyed the middle class. (The exchange rate of Austrian crowns for one US$ inflated from 16 to over 70,000 between 1919 and 1923.[13]) Von Hayek became a key developer of the Austrian School of Economics of Ludwig von Mises, and joined Lionel Robbins as a professor in LSE's Economics Department in 1931. Von Hayek addressed *The Road to Serfdom* to 'socialists of all parties' and argued that: 'Few are ready to recognize that the rise of fascism and Nazism was not a reaction against the socialist trends of the preceding period but a necessary outcome of those tendencies.'[14] Von Hayek set out the ideological foundations for rolling back the state and abandoning Keynesian economics. Whereas classical liberalism prioritised political institutions, neoliberalism in Britain followed von Hayek's argument that impersonal markets are the chief means of securing popular welfare and personal liberty.[15]

In 1945 von Hayek was lionised in the US as a protagonist in the fight against Franklin Roosevelt's New Deal of the 1930s: the *Reader's Digest* published a condensed version of *The Road to Serfdom*.[16] Thousands came to hear his public lectures.[17] Gary Gerstle summarised neoliberalism in the US as 'grounded in the belief that market forces had to be liberated from government regulatory controls that were stymieing growth, innovation and freedom'.[18] Roosevelt had put into practice Keynes's ideas to end the slump,

> founded on the conviction that capitalism left to its own devices spelled economic disaster. It had to be managed by a strong central state able to govern the economic system in the public interest.[19]

The economics of Keynes was, for Aneurin Bevan, an existential threat to socialism (see Chapter 3). But in the US the first American university textbook to set out Keynes's ideas, *Elements of Economics*, was described as 'a sort of second edition of Karl Marx's book "*Capital*"' and under pressure dropped from the curricula of American universities and ceased publication.[20] The febrile antagonism to communism in the 1940s and 1950s culminated in hearings of the House Un-American Activities Committee (HUAC), where US Senator Joseph McCarthy of Wisconsin notoriously asked: 'Are you now or have you ever been a member of the Communist Party of the United States?' A Republican congressman requested that HUAC launch an investigation into the author of *Elements of Economics*.[21]

In 1947, von Hayek invited like-minded individuals to the Swiss mountain village of Mont-Pèlerin and 39 thinkers came. That turned out to be the inaugural meeting of the Mont Pèlerin Society (MPS).[22] Lionel Robbins drafted its Statement of Aims, which began 'The central values of civilization are in danger'.[23] The statement identified as threats to these values 'a decline of belief in private property and the competitive market', because 'without the diffused power and initiative associated with these institutions it is difficult to imagine a society in which freedom may be effectively preserved'. It continued that 'a decline of belief in private property and the competitive market' posed threats to 'the central values of civilization'.[24] By November 1947, the MPS was formally registered in the United States as a non-profit corporation with the purpose:

> To study and promote the study of political, economic, historical, moral and philosophic aspects of civil society having a bearing upon the institutional and organizational conditions compatible with freedom of thought and action.[25]

The MPS played a vital role in defining neoliberalism.[26] One later influential member of the MPS was Sir Antony Fisher, who founded the UK's Institute for Economic Affairs (IEA) in 1955.[27] And, in 1981, he founded the Atlas Economic Research Foundation, which became an international network of over 500 right-wing think tanks in 90 countries, who share the vision 'of a free, prosperous, and peaceful world where the principles of individual liberty, property rights, limited government, and free markets are secured by the rule of law'.[28]

Von Hayek's contribution to neoliberalism was ideological: to assert the primacy of markets, and the need for rolling back the state and abandoning Keynesian economics. In 1950, he moved to a chair at the University of Chicago but was not deemed appointable in the Economics Department.[29] In 1974, he was awarded the Nobel Prize in Economics for his 'penetrating analysis of the interdependence of economic, social and institutional phenomena'.[30] The institutions of neoliberal capitalism were shaped by Nobel Prize-winning economists who had taught and studied in the Chicago Economics Department: Milton Friedman, Robert Lucas and Myron Scholes.

5.2 Monetarism

In 1976 (the year the British government needed an IMF loan), Friedman's award for the Nobel Prize in Economics cited as his major work *A Monetary History of the United States, 1867–1960*.[31] It praised Friedman and the Chicago School for the emergence of monetarism and giving us the terms 'money matters' or, even, 'only money matters'.[32] In his 1964 review, Charles Goodhart (who became the Bank of England's resident 'monetary economist') praised *A Monetary History of the United States, 1867–1960* for its statistical and historical aspects'. But he criticised the authors for basing 'their formal analysis completely and without compromise upon the neo-classical quantity theory of money, as reinterpreted by the Chicago school'. His judgement was that 'the authors do not really provide or refer the reader to evidence of sufficient weight to support the reliance that they place upon the classical price-specie [i.e., money] flow mechanism'.[33]

Paul Krugman points out that Margaret Thatcher 'was surrounded by men who had been really convinced by Milton Friedman'.[34] From 1979 to 1986, her government 'did not announce policy goals for output, employment or inflation; it simply announced targets for a broad monetary aggregate M3 (notes and coins and bank lending)'.[35] Goodhart correctly warned the Conservative Party, both before they won the 1979 election and after they had been elected as the new government, that 'monetarism' would fail in the UK's monetary and banking system.[36] James Forder's 2019 book on Milton Friedman points out that the attempt by Friedman and Schwartz to replicate their study of the US for the UK was heavily criticised for its failure to take into account their institutional differences (and its weak methodology).[37] Goodhart argued that a historic relationship between aggregate measures of money and subsequent inflation would breakdown when governments try to control the money supply. Goodhart's law is that 'any observed regularity will tend to collapse once pressure is placed upon it for control purposes'.[38]

Figure 5.3 gives the percentage increases in the measures of money supply (based on various money measures) and the Consumer Price Index two years later for the first 50 years of the post-war period. It shows that, with one notable exception, there was virtually no relationship between the money supply and inflation. The exception is the monetary incontinence of the Barber boom, from 1970 to 1974 (see Chapter 4), which was followed by an alarmingly high rate of inflation. Charles Goodhart explained to me that:

> if you take a period which includes very volatile and extreme changes in the money stock, you will find a close relationship in a regression; but if you take a period in which the money stock has fluctuated over a relatively small range, then you are likely to find no relationship between monetary growth and nominal incomes.[39]

Figure 5.3 also shows that the Bank of England's attempts to control the money supply failed. That policy was abandoned in 1986. Friedman blamed the failure of 'monetarism' in Britain on the 'gross incompetence' of the Bank of England. As James Forder points out, Friedman's policy of 'monetarism', of targeting the quantity of money, 'has been rejected almost completely'.[40]

Within 18 months of Thatcher taking office, outputs in the manufacturing sector collapsed.[41] Alec Chrystal argued, however, that the primary cause of the reduction in inflation and deindustrialisation was not 'monetarism' but the 'Dutch disease' from the impact of North Sea oil.[42] In the Netherlands, in the 1960s, the discovery of natural gas had increased the value of its currency, which damaged its manufacturing industry and increased unemployment. Figure 5.4 shows the sharp increase in value of the pound sterling to above US$2.30 in 1980. In 1988 Hilde Bjørnland examined the impacts of North Sea oil on the economies of Britain and Norway. She explained that, although the 'Dutch disease' would have been expected to have caused a greater increase in unemployment in Norway, manufacturing declined in the

Figure 5.3: Annual percentage increases (%) in the UK money supply and in price levels (two years later), from 1946 to 2016

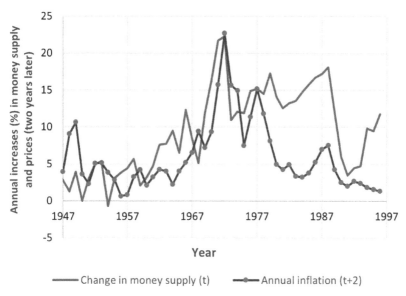

Source: Bank of England.[43]

Figure 5.4: The exchange rate of the pound in terms of US dollars

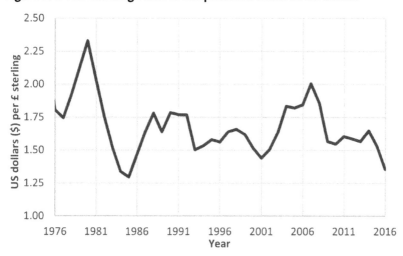

Source: Bank of England.[44]

UK and increased in Norway. She argued that these outcomes resulted from differences in government policies. The Norwegian government directed subsidies to maintain manufacturing output over the transitional period of North Sea oil. In the UK, much of the revenue from the North Sea went into paying social security payments (and existing external debts).[45]

In 1987, James Alt came to the same conclusion.[46] He identified vital differences in the key players, their institutional capabilities, and their governments deciding whether the key economic problem was unemployment or inflation.

- *Norway.* The government acted as a small country and set out to counter its vulnerability to currency speculation. Trade unions played a vital role in working with government on managing the transition

Figure 5.5: The distribution of UK employment across industrial sectors from 1996 to 2016

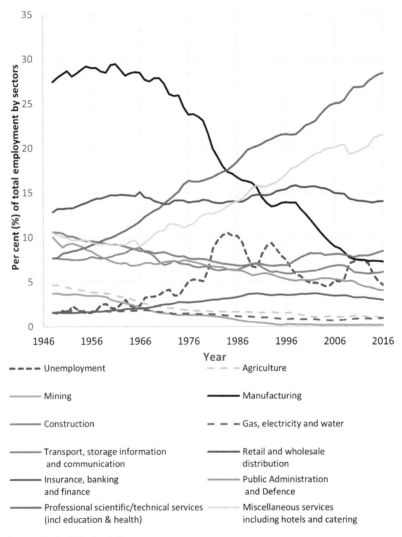

Source: Bank of England.[47]

to maintain jobs. The government had the institutional capacity on the supply side to target subsidies to the sectors of its economy under greatest threat.

- *Britain.* The government acted as a big country in which financial interests were paramount and their impact on the appreciation of the pound sterling was welcomed as an effective means of driving down inflation. Figure 5.4 shows that sterling's rate against the US dollar increased by a third, from 1.75 in 1977 to 2.33 in 1980. Alt argues that, even if there had been a Labour government, it would have lacked the institutional capacity on the supply side to target subsidies in the sectors and towns where they were most needed.

Figure 5.5 shows the changes over 70 years in the patterns of employment and unemployment in Britain. The two major sectors of employment at the start of the 20th century, agriculture and mining, had declined to account for less than 10 per cent by 1946. Figure 5.5 also shows that, from 1979, there was a sharp reduction in employment in the manufacturing industry, an increase in unemployment, and growth in services. The strongest growth was in professional and scientific services, and miscellaneous services (which include hotels and catering). The groups that were relatively stable were transport, storage, information and communication, and retail and wholesale distribution. Although the percentage working in insurance, banking and finance almost doubled, it accounted for only 3 per cent in 2016.

5.3 The Global Financial Crisis: made in Chicago?

For Milton Friedman, the principle that 'only money matters' was the basis of his 'fundamentally subversive doctrine', as he argued in an influential leader in the *New York Times* in 1970:

> there is one and only one social responsibility of business – to use its resources and engage in activities designed to increase its profits so long as it stays within the rules of the game, which is to say, engages in open and free competition without deception fraud.[48]

He went on to say that businessmen who interpret the 'social responsibilities' of business to include 'providing employment, eliminating discrimination, avoiding pollution … are … preaching pure and unadulterated socialism'. A risk to this slant was that senior executives might not agree: they might believe that their corporations also ought to serve stakeholders other than shareholders, such as customers, employees, creditors and the environment. In 1976 the economists Michael Jensen and William Meckling aimed to offer a solution to that problem by linking the remuneration of senior executives to increases in shareholder value.[49]

Figure 5.6: Five ways to maximise shareholder value (MSV)

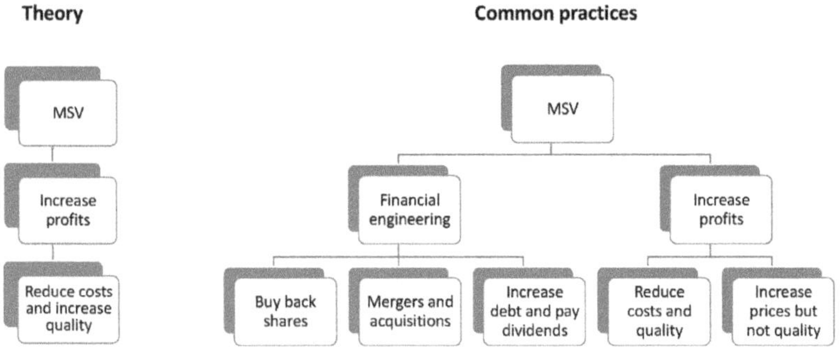

Source: Author.

In the neoliberal world of perfectly competitive markets, economic insti-tutions supposedly create incentives to reduce costs and improve quality, as illustrated in the left part of Figure 5.6. That has not been the consequence when corporations are governed with the sole objective of maximising share-holder value (MSV), as described by Rana Foroohar in the US[50] and Mariana Mazzucato in the UK.[51] The right part of Figure 5.6 illustrates the dysfunc-tional outcomes. For example, what ought a firm do with its profits: invest in the company or buy back shares? The former is risky, but the latter is a sure way of increasing shareholder value. (By definition, the value of a share is the total value of the firm divided by the number of shares.) General Electric (GE) used to be a $600 billion behemoth in the US. William Cohan attributes its demise, via being broken up for disposal, to cost-cutting, outsourcing and financial speculation.[52] The next chapter gives examples of how financial engi-neering by financing dividends by increasing debt undermined the outsourc-ing of care homes and the privatisation of water in England. As Martin Wolf argues, the consequences of corporations becoming 'appendages of financial markets' changed 'every aspect of corporate behaviour – its goals, its internal incentives, and the identity of those in charge'.[53]

In the US, financial services were deregulated from 1987, under Alan Green-span as chairman of the US Federal Reserve. This sea-change was justified by the theory of 'rational expectations', developed by Robert Lucas, for which he was awarded the Nobel Prize in Economics in 1995. His theory is based on the 'efficient-market hypothesis': the price of a financial asset reflects all relevant generally available information.[54] In 1973, Fischer Black and Myron Scholes developed a formula that could put a price on a financial contract when it still had years to run, for example a 20-year mortgage. The Black–Scholes formula takes into account four variables: the time the mortgage has to run, the price of the house on which the mortgage is secured, the risk-free interest rate, and volatility over what the future price of the house might be.[55] In 1994, Robert Merton (another option-pricing expert) joined Myron Scholes as partners in the hedge fund Long-Term Capital Management. In 1995, Fischer Black died.

In 1997, Scholes and Merton shared the Nobel Prize in Economics 'for a new method to determine the value of derivatives'.[56] In 1998, Long-Term Capital Management (LTCM) collapsed. Alan Greenspan, the then chairman of the Federal Reserve, organised LTCM's rescue by a consortium of banks.[57] Naseem Taleb argued that LTCM's collapse clearly showed that the way the Black–Scholes formula modelled volatility was vulnerable to 'highly improbable' outcomes – 'black swans'.[58]

Two great economists of the 20th century had emphasised the vital distinction between *risk*, which can be quantified and modelled (for example, the likelihood of outcomes of throws of a dice), and future *uncertainty*, which cannot (for example, the future state of the economy). One was Frank Knight at the University of Chicago.[59] (He had opposed von Hayek's appointment to its Economics Department because the market could be equally inefficient as government.[60]) The other was John Maynard Keynes in *The general theory of interest, employment and money*.[61] John Kay and Mervyn King point out that Milton Friedman decided that Knight and Keynes were wrong: Friedman asserted that uncertain outcomes could be modelled using probability theory.[62] Kay and King highlight how those who followed Friedman in developing derivatives were incapable of recognising the vital distinction between their models of risk and uncertainty.[63] On 13 August 2007, as the Global Financial Crisis began to bite, David Viniar, the chief financial officer of Goldman Sachs, claimed that they were seeing market outcomes each day that were 25 standard deviations from their mean prediction. Kay and King point out that there are not enough days in the history of our universe for an outcome with that daily probability to happen.[64]

In 2003, Robert Lucas began his presidential address to the American Economic Association by stating that the 'central problem of depression prevention has been solved, for all practical purposes, and has in fact been solved for many decades'.[65] In that year, John Kay had asked whether 'history will judge whether Greenspan was the man who made millions of American rich – or the man who couldn't bear to tell them they had only imagined it?'[66] In 2005, the US monetary and financial elite met to celebrate Greenspan's retirement at their annual conference at Jackson Hole, Wyoming. Raghuram Rajan had the temerity to present his paper at that conference, asking, 'Has Financial Development Made the World Riskier?'[67] He argued that the deregulated financial system was vulnerable to a catastrophic meltdown. Larry Summers, a former Treasury secretary, described Rajan's advocacy of increased financial regulation as Luddite – like advocating giving up air travel because of a fear of crashes.[68] For the rest of the conference, Rajan felt like 'an early Christian who had wandered into a convention of half-starved lions'. What troubled him most was that his 'critics seemed to be ignoring what was going on before their eyes'.[69] Rajan argues that successive federal governments in the US, under Presidents Bill Clinton and George W Bush, used subprime mortgages to enable the poor to buy houses that would increase in price and make them feel better off.[70] This was the neoliberal solution to the problem of stagnant or declining median incomes and the creation of the precariat: the 'large swathe of low-wage, low-skill, low-progression service-sector employment, often with poor labour standards'.[71]

Markovits describes how decisions on whether to offer a mortgage used to be made deliberatively in the US, by an army of mid-skilled professional loan officers who had the 'educational and social background commensurate to their solidly middle class status'.[72] They exercised 'independent judgement about the economic wherewithal and reliability of particular borrowers and the value of particular houses to ensure that each loan was providently made'. They took into account not only taxable income and loan-to-value ratio but also assessments of the 'borrower's character and standing in the community'.[73] Under those institutional arrangements, few investments were as 'safe as houses' as prices reflected ability to pay. After financialisation, the decisions to offer mortgages changed radically:

> A rump of gloomy Main Street workers collect data to fill in boilerplate loan applications. And a small elite of Wall Street workers 'correct' for the inaccuracies of initial loan decisions by repackaging loans into complex derivatives that quantify, hedge, and reallocate the risks of improvident originations.[74]

Naseem Taleb had expected that the collapse of Long-Term Capital Management would end the use of the Black–Scholes formula to value risk in financial derivatives. But, as Katharina Pistor explains, the way the institutions of financialisation work, banks kept the profits when their risk models worked and governments socialised the losses when they failed.[75] That is why, as Ian Stewart described, banks hired mathematically talented analysts to develop the Black–Scholes formula into 'ever-more complex financial instruments whose value and risk were increasingly opaque'.[76] As Pistor argues, the credit rating agencies gave derivatives credibility and have 'largely escaped liability for their use of misleading labels'. Their core argument is 'that they are in the business of offering opinions, and their utterances should therefore enjoy the protection of free speech under the US constitution's First Amendment'.[77] By 2007, the international financial system was trading derivatives valued at one quadrillion dollars (that is, $1,000,000,000,000,000) per year. (This is 10 times the total worth, adjusted for inflation, of all products made by the world's manufacturing industries over the last century.)[78] Even with Pistor's example of a credit risk manager charging the seemingly modest fee of 0.015 per cent, that would generate $15 billion in annual fees.

Financialisation changed the price mechanism for American houses from being determined in a normal market, in which increases in prices reduced demand, to a speculative market, in which increases in prices fuelled demand. When people with subprime mortgages were unable to make their monthly payments, the house of cards of financial derivatives progressively collapsed.[79]

On 15 September 2008, the scale of exposure of US investment bank Lehman Brothers to defaults on subprime mortgages resulted in its bankruptcy and the Global Financial Crisis became locked in.[80] In October 2008, Alan Greenspan, in his evidence to Congress, recognised that there had been a 'flaw' in his thinking. But he believed that the kind of heavy regulation that could have prevented the crisis would have damaged US economic growth.[81]

In December 2009, Paul Volcker, Greenspan's predecessor as chairman of the US Federal Reserve, said that he wished 'somebody would give me some shred of evidence linking financial innovation with a benefit to the economy' – his favourite financial innovation was the ATM.[82] Mariana Mazzucato points out that, before the 1970s, in economics, the financial sector was treated as 'a value extractor'.[83] Paradoxically, by the time of the Global Financial Crisis of 2008, that had changed in the national accounts of most countries so that the sector added value.[84] Martin Wolf lays out the impact of the Global Financial Crisis on trust in the institutions of capitalism:

> Many members of the public came to believe that these failings were the result not of stupidity but of the intellectual and moral corruption of decision makers at all levels – in the financial sector, regulatory bodies, academia, the media and politics. They also saw the resources of the state used to rescue both banks and bankers – the architects as they saw it of the disaster – whilst they (and those they loved) suffered large losses through foreclosure, unemployment, a prolonged period of stagnant or declining real wages and fiscal austerity. Finally, they also saw that while institutions were forced to pay huge fines, essentially nobody (or nobody of any importance) was punished for what had happened.[85]

Katharina Pistor explains that this is what the legal rules of the game that underpin the financialised institutions of capitalism were designed to do.[86] She cites the analysis by the late legal historian Bernard Rudden. He argued that, although the common law of property originated in extractive feudal societies, its 'feudal calculus still lives and breeds, but its habitat is wealth not land'.[87] The law of limited liability is designed to protect the wealth of shareholders so that their exposure to risk from investing in a firm is limited to the price they paid for their shares: that is, shareholders have legal protection to retain all dividends paid prior to when a firm goes bankrupt. Katharina Pistor describes how financialisation has offered opportunities for creative use of the law of limited liability, so a holding company is protected from having to repay dividends from its subsidiaries when they go bankrupt.[88] Tooze quotes the CEO of Citigroup telling journalists in the summer of 2007: 'as long as the music is playing you've got to get up and dance. We're still dancing.'[89] When the music stopped, the banks in the US were made offers so attractive that they would have been unwise to refuse.[90]

In 1982, Lehman Brothers in the US was the first major investment bank to convert from a partnership to a public company. It 'along with other financial intermediaries developed the legal partitioning of assets with the help of corporate law into an art form'.[91] The parent holding company of Lehman Brothers had 209 subsidiaries in 26 jurisdictions. Sixty were in the US state of Delaware, which has particularly 'nimble' rules that allow a corporation to pay dividends to shareholders 'even when this may be detrimental for its long term survival'.[92] During the financial crisis of 2008 the purpose of the US government's Troubled Asset Relief Program (TARP) was to implement programmes to stabilise the financial system. Viral Acharya et al found that, 'in the 2007–2009 period, all the banks which had received TARP funding [Congressional relief payments] had paid at least 45 per cent of the amount as dividends in 2007–2009'.[93] Pistor describes how the elaborate scheme developed by Lehman Brothers, its Regulation and Administration of Safe Custody and Local Settlement (RASCALS), was designed to protect a new company, LBF, against claims of creditors after Lehman Brothers went bankrupt. The case was brought in a London Chancery Court and presided over by the Chancellor, and:

> When the creditors argued that the entire scheme was a scam and should simply be set aside, the Chancellor was in disbelief … Like the chancery courts of the eighteenth century, which had sided with the landed elites, he had few qualms about parties using the law to their own private benefits, even if this put the entire system at risk.[94]

In March 2023, the Silicon Valley Bank collapsed. Paul Krugman in the *New York Times* observed:

> Just a few years ago, S.V.B. was one of the midsize banks that lobbied successfully for the removal of regulations that might have prevented this disaster, and the tech sector is famously full of libertarians who like to denounce big government right up to the minute they themselves needed government aid.[95]

John Thornhill in the *Financial Times* observed:

> [The] fiasco also shines an unforgiving spotlight on the hypocrisy of some of the biggest venture capital players on both sides of the Atlantic, who privately urged their portfolio companies to pull their money from the bank and then later publicly called for government support … Just like many of the banking titans after the global financial crisis of 2008, tech tycoons appear to favour the privatisation of profits and the socialisation of losses.[96]

5.4 The financialisation of the UK's economy after Thatcher

Eichengreen's explanation of why Britain had descended in rankings of real per capita incomes, from second in 1950 to 10th by 1979, was the country's lack of networks of investment banks lending to large enterprises that challenged unions in implementing the technologies of modern mass production.[97] What changed after 1979 was financialisation, with the dysfunctional outcomes summarised in Figure 5.6.[98] Anthony Warwick-Ching describes how, in the 1980s, many UK companies were acquired by European enterprises in transactions that were generously remunerative to those in Britain who organised them.[99] And John Kay showed how acquisitions and mergers resulted in the demise of the chemical giant ICI.[100] Financial services were deregulated in the UK in 1986, following the 'big bang' in the City of London.

Kay has set out how financialisation destroyed the mutual financial institutions and partnerships (such as building societies in the UK) that used to play a vital role in every country as trusted providers of retail financial services. For their partners and members, this realised financial returns in the short term but it resulted in the loss of goodwill and trust that had been established in these institutions over many years. There was a transformation from a 'risk-averse culture of mutual and partnership' to the 'competitive machismo in the public company'.[101] Simon Lee has pointed out that in the UK, after the demutualisation of the building society Northern Rock in 1997, the new housing bank financed an aggressive sixfold increase in its assets over the following decade through borrowing and debt. During the first half of 2007, Northern Rock accounted for nearly 10 per cent of total mortgage lending in the UK. As 80 per cent of its funding was from wholesale markets used by banks, it faced an impending crisis as that market froze in August 2007. After the BBC reported its problems there was, in September 2007, the first run on the deposits of a bank in the UK since 1878.[102] But the primary cause of the UK's subsequent homegrown financial crisis was the loss of £24 billion accumulated from a disastrous series of takeovers by the Royal Bank of Scotland, led by Sir Fred Goodwin, who retired early at age 50 with a pension fund of £17 million.[103]

In 1997, Gordon Brown had a recurrent dream that his economic policies based on 'the bedrock of prudent and wise economic management for the long term' would avoid 'the shifting sands of boom and bust' and create the 'firm foundations [to] raise Britain's underlying economic performance'. He repeated variations on that dream in speeches every year to 2007, when he described his mission to build a 'dynamic and competitive enterprise economy' by 'building on our hard-won stability'.[104] In 2006, when the price of a typical house increased by £45 a day, Gordon Brown described the UK's 'light touch system of regulation' as 'fair, proportionate and increasingly risk based'.[105] In 2007, he envisaged 'a new golden age for the City of London' enabling Britain to become 'one of the greatest success stories in the new global economy.[106]

Michael Barber (an adviser to both the Blair and Cameron governments) likened Treasury forecasts to Joseph's interpretation of Pharoah's dream in the Bible:[107] 'Seven thin kine [cows] ate seven fat kine, and thin ears of wheat devoured good ears of wheat.'[108] Joseph's interpretation of Pharoah's dream was that there would be seven years of feast to be followed by seven years of famine. Pharoah asked Joseph to put into practice Keynes's principle of balancing the Egyptian economy over the economic cycle: to 'gather all the food of those good years that come, and lay up corn ... And that food shall be for store to the land against the seven years of famine.' In the years of famine, 'all countries came into Egypt to Joseph for to buy corn; because that the famine was so sore in all lands'.[109] Pharoah's dream correctly predicted an economic cycle, but Treasury forecasts did not. In November 2008, Queen Elizabeth opened LSE's New Academic Building, and famously asked the assembled economists about the Global Financial Crisis of 2008: 'Why did nobody see this coming?'[110]

Simon Lee points out that, prior to the Global Financial Crisis, the UK enjoyed 59 successive quarters of sustained economic growth, which was driven mainly not by investment but by consumer demand financed by debt.[111] Hence the need for a prudent economic policy to build up a surplus to help cushion the economy through the Global Financial Crisis. That economic sin of omission allowed the Conservative–Liberal Democrat government (2010–15) to blame the Blair/Brown governments for the crisis, attributing it to their profligacy in public spending in order to justify their policy of austerity. Martin Wolf argues that its excessive severity undermined our public services and prolonged the recession in the UK, and its devastating impacts on the areas 'left behind' is why people there voted for Brexit, which then worsened their plight.[112]

Figure 5.7 compares the UK's GDP per capita as a percentage of that of Germany, France and Italy between 2016 and 2022. It shows that, after Brexit, it is not just parts of the UK areas that are now left behind but the whole country. The UK has lacked the economic growth so vital to generate the funding to repair the damage austerity has inflicted on our fragile public services. Economic growth depends on increases in productivity. Nicholas Crafts and Terence Mills found that, over the decade to 2018, the UK's productivity was 20 per cent below the pre-2008 trend. That fall is without precedent in the past 250 years.[113] Anna Stansbury, Dan Turner and Ed Balls attributed the UK's low productivity to a shortage of degrees in science, technology, engineering and mathematics; inadequacies in transport; and support for innovation outside, and unaffordable housing within, England's golden triangle.[114] Indeed, as Martin Wolf argued, given the UK's unprecedented decade of a low increase in productivity, the only way that the UK looks like solving the long-standing problem of regional inequalities is by levelling down.[115]

Figure 5.7: GDP per capita for the UK as a percentage (%) of that in Germany, France and Italy, in 2016 and 2022

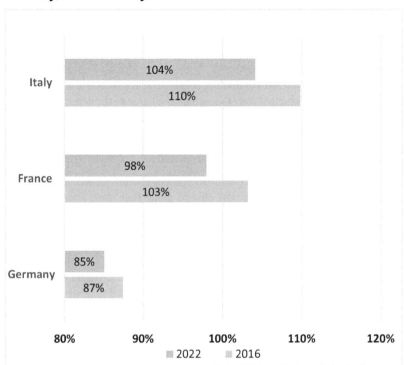

Source: OECD.[116]
Note: GDP per capita was measured here in US $ at current prices and current purchasing power parities.

In 2021, the UK was ranked by the OECD as 20th for real GDP per capita (just ahead of Malta) and eighth for income inequality.[117] Britain is now a relatively poor, unequal country. Analyses by *Financial Times* journalist John Burn-Murdoch showed that the rich are doing fine. In 2019 (pre-Covid-19), the top 10 per cent of households in the UK and Germany had similar incomes, of over $120,000 (in US dollars at 2020 purchasing power parity). But the incomes of the bottom 5 per cent of people in the UK was $15,900, over 20 per cent lower than the same group in Germany.[118] By 2023, the US and the UK were outliers in inequality and getting worse:

> Real wages in the UK are below where they were 18 years ago. Life expectancy has stagnated, with Britain arcing away below most other developed countries, and avoidable mortality — premature

deaths that should not occur with timely and effective healthcare — rising to the highest level among its peers, other than the USA, whose opioid crisis renders it peerless.[119]

5.5 Financialisation of housing in the UK

After Aneurin Bevan's dream of making public housing as central to the people of Britain as his NHS turned sour (see Chapter 4), one of the central planks of Thatcher's appeal to voters was the right to buy scheme, which seemed to give tenants of council-owned housing autonomy from badly run councils and standard-colour front doors. Depending on the duration of their tenancy, the scheme allowed council tenants discounts ranging from 33 per cent of market value (at three years) to 50 per cent (at 20 years or more).[120] The sitting tenants who bought their houses were now able to make their own alterations and improvements more easily. If they wanted to move on elsewhere, to another city or just a smarter part of town, they could sell up and recoup the full value of their house – creating over time a massive increase in family finances. Under the Thatcher governments, the number of new council houses built in England fell from 75,000 in 1979 to 8,000 in 1991; and under subsequent Conservative and Labour governments it further reduced to a rump.[121] Owner-occupation in the UK peaked at 72 per cent in 2001 and, by 2006, the stock of council and socially rented homes had almost been halved.[122] This chapter concludes by looking at the consequences of Margaret Thatcher's 'right to buy' scheme after the housing market became financialised. This has enabled the children of the rich, with access to the bank of mum and dad, to afford to take up offers of 'glossy' jobs in England's golden triangle, and thus entrenched geographical inequalities.

Anna Minton has argued that the country's crisis from the lack of affordable homes is chiefly due to three policies enacted by the Blair–Brown governments (1997 to 2010).[123] First, they continued the right to buy. Many former council houses and flats were then bought by new generations of private landlords who rented them out, at the bottom of the market, often to people who qualified for housing benefit welfare payments. By December 2022, private rents in 48 council areas were classed by the Office for National Statistics as unaffordable when compared with average wages.[124] Second, New Labour reduced the building of council houses to less than half those of the Thatcher years (below 8,000 homes per year on average). From 1991, local authorities accounted for at most 1 per cent of completions (see Figure 4.4 in Chapter 4). Third, they expanded private renting by encouraging 'buy to let mortgages'. These increased in number and value from under 50,000 and £4 billion in 2000, to 350,000 and £46 billion in 2007.

The Global Financial Crisis reduced the number of new houses completed by private builders in England from 150,000 in 2007 to 83,000 in 2010. In 2012, the number of new houses built was still only 60 per cent of the number in 2007.[125] In 2013, the UK government introduced a 'Help to Buy' equity loan scheme for a new-build house or flat worth up to £600,000 that was to be the owner's primary residence. In 2019, the National Audit Office (NAO) found that the scheme increased housing supply and home ownership and had a negligible impact on house prices, but fewer than 40 per cent of buyers using the scheme actually required it.[126] When the Chancellor of the Exchequer, George Osborne, launched the 'Help to Buy' scheme he promised that this would deliver 'a great deal for homebuyers' and 'a great support for home-builders'. As the *Financial Times* observed, it 'certainly delivered on the second'.[127] The NAO found that '[t]he scheme has supported five of the six largest developers in England to increase the overall number of properties they sell year on year, thereby contributing to increases in their annual profits'.[128] One of them, Persimmon, received the largest individual share (nearly 15 per cent of Help to Buy sales between 2013 and 2018), with 60 per cent of all its sales financed by the scheme.[129] Its share price-linked bonus scheme made Persimmon's chief executive, Jeff Fairburn, 'the UK's highest paid chief according to annual reports' in 2017. His pay and bonuses were: £2 million in 2016, nearly £46 million in 2017, and £39 million in 2018. Total payments to Persimmon's executives from share price-linked bonus scheme were £444 million.[130]

Did this high pay reflect the quality of Persimmon's products? In April 2019, the *Financial Times* reported that Persimmon 'recently scored the lowest of all the major housebuilders in the Home Builders Federation's annual customer satisfaction survey'. Following its executive pay scandal and concerns over build quality, the new chairman of the board of Persimmon announced 'an independent review of its culture, workmanship and customer care'.[131] When the findings of the independent review were published, a leader article in the *Financial Times* described the report as 'devastating' and highlighting all that was wrong with a company driven only by the pursuit of profit, shareholder value and remuneration of senior executives:

> It has laid bare a corporate culture driven by greed, one with a focus on buying as much land as possible and selling the houses it built as quickly as possible rather than on building quality homes. It lays bare a litany of failings, from a reliance on box-ticking to the absence of systems to inspect work in progress. Even worse, the company had a 'nationwide problem of missing and/or incorrectly installed cavity barriers in its timber frame properties' to help to prevent the spread of fire. Given that the company has in the past 10 years achieved stellar stock market success, and in the process made Mr Fairburn and other executives extremely rich, it is doubly telling that careful independent scrutiny has found that it has no central purpose. The only purpose, it might be inferred, has been the creation of that wealth.[132]

The financialisation of housing generates high profits for builders, with unprecedented levels of returns to shareholders through dividends. Jonathan

Eley reported in the *Financial Times* that BP's return of 30 per cent on average capital employed, for 2022, was similar to that for the UK's largest house-builder, Barratt Developments, for the half-year to December. As he observed,

> The profitability of the companies that turn patches of earth into habitable dwellings has attracted less attention than that of the oil titans who turn hydrocarbon sludge into fuel, but it has been no less remarkable.[133]

Tom Archer and Ian Cole pointed out that the Persimmon deal was 'just one end of a spectrum in the trend of rapidly inflating pay outs for senior executives across the housebuilding sector'.[134] They estimated that, after the Global Financial Crisis, the average profit by private builders on each completed house increased from £6,000 in 2009 to over £60,000 in 2017.[135] That profit is about twice the median family income.[136]

The UK's financialised housing market is designed to create shortages. The supply is restricted, because, in seeking to maximise shareholder value, builders require a high hurdle for returns on investment.[137] Demand is restricted because the prices of 'affordable' housing are defined with reference not to earnings but to prevailing market rates – up to 80 per cent.[138] Wendy Wilson and Cassie Barton estimated that, in 2021, median house prices in England were over nine times higher than median full-time earnings.[139] The least affordable area was the London borough of Kensington (where Grenfell Tower burnt down) where median house prices were 28 times higher than median full-time earnings.[140] Oliver Bullough devotes a chapter in *Moneyland* to high-end property, pointing out that, over 22 years from January 1995, 'the average price of a property bought in Kensington and Chelsea rose from £180,000 to more than £1.8 million'.[141]

High-end property is one of the commodities of Ajay Kapur's 'plutonomy', that is, an economy, like those of the US and UK, that is 'driven by massive income and wealth inequality ... where the rich are so rich that their behavior ... overwhelms that of the "average" or median consumer'. He foresaw that, in a plutonomy, these inequalities 'would likely drive a positive operating environment for companies selling to or servicing the rich' where 'rising tides lift yachts'.[142] Kapur showed that over 30 years from 1976 the rate of increase in prices of luxury goods items was twice that of general inflation. Plutonomy explains why, as Minton observes, the incentives generated in the UK's housing market are to build complexes of small luxury apartments in London that are sold off plan to foreign investors. They are unaffordable to most Londoners, let alone people in the rest of the country.[143] She quotes property consultants Savills's description of the 'champagne tower effect':

> Billionaires displace multi-millionaires from the top addresses, so they in turn displace millionaires. Equity migrates to the more

peripheral areas of the capital and, eventually, out of the capital to the rest of the UK.[144]

A January 2020 *Guardian* leader on the UK's housing crisis drew attention to the rows of 'ghost houses' in London and pointed out that additional levies for foreign buyers of houses is one way in which governments in Canada, Singapore and Australia tackle their housing crises and 'create a win-win situation for everyone'.[145] It would lead to foreign investors leaving, a cooling of house prices, and hence more affordable homes. But a British government that succeeded in reducing the price of houses would not appeal to the many voters who have had the good fortune to have been able to invest in their own house.

Conclusions

Instead of a new social peace, the forging of a whole new policy settlement begun by the Thatcher governments resulted in such despair that there were riots of a kind highly unusual in the UK. Under Thatcher, neoliberalism delivered Friedman's impressive triad of toxic legacies: first, a post-war record for unemployment in the UK following monetarist policies; second, the demise of great enterprises forced to focus only on maximising profits and shareholder value; and third, the nemesis of global financial crisis from opaque financial instruments that hubristically modelled radical uncertainty.

The malign impact of financialisation on markets that used to work is exemplified by what happened to housing. In the 1980s, the 'right to buy' of council houses was touted as a solution to a socialised system that ended in the slum clearance/high-rise period building 'slums in the sky'. But, 40 years on, the financialisation of the housing market has contributed to insufficient numbers of houses being built in a global market where sellers aim to sell assets to the highest bidder. That makes homeownership unaffordable to many. As Paul Johnson notes, one consequence of high rents, high house prices and inadequate social housing has been a doubling in the annual Housing Benefit Bill over 20 years, to £22 billion in 2019. That is 'the very expensive canary in the coalmine'.[146]

Yet financialisation policies have shown the cockroach's capacity to survive the havoc they have caused. In 2023 (as I write), they still seem almost untouchable politically. There has been no reshaping of the legacies of the Thatcher settlement to combat the adverse effects of financialisation. The next chapter examines the way the Thatcher governments used private markets to roll back the state through outsourcing and the privatisation of nationalised industries, and how these innovations then degenerated from inadequacies in contracting and regulation. Chapter 7 considers the dysfunctional consequences of marketisation in a policy sphere that proved far harder for the state to shrug off, school education and the universities. Chapter 8 explains why, despite attempts by governments in the 1990s, 2000s and 2010s to intro-duce varieties of a 'quasi-market' within the NHS, that policy has been aban-doned.

Endnotes

[1] Coase, Ronald (1964) 'Papers and proceedings of the Seventy-Sixth Annual Meeting of the American Economic Association', *The American Economic Review*, vol. 54, no. 3, pp.194–95. https://www.jstor.org /stable/1818503. Cited by Williamson, Oliver (1985) *The economic institutions of capitalism*, UK: The Free Press, p.327.

[2] Ramishvili, Levan (2017, 16 January) 'Margaret Thatcher reciting St Francis of Assisi's prayer' [Video]. YouTube. https://www.youtube.com/watch?v=UhXlAGmUitU

[3] Margaret Thatcher Foundation (2019) "And I would just like to remem-ber some words of St. Francis of Assisi…". https://perma.cc/SU8H-6MBX

[4] King, Anthony and Crewe, Ivor (2013) 'A tax on heads', Chapter 4 in *The blunders of our governments*, UK: Oneworld.

[5] Minister for Reconstruction (1944) *Employment policy*, UK: HMSO, Cmd 6527, p.3.

[6] The Conservative Party/Saatchi & Saatchi (1979) 'Labour isn't working: Britain's better off with the Conservatives'. Available from: https://image.guardian.co.uk/sys-images/Politics/Pix/pictures/2001/03 /10/pub_notworking.gif

[7] Bank of England (2016) 'A millennium of macroeconomic data'. https://www.bankofengland.co.uk/statistics/research-datasets

[8] Turner, Alwyn (2010) *Rejoice! Rejoice! Britain in the 1980s*, UK: Aurum Press, pp.4–25.

[9] Turner, Alwyn, *Rejoice!* pp.26–75.

[10] Tuohy, Carolyn (1999) *Accidental logics: The dynamics of change in the health care arena in the United States, Britain, and Canada*, UK: Oxford University Press.

[11] Von Hayek, Friedrich (1944) *The road to serfdom*, UK: Routledge.

[12] Margaret Thatcher Foundation (n.d.) 'Thatcher, Hayek & Friedman'. https://perma.cc/HN46-M5T4

[13] Wapshott, Nicholas (2011) *Keynes Hayek: The clash that defined modern economics*, UK: WW Norton & Company, p.22.

[14] Von Hayek, *The road to serfdom*, p.3.

15 Tribe, Keith (2015) 'Liberalism and neoliberalism in Britain'. In Mirowski, Philip and Plehwe, Dieter (eds) (2015) *The road from Mont Pèlerin: The making of the neoliberal thought collective, with a new preface*, UK: Harvard University Press, p.75. https://doi.org/10.4159/9780674495111

16 Von Hayek, Friedrich A. (1999) *The condensed version of The Road to Serfdom by F. A. Hayek as it appeared in the April 1945 edition of Reader's Digest*, UK: The Institute of Economic Affairs. https://iea.org.uk/publications/the-road-to-serfdom/

17 Wapshott, Nicholas, *Keynes Hayek*, p.207.

18 Gerstle, Gary (2022) 'Part I The New Deal order', in *The rise and fall of the neoliberal order: America and the world in the free market era*, UK: Oxford University Press, p.2. https://doi.org/10.1093/oso/9780197519646.001.0001

19 Gerstle, Gary, *The Rise and Fall of the Neoliberal Order*, p.2.

20 Carter, Zachary (2021) *The price of peace: money, democracy, and the life of John Maynard Keynes*, US: Penguin, pp.376, 378.

21 Carter, Zachary, *The price of peace*, p.377.

22 Carter, Zachary, *The price of peace*, p.383.

23 Mirowski, Philip and Plehwe, Dieter (eds) (2015) 'Introduction', in *The road from Mont Pèlerin*, p.24.

24 Tribe, Keith, 'Introduction', in *The road from Mont Pèlerin*, pp.24–25.

25 Butler, Eamonn (n.d.) *A short history of the Mont Pelerin Society*. https://perma.cc/7HLA-WDP5

26 Mirowski, Philip (2015) 'Postface: Defining neoliberalism'. In *The road from Mont Pèlerin*, pp.417–55.

27 Mirowski, Philip, 'Postface'.

28 Atlas Network (n.d.) 'Over 500 partners in almost 100 countries around the globe'. https://perma.cc/K4Q5-C3TM

29 Wapshott, Nicholas, *Keynes Hayek*, p.217.

30 The Nobel Prize (2023) 'Friedrich August von Hayek – Facts'. https://perma.cc/QU25-CH9S

31 Friedman, Milton and Schwartz, Anna (2008) *A monetary history of the United States, 1867–1960*, US: Princeton University Press. https://muse.jhu.edu/pub/267/monograph/book/36656

32 The Nobel Prize (1976) 'Milton Friedman - Press Release'. https://perma.cc/A447-YJEH

[33] Goodhart, Charles (1964) 'A monetary history of the United States, 1867–1960', *Economica*, New Series, vol. 31, no. 123, p.314. https://www.jstor.org/stable/2550627

[34] Krugman, Paul (1994) *Peddling prosperity: Economic sense and nonsense in the age of diminished expectations*, UK: WW Norton & Company, p.173.

[35] Krugman, Paul, *Peddling prosperity*, p.174.

[36] Goodhart, Charles (1997) 'Whither now?' *PSL Quarterly Review*, vol. 50, no. 203, pp 400, 405–06. https://rosa.uniroma1.it/rosa04/psl_quarterly_review/article/view/10583

[37] Forder, James (2019) 'Monetary trends in the United States and the United Kingdom'. Chapter 17 in *Milton Friedman*, UK: Palgrave Macmillan, pp.307–13.

[38] Goodhart, Charles (1984) *Problems of monetary management: The UK experience*, UK: Macmillan Education, pp.91–121.

[39] Goodhart, Charles (2023) Email to Gwyn Bevan, 4 January.

[40] Forder, James, *Milton Friedman*, p.411.

[41] Coutts, Ken; Tarling, Roger; Ward, Terry; and Wilkinson, Frank (1981) 'The economic consequences of Mrs Thatcher', *Cambridge Journal of Economics*, vol. 5, no. 1, pp.81–93. https://www.jstor.org/stable/23596658

[42] Chrystal, K. Alec (1984) 'Dutch disease or monetarist medicine?: The British economy under Mrs. Thatcher', *Federal Reserve Bank of St. Louis Review*, vol. 66, no. 5, pp.27–37. https://perma.cc/Y3KG-BLZH

[43] Bank of England (2016) 'A millennium of macroeconomic data'. https://www.bankofengland.co.uk/statistics/research-datasets

[44] Bank of England (2016) *A millennium of macroeconomic data*. https://www.bankofengland.co.uk/statistics/research-datasets

[45] Bjørnland, Hilde (1998) 'The economic effects of North Sea oil on the manufacturing sector', *Scottish Journal of Political Economy*, vol. 45, no. 5, p.582. https://doi.org/10.1111/1467-9485.00112

[46] Alt, James E. (1987) 'Crude politics: Oil and the political economy of unemployment in Britain and Norway, 1970–85', *British Journal of Political Science*, vol. 17, no. 2, pp.149–99. https://doi.org/10.1017/S0007123400004695

[47] Bank of England, *A millennium of macroeconomic data*.

[48] Friedman, Milton (1970) 'The first and core principle is that "the social responsibility of business is to increase its profits"', *New York Times*. https://perma.cc/7MMB-67DY

[49] Mazzucato, Mariana (2018) *The value of everything: Making and taking in the global economy*, UK: Hachette, p.166; Jensen, Michael and Meckling,

William (1976) 'Theory of the firm: Managerial behavior, agency costs and ownership structure', *Journal of Financial Economics*, vol. 3, no. 4, pp.305–60. https://doi.org/10.1016/0304-405X(76)90026-X

50 Foroohar, Rana (2016) *Makers and takers. How Wall Street destroyed Main Street*, US: Currency, p.62.

51 Mazzucato, Mariana, *The value of everything*, pp.163–70.

52 O'Brien, Hettie (2022) 'Power Failure by William D Cohan review – pulling the plug'. *The Guardian*, 17 November. https://perma.cc/ATG6-URSE

53 Wolf, Martin (2023) *The crisis of democratic capitalism*, UK: Penguin, pp.148, 153.

54 The Nobel Prize (2023) 'Robert E. Lucas Jr. – Facts'. https://perma.cc/QC8D-WHXV

55 Black, Fischer and Scholes, Myron (1973) 'The pricing of options and corporate liabilities', *Journal of Political Economy*, vol. 81, no. 3, pp.637–54. https://www.jstor.org/stable/1831029

56 The Nobel Prize (2023) 'The Sveriges Riksbank Prize in Economic Sciences in Memory of Alfred Nobel 1997'. https://perma.cc/DK36-K5QB

57 Pistor, Katharina (2019) *The code of capital. How the law creates wealth and inequality*, US: Princeton University Press, pp.101, 105. https://muse.jhu.edu/pub/267/monograph/book/64439

58 Taleb, Nassim (2007) *The black swan: The impact of the highly improbable*, UK: Penguin, p.282.

59 Knight, Frank (1921) *Risk, uncertainty and profit*, US: Houghton Mifflin.

60 Wapshott, Nicholas, *Keynes Hayek*, p.217.

61 Keynes, John Maynard (1973) *The general theory of interest, employment and money*, UK: Macmillan.

62 Kay, John and King, Mervyn (2020) *Radical uncertainty. Decision-making beyond the numbers*, UK: Bridge Street Press, p.74.

63 Kay, John and King, Mervyn, *Radical uncertainty*, pp.366–68.

64 Kay, John and King, Mervyn, *Radical uncertainty*, p.6.

65 Lucas Jr, Robert E. (2003) 'Macroeconomic priorities', *American Economic Review*, vol. 93, no. 1, pp.1–14. https://doi.org/10.1257/000282803321455133

66 Kay, John (2003) *The truth about markets: Why some nations are rich but most remain poor*, UK: Allen Lane, pp.5–6.

[67] Rajan, Raghuram (2005) *Has financial development made the world riskier?* NBER Working Paper Series, No 11728, US: National Bureau of Economic Research. https://www.nber.org/papers/w11728.pdf

[68] Tooze, Adam (2018) *Crashed: How a decade of financial crises changed the world*, UK: Penguin, p.67.

[69] Rajan, Raghuram (2011) *Fault lines*, US: Princeton University Press, p.3. https://doi.org/10.1515/9781400839803

[70] Rajan, Raghuram, *Fault lines*, pp.34–36.

[71] Muellbauer, John and Soskice, David (2022) *The Thatcher legacy. Lessons for the future of the UK economy*, UK: The Resolution Foundation, p.25. https://perma.cc/7G84-87LN

[72] Markovits, Daniel (2019) *The meritocracy trap*, UK: Penguin, p.165.

[73] Markovits, Daniel, *The meritocracy trap*, p.167.

[74] Markovits, Daniel, *The meritocracy trap*, p.167.

[75] Pistor, Katharina, *The code of capital*.

[76] Stewart, Ian (2012) 'The mathematical equation that caused the banks to crash'. *The Observer*, 11 February, https://perma.cc/SV8J-N2XF

[77] Pistor, Katharina, *The code of capital*, p.86.

[78] Stewart, Ian, *The mathematical equation*.

[79] Tooze, Adam, 'Subprime', Chapter 2 in *Crashed*, pp.42–71.

[80] Tooze, Adam, 'Subprime'; 'The worst financial crisis in global history', Chapter 6, pp.143–65.

[81] Beattie, Alan and Politi, James (2008) '"I made a mistake," admits Greenspan'. *Financial Times*, 23 October. https://perma.cc/7VX4-323H

[82] *WSJ London* (2009) 'Volcker praises the ATM, blasts finance execs, experts', *Wall Street Journal*, 8 December. https://perma.cc/T2HS-XEXH

[83] Mazzucato, Mariana, *The value of everything*, p.110.

[84] Mazzucato, Mariana, *The value of everything*, p.108.

[85] Wolf, Martin, *The crisis of democratic capitalism*, p.103.

[86] Pistor, Katharina, 'Cloning legal persons', Chapter 3 in *The code of capital*, pp.47–75.

[87] Rudden, Bernard (1994) 'Things as thing and things as wealth', *Oxford Journal of Legal Studies*, vol. 14, no. 1, pp.82–83. Cited in Pistor, Katharina, *The code of capital*, p.5.

[88] Pistor, Katharina, *The code of capital*, p.52.

[89] Tooze, Adam, *Crashed*, p.71.

[90] Tooze, Adam, *Crashed*, p.198.

[91] Pistor, Katharina, *The code of capital*, p.52.

[92] Pistor, Katharina, *The code of capital*, p.61.

[93] This excluded government-sponsored enterprises (GSEs). See Acharya, Viral; Gujral, Irvind; Kulkarni, Nirupama; and Shin, Hyun (2011) *Dividends and bank capital in the financial crisis of 2007–2009*, US: National Bureau of Economic Research (No. w16896). https://perma.cc/5PDS-S3KP

[94] Pistor, Katharina, *The code of capital*, pp.73–75.

[95] Krugman, Paul (2023) 'How bad was the Silicon Valley Bank bailout?' *The New York Times*, 14 March. https://perma.cc/7DGK-YCC8

[96] Thornhill, John (2023) 'SVB shows that there are few libertarians in a financial foxhole', *The Financial Times*, 13 March. https://perma.cc/7W2J-XVY9

[97] Eichengreen, Barry (1996) 'Explaining Britain's economic performance: A critical note', *Economic Journal*, vol. 106, no. 434, p.213. https://doi.org/10.2307/2234944

[98] Mazzucato, Mariana, *The value of everything*, pp.163–70.

[99] Warwick-Ching, Anthony (2020) *Stolen heritage: The strange death of industrial England*, UK: Troubador.

[100] Kay, John (2015) *Other people's money*, UK: Profile Books, p.45.

[101] Kay, John, *Other people's money*, p.30.

[102] Lee, Simon (2009) *Boom and bust: The politics and legacy of Gordon Brown*, UK: Oneworld, pp.234, 227.

[103] Lee, Simon, *Boom and bust*, p.238.

[104] Summers, Deborah (2008) 'No return to boom and bust: what Brown said when he was chancellor', *The Guardian*, 11 September. https://perma.cc/8HM5-GC3H

[105] Lee, *Boom and bust*, p.97.

[106] Lee, *Boom and bust*, pp. 224–25.

[107] Barber, Michael (2015) *How to run a government so that citizens benefit and taxpayers don't go crazy*, UK: Penguin Books, p.251.

[108] Genesis, Chapter 41, verses 15–24. *The Bible* (King James Version). https://perma.cc/U9KP-5DHV

[109] Genesis, Chapter 41, verse 57.

110 Giles, Chris (2008) 'The economic forecasters' failing vision'. *Financial Times*, 25 November. https://perma.cc/FJ7L-4RMY

111 Lee, Simon, *Boom and bust*, p.68.

112 Wolf, Martin, *The crisis of democratic capitalism*, p.112.

113 Crafts, Nicholas and Mills, Terence (2020) 'Is the UK productivity slowdown unprecedented?' *National Institute Economic Review*, vol. 251, pp.R47–R53. https://doi.org/10.1017/nie.2020.6

114 Stansbury, Anna; Turner, Daniel; and Balls, Ed (2023) *Tackling the UK's regional economic inequality: Binding constraints and avenues for policy intervention*. M-RCBG Associate Working Paper Series, US: Harvard University's DASH repository. https://nrs.harvard.edu/URN-3:HUL.INSTREPOS:37374470

115 Wolf, Martin (2023) 'The UK economy has two regional problems, not one', *Financial Times*, 8 March. https://perma.cc/9EAN-53SA

116 OECD (2023) *Gross domestic product (GDP): GDP per capita, USD, current prices and PPPs*. https://stats.oecd.org/index.aspx?queryid=61433

117 OECD (2022) 'OECD Data: United Kingdom'. https://data.oecd.org/united-kingdom.htm

118 Burn-Murdoch, John (2022) 'Britain and the US are poor societies with some very rich people', *Financial Times*, 16 September. https://perma.cc/GVX4-QWFY

119 Burn-Murdoch, John (2022) 'Britain's winter of discontent is the inevitable result of austerity', *Financial Times*, 22 December. https://perma.cc/N9DQ-4KMF

120 Muellbauer, John and Soskice, David, *The Thatcher legacy*, p.13.

121 Office of National Statistics (2023) 'Table 3b – House building: permanent dwellings started and completed, by sector, England, historical calendar year series', *House building, UK: permanent dwellings started and completed by country*. https://www.ons.gov.uk/peoplepopulationandcommunity/housing/datasets/ukhousebuildingpermanentdwellingsstartedandcompleted

122 Muellbauer, John and Soskice, David, *The Thatcher legacy*, p.13.

123 Minton, Anna (2022) 'From gentrification to sterilization? Building on big capital', *Architecture and Culture*, pp.1–21. https://doi.org/10.1080/20507828.2022.2105573

124 Booth, Robert and Goodier, Michael (2022) 'Soaring rents making life "unaffordable" for private UK tenants, research shows', *The Guardian*, 1 December. https://perma.cc/57XB-A3DB

125 Office of National Statistics, 'Table 3b - House building: permanent dwellings started and completed, by sector, England, historical calendar year series'.

126 Comptroller and Auditor General (2019) *Help to Buy: Equity Loan scheme – progress review.* https://www.nao.org.uk/reports/help-to-buy-equity-loan-scheme-progress-review/

127 Hammond, George (2019) 'Help to Buy offers biggest hand to house-builders', *Financial Times*, 1 March. https://perma.cc/Y8ZQ-CMR2

128 Comptroller and Auditor General (2019) *Help to Buy: Equity loan scheme – progress review.* (HC 2216), UK National Audit Office, p.9. https://www.nao.org.uk/reports/help-to-buy-equity-loan-scheme-progress-review/

129 Williams, Aime (2018) 'Persimmon boosted by scheme to help first-time buyers', *Financial Times*, 21 August. https://perma.cc/SB8E-YA2P

130 Evans, Judith (2019) 'Former Persimmon boss was paid £85m in two years', *Financial Times*, 18 March. https://perma.cc/SKG6-SMW2

131 Hammond, George (2019) 'Housebuilder Persimmon to launch wide-ranging independent review', *Financial Times*, 5 April. https://perma.cc/3VX8-J54P

132 Editorial (2019) 'Persimmon report shows capitalism at its worst', *Financial Times*, 19 December. https://perma.cc/K69S-NG4G

133 Eley, Jonathan (2023) 'UK housebuilders' profitability no less remarkable than BP's returns', *Financial Times*, 9 February. https://perma.cc/X485-T3KE

134 Archer, Tom and Cole, Ian (2021). 'The financialisation of housing production: exploring capital flows and value extraction among major housebuilders in the UK', *Journal of Housing and the Built Environment*, vol. 36, p.1376. https://doi.org/10.1007/s10901-021-09822-3

135 Archer, Tom and Cole, Ian, 'The financialisation of housing production', p.1377.

136 Office for National Statistics (2021) 'Average household income, UK: financial year ending 2021'. https://www.ons.gov.uk/peoplepopulationandcommunity/personaland householdfinances/incomeandwealth/bulletins/householddisposablein comeandinequality/financialyearending2021

137 Archer, Tom and Cole, Ian, 'The financialisation of housing production', p.1383.

138 Wilson, Wendy and Barton, Cassie, *What is affordable housing?* House of Commons Briefing Paper, p.12. https://researchbriefings.files.parliament.uk/documents/CBP-7747/CBP-7747.pdf

[139] Wilson, Wendy and Barton, Cassie, *What is affordable housing?* p.21.

[140] Wilson, Wendy and Barton, Cassie, *What is affordable housing?* p.22.

[141] Bullough, Oliver (2018) *Moneyland: Why thieves and crooks now rule the world and how to take it back*, UK: Profile, p.222.

[142] Kapur, Ajay (2006) 'The plutonomy symposium — rising tides lifting yachts', *The Global Investigator*, Citigroup 29 September, p.8. https://perma.cc/SD59-4TP8

[143] Minton, Anna, 'From Gentrification to Sterilization?' p.5.

[144] Minton, Anna, 'From Gentrification to Sterilization?' p.5.

[145] Editorial (2020) 'The Guardian view on the UK housing crisis: No plan to fix it', *The Guardian*, 5 January. https://perma.cc/Z8TS-XDHE

[146] Johnson, Paul (2019) *Doubling of the Housing Benefit bill is a sign of something deeply wrong*, UK: Institute for Fiscal Studies. https://ifs.org.uk/publications/13940

6. The 'make or buy' decision: the UK's 'parastate' after privatisation and outsourcing

> In the last 20 years, governments in market economies through-
> out the world have privatized the very state firms in steel, energy,
> telecommunications and financial services that the Nobel laureates
> approvingly saw nationalized a few decades earlier. Communism
> has collapsed almost everywhere in the world, and reform govern-
> ments throughout the formerly socialist world have embarked on
> massive privatization programs. The economic policies of devel-
> oping countries turned squarely to private ownership. In market
> economies, government provision of such basic services as garbage
> collection and education has come into question, and has increas-
> ingly been replaced with private provision, though still paid for
> largely from tax revenues.
>
> Andrei Shleifer (1998)[1]

Neoliberal arguments over the role of the state in steering the economy were
critical in the breaking of the Attlee settlement. Chapter 5 showed how the
accidental logic of neoliberalism played out under the Thatcher settlement for
financialisation, including in the housing market. Its initial promise, under
the right to buy scheme in the 1980s, was when the market worked. It became
dysfunctional with the further development of financialisation. In this chapter
I explore the similar fates of privatisation and outsourcing after they were first
introduced with the promise of effective use of these markets in the 1980s.

Robert Lucas's theory of rational expectations justified and enabled the
financialisation of the Thatcher settlement. It appealed to neoliberal economists for two reasons. First, it 'proved' that any government intervention
in the economy would be counterproductive. Second, it healed the division
that Keynes had introduced into economics between macroeconomics (steering the economy) and microeconomics (the theory of the firm).[2] But there
is a puzzle: if markets are as efficient and effective as required by theory of
rational expectations, why do firms exist? Furthermore, as Alfred Chandler

---

How to cite this book chapter:

Bevan, Gwyn (2023) *How Did Britain Come to This? A century of systemic failures
of governance*, London: LSE Press, pp. 139–172.
https://doi.org/10.31389/lsepress.hdb.f License: CC BY-NC

argued in *The Visible Hand*, the economy of the US in the 20th century was shaped by large integrated firms that were run as hierarchies.[3] Why didn't they buy what they needed in 'spot' markets at the lowest obtainable prices? The way Ronald Coase resolved that puzzle enabled the development of the neoliberal approaches that reduced the role of the state through privatisation and outsourcing.

In the summer of 1932, when Coase was 21, he formulated the key ideas of his article on 'The Nature of the Firm', which was published five years later.[4] It laid the foundation of institutional economics, and was one of the two cited in Coase's award of the Nobel Prize in Economics in 1991.[5] In that paper Coase argued that the reason why firms exist is that there are transaction costs of using the market, which include:

- working out the price;
- writing a contract to specify what is to be delivered;
- sharing risks over future uncertainties; and
- monitoring contracts.

Markets work effectively when none of these seem to matter – that is, when these transaction costs are low, as in Adam Smith's famous observation in his *Wealth of Nations*, published in 1776: 'It is not from the benevolence of the butcher, the brewer, or the baker, that we expect our dinner, but from their regard to their own interest'.[6] These simple commodities illustrate Coase's argument that it often makes sense to use a market for goods. Food is an exemplar of where markets work well. Although the production of food is often supported by government subsidies and subject to special public health regulations, there are some terrible lessons from when governments overreach and try to control its production and distribution. They include the horror of the Holodomor (famine) in 1930s Ukraine under Soviet control, with nearly four million deaths[7] (see Chapter 2), and, in China, about 30 million died between 1958 and 1962, during the 'Great Leap Forward' effort to collectivise farms under Chairman Mao.[8]

Bowles points out that the market works when it is possible to specify what is to be supplied in complete contracts.[9] That is easier to do for goods than for services; for example, a contract with a lawyer is inevitably incomplete. One of Oliver Hart's many papers on the subject of incomplete contracts can be summarised by this equation:

Incomplete contract + intense pressure on costs = quality problems.[10]

Coase's 1937 paper criticised the then extant microeconomic theories of the firm for considering costs of production only, which justified the existence of large firms in terms of the economies of scale of production. Hence his question 'why is not all production carried out in one big firm?'[11] to which his answer was that such a firm would be unmanageable (as shown by the Soviet centrally planned economy – see Chapter 2). Coase argued that micro-economics had neglected the *transaction costs* of organising production of a good or delivery of a service in the 'make or buy' decision. For example, should BMW make the steel and run dealerships for its own cars, or should it buy steel from other firms and sell its cars to dealers on open markets? Most firms that make cars tend to contract for the steel they need in the market, but manage the service of selling cars through dealership networks.

In 1937 Coase was disappointed that his 'elders and betters' at LSE, including the leading protagonists of neoliberalism in the UK, Lionel Robbins and Friedrich von Hayek, showed 'a complete lack of interest' in the publication of his article.[12] Chandler argued, in 1977, that 'until economists analyze the function of administrative coordination, the theory of the firm will remain essentially a theory of production'.[13] In 1988, Coase observed that his article 'had little or no influence for thirty or forty years after it was published'.[14] In the years of the Attlee government, and its 1950s successors, the experience of wartime planning still predominated and was seen as critical in modernising and refounding industries of strategic national importance. One of the perceived advantages of nationalising coal, and later steel, was the promise of economies of scale. Yet gradually the importance of transaction costs was recognised in the development of institutional economics, with profound implications for public ownership.

An influential later framework for analysing the transaction cost economics of 'make or buy' decisions was developed by Oliver Williamson, for which he was awarded the Nobel Prize in Economics in 2009.[15] Figure 6.1 is derived from Williamson's analysis of transaction costs and shows where transaction costs are low and indicates where markets are expected to work well (for example for food, meat and beer).[16]

Working out the implications of the Coasian approach for public sector organisations took time. The 'make or buy' decision of private firms was translated via the influence of US privatisation exponents (like Shleifer quoted at the start of this chapter) and neoliberal think tanks into a 'new public management (NPM)' approach for governments.[17] This doctrine asked of every state activity whether the government should be 'rowing or steering' – where rowing meant directly producing services with its own staff, and steering meant allocating contracts to other suppliers (such as firms or perhaps non-governmental organisations).

This chapter applies the economics of transaction costs to explore the implementation of new public management in the UK. The first two sections look at the privatisation of state-owned enterprises and consider the more problematic privatisation of vital services. The third section illustrates how some general problems of government outsourcing contributed to the catastrophic failure of NASA with the *Challenger* tragedy – notably, the 'fundamental transformation' from there being competition in bidding for a contract, but a bilateral monopoly after the contract has been awarded, plus the pressure to

Figure 6.1: A market with low transaction costs

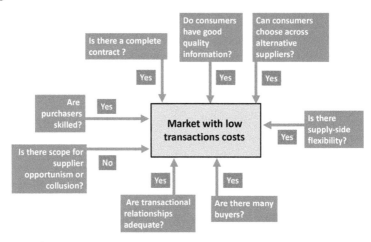

Source: Author.

economise on an incomplete contract. The final section identifies some key problems of the UK's 'parastate' as government has become so dependent on outsourcing to contractors.

6.1 Privatising industries – coal and steel

Figure 6.1 indicates that for industries like coal or steel there would be low transaction costs from using the market to supply what the country needs. So was the Attlee government mistaken in deciding on nationalisation because they were vital as 'the commanding heights of the economy'? My first job, in the late 1960s, was working for the National Coal Board (NCB). I had huge admiration for the exceptional individuals who had risen to be managers of collieries and of the West Wales area. I remember Ron Walker, who had left his elementary school at age 14, and, as the general manager of Wyndham Western colliery in Ogmore Vale, turned round its performance from losing £0.5 million a year to making a profit of £0.5 million a year. I learnt that the NCB served three vital functions for the UK that are omitted from analysis of the transaction costs of the 'make or buy' decision.

First, the reason I joined the NCB was that its Operational Research Executive offered one of the best training schemes in mathematical modelling. Alf Robens, the then chairman of the NCB, argued that it was quite appropriate for a *nationalised* industry to produce not only coal but also skilled manpower for other industries in Britain through its apprenticeships. That ended with privatisation.

Second, the NCB was required to operate in the 'public interest' by meeting the nation's need for coal and breaking even financially over good and bad years. The NCB was established on 1 January 1947, at a time when there was no alternative of oil or gas. In its early years the NCB was required to import coal and sell it at a loss. In planning its production to meet the future need for coal in the 1960s, it made good forecasts of the total demand for energy but underestimated the growth in the supply of oil. The excess investment in the coal industry can be seen as a cost of making the UK resilient to an uncertain future. Whether planned investments turn out to be 'economic' depends on unforeseeable developments, as we have been forcefully reminded after Russia invaded Ukraine in February 2022 and put at risk the gas supplies to Europe.

Third, in the planning of colliery closures, the NCB tried to maintain employment in the economically vulnerable areas of Britain: Scotland, the North East and North West of England, and Wales. These areas were where successive post-war governments had failed to diversify industry, as recommended by the 1944 White Paper (see Chapter 3). Unfortunately, because of the geology of Britain, they were also where the uneconomic collieries were concentrated. The most economic UK mines were in the Midlands (Nottinghamshire and Derbyshire), where the coal seams were thicker and had few geological faults. In the older coal seams in the rest of Britain, geological faults meant mechanised coal faces had to stop whenever the coal seam suddenly disappeared. The colliers would then be unable to produce coal until the seam was refound, new underground roadways developed and the machinery to cut coal and take it away had been reinstalled.

Figure 6.2 shows that the NCB's output peaked at 211 million tons of coal in 1955, and then was reduced to around 100 million tons by the start of

Figure 6.2: UK coal production (in millions of tons), from 1945 to 2003

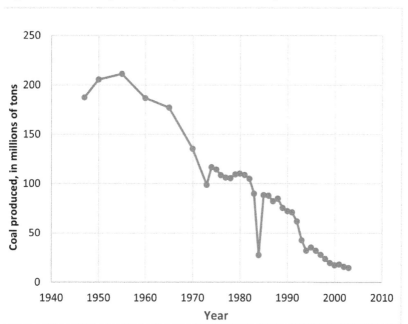

Figure 6.3: The numbers of coal mines and thousands of mining employees, from 1945 to 2003

Source: Access to Mineral Heritage.[19]

the 1970s. Figure 6.3 shows how the decline in production was accompanied by much greater reductions in the numbers of collieries and employees, with sharp reductions in the 1960s. The average outputs per mine and employee in 1947 were 196,000 and 266 tons, and in 1970 were 475,000 and 463 tons. The NCB had managed the decline of employment in the coal industry from over 700,000 in 1948 to around 200,000 in the early 1980s without devastating mining communities. The nationalised Central Electricity Generating Board had bought 40 per cent of the NCB's coal in long-run contracts.

In the 1980s, the privatised distributors of electricity were troubled about the security of supplies of coal. Krugman describes how the privatised gas industry enjoyed 'very lax control over prices'. So the privatised electricity companies, 'in a dash for gas', developed their own supplies, which rang the death knell of the coal industry.[20] Figures 6.2 and 6.3 show its demise after the strike in 1984 to its privatisation in 1994.

In the early 1970s, the coal and steel industries employed 320,000 and 250,000. By 2020, each employed 44,000.[21] That chaotic reduction ripped the hearts out of communities that became known much later as 'left behind', in Scotland, Wales and the North West and North East of England. The Thatcher government's combination of a high exchange value for pound sterling and privatisation increased unemployment to its peak in the mid-1980s. The South East, East Anglia and the South West were the regions with unemployment rates lower than the national average. John Muellbauer and David Soskice highlight the way in the 1980s that job losses were geographically concentrated, with 12 local authorities losing over 20 per cent of their jobs.[22]

In 2021, Aaron Atteridge and Claudia Strambo, for the Stockholm Environment Institute, looked back at the long and steady decline of the steel industry across the UK. They argued that replacing well-paid, highly skilled jobs with low-paid, unskilled jobs (for example, call centres and distribution centres) showed no change in unemployment statistics. But the communities lost their engines of prosperity and the workers their identity. Atteridge and Strambo were bewildered that, after the closures of steelworks at Corby in 1979 and Consett in 1980, there was no development of the railway infrastructure needed to take advantage of Corby's proximity to London, and Consett lost its railway line when male unemployment was almost 100 per cent.[23]

Yet Atteridge and Strambo argued that in the 2020s Western governments would be mistaken to try to stem the further decline of the steel industry. In 2019, John Collingridge pointed out in *The Times* that the metals tycoon Sanjeev Gupta was now the main owner of UK steel manufacturing. He was born in India. In the early 1990s, he began studying economics at Cambridge but switched to economics and business management to free up time to work on starting up his company selling chemical products to Nigeria, making £1 million a day.[24] In 2019, Collingridge described Gupta's steel empire as built on:

a fragile and interdependent ecosystem: politicians desperate to save jobs in tired industries, companies keen to shed problematic assets, financiers eager to package and sell government subsidies, and investors hunting for yield in the ultra-low rates environment.[25]

In April 2021, the Scottish government took a £161 million provision against a guarantee of £586 million in December 2016 that 'allowed Gupta's family business to acquire the smelter in Lochaber, near Fort William, and two nearby hydropower plants from Rio Tinto'. (The total size of that guarantee only emerged after a nearly two-year freedom of information campaign by the *Financial Times*.[26]) In July 2022, the *Sunday Times* pointed out that Gupta's business empire had 'contributed less than £5 towards the £330 million purchase of a smelting plant in the Highlands'.[27] On 30 June 2021, Liz Truss (then international trade secretary), under pressure from Kwasi Kwarteng (then business secretary), overruled the recommendation made two weeks earlier by the Trade Remedies Authority and introduced emergency legislation to protect privatised domestic steel producers from a flood of cheap imports.[28] In January 2023, the *Financial Times* reported that the government was:

poised to sign off a support package for British Steel and Tata Steel UK worth over half a billion pounds in a move that will be tied to Britain's two biggest steel manufacturers switching to green technology.[29]

There have been a number of issues with Gupta's GFG Alliance companies. Its long-time auditor, King & King, 'resigned from its role at his UK steelworks after it was blocked from stating there was insufficient information to complete its work', and King & King was 'under investigation for previous audits of Gupta's companies'.[30] The UK's Serious Fraud Office and French police were 'investigating over suspected fraud and money laundering. GFG has consistently denied any wrongdoing'.[31]

6.2 Privatising key service industries

Williamson's framework (see Figure 6.1) suggests that privatising coal and steel is straightforward compared with privatising *public service industries*, where there were either small numbers of competitors (for example, electricity, gas, railways) or a natural monopoly (only one enterprise can deliver water to any given house or enterprise). In these and other industries there are strong network effects or economies of scale. The Thatcher governments believed that, as the privatisation proponent Shleifer had argued, these potential market failures could all be handled by careful design of contracts and regulation. And, in the 1980s, the privatisation of electricity, gas and water seemed to be working. But two problems developed from financialisation of the providers. First, the focus on making profits and increasing shareholder value encouraged opportunism and mergers and acquisitions that reduced competition. Second, there were weaknesses from 'light-touch' regulation. In agrarian societies it paid poachers to turn gamekeepers, but the remuneration packages offered to senior executives in privatised public services far outstripped the salaries paid to the regulators.

Privatisation of energy. The regulator, OFGEM, aimed to enable competition and to drive down prices and develop new products and services for consumers by encouraging new entrants into the delivery of electricity to users.[32] Unfortunately, OFGEM neglected the importance of supplier resilience. OFGEM's strategy to increase the number of competitors resulted in 26 small and medium-sized operators going bankrupt, by February 2022, from the energy price spike during the Russo-Ukraine war.[33] The cost to the taxpayer for finding alternative suppliers to take on customers from just one of these firms (Bulb) was estimated by the Office for Budget Responsibility, in November 2022, to be *£6.5 billion*.[34] OFGEM's chief executive, Jonathan Brearley, recognised that they should have been 'more careful' about the financial resilience of new entrants, and that 'with hindsight we would have done something differently'.[35]

In 2018 and 2019, Toshiba and Hitachi decided to abandon construction of new nuclear plants in Cumbria and North Wales.[36] In April 2022, the government published a policy paper, *British Energy Security Strategy*.[37] Michael Grubb's expert commentary in the *Financial Times* highlighted its failures in meeting the challenges of the short-term crisis over the supply of gas and the longer-term reconciliation of meeting the nation's energy needs and reducing greenhouse gas emissions.[38] Gas accounts for a large amount of electricity generation in the UK. In 2017, Centrica, the privatised UK energy group owning British Gas, decided to close Rough, its large gas storage facility off the Yorkshire coast, because failures in its ageing wells meant that it could no longer be operated safely. This facility accounted for 70 per cent of UK's gas storage capacity. That year, Andrew Ward reported in the *Financial Times* that:

> officials at the Department for Business, Energy and Industrial Strategy said they were neither surprised nor worried by the loss of Rough, arguing that the market had coped well without it over the past year,

and that:

> National Grid, which operates the UK gas transmission system, said in its annual winter outlook last week that it was confident there would be adequate gas supplies this winter despite the absence of Rough.[39]

In November 2022, Nathalie Thomas noted in the *Financial Times* that Rough had been reopened, but could operate only at about a fifth of its previous capacity. Prior to that change, the UK's total storage capacity could meet five days of gas demand, compared with 112 days for France, 111 in Germany and 97 in Italy.[40]

Privatisation of the rail industry. In 1996, the two objectives of the Major government when privatising rail were, according to Michael Moran's *The British Regulatory State*: to extract maximum short-term revenue, and to head off public ownership by a Labour government in anticipation of the 1997 general election.[41] The first reason is why the country has its current system of rail operators.[42] The second reason explains the haste with which privatisation was enacted in 1996, and 'the sketchiness of the preparation with which complex institutional changes were implemented'.[43] Richard Wellings pointed out that:

> In terms of transactions cost economics, the UK railway experiment suggests that integration is indeed superior to fragmentation as a mode of railway operation, and that it was no accident that railways developed as vertically integrated entities under market conditions. The key transaction costs of opportunism (in this case, reducing inputs by the seller), bounded rationality (limited awareness of this reduction on the part of the buyer), and the dissipation of asset-specific (i.e. railway) skills actually increased rather than decreased under the new approach.[44]

In 2003, Moran described the 'catastrophic condition' of the British railway system: the lack of a reliably timed railway network, the highest rail fares in Western Europe, railways more deeply in debt than the old nationalised British Rail, and a bankrupt manager of the rail network infrastructure (Railtrack, which had to be renationalised as Network Rail). The 2021 review of the privatised railway system stated that 'Around half of trains in northern England and a third of trains nationally were late in 2019/20. This has barely improved in the past five years'.[45] The current regulator, the Office of Rail and Road (ORR), aims to make the rail industry competitive and fair.[46] Helen Pidd reported in *The Guardian* that, under the rules of the ORR, when a rail company pre-emptively cancelled trains up to 10pm the night before, these were excluded from the company's reported performance.

> Figures obtained by the Guardian show that during the October half-term holiday, TransPennine Express (TPE) cancelled 30 per cent of all trains, and at least 20 per cent each subsequent week until 20 November … Yet when it submits its performance statistics to the [ORR], TPE will report cancellations of between 5.6 per cent and 11.8 per cent for the same period.[47]

On 27 October 2022, the Mayors of West Yorkshire, Greater Manchester, South Yorkshire, North of Tyne, and the Liverpool City Region issued a joint statement on the parlous state of the privatised railway services in their areas:

> Thousands of last-minute cancellations continue to make life miserable for people in the North, and cause serious damage to the economy … We need an urgent meeting with Ministers to agree a long-term plan for the future. Our transport network has been starved of support for years. This is derailing our plans for a strong Northern economy. We need to explore potential for more devolved and local control of our railways so they can be integrated into public transport systems within city-regions. If 'levelling up' is to be more than a slogan under the new Prime Minister, then he must give us the rail funding and powers we need to deliver.[48]

Privatisation of water and sewage. On 8 August 1989, on his appointment as director general of water services (Ofwat), Ian Byatt explained that his primary duty was:

> to ensure that the functions of water and sewage undertakers are properly carried out and that Appointees can finance them. Subject to that I must protect customers, facilitate competition and promote economy and efficiency. … But, because of the limitations on direct competition, consumers cannot look to market mechanisms

to protect them from unnecessarily high charges or a poor service or both. My objective will be to achieve through regulation the same balance as would otherwise be achieved by competitive markets.[49]

On 30 June 2023, a leader in the *Financial Times* observed that:

Running a water utility — a natural monopoly selling a basic necessity to a captive market — ought not to be difficult. The terms of England's experiment with privatising former publicly-owned regional water companies, where they started out with zero debt, seemed especially propitious.[50]

When 10 English regional water companies were privatised, in 1989, they were listed on the London Stock Exchange. In May 2023, *The Guardian* reported that, in 2002, Chris Goodall had highlighted the regulatory risks from the takeover of Southern Water by private equity (PE) shareholders and that, although that report would normally have been released under the 20-year rule, it was being kept secret. Goodall had predicted that:

Large external private equity shareholders would load the company with debt and Ofwat inevitably would lose any regulatory control. For example, it would prove extremely difficult to ensure that water companies invested enough in sewage control.[51]

In his review of Byatt's book in the *Financial Times*, in 2020, Max Wilkinson points out that takeovers by private equity and sovereign wealth funds:

resulted in opaque and labyrinthine ownership structures, blurred lines of responsibility, subsidiaries in the Cayman Islands, a delisting of most companies and a sense that financial engineering had become more important than providing a service.[52]

Chapter 1 showed that regulatory failure over the neglect of patients at Mid Staffordshire NHS Foundation Trust was in part a result of two regulators established at different times with different remits working independently of each other. This chapter has also identified regulatory failure in the privatised energy industries to secure the UK's future supply. Both kinds of failure apply to regulation of the financialised water industry by Ofwat and the Environment Agency. Dieter Helm described the 'spectacular failure' of the:

belief in light-touch regulation. So, regulators decided that the balance sheets were a matter best left to the companies, and, even worse, positively incentivised them to borrow by mortgaging the assets and paying out the proceeds to investors.[53]

Oliver Bullough, writing in *The Guardian*, in August 2022, on 'Sewage sleuths: the men who revealed the slow, dirty death of Welsh and English rivers', observed:

> I mainly write about corruption and kleptocracy, but what's extraordinary is how similar the situation around environmental enforcement is to that around financial crime. On paper, the laws are perfectly acceptable and regularly updated. The problem is that they are rarely, if ever, enforced. The result is government by press release; Potemkin enforcement; regulatory theatre; decriminalisation by underresourcing.[54]

Ofwat's statutory duties include: protecting the interests of consumers; promoting effective competition; ensuring the supply of water and disposal of sewage is properly carried out and that their systems are resilient to long-term needs.[55] Evidence to the House of Lords Industry and Regulators Committee highlighted the problem of ambiguity over resilience given the pressure to keep prices low: these have been falling in real terms for 25 years.[56] The outcome has been that 'Under present plans, the UK will not have built a single new major reservoir between 1991 and 2029'.[57] The Environment Agency was established in 1996 from the staff of Her Majesty's Inspectorate of Pollution, National Rivers Authority and 83 Waste Regulation Authorities from local authorities. There is ambiguity over its primary role as a 'champion' of sustainable development or the environment.[58] The report from the House of Lords Industry and Regulators Committee, in 2022, concluded that there has been 'a clear lack of effective co-ordination on issues such as Environment Agency outputs not aligning with what Ofwat deems financeable, and ineffective information-sharing'.[59] The development of a reservoir now recognised 'as important strategic water resource for water security in the south-west of England' (Cheddar) was refused by Ofwat, after its development had been approved by the Environment Agency in 2014.[60]

In his evidence to the House of Lords Industry and Regulators Committee, Professor Ian Barker stated that 'there has progressively been a reduction in the grant in aid given to the Environment Agency', which means that it 'does not have adequate resources to monitor and enforce'.[61] The House of Lords Report identified the problem of over-reliance by Environment Agency on self-monitoring by water companies.[62] The report showed that Ofwat and the Environment Agency have been playing catch-up for past failures to tackle growing problems:

> In 2019 Ofwat fined Southern Water £126 million after concluding that it had underinvested in a number of its works, leading to equipment failures and sewage spills. The company had also 'manipulated its wastewater sampling process' to avoid revealing the sites' performance and so avoid penalties under Ofwat's incentive scheme.

Separately, in 2021 the Environment Agency prosecuted Southern Water for breaches of the conditions of its permits which had resulted in the dumping of *billions of litres of raw sewage* into the sea over several years. The company admitted *6,971 unpermitted spills* from 17 sites in Hampshire, Kent and West Sussex between 2010 and 2015. The £90 million fine for the spills was the highest ever awarded by a court for a sewage discharge permit breach.[63] (emphasis added)

In July 2022, the Environment Agency's report for 2021 gave this damning assessment of the environmental performance of England's water and sewerage companies:

In 2021, the environmental performance of England's 9 water and sewerage companies was the worst we have seen for years. Measured against our four-star rating, most of them went the wrong way: down. Four companies (Anglian, Thames, Wessex, Yorkshire Water) were rated only 2 stars, which means they require significant improvement. Two (Southern and South West Water) fell to 1 star, the bottom of our star ratings, meaning their performance was terrible across the board.[64]

Numerous press reports in 2022 highlighted the issue of sewage dumping in places like Cornwall.[65] The Environment Agency called for a major strengthening of its enforcement powers, including:

- Courts should be able to impose much higher fines for serious and deliberate pollution incidents – although the amount a company can be fined for environmental crimes is unlimited, the fines currently handed down by the courts often amount to less than a chief executive's salary.
- Prison sentences should apply for chief executives and board members whose companies are responsible for the most serious incidents.
- After illegal environmental damage, company directors should be struck off so they cannot simply move on in their careers.[66]

In June 2023, Thames Water, which featured prominently in Oliver Bullough's article, was described by a leader in the *Financial Times* as:

a specially problematic case. Years of poor performance have combined with the rising costs of servicing its £16bn debt – in part a legacy of its previous ownership by Australia's Macquarie, which extracted supersized returns to leave it unable to fund all of its projected spending in coming years ... News this week that the government is on standby to take Thames Water into temporary public ownership in case of its potential collapse is another sign that the great experiment has failed.[67]

Gill Plimmer and Nic Fildes, in the *Financial Times*, described how Macquarie had had 'extracted supersized returns' from owning Thames Water from 2006 to 2017. Over that period, it took £2.7 billion in dividends and £2.2 billion in loans, increased the pension deficit from £18 million to £380 million in 2017, and increased Thames Water's debt from £3.4 billion to £10.8 billion.[68] They also pointed out that:

> Macquarie's decision to take over Southern Water — another UK water utility facing huge investment challenges — as it teetered on the brink of bankruptcy in 2021 was *welcomed by the water regulator Ofwat.* (emphasis added)

6.3 The makings of the Challenger tragedy

In the 1930s, Coase considered the 'make or buy' decision from the perspective of a firm, as detailed at the start of this chapter. Writing 50 years later, Andrei Shleifer argued that the same questions were just as relevant for government:

> Suppose that the government wants to have a good or service delivered to some consumers. The product can be food or shelter, steel or phone service, education, health care or incarceration. The government might wish to pay for some of this good and service out of its budget, or it may have views on the characteristics of this good, such as the price, even though the consumers buy it on their own. Should the government hire its own employees to deliver the service, or should it relinquish the provision to a (possibly regulated) private supplier? Does the mode of provision matter even when the government pays?[69]

Shleifer developed three arguments. First, public finance does not entail public ownership. Moving from public to private ownership in delivering public services brings a drive to seek economy, which Shleifer recognises also brings the risk of this being done at the expense of unacceptable reductions in quality. Second, in principle, governments can ensure private firms deliver on social goals through the design of their outsourcing contracts. Third, private ownership 'is the source of capitalist incentives to innovate'.[70] Schleifer concluded that government ought to restrict managing the delivery of a good or service only to those where the alternative of using a market would be clearly expected to fail. To illustrate the limited scope of that residual category he gives an example where innovation is unimportant – Air Force One, the aeroplane used by the president of the US.

Although Shleifer envisaged the private sector to have a monopoly on innovation, Mazzucato has argued on the contrary that many transformational innovations originate from substantial investment by government, including the technology that underpinned the iPhone, the internet, GPS navigation systems, touchscreens, pharmaceuticals, energy (nuclear, solar and fracking), battery storage, and Google's algorithm. In all these areas the private sector has been good at exploiting government-funded breakthroughs in technology for private gain and taking the credit.[71] The NASA space programme has resulted in an impressive set of technological innovations.[72]

On 12 September 1962, John F Kennedy declared 'We choose to go to the Moon in this decade and do the other things, not because they are easy, but because they are hard'.[73] And, with five months to spare, NASA delivered: its Apollo programme succeeded in putting a man on the Moon on 20 July 1969, relying on multiple different private contractors work across multiple aspects.

Richard Feynman describes how, paradoxically, that stunning success of the Apollo programme created a problem: the federal government could justify neither firing the people working for NASA nor maintaining its continuing astronomic claim on taxpayers' money. The new political settlement that the president and Congress reached with NASA required it to demonstrate economy and regularly put astronauts into space in earth orbits. The space shuttle was the logical outcome of that new settlement: its vehicle (but not its booster rockets) could be reused to enable a schedule of regular launches. Feynman argued that to convince Congress of the programme's viability NASA needed to exaggerate the economy and safety of the shuttle and how often it could fly.[74]

NASA decided that the best way to ease its severe budgetary constraints was to win political support for increasing its funding by putting a teacher in space. After President Ronald Reagan announced that to be NASA's objective, in his State of the Union address of 28 January 1985, the clock started ticking for the agency.[75] Failing to meet that objective before the next year's address would raise questions about its capability. NASA's ploy certainly captured the public's imagination: 11,000 people applied to be the teacher in space.[76] Christa McAuliffe, who was chosen for *Challenger* flight 51-L, was going to conduct experiments and teach two lessons from the space shuttle. NASA gained publicity to dream about: pupils in schools across the nation would watch the launch live on television.

The shuttle's launch rockets were designed and built by the major system integrator company Morton Thiokol. They employed a two-piece design for fixing two booster rockets to the main rocket bearing the shuttle. This 'Tang and Clevis' equipment moved apart during the launch and its two rubber O-rings needed to be flexible to seal off the gap between them and its fuel tanks from the hot gases emitted by the rocket (see Figure 6.4). However, Thiokol found that for launches at cooler temperatures, because the rubber O-rings were less flexible, they eroded, increasing the risk of explosion. To fix that problem would incur costs and cause delays, which conflicted with the overriding objectives of NASA's top management. Hence these problems were ignored in what Diane Vaughan memorably described as the 'normalisation of deviance'.[77] Although erosion of O-rings was not allowed for as part of the original design, this came to be 'normalised'. The company's stance continued even after it was discovered in April 1985 that the primary O-ring seal had been so eroded that it did not seal and this had caused the secondary O-ring to begin to erode.[78]

Figure 6.4: NASA diagram showing tang, clevis and O-rings in its *Challenger* booster rocket

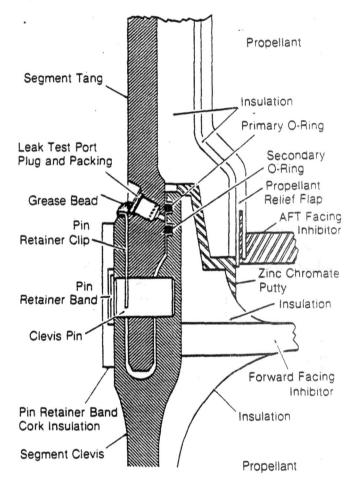

Source: Presidential Commission on the Space Shuttle Challenger Accident. Public domain.[79]
Note the tang is labelled 'segment tang', the O-rings are 'primary O-ring' and 'secondary O-ring' and the clevis 'segment clevis'

Challenger flight 51-L was originally scheduled for July 1985. It was postponed to November 1985, and then five more times to January 1986. On 27 January, the day before President Reagan's planned State of the Union address, events unfolded as follows (all at Eastern Standard Time):

2pm: NASA decided to postpone the *Challenger* launch *yet again* to the following morning.

2.30pm: NASA asked Morton Thiokol to review the risks given the forecast of an overnight low of 18°F (−8°C). Their engineers believed this could mean that the O-rings would be too stiff to be effective.

8.45pm: At the teleconference between NASA and Morton Thiokol, the company's vice president for the shuttle boosters, Joe Kilminster, said that he could not recommend a launch at any temperature below the limit of their experience (i.e. below 53°F). NASA responses were 'appalled': 'The eve of a launch is a hell of a time to be inventing new criteria'; 'My God, Thiokol, when do you want me to launch, next April?' Kilminster asked for a five-minute offline caucus for the Thiokol personnel, which lasted for half an hour, in which one of them was told he had to 'Take off his engineer's hat and put on his manager's hat'.[80]

10.30pm: Thiokol decided to recommend the launch.[81]

So, on the morning of 28 January, children in schools across the US watched *Challenger* launch at 11.38am and explode 73 seconds later, killing all seven crew members instantly.

This chapter has applied Oliver Williamson's conceptual framework to examine how Shleifer's argument has worked in the UK in outsourcing public services. Figure 6.5 uses that framework to formulate seven questions that indicate why using a market can fail because of high transaction costs. Each is grounded in departures from the assumptions required by models that 'prove' markets work best: the buyer has perfect information and can write a complete contract; there are so many buyers and many sellers (with no barriers to entry) so that the departure of any single buyer or seller has no impact on the functioning of the market; and a transactional relationship does not impair the 'atmosphere' in which a service is provided (for example, professionally or voluntarily).

Figure 6.6 uses the seven questions from Figure 6.5 to identify where the decision to outsource has high transaction costs and hence may fail. All of these conditions applied to NASA's contract with Morton Thiokol, which had five primary causes of market failure:

1. Although four firms competed for the initial contract, after it was awarded to Morton Thiokol there was what Williamson describes as a 'fundamental transformation' to Thiokol having a monopoly.

Figure 6.5: Seven questions that indicate where a market may fail

Question	High transaction costs in using a market
1. Can a complete contract be specified?	No. This could be because: – the buyer is uncertain over when and at what scale a service will be needed; or – the service needed is too complex to be specified in advance; or – the buyer is uncertain *and* the service needed is complex.
2. Is the buyer able to assess the adequacy of the quality and costs of what is supplied?	No, and they would find it costly to try to find out if the supplier is overcharging for the volume and quality of services supplied.
3. Is there supply-side flexibility?	No: there is a small number of suppliers, those that fail do not exit the market, and the dominant suppliers are not challenged by new entrants.
4. Are there many buyers?	No: the supplier in the contract has had to invest in assets (equipment and staff) that are specific to the buyer.
5. Is the transactional relationship between buyer and supplier adequate to cover all aspects?	No: the buyer's experience of the quality of service supplied is impaired by a transactional relationship – 'atmosphere' matters.
6. Is there scope for suppliers to behave with opportunism?	Yes: the buyer is vulnerable to being exploited by being overcharged for an excessive or inadequate volume of services of poor quality.
7. Is the buyer a skilled purchaser?	No. This could be because: – the suppliers bring their 'five star generals' to negotiate with the buyer's junior staff; – the contract is one-off; or – the service is so complex and uncertain that there is no 'learning by doing' from contracting over time.

2. Thiokol's assets in this area were specific to NASA: there were no other buyers for a booster rocket for the space shuttle.

3. The contract for the costly research and development to develop and produce the booster rocket was a one-off contract, so NASA had no opportunity to do repeated 'learning by doing' and develop into a skilled purchaser.

4. Research development is complex and uncertain so NASA could not write a complete contract to specify what Morton Thiokol ought to do. And when NASA most needed to launch *Challenger* they were dismayed at Morton Thiokol introducing new criteria that it would not be safe to do so: the need to launch in cold weather was not specified in the initial contract.

Figure 6.6: A market with high transaction costs

Source: Author.

NASA chose Morton Thiokol because it could 'do a more economical job than any of the other proposers in both the development and the production phases of the program'. But Thiokol's proposal ranked worst amongst the four bidders in terms of 'design, development and verification'.[82] Vaughan found that NASA's contract was designed to generate financial incentives for Thiokol that 'prioritized cost saving and meeting deadlines over safety'.[83] Budgetary pressure on an incomplete contract always requires careful monitoring of quality, but that pressure also makes that difficult to do, as in this case.

The Rogers Commission described how NASA's 'silent safety program' developed:

> The unrelenting pressure to meet the demands of an accelerating flight schedule might have been adequately handled by NASA if it had insisted upon the exactingly thorough procedures that were its hallmark during the Apollo program. An extensive and redundant safety program comprising interdependent safety, reliability and quality assurance functions existed during and after the [1960s] lunar program to discover any potential safety problems. Between that period and 1986, however, the program became ineffective.[84]

When there are many buyers and sellers, failing suppliers exit the market over time. But the 'fundamental transformation' meant that NASA and Morton Thiokol were locked into a bilateral monopoly. Diane Vaughan has analysed in detail what the consequences were for these two parties after catastrophic public failure. NASA did not terminate its contract with Thiokol: to have done that would have meant finding another supplier, with increased costs and delays to the launch schedule.[85] If Thiokol had accepted legal liability for the accident, this would have brought social stigma, limited its ability to compete successfully for future government contracts, and left it vulnerable to being sued by private parties. So, after the accident, NASA and Thiokol agreed to avoid litigation of that issue to avoid incurring additional costs.

NASA paid Thiokol $800 million in its initial contract, and $505 million (at no profit) 'to redesign the field joint, rework existing hardware to include the redesign, and replace the reusable hardware lost in the Challenger accident'.[86] Thiokol agreed to a $10 million reduction in the incentive fee it had earned under the contract at the time of the accident[87] (approximately $75 million).[88] My estimate is that the cost to Thiokol of the accident was less than 1 per cent of NASA's total payments.

Now consider two thought experiments of different arrangements for booster rockets:

1. Thiokol was one of a large number of suppliers in a mass market, and
2. NASA managed its own rocket development and production in-house.

In the first thought experiment, the overriding objective concern of Thiokol's managers would have been to preserve their market share. So, it is likely that they would have told NASA it was not safe to launch on 27 January 1986. Where the market works, as Samuel Bowles argued, 'prices do the work of morals, recruiting shabby motives to elevated ends'.[89] In the second thought experiment, we know NASA managers were driven by making economies and meeting the demanding schedule for launches – not the safety of the astronauts. So, with in-house production it is likely that they would have gone ahead with the launch on 27 January 1986. (Recall here that Chapter 1 described how the managers at Mid Staffordshire NHS Foundation Trust were driven by making economies and meeting waiting time targets, not the care of patients –with catastrophic consequences.)

6.4 Outsourcing and the UK's parastate

In England in the 2020s, about a third of what the government spends on goods and services is outsourced. Brilliant economists have described how policymakers ought to aim to:

1. *Develop into a skilled purchaser* able to choose between competing outsourcers that all have the capability to deliver at the scale and quality required.
2. *Develop effective systems for contracting and monitoring* to ensure that providers do not act opportunistically (for example, via quality-shading once a contract is let).
3. *Set fair prices* to enable private firms to make reasonable profits when they deliver goods and services of high quality, and avoid creating either opportunities for excess profits or putting such intense pressure on costs that quality suffers.

4. *Develop effective competition*: outsourcers ought to compete on price and quality so that a failing supplier can exit the market and be easily replaced. This requires ensuring there is a sufficient number of suppliers. Where that is not possible effective contract monitoring is even more vital than normal.

These conditions require senior civil servants to take commissioning and managing contracts seriously. But Margaret Hodge, who chaired the UK Parliament's Public Accounts Committee (PAC) from 2010 to 2015, concluded that they see these tasks as beneath their pay grade.[90] She described 'too many disasters' in government outsourcing, with examples including failures on:

- *Skilled purchasing.* A company with a credit rating for a contract up to £1 million only was nonetheless awarded a £42 million contract for interpreting services in law courts. They were able to supply only 280 out of the 1,200 interpreters needed.[91]
- *Effective contracting and monitoring.* Like NASA's 'silent safety' system, in contracts for electronic tagging for people convicted of crimes serving sentences in the community, the UK government allowed two large contractors, G4S and SERCO, to behave opportunistically. The firms billed and charged the government for tagging people who had ceased to be tagged, either because their sentence period was up or sometimes when they had died.[92]
- *Effective competition.* Hodge gave an example of one tender that required a company to supply 12 A4 boxes of information, which took 80 hours to print.[93] The government's heavy-handed bureaucracy is perfectly designed to create a formidable barrier to small players entering procurement competitions.

These weaknesses on the demand side of outsourcing have been exacerbated by financialisation of the supply side with failures by the UK government to develop competition and set fair prices. Gill Plimmer pointed out in the *Financial Times* that, to deliver increases in shareholder value, and the remuneration it brought them, senior executives drove up the growth in the size of the big firms that received large public contracts for outsourced services. Successful contractors borrowed heavily to grow through acquisitions of smaller firms, even though these often operated in sectors and countries in which the new parent owners lacked experience and expertise.[94] Strong targeting that aimed to increase shareholder value resulted in firms making losses, when the big outsourcers were caught in a price war as a result of the Conservative–Liberal Democrat government's austerity policies after 2010.

Some key firms gained first-hand experience of what is meant by 'the winners curse' from winning contracts at low prices where they lacked expertise and experience to fulfil them.[95] Plimmer has reported how the stock market value of their shares fell steeply. SERCO was unable to deliver appropriate care to patients on three different types of NHS contracts: out-of-hours GP services (Cornwall), community services (Suffolk) and a community hospital (Braintree).[96] Its shares fell in value from 674p a share in July 2013 to 215p in November 2014.[97] Over the year to November 2020, Capita's shares plunged in value by 73 per cent.[98] Financialisation of the outsourcing of government services enabled a few executives and managers to recoup extremely large financial rewards unrelated to any social value, whilst the staff who delivered goods and services struggled to make ends meet. Kier was planning to pay its chief executive 'more than £1m in bonuses' after their shares had lost 90 per cent of their value – this was opposed by shareholders.[99] But the most egregious example was Carillion.

From 2012 to 2016, Carillion had financed payments of dividends to its shareholders that exceeded its profits, a feat accomplished by selling assets worth £217 million and running up debts. Although it was a signatory to the government's Prompt Payment Code, it failed to fulfil that commitment to pay 95 per cent of invoices within 60 days (unless there are exceptional circumstances).[100] Carillion's standard terms were payments within 120 days – those suppliers wanting earlier payment were required to accept a discount. In July 2017, after Carillion's share value had fallen by 70 per cent and it had issued its first profit warning, the government awarded Carillion transport infrastructure contracts related to HS2 (high speed rail) worth £1.34 billion. In November 2017, after Carillion's third profit warning and its announcement that it was heading towards a breach of its debt covenants, the government still awarded Carillion a contract worth £130 million for the London–Corby rail electrification project.[101] In January 2018 Carillion went into liquidation. After the firm's collapse, the prisons it had been contracted to maintain were found to be in a bad way from lack of investment, severe staff shortages and a backlog of work.[102] The buildings of its new hospitals in Liverpool and Birmingham were found to have serious structural faults; there was huge disruption for departments, agencies and customers relying on its services; its pension schemes had liabilities of around £2.6 billion; its 30,000 subcontractors were owed £2 billion; and over 2,000 people lost their jobs.[103] Four supervising institutions that failed to protect the interests of all of these Carillion stakeholders were the subject of a coruscating joint report, published, in 2018, from two select committees of the House of Commons, the Business, Energy and Industrial Strategy and Work and Pensions Committees.[104] These were:

Carillion's remuneration committee (RemCo). Its role according to the Institute of Directors is to 'make sound decisions on levels of remuneration, on the link between remuneration and performance'.[105] Alexander Pepper has criticised the outcomes of that system as being quite incapable of making fair settlements. This is because remuneration committees seek to resolve the collective action problem when posed with the rhetorical question: do we want our chief executive to be paid less than the average?

There is no ethical justification for paying economic rents in the form of excessive remuneration. Executives and investors, along with governments and major institutions, all share a moral responsibility for ensuring that there is distributive justice in society. But the problem of high pay will not be solved by technical means alone – the various parties involved must also recognise their ethical obligations. When it comes to top pay, for too long companies have behaved as if they are in the equivalent of an arms race. It is a mad, bad system, and it needs to change if inflation in executive pay is to be brought under control.[106]

Carillion's chief executive recalled that his total remuneration in 2016 'jumped from something like £1.1 million or £1.2 million to £1.5 million.'[107] That was 70 times the UK's median pay for full-time jobs.[108] He was also paid 'a bonus of £245,000 (37 per cent of his salary) despite meeting none of his financial performance targets.'[109] The joint report's verdict:

> In the years leading up to the company's collapse, Carillion's remuneration committee paid substantially higher salaries and bonuses to senior staff while financial performance declined. It was the opposite of payment by results. Only months before the company was forced to admit it was in crisis, the RemCo was attempting to give executives the chance for bigger bonuses, abandoned only after pressure from institutional investors. As the company collapsed, the RemCo's priority was salary boosts and extra payments to senior leaders in the hope they wouldn't flee the company, continuing to ensure those at the top of Carillion would suffer less from its collapse than the workers and other stakeholders to whom they had responsibility.[110]

The Pensions Regulator is a state agency that promises: 'We protect the UK's workplace pensions. We make sure employers, trustees, pension specialists and business advisers can fulfil their duties to scheme members.'[111] The joint report's verdict was very different:

> The Pensions Regulator failed in all its objectives regarding the Carillion pension scheme. Scheme members will receive reduced pensions. The Pension Protection Fund [a state agency that is compensator of last resort to ill-served pensioners] and its levy payers will pick up their biggest bill ever. Any growth in the company that resulted from scrimping on pension contributions can hardly be described as sustainable. Carillion was run so irresponsibly that its pension schemes may well have ended up in the PPF regardless,

but the Regulator should not be spared blame for allowing years of underfunding by the company.[112]

Carillion's auditor, KPMG. Two of the auditing giant's core values were 'Integrity – we do what is right' and 'Courage – we think and act boldly'.[113] The joint report's verdict was damning:

> KPMG audited Carillion for 19 years, pocketing £29 million in the process. Not once during that time did they qualify their audit opinion on the financial statements, instead signing off the figures put in front of them by the company's directors. Yet, had KPMG been prepared to challenge management, the warning signs were there in highly questionable assumptions about construction contract revenue and the intangible asset of goodwill accumulated in historic acquisitions. These assumptions were fundamental to the picture of corporate health presented in audited annual accounts. In failing to exercise—and voice—professional scepticism towards Carillion's aggressive accounting judgements, KPMG was complicit in them. It should take its own share of responsibility for the consequences.[114]

The Financial Reporting Council (FRC). The FRC aims to 'promote transparency and integrity in business' for 'investors and others who rely on company reports, audit and high-quality risk management'.[115] The joint report's verdict:

> The FRC was far too passive in relation to Carillion's financial reporting. It should have followed up its identification of several failings in Carillion's 2015 accounts with subsequent monitoring. Its limited intervention in July 2017 clearly failed to deter the company in persisting with its over-optimistic presentation of financial information. The FRC was instead happy to walk away after securing box-ticking disclosures of information. It was timid in challenging Carillion on the inadequate and questionable nature of the financial information it provided and wholly ineffective in taking to task the auditors who had responsibility for ensuring their veracity.[116]

In early 2022, after hearings at a tribunal, the FRC 'ruled that during the inspections KPMG auditors created documents, including meeting minutes, spreadsheets and assessments of goodwill'. KPMG was fined £14.4 million.[117]

Plimmer reported in the *Financial Times* how the financial difficulties of Carillion and Interserve created opportunities for financial speculators to make millions of pounds. In 2018, Coltrane Asset Management (a New York-based hedge fund) made £4 million by betting on Carillion's shares losing value (short-selling), and in 2019 it attempted to derail the rescue plan for Interserve. Emerald (a private equity fund) bought 'about £140 million of

Interserve's debt in the secondary market last year [*2022*] for as little as 50p in the pound' and stood 'to gain millions if the debt-for-equity swap is agreed'.[118]

The Carillion fiasco clearly sits in a parallel universe from Shleifer's vision of governments effortlessly contracting with dedicated private enterprises to reliably deliver social goals. But UK citizens rightly expected the UK government to have been more aware of Carillion's precarious financial position than a hedge fund based in New York, to ensure Carillion did not neglect the prisons it was contracted to maintain and that it built safe hospitals, and to require compliance with the government's own Prompt Payment Code. Citizens would clearly expect the Pensions Regulator to ensure the security of Carillion's pensions schemes. The FRC exists because too often an auditor has found nothing wrong with a firm's financial position prior to its collapse. So, we would have expected FRC to have acted promptly on discovering the failures of KPMG.

There are also similar stories from outsourcing of social care for the elderly in the 1980s by local government in the UK to experienced local firms and entrepreneurs. Outsourcing was supposed to break up a 'provider' monopoly by government agencies but, by the 2000s, mergers and acquisitions undermined what used to be a competitive market. The local suppliers often found it hard to compete against large financialised companies. By 2004 two firms, Southern Cross and Four Seasons Health Care, dominated the social care market. In 2003, Southern Cross owned more than 100 care homes and 'was attracting the attention of investment bankers'. It was acquired in 2004 by the US private equity group Blackstone, which made a profit of £1.1 billion by selling off, first its property assets and then its shares. In 2011, when Southern Cross owned 750 care homes, it went into administration. Its 31,000 residents all needed to be cared for.[119] In 1999, Four Seasons Health Care started out as a small Scottish chain of care homes. It grew, was acquired by, and passed through, five funds: Alchemy Partners, Allianz Three Delta, Terra Firma and H/2 Capital Partners.[120] Mazzucato points out that by 2008 (just nine years later) Four Seasons Health Care had a debt burden that required a weekly interest charge of £100 per bed.[121] The firm subsequently went into administration in 2019, when it owned and ran over 320 care homes and cared for thousands of residents.[122]

Conclusions

The extreme neoliberal nostrum that government ought to privatise or outsource all except for a residual category like Air Force One was tested to destruction in post-Thatcherite Britain. Williamson's framework suggests that privatisation of the coal and steel industries would bring gains without losses. But they removed a means through which training and employment was maintained in the areas that have since been left behind. Hence the generous government support given to private industry for the rump that remains of the UK's steel industry. The nationalised coal industry aimed to secure the resilience of the UK to what was a vital source of energy. Privatised suppliers of energy have no interest in developing resilience when that conflicts with making profits.

Adam Smith's examples, of the butcher, brewer and baker, are of markets that worked so well because they satisfied a stringent set of conditions. Each was a small self-managed enterprise and whether it thrived or failed depended on its local reputation. Each market was contestable; it was easy for new entrants to replace the suppliers failing on quality and price. Consumers were skilled repeat buyers who knew what they wanted, their willingness to pay, and easily assessed the price and quality of what was on offer. They exemplified Smith's famous metaphor of working like an 'invisible hand'.[123] Governments could only make privatisation and outsourcing work for services that do not satisfy those stringent conditions through the visible mechanisms of regulation and written contracts. But the vulnerability of those mechanisms has been exposed by another institution of neoliberalism, namely financialisation. The UK government has failed to make privatisation work for gas, electricity, railways and water. Katharina Pistor's *The code of capital* (see Chapter 5) explains why, as Dieter Helm argued, 'light-touch' regulation of financialised water companies failed so spectacularly because it assumed that 'balance sheets were a matter best left to the companies' and allowed 'The horses [to] have bolted with their dividends'.[124] The UK government has also failed to create an effective market in outsourcing.

Education and healthcare, however, were too politically salient to be marketised in the same way by the Conservative, and New Labour, governments who bought into new public management doctrines advocated by neoliberal think tanks. The next two chapters, 7 and 8, examine the policy of decentralised quasi-markets run under state control and micro-local agencies (individual schools, universities or hospitals) that were required to compete in order to attract customers (parents, students or patients).

Endnotes

[1] Shleifer, Andrei (1998) 'State versus private ownership', *Journal of Economic Perspectives*, vol.12, no. 4, pp.133–50. https://doi.org/10.1257/jep.12.4.133

[2] Krugman, Paul (1994) 'Rational expectations', in *Peddling prosperity: Economic sense and nonsense in the age of diminished expectations*, UK: WW Norton & Company, pp.47–53.

[3] Chandler Jr, Alfred D. (1977) *The visible hand*, US: Harvard University Press. http://library.mpib-berlin.mpg.de/toc/z2010_942.pdf

[4] Coase, Ronald (1988) '1. The nature of the firm: Origin', *The Journal of Law, Economics, and Organization*, vol, 4, no. 1, pp.3–17. https://doi

.org/10.1093/oxfordjournals.jleo.a036946; Coase, Ronald. (1937) 'The nature of the firm', *Economica*, vol. 4, no. 16, pp.386–405. https://doi.org/10.1111/j.1468-0335.1937.tb00002.x

5 The Royal Swedish Academy of Sciences (1991) 'Press Release: Nobel Prize awarded to Ronald H. Coase', *The Nobel Prize*. https://perma.cc/HS7L-X3YH

6 Smith, Adam (1976) *The Wealth of Nations*, US: University of Chicago Press.

7 Applebaum, Anne (2022) 'Holodomor', *Encyclopedia Britannica*, 8 May. https://perma.cc/RP5H-ZM6Y

8 Brown, Archie (2010) *The rise and fall of communism*, UK: Vintage, p.337.

9 Bowles, Samuel (2008) 'Policies designed for self-interested citizens may undermine "the moral sentiments": Evidence from economic experiments'. *Science*, vol. 320, no. 5883, pp.1605–09. https://doi.org/10.1126/science.1152110

10 Hart, Oliver (2008) 'Economica Coase lecture: Reference points and the theory of the firm', *Economica*, vol. 75, no. 299, pp.404–11. https://doi.org/10.1111/j.1468-0335.2007.00659.x

11 Coase, Ronald, 'The nature of the firm', p.394.

12 Coase, Ronald (1988) '3. The nature of the firm: Influence', *The Journal of Law, Economics, and Organization*, vol. 4, no. 1, p.33. https://doi.org/10.1093/oxfordjournals.jleo.a036947

13 Chandler, Alfred, *The visible hand*, p.490.

14 Coase, Ronald, '3. The nature of the firm: Influence', pp. 33-34.

15 The Nobel Prize (2023) 'Oliver E. Williamson – Facts.' https://perma.cc/UX8B-46LP

16 Williamson, Oliver (1975) *Markets and hierarchies: Analysis and anti-trust implications*, UK: The Free Press; Williamson, Oliver (1985) *The economic institutions of capitalism. Firms, markets, relational contracting*, UK: The Free Press.

17 Dunleavy, Patrick and Hood, Christopher (1994) 'From old public administration to new public management', *Public Money & Management*, vol. 14, no. 3, pp.9–16. https://doi.org/10.1080/0954096940 9387823; Hood, Christopher (1995) 'The "new public management" in the 1980s: Variations on a theme', *Accounting, organizations and society*, vol. 20, no. 2–3, pp.93–109. https://doi.org/10.1016/0361-3682(93)E0001-W

18 Access to Mineral Heritage (2005) *Underground coal production and manpower from 1947*.

https://web.archive.org/web/20140714165303/http://mininghistory
.thehumanjourney.net/edu/UndergroundCoalProductionPost1947.shtml

[19] Access to Mineral Heritage, *Underground coal production.*

[20] Krugman, Paul, *Peddling prosperity*, p.181.

[21] Atteridge, Aaron and Strambo, Claudia (2021) *Decline of the United Kingdom's steel industry*. Sweden: Stockholm Environment Institute. https://euagenda.eu/upload/publications/decline-of-the-steel-industry -in-the-uk.pdf; Access to Mineral Heritage, *Underground coal production and manpower from 1947.*

[22] Muellbauer, John and Soskice, David (2022) *The Thatcher legacy. Lessons for the future of the UK economy*, UK: The Resolution Foundation, p.19. https://perma.cc/7G84-87LN

[23] *BBC News* (2019) 'Corby: "Devastating" steel works closure remembered 40 years on'. https://perma.cc/ET4X-P93M

[24] Doshi, Vidhi (2016) 'Sanjeev Gupta: From college dorm deals to UK steel's great hope', *The Guardian*, 6 April. https://perma.cc/8KYQ-4LR2

[25] Collingridge, John (2019) 'How Sanjeev Gupta built an empire on risky alchemy', *The Times*, 7 July. https://perma.cc/W22Q-V6CG

[26] Smith, Robert; Fletcher, Laurence; and Dickie, Mure (2021) 'Scottish government raises provision on Gupta guarantee to £161m', *Financial Times*, 17 December. https://perma.cc/ZRA6-PFBU

[27] Glackin, Michael (2022) 'New disclosures over Sanjeev Gupta's smelter turn heat on the SNP', *The Sunday Times*, 23 July. https://perma.cc/6VET-8QU8

[28] Trade Remedies Authority (2021) 'TRA publishes final recommendation on steel safeguard measures', 11 June. https://www.gov.uk/government/news/tra-publishes-final-recommendation -on-steel-safeguard-measures

[29] Jim, Pickard and Pfeifer, Sylvia (2023) 'Jeremy Hunt set to sign off on support for UK steel groups', *Financial Times*, 20 January. https://perma.cc/TT6A-WCJK

[30] Smith, Robert; Pfeifer, Sylvia; and O'Dwyer, Michael (2022) 'Sanjeev Gupta's auditor quit after lack of evidence to complete work', *Financial Times*, 20 September. https://perma.cc/YE5T-8ABM

[31] Walker, Owen; Pfeifer, Sylvia; and Smith, Robert (2022) 'Sanjeev Gupta's Liberty Steel nears deal with creditors led by Credit Suisse', *Financial Times*, 15 November. https://perma.cc/2H5B-2L5D

[32] Ofgem (n.d.) 'Our role and responsibilities'. https://perma.cc/U8CY-FUZZ

33 Thomas, Nathalie (2022) 'Ofgem admits failings in oversight of UK retail energy market', *Financial Times*, 8 February. https://perma.cc/FL86-A77R; Thomas, Helen (2022) 'UK energy crisis needs fighting on multiple fronts'. *Financial Times*, 5 January. https://perma.cc/4DD5-RF2E

34 Office for Budget Responsibility (2022) *Economic and Fiscal Outlook*, UK: HMSO. https://perma.cc/U7UG-ZS4G

35 Thomas, Nathalie, 'Ofgem admits failings in oversight of UK retail energy market'.

36 Thomas, Nathalie (2021) 'UK's ageing reactors bring nuclear question to a head', *Financial Times*, 14 July. https://perma.cc/2JTD-TUFU

37 UK Government (2022) *British energy security strategy*. https://www.gov.uk/government/publications/british-energy-security -strategy/british-energy-security-strategy

38 Grubb, Michael (2022) 'The UK energy strategy is both cowardly and incoherent', *Financial Times*, 10 April. https://perma.cc/3EQY-FQ4P

39 Ward, Andrew (2017) 'Centrica to close UK's largest gas storage site', *Financial Times*, 20 June. https://perma.cc/BEH8-PBQ7

40 Thomas, Nathalie (2022) '"We can't take energy security for granted": UK races to boost gas storage capacity', *Financial Times*, 1 December. https://perma.cc/7PK9-ECT4

41 Moran, Michael (2003) *The British regulatory state: high modernism and hyper-innovation*, UK: Oxford University Press. https://epdf.pub/the-british-regulatory-state-high-modernism-and-hyper -innovation.html

42 Moran, Michael, *The British regulatory state*, p.178.

43 Moran, Michael, *The British regulatory state*, p.177.

44 Wellings, Richard (2014) 'The privatisation of the UK railway industry: An experiment in railway structure', *Economic Affairs*, vol. 34, no. 2, pp.255–66. https://doi.org/10.1111/ecaf.12083

45 Secretary of State for Transport (2021) *Great British Railways. The Williams-Shapps Plan for Rail*. CP 423, UK: HMSO, p.13.

46 ORR (2023) 'About ORR'. https://perma.cc/NJK9-L8TA

47 Pidd, Helen (2022) 'Revealed: North of England train line vastly under-reports cancellations', *The Guardian*, 27 November. https://perma.cc/MLS5-PWY2

48 Brabin, Tracy; Burnham, Andy; Coppard, Oliver; Driscoll, Jamie; and Rothcram, Steve (2022) 'Joint Northern Mayors statement as rail services in the North grind to a halt', *West Yorkshire Combined Authority*, 27 October. https://perma.cc/6UNC-QASS

[49] Byatt, Ian (2019) *A regulator's sign off: Changing the taps in Britain*, UK: Short Run Press Ltd, p.30.

[50] The Editorial Board (2023) 'England's ill-fated experiment with privatising water', *Financial Times*, 28 June. https://perma.cc/L3WU-5G8W

[51] Laville, Sandra (2023) 'Revealed: Warning to ministers over privatised water kept secret since 2002', *The Guardian*, 20 May. https://perma.cc/CH4Q-YLH5

[52] Wilkinson, Max (2020) 'A Regulator's Sign Off: Changing the Taps in Britain, by Ian Byatt', *Financial Times*, 6 January. https://perma.cc/TE3K-4SA6

[53] Helm, Dieter (2023) 'Lessons from the Thames Water debacle', *Financial Times*, 2 July. https://perma.cc/BT8R-3524

[54] Bullough, Oliver (2022) 'Sewage sleuths: The men who revealed the slow, dirty death of Welsh and English rivers', *The Guardian*, 4 August. https://perma.cc/2X7H-3TD6

[55] House of Lords Industry and Regulators Committee (HLIRC) (2023) *The affluent and the effluent: Cleaning up failures in water and sewage regulation.* HL Paper 166. p.15.

[56] HLIRC, *The affluent and the effluent*, pp.15–17.

[57] HLIRC, *The affluent and the effluent*, p.65.

[58] Bell, Derek and Gray, Tim (2002) 'The ambiguous role of the environment agency in England and Wales', *Environmental Politics*, vol. 11, no. 3, pp.78–79, 93.

[59] HLIRC, *The affluent and the effluent*, p.12.

[60] HLIRC, *The affluent and the effluent*, p.65.

[61] HLIRC, *The affluent and the effluent*, p.46.

[62] HLIRC, *The affluent and the effluent*, p.75.

[63] HLIRC, *The affluent and the effluent*, p.46.

[64] Environment Agency (2022) *Water and sewerage companies in England: environmental performance report 2021.* https://www.gov.uk/government/publications/water-and-sewerage -companies-in-england-environmental-performance-report-2021/water -and-sewerage-companies-in-england-environmental-performance -report-2021

[65] Wace, Charlotte (2022) 'Sewage and mud spill taints the beauty of one of Cornwall's most beautiful beaches', *The Times*. 1 November. https://perma.cc/S3UV-DEAT

[66] Environment Agency, *Water and sewerage companies in England: Environmental performance report 2021.*

[67] The Editorial Board, 'England's ill-fated experiment with privatising water'.

[68] Plimmer, Gill and Fildes, Nic (2023) 'Managed by Macquarie: the Australian group with a grip on global infrastructure', *Financial Times*, 27 June. https://perma.cc/BV3G-BMKE

[69] Shleifer, Andrei, 'State versus private ownership', p.136.

[70] Shleifer, Andrei, 'State versus private ownership', p.135.

[71] Mazzucato, Mariana (2018) *The value of everything: Making and taking in the global economy*, UK: Hachette, p.194.

[72] *Wikipedia* (n.d.) 'NASA spinoff technologies'. https://perma.cc/PF2T-MPYV

[73] JFK Library (2019) 'Address at Rice University, September 12, 1962' [Video]. YouTube, 28 June. https://www.youtube.com/watch?v=iiC-E8vl7Fw

[74] Feynman, Richard (1989) 'Afterthoughts and Appendix F, Personal observations on the reliability of the Shuttle', in *What do you care what other people think?* UK: Bantam, pp.212–37.

[75] Wagner, Dennis (2016) '1986 Ronald Reagan – Space Shuttle Challenger Explosion', *State of the Union History*, 28 January. https://perma.cc/KM66-MF8U

[76] Challenger Center for Space Science Education (2009) *The Challenger story: Teacher in space.* https://web.archive.org/web/20090125080418/http://www.challenger.org/about/history/index.cfm

[77] Vaughan, Diane (1996) *The Challenger launch decision. Risky technology, culture, and deviance at NASA*, US: University of Chicago Press.

[78] Rogers, William (Chair) (1986) *Report to the president by the Presidential Commission on the Space Shuttle Challenger Accident.* https://sma.nasa.gov/SignificantIncidents/assets/rogers_commission_report.pdf, p.138.

[79] Rogers, William, *Report to the president*, Figure 14.

[80] Herkert, Joseph (1991) 'Management's hat trick: Misuse of "engineering judgment" in the Challenger incident', *Journal of Business Ethics*, vol. 10, pp.617–20. https://www.jstor.org/stable/25072193

[81] Bell, Trudy and Esch, Karl (1987) 'The fatal flaw in flight 51-l', *IEEE Spectrum*, vol. 24, no. 2, pp.36–37. https://doi.org/10.1109/MSPEC.1987.6448023

[82] Rogers, William, *Report to the president by the Presidential Commission on the Space Shuttle Challenger Accident*, p.121.

[83] Vaughan, Diane (1990) 'Autonomy, interdependence, and social control: NASA and the space shuttle Challenger', *Administrative Science Quarterly*, vol. 35, no. 2, p.247. https://doi.org/10.2307/2393390

[84] Rogers, William, *Report to the president*, p.153.

[85] Vaughan, Diane, 'Autonomy, interdependence, and social control', p.249.

[86] Vaughan, Diane, 'Autonomy, interdependence, and social control', p.250.

[87] Vaughan, Diane, 'Autonomy, interdependence, and social control', p.249.

[88] Vaughan, Diane, 'Autonomy, interdependence, and social control', p.248.

[89] Bowles, Samuel, 'Policies designed for self-interested citizens'.

[90] Hodge, Margaret (2017) *Called to account: How corporate bad behaviour and government waste combine*, UK: Little, Brown.

[91] Hodge, Margaret, *Called to account*, pp.317–19.

[92] Hodge, Margaret, *Called to account*, p.309.

[93] Hodge, Margaret, *Called to account*, p.345.

[94] Plimmer, Gill (2018) 'UK contractors have "bankrupt" business models, says vetting group', *Financial Times*, 2 December. https://perma.cc/9MPW-XFM5

[95] Plimmer, Gill (2020) 'Capita in talks to sell education business to tackle £1bn debt', *Financial Times*, 27 November. https://perma.cc/D4AD-U6FW

[96] Hodge, Margaret, *Called to account*, pp.338–39.

[97] Plimmer, Gill and Aglionby, John (2014) 'Serco plans £550m rights issue after profit warning', *Financial Times*, 10 November. https://perma.cc/93HK-WMFF

[98] Plimmer, Gill, 'Capita in talks to sell education business to tackle £1bn debt'.

[99] Plimmer, Gill (2019) 'Kier investors rebel over chief's potential £1m bonus', *Financial Times*, 15 November. https://perma.cc/H8B6-DYP3

[100] Hajikazemi, Sara; Aaltonen, Kirsi; Ahola, Tuomas; Aarseth, Wenche; and Andersen, Bjorn (2020) 'Normalising deviance in construction project organizations: A case study on the collapse of Carillion', *Construction Management and Economics*, vol. 38, no. 12, p.1128. https://doi.org/10.1080/01446193.2020.1804069

[101] Hajikazemi, Sara et al, 'Normalising deviance in construction project organizations', p.1113.

[102] Plimmer, Gill (2019) 'Standards in jails run by Carillion criticised', *Financial Times*, 23 October. https://perma.cc/578M-FE63

[103] Comptroller and Auditor General (2020) *Investigation into the rescue of Carillion's PFI hospital contracts*, Session 2019–20, HC23. https://www .nao.org.uk/reports/investigation-into-the-rescue-of-carillions-pfi -hospital-contracts/1; House of Commons Business, Energy and Industrial Strategy and Work and Pensions Committees (2018) *Carillion: Second joint report from the Business, Energy and Industrial Strategy and Work and Pensions Committees*, Session 2017–19 HC 769, The Stationery Office. p.3. https://publications.parliament.uk/pa/cm201719/cmselect/cmworpen /769/76903.htm

[104] House of Commons, *Carillion*.

[105] Institute of Directors (2022) *What is the role of the remuneration committee?* https://www.iod.com/resources/factsheets/company-structure/what-is-the -role-of-the-remuneration-committee/

[106] Pepper, Alexander (2022) *If You're So Ethical, Why Are You So Highly Paid?: Ethics, Inequality and Executive Pay*, UK: LSE Press, p.135. https://doi.org/10.31389/lsepress/eth

[107] House of Commons, *Carillion*, p.32.

[108] Office for National Statistics (2016) UK *gross and net weekly median pay for full time and part time workers 2015/2016 based on APS and LFS data*. https://www.ons.gov.uk/employmentandlabourmarket/peopleinwork /employmentandemployeetypes/adhocs/006144ukgrossandnetweeklyme dianpayforfulltimeandparttimeworkers20152016basedonapsandlfsdata

[109] House of Commons, *Carillion*, p.33.

[110] House of Commons, *Carillion*, pp.33–34.

[111] The Pensions Regulator (2022) https://perma.cc/725S-CHZA

[112] House of Commons, *Carillion*, pp.59–60.

[113] KPMG (2022) *What are our values?* https://perma.cc/CK8J-WH7G

[114] House of Commons, *Carillion*, p.53.

[115] Financial Reporting Council (2022) *About the FRC*. https://www.frc.org.uk/about-the-frc

[116] House of Commons, *Carillion*, p.61.

[117] O'Dwyer, Michael (2022) 'KPMG faces £14.4mn fine for misleading UK regulators over Carillion audit', *Financial Times*, 12 May. https://perma.cc/JAW2-KX33

[118] Plimmer, Gill (2019) 'Hedge fund in Interserve feud profited from Carillion collapse', *Financial Times*, 8 February. https://perma.cc/6EDA-TDTE

[119] Wachman, Richard (2011) 'Southern Cross's incurably flawed business model let down the vulnerable', *The Guardian*, 16 July. https://perma.cc/GK2H-SYG7

[120] Neville, Sarah; Plimmer, Gill; and Espinoza, Javier (2019) 'Four Seasons woes expose private care home risks', *Financial Times*, 6 May. https://perma.cc/6J7T-N9CJ

[121] Mazzucato, Mariana, *The value of everything*, p.169.

[122] Neville, Sarah et al, 'Four Seasons woes expose private care home risks'; Davies, Rob (2019) 'Four Seasons care home operator collapses into administration', *The Guardian*, 30 April. https://perma.cc/QEL7-ZJRX

[123] Rothschild, Emma (1994) 'Adam Smith and the invisible hand'. *The American Economic Review*, vol. 84, no. 2, pp.319–22. https://www.jstor.org/stable/2117851

[124] Helm, Dieter, 'Lessons from the Thames Water debacle'.

7. Marketisation in education

> Health, education, some incarceration, some military and police
> activities, and some of what now is presumed to be 'social' insur-
> ance like [US] Social Security, can probably be provided more
> cheaply and attractively by private firms. It is plausible that 50
> years from now, today's support for public provision of these
> services will appear as dirigiste as the 1940s arguments for state
> ownership of industry appear now. A good government that wants
> to further 'social goals' would rarely own producers to meet its
> objectives.
>
> Andrei Shleifer (1998)[1]

School education is a quintessential public service, serving a wide range of
social values and enjoying firm support from citizens and voters in all advanced
liberal democracies. That applies even in the US, where the state's role in
healthcare has remained contested. For Milton and Rose Friedman, however:

> The history of schooling in the United States, the United Kingdom,
> and other countries has persuaded us that compulsory attendance
> at schools is not necessary to achieve that minimum standard of
> literacy and knowledge.[2]

And the reason governments got involved was not because of concerns from
parents but because teachers and government officials could be 'expected to
enjoy greater certainty of employment, greater assurance that their salaries
would be paid, and a greater degree of control if government rather than
parents were the immediate paymaster'.[3] They made that argument in *Free to
Choose*, their neoliberal playbook written for a British readership.[4]

Walter Armytage gives a different historical account of the origins of
the 1870 Education Act, which introduced compulsory education in England in response to pressure from the civil service, industry and organised

How to cite this book chapter:

Bevan, Gwyn (2023) *How Did Britain Come to This? A century of systemic failures
of governance*, London: LSE Press, pp. 173–196.
https://doi.org/10.31389/lsepress.hdb.g License: CC BY-NC

labour. It attracted support in Parliament from 174 MPs, eight bishops and 26 peers, and the only opposition expressed was that the legislation did not go far enough.[5] The system of schools in England and Wales later developed greatly under the Attlee settlement to tackle Beveridge's giant of Ignorance, 'which no democracy can afford amongst its citizens' (see Chapter 4).[6] In the 1940s, a good education was not seen as a key route to the prosperity of individuals or countries. It is now. Good schools enable students to gain access to higher education, and then move on to glossy jobs and all the benefits they bring.

The Friedmans' proposed remedy to (what they saw as) the UK's flawed system of state schooling was to introduce a voucher system to empower parents as consumers. The first section of this chapter looks at that policy and the consequences after it was implemented by the Pinochet-led government in Chile. Section 7.2 looks at the way a voucher system was modified into a 'quasi-market' for schools in England. This scheme claimed to offer a remedy for failures of the Attlee settlement in which governance of schools was based on entrusting teachers with professional autonomy in their 'secret garden' – a system that lacked choice, incentives, equitable funding, and sanctions for failure. Under the Thatcher settlement the aim was to empower parents by giving them a real and equal choice of alternative schools, in a market-like setting where competition between schools would generate incentives on teachers to improve their performance. To inform choice by parents the national government also began to publish league tables of schools, comparing their performance in public exam results and in test scores for earlier-years children.

The third section of the chapter considers the remodelling of undergraduate university education in England and other UK countries. Under the Attlee settlement, undergraduate university education (UUE) was 'free' with (means-tested) grants to cover living costs. Only 5 per cent of young people went to university up to the 1960s. By the 1990s, that proportion increased to over 30 per cent.[7] Yet increasing enrolment without changing the tax-based system of finance meant either constraining the expansion of higher education or reducing its quality or both. Hence governments faced a need to redesign the system to try to optimise the size and quality of the university sector and deliver equity of access (according to ability to benefit). Again, the neoliberal approach was to attempt to develop a better system via a competitive market, financed by students paying fees to universities, for which they took out income-contingent loans from a state agency.

The final section of the chapters looks at the difference that devolution in 1990 made to education. The governments in Wales and Scotland partly moved back to systems of the Attlee settlement. Wales stopped publication of league tables of schools' exam results and Scotland abolished tuition fees (for Scottish students going to Scottish universities). I assess the impacts of these changes by comparing England with Wales and Scotland; and looking also at outcomes in Germany, which first introduced and then abandoned tuition fees for undergraduate education.

7.1 Designing social segregation by schools in Chile's voucher system

On 9 September 1973, a clandestine CIA officer, Jack Devine, was eating lunch at an Italian restaurant in Santiago, Chile, when a colleague joined his table to whisper in his ear, 'Call home immediately; it's urgent.' When he did so, his wife told him of a call from a CIA source that he was about to leave the country from the airport because the Chilean military had set a coup in motion.[8] The country was in chaos after three years of President Allende's implementation of a Marxist programme of reforms: nationalisation of US copper companies (without compensation) and 90 per cent of the banking system; expropriation of many large and medium-sized farms; the administrative takeover of some 300 factories; and introduction of workers control in socialised enterprises.[9] In retaliation, the US imposed a credit blockade that resulted in all kinds of shortages. Black markets were rampant, state-owned buses could not run, government debt soared with hyperinflation, and bombs rocked the capital.

After the military coup and the assassination of President Allende, General Pinochet took over as the head of a military dictatorship. Those advising Pinochet's government on its programme of neoliberal reforms included Milton Friedman and the 'Chicago boys', Friedrich von Hayek, and other members of the Mont Pèlerin Society (a neoliberal organisation founded by von Hayek in 1947 – see Chapter 5).[10] They seem to have been untroubled by the Pinochet government's appalling brutal record of repressing dissent: more than 35,000 people were tortured and over 100 were 'disappeared' or were executed.[11] (Forder suggests that, later, Friedman was keen to downplay his influence on Pinochet's government, and overplay that on Margaret Thatcher's.[12])

The Friedmans recognised that returning to their Arcadian vision of abolition of state schooling was not politically feasible. So, their second-best solution was a voucher system to enable parents to top-up state funding so as to secure better education for their children. Figure 7.1 outlines the traditional state schooling system, the Friedmans' voucher system, and its modification in a quasi-market (see Section 7.2). In each system there are independent schools for which parents pay their full costs. The voucher system implemented in Chile enshrined three cardinal principles of neoliberalism:

1. Public finance of a service does not mean public provision.
2. Public services ought to be organised in a market where the funding of providers follows consumer choice (in this case parents' choices).
3. The market for public services ought to be designed so that those who want to spend more to gain better services can easily do so.

Figure 7.1: Private schools and three state systems

Key features	Private school system	Publicly funded systems		
		Conventional	Voucher system	Quasi-market
Types of school	Independent	Public	Public and private	Public and self-governing
Provider organisation	Autonomous, self-governing	Bureaucratically run by local governments	Autonomous	Regulated NGO/firm single school trust, or chain of schools
Funding source	Wholly parents' fees	Taxes	Taxes fund vouchers plus top-up fees paid by parents	Taxes and some funded by corporate sponsors
Parental choice	Competitive market with choice based on quality, accessibility and cost	Local monopoly. No choice*	Competitive market with choice based on quality, accessibility, and cost	Competitive market with choice based on quality, and accessibility
School income	Depends on numbers of pupils and the fees charged	Annual school budgets set with incremental changes over time**	Depends on numbers of pupils and top-up fees from parents	Determined by formula that takes into account numbers of pupils and their needs

Notes: *Limited right to appeal against the school that is allocated. **Budgets are set by staffing levels, without considering the numbers and needs of pupils, or school performance.

Voucher systems could tackle four constraints of the traditional arrangements of the UK's Attlee settlement:

- Schools were subject to bureaucratic and political control (by local governments).
- Parents had almost no choice – the school their children went to was determined by its catchment area (set by local government).
- The funding for each school was based on its current size and staffing, with only incremental changes to past budget without having to take into account changes in the numbers and needs of its pupils.
- The state allowed parents freedom to spend money as they wished in other aspects of their lives, but did not allow them to pay more than the state's allocation for their children to go to a better school.

A fundamental rationale of economics that justified the voucher systems is that systems that are designed to increase choice will also increase welfare. Vouchers were also claimed to democratise access to independent schools, while wholly private schools are the prerogative of the rich. Neoliberals also questioned the fairness of a system in which parents who send their children to independent schools also have to pay taxes for state schools that they do not use. (Schooling is quite different from defence, which conventional economics defines as a 'public good' because its outputs are indivisible.)

In the voucher system, from the start schools that charged a top-up would obviously have more money to spend per pupil, and hence be attractive to middle-class parents who could easily afford to pay more. But that also means the top-up schools have pupils that are easier to teach than the average, and the voucher schools pupils who are harder to teach than the average. This will result in the sorting of able pupils and good teachers to the top-up schools. Over time this strong 'club effect' sets in train a widening gulf in the capacity of pupils to benefit from each type of school.

The parents who care the most about their children's education will exit from voucher schools and send their children to a top-up school wherever they can, even if this requires forgoing luxuries and a struggle to live within their incomes. These parents will tend to have greater ability to assess the quality of their children's education and the performance of schools, and more capable and powerful 'voice' to put pressure on school heads and governors if quality were to falter. They will stay loyal to strongly performing schools and support teachers more. The children who end up in the voucher schools will have parents who either do not care about the quality of their children's education or who do care but do not have enough income to exit to a top-up school. The voucher schools will have to manage with less to spend on pupils who are harder to teach.

The fully independent schools will have the most socially exclusive peer group of pupils and parents with strong loyalties to them and the most powerful capabilities to secure good school performance through choice and voice. (As illustrated by the Royal Commission established in England, in 1864, to review the nine top independent schools – see Chapter 3.) The Friedmans' voucher system exemplifies Hirschman's powerful conceptual analysis in his classic short seminal book, *Exit, Voice, and Loyalty*, published 50 years ago, in which he explained why nothing was done about the appalling railway service in Nigeria that was used by the poor (the rich and influential used roads).[13] A damning but realistic one-sentence summary of systems with the characteristics of exit, voice and loyalty attributed to Richard Titmus is: 'Show me a service that only the poor use, and I will show you a poor service.'

The way that the voucher system was implemented in Chile resulted in the 'Penguin Revolution' of May 2006, when thousands of high school students protested on the streets wearing their black and white uniforms.[14] The country's voucher system distributed resources in much the same way as Julian Tudor Hart's inverse care law predicts for healthcare: available resources were *inversely* related to need.[15] Although the libertarian argument for vouchers with top-up fees was framed as letting parents spend more on their children's education, it proved perfectly designed to entrench inequalities in schooling – with consequential inequalities around students' 'meritocratic' eligibility for elite higher education.

7.2 Did England's quasi-market for schools deliver equity through choice?

The Friedmans' arguments highlighted flaws in the traditional design of state schooling systems. Julian Le Grand proposed instead a quasi-market that retained attractive features of voucher systems (parental choice, autonomy and relating funding to the number of pupils) but was designed with an equitable system of school funding (summarised in the final column of Figure 7.1). The concept aimed to harness the invisible hand of the market without 'consumers' using their own money to pay for schooling. Instead, parents chose the school that was right for their child, and then the number of pupils that each school attracted determined their funding. Le Grand advocated augmenting the standard per capita rate of funding per pupil with a pupil premium for those pupils that are harder to teach.[16]

The Thatcher government considered introducing a voucher system for schools, but instead the 1988 Education Reform Act introduced a quasi-market in England and Wales in 1989.[17] Figure 7.1 indicates that, in addition to changes in choice and funding, the move to a quasi-system entailed replacing control by local authorities with regulation by central government. This included the introduction of a National Curriculum[18] and nationally set key stage testing at three points in school students' careers (over and above the mandatory public exams for GCSEs at (around) age 16 and for A levels or BTEC qualifications at (around) age 18).[19] School performance testing was justified by the need to provide parents with objective information on school performance and quality to help them make informed choices, to be accomplished by the government publishing rankings of all schools' performance in tests and public examinations in league tables. This huge surveillance effort was introduced from 1992 by the governments in England and Wales.[20]

Figure 7.2 gives the standard per capita rate in England's school funding formula, for 2023–24, for pupils in primary, junior and senior secondary schools (Basic for primary, Basic I and II for secondary), and the extra funding per pupil for those who are eligible for free school meals (in the year or over the past six years), who live in a deprived area (highest rate shown), with low prior attainment, or who lack English; and for schools with more than 6 per cent of pupils joining during the school year.[21]

Figure 7.2: England's school funding formula

(a) Primary schools

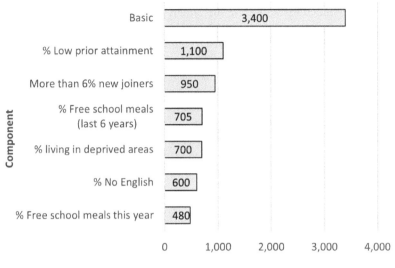

Funding per pupil in £s

(b) Secondary schools

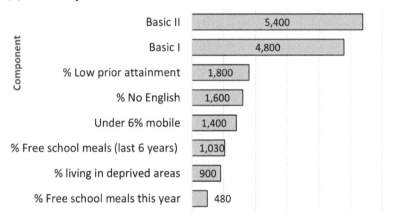

Funding per pupil in £s

Source: Department of Education.[22]

The problem of designing a *proportionate* care law to match funding of a service to need has been extensively researched in healthcare.[23] That research shows that using a formula to estimate relative need works better the larger the population, and that, although we can easily identify indicators of increased need, how much extra funding ought to allocated cannot be determined by empirical research. Eligibility for free school meals (FSMs) is known to be a good indicator for household poverty, but there remains the problem of determining how much extra funding that ought to bring, which surely depends on the scale and degree of poverty of pupils in a school. This suggests that a need-based formula ought to be used to inform judgement by a local organisation held to account for delivering equity in the educational achievements of schools. Farquharson et al found that, despite the extra funding in England for children eligible for FSMs, their success rates were about half those of non-FSM students in achieving good grades at GCSE in English and maths at age 16, and two or more A levels at age 19.[24]

Carolyn Hoxby identified three requirements for a policy of competition between schools to be an effective policy instrument of improving the quality of schools for all students:

- Money follows parental choices.
- The heads of schools are free to manage their own resources and policies. And
- There is supply-side flexibility.[25]

The third requirement means that: new schools are free to enter the system and compete with existing providers; successful schools are free to expand; and failing schools lose pupils and close from reduced incomes.[26] Yet, in practice, governments in England have been unwilling to fund the spare school capacity needed to enable such a dynamic system to operate. Pressure on budgets results in funding the number of school places to match the number of school-age students. The Institute of Fiscal Studies explains how the lack of supply-side flexibility in England meant that poorly performing schools did not exit the market but became 'sink schools', with peer groups of children whose parents were neither interested in nor capable of using the system to send their children to a better school. That was Lynsey Hanley's experience for schools serving the Chelmsley Wood estate (see Chapter 4).[27] As Fred Hirsch argues (see Chapter 4), education is a positional good and derives value from its exclusiveness.[28] If a good school were to expand its intake, that could reduce the degree to which it is oversubscribed, and hence worsen public perception of its quality. In a system of school competition without supply-side flexibility, instead of parents choosing schools, it is schools who choose parents with children that are likely to be easy to teach and do well.[29] Recruiting better students from the outset reduces the school's costs of teaching, and improves its ranking within the government-mandated 'league tables' of schools' examination performance that are fundamental to quasi-market systems.

Figure 7.3 applies Oliver Williamson's criteria for analysing transaction costs (see Chapter 6) to contracting for schools. This quasi-market has low transaction costs on five of the seven criteria: there is good information (from

Figure 7.3: Requirements for an effective quasi-market for schools on Williamson's criteria

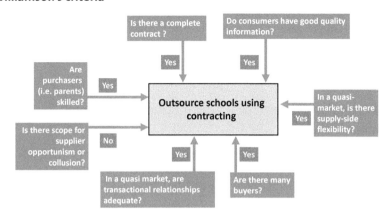

Source: Author.

OFSTED reports and league tables of exam results); scope for opportunism is constrained by inspections and testing; well-educated parents are skilled purchasers; the contract is specified by the National Curriculum; and there are many buyers (parents). The causes of high transaction costs come from wanting our schools to do more than 'teach to the test' in a transactional relationship; and the fundamental problem of 'site asset specificity'. To put this more simply, parents want their children to go to locally accessible schools. This inevitably restricts the degree of competition in towns and cities, and creates monopolies in rural areas, especially at secondary level.[30] It also makes it problematic to close a failing school.

Burgess et al found that, after the introduction of England's policy of school choice in 1988, geographic proximity continued largely to determine access to high-performing schools that were oversubscribed.[31] This was because proximity was the main criterion used in selecting their pupils. (Julian Le Grand acknowledges this problem in his plaintive observation: 'If real choice were available, this would reduce the influence of simply living near good schools, and hence go some way towards rectifying this imbalance.'[32]) Houses near good schools sell at a premium.[33] In England, the longer-term consequence of the abolition of the 11-plus exam and the development of comprehensive schools was to change how students got into secondary schools from selection by exams to instead selection by the price of property. In 1956, Charles Tiebout described where people choose to live as 'the local public-goods counterpart to the private market's shopping trip'.[34]

One way to make the school systems more equitable would be to move to a lottery system for all school places. Burgess et al recognise that this would face a hostile reception from families who have struggled to pay more for their house to ensure their children have access to a good school (England's equivalent to the pressure on parents in Chile to find the money to pay for their children to go to a voucher school). Introducing a lottery would mean that struggle had been in vain and reduce the value of their house. So, instead, Burgess et al propose only a proportionate change in which a percentage of places, say 20 per cent, would be allocated by a lottery, with 80 per cent being allocated as now.[35]

7.3 England's search for an optimal and equitable university system

A 2017 World Bank report on higher education (in Latin America and the Caribbean) made a clear case that mass higher education is vital for the futures of children across all countries:

> In the pursuit of growth and equity, no country can afford to ignore higher education. Through higher education, a country forms skilled labor and builds the capacity to generate knowledge and innovation, which boosts productivity and economic growth. Since acquiring greater skills raises a person's productivity and her expected earnings, a good education system is also the basis for achieving greater equity and shared prosperity on a societal level. Particularly in societies mired with persistent and profound inequality, high-quality education can act as 'the great equalizer': the ultimate channel of equal opportunities, and the ultimate hope for parents who long for a better future for their children.[36]

Under the post-war Attlee settlement there was a generous system for those going to university in which governments paid tuition fees and grants (on a means-tested basis). Although that system funded well-off households, it played a vital role, until the late 1970s, in expanding the numbers of working-class children going to university. LSE academic Nicholas Barr identified two disadvantages of funding 'free' undergraduate university education through taxes. First, it is paid for by taxpayers who may never have been to a university and whose children may be excluded. (The same argument applies to 'free' selective grammar school education.) Second, it has to compete in claims for future spending with all other central government priorities – for example, the NHS, social care, relief of poverty, schools, defence, and law and order. There is an important spillover benefit from university education to a country from having well-educated citizens, and this is the economic argument for a government subsidy – but one that has to compete for public funds with other claims on the Exchequer. The normal outcome from tax-based finance will be tight budgetary constraints that constrain the university sector from improving its quality or growing in size or both. Reform critics (both neoliberals and many 'New Labour' voices) argued for introducing tuition fees. The Blair government, in 1998, introduced low annual tuition fees: £1,000 for students whose parents were in the top third of the income distribution, £500 for the middle third of parents, and no fee for the bottom third. Students financed their living costs with income-contingent loans (which graduates repaid with 9 per cent of their income when earning more than £10,000 a year).[37] There were some maintenance grants for students from the lowest-income households.

In England, the UK's self-appointed elite Russell Group of universities successfully lobbied the Blair government in 2003 to increase the annual tuition fee to a new level, which was set at £3,000 a year.[38] Their justification was that the change was vital to arrest the decline of England's elite universities in international rankings. In the QS World University Rankings for 2004, there were seven British universities in the top 50: six in England and one in Scotland.[39] (The reliability of those rankings was, however, questionable because of serious weaknesses in their methods and data.[40]) The Blair government (but not all Labour MPs) was persuaded by Barr's argument for financing the increased tuition fees by income-contingent loans.[41] Barr argued that the three desirable objectives of a university system are high quality, optimal size, and equity of access by ability to benefit (and not ability to pay for it). He developed a lucid exposition of the economic logic of financing mass undergraduate university education by using income-contingent loans.[42] This is because, as the people who are awarded degrees benefit the most from them, they ought to bear most of the costs (although there are also national welfare spillover gains). Private arrangements for loans will not achieve equity in access, because most undergraduates lack collateral (unlike in a mortgage for a house). Hence Barr's elegant solution requires governments to organise a system of income-contingent loans for undergraduates to finance their tuition with the promise that:

- Tuition fees charged by universities would vary with each institution's perception of the quality and nature of what it is offering.
- Competition between universities to attract students would create incentives to raise quality, with student choices weeding out, or leading to reform of, weak degrees, and constant innovation being encouraged.
- The size of the sector would be determined by choices made by students and universities. Government's role is to steer that market with incentives to attract more students to subjects deemed 'worthy' or national priorities, such as for science, technology, engineering and mathematics in England.
- Finally, the total costs of undergraduate education would be financed mainly by loan repayments, with only limited financial support from taxpayers to recognise the positive national spillover benefits.

The Blair government was able to win the vote in the Westminster Parliament for this change, in 2003, in *England*, but only with the support of Labour MPs from *Scottish* constituencies (who escaped scot-free from any loss of support from their constituents, who were unaffected).[43] In the 2010 general election campaign in the UK, Nick Clegg, the leader of the Liberal Democrats, signed a pledge to vote against any increase in the £3,000 tuition fees in England. Moreover, the Party's manifesto made a commitment to 'Scrap unfair university tuition fees for all students taking their first degree' with 'a financially responsible plan to phase fees out over six years'. And every Liberal Democrat MP was photographed for their election leaflets alongside the fees pledge.[44] However, when Nick Clegg became deputy prime minister in the Conservative–Liberal Democrat coalition government (formed in 2010), he led the Liberal Democrats in voting to *treble the maximum annual fee* for undergraduate education, in England (from £3,000 to £9,000). Liberal Democrat support in opinion polls fell precipitously from 23 per cent in 2010 to around 7 per cent after this change. At the next general election, in 2015, the number of Liberal Democrat MPs fell from 57 to 8 and Nick Clegg resigned as their leader.[45] In the 2017 general election, Nick Clegg lost his seat for the constituency of Sheffield Hallam. To continue his career, he moved to Facebook, where he rose to become president of global affairs in 2022.[46] After the fee increases, the QS World University Rankings for 2022 shows improvement in the rankings of some of the eight British universities in the top 50 as compared with those of 2003.[47]

Figure 7.4 compares the desired and actual outcomes of the English market for undergraduate university education. It shows that the English system allowed universities ample scope for gaming – a form of behaviour that Williamson describes as opportunism. This includes inflating the proportion of students being awarded first-class degrees, and making 'conditional unconditional' offers (a practice now been banned by the government's regulator, the Office for Students). Another disappointing outcome of the market for universities has been the lack of innovation. John Muellbauer and David Soskice identify the continuing absence of two-year, vocationally oriented degrees and the dominance of narrow, specialised degrees. They also see weaknesses in professional education for business, public policy, law, medicine, IT and engineering, and in the development of biogenetics and IT with close links to start-ups.[48] Another disappointment is the lack of flexible options for part-time study so that people can acquire skills along a time path of their choosing. Farquharson et al found that:

> the UK has one of the lowest rates of adults taking advanced vocational qualifications in OECD countries, and spending on adult education in 2019–20 was nearly two-thirds lower in real terms than in 2003–04.[49]

Figure 7.4: The desired and actual outcomes of the English market for undergraduate education

Desired outcome	Actual outcome
Tuition fees should vary according to the quality of a university and a course.	The maximum fee has become the fee that all universities charge: e.g. the tuition fee of £9,250 was charged for 2022/23 for accountancy at the University of Bolton and for accounting and finance at LSE.[50]
Good information is available to students (and parents) on quality and costs.	Information on the quality of degrees and universities is available in regulators' annual league tables (covering teaching and research separately) and various private sector guides (giving different results). Students know tuition fees, but not what they will pay back because of uncertainty about their future incomes and the complexities of the scheme.
Competition drives up quality, and drives out weak degrees.	Two main tactics by universities have undermined this mechanism: 1. In 2019, according to the BBC, 'A record one in four university applicants received a "conditional unconditional" offer'.[51] These applicants were guaranteed a place on a degree course (not conditional on their performance at A levels), provided they made that university their first choice – a practice no longer allowed by the regulator.[52] 2. The proportion of first-class degrees awarded doubled over eight years: from 14 per cent in 2009/10 to 28 per cent in 2017/18.[53] A detailed study by the Office for Students found that, e.g., 'graduates who entered higher education with the equivalent of grades CCD or below at A-level were almost three times more likely to graduate with first class honours in 2016–17 than in 2010–11'.[54]
Competition encourages innovation.	Innovation has largely been absent (see main text).
No unplanned government debt.	At the end of March 2021, the total value of outstanding student loans was £160 billion. Government projections show this will increase to £560 billion (at constant 2020/21 prices) by the middle of the century. It is officially expected that only 25 per cent of loans will be fully repaid.[55]

Figure 7.4 makes clear that the system financed by income-contingent loans has failed to act as a price mechanism in which universities charged fees that reflected the quality of their degrees, and has accumulated vast public debt. In 2021, the payment of debt interest on the student loan debt of

£160 billion was £6.4 billion (at the annual interest rate of 4 per cent set by the Bank of England).[56] That was 16 per cent of public expenditure on primary and secondary education in 2020/21 (£41 billion a year).[57]

If the fee charged signalled what students are expected to repay, then a low-ranked university that charges high fees for its low-quality degrees would attract few applicants. The system of income-contingent loans is designed to encourage the brightest students to apply to the best universities, regardless of the financial support their families can afford. That design also encourages low-ranked universities to charge the maximum tuition fees. If their graduates with weak degrees earn less than the income threshold, they do not have to pay back their loans. If a university were to charge low fees, that would signal to potential applicants that it recognises its degrees are of low quality. The system of income-contingent loans, which insures graduates against the risk of not earning enough to pay back their loans, brings the problem of moral hazard, as when we take our car to be repaired after a bump and we are asked: 'is this an insurance job or are you paying yourself?' In England, after the 2010 election, the intrinsic problem of moral hazard was exacerbated by the demand of the Liberal Democrats in the governing coalition that the income threshold for the repayment of the tuition fee loans should be raised so as to try to allay public criticisms of them for having had to completely abandon their promises on fees.[58]

Furthermore, fees that are published do not signal the future liabilities of graduates in a system of income-contingent loans that aims for fiscal neutrality. That requires high-earning graduates from elite universities with high-quality degrees to pay back more than the borrowing costs of their own fees. Only in that way can total repayments cover the costs of the loan scheme. Hence the fees charged by the best universities only indicate in part the future liabilities of their graduates.

Pressure has mounted on the UK's elite universities to take more children with lower educational achievements from lower social classes because it is well known that the achievements of school leavers do not fairly reflect their abilities. There is strong evidence that for children from low-income households the key obstacle to realising their potential through university education comes not from fees and loans but from their lower prior educational attainment.[59] That is why Barr's review of the 2012 reforms to undergraduate funding support in England described as 'unspeakable' the decisions by the Cameron–Clegg coalition government to abandon or curtail three policies launched under Blair that were directed at improving educational attainment by children from disadvantaged backgrounds.[60] First, the Education Maintenance Allowance was abolished. This was launched in 1999 to provide up to £30 per week for students from low-income households to encourage them to stay in education at ages when it was no longer compulsory.[61] Second, the Aimhigher programme was scrapped. This was established to widen participation in higher education, mainly focused on pupils in school years

10–12 (ages 14–16) – for example, offering summer school experience on university campuses, master classes, campus visits, guest lectures and mentoring.[62] Third, cuts were made to Sure Start, launched in 1999 as a programme of early interventions for the under-fives in the 20 per cent most deprived areas in England.[63] Evaluations of these schemes found that none of them was 'transformative'. But, given the scale of the challenge posed by educational inequalities, that was to be expected. What was so disappointing is the way these initiatives were abandoned or curtailed without learning from them how to deliver better access to higher education for the key groups that they targeted.

7.4 Back to the Attlee settlement?

Would it therefore be a mistake to go back to something closer to the Attlee settlement? To answer this, consider how that played out when the devolved governments in Wales decided to do that for schools and Scotland for university undergraduate education. After devolution (in 1999), following pressure from the National Union of Teachers, and a public consultation, the Welsh government stopped the publication of school league tables from 2002.[64] There were no other major policy differences between England and Wales. Figure 7.5 shows the consequences of that 'natural experiment' in the percentages of schoolchildren achieving five good grades (from A to C) at GCSE. After 2002, schoolchildren in Wales did not improve at the same rate as those in England. Burgess et al made a careful econometric study based on matching schools in England and Wales.[65] They found that, for every year that Wales did not publish a league table, a pupil in Wales would *lose two GCSE grades* compared with a similar pupil in England. If Wales wanted to match its schools' performance to those in England, they estimated that its class sizes would need to be *30 per cent smaller*. These differences were not explained by 'gaming' in England ('teaching to the test'). Wales was found to be much worse than England in the different tests used by OECD in its Programme for International Student Assessment (PISA). The PISA scores of school performance at age 18 for 2018 have significantly higher mean scores for science and mathematics in England than the devolved countries, and the scores for reading in Wales were significantly lower than in the other countries of the UK.[66] Nor did markets cause the disparity in GCSE grades between England and Wales, because many schools in both countries were in rural areas where there was no secondary school competition.[67]

The Burgess et al study also showed that the Welsh pupils who had lower performance than their English peers were from poor families going to the schools with the poorer outcomes. Stopping publication of school league tables in Wales had no significant impact on the characteristics of those going to the best 25 per cent of schools.[69] A study comparing GCSE results

Figure 7.5: The percentage (%) of students achieving more than five good grades in GCSE at 16 in England and Wales, from 1993 to 2007

Source: Office for National Statistics.[68]
Note: The Welsh Assembly Government stopped the publication of school league tables from 2002.

between England and Wales by Joanne Cardim-Dias and Luke Sibieta also found that in England the percentage of students eligible for free school meals who achieved five good grades increased from 50 per cent in 2006 to over 60 per cent from 2010.[70] But in Wales the same improvement was from below 20 per cent in 2006 to below 30 per cent in 2012. This dramatic impact of publishing information on school performance was not from choice in a market but making schools accountable to those living locally; in that way, it put pressure on schools shown to have poor results to improve.

In 1999, university financing for the devolved nations was transferred to the Scottish and Welsh governments. In 2001, the Scottish Parliament replaced the up-front tuition fee with a 'graduate endowment fee' of £2,000, to be paid after graduation to fund bursaries for poorer students from Scotland going to Scottish universities.[71] In 2008, when the Scottish National Party led by Alex Salmond won a majority in the Scottish Parliament, they won the vote to abolish the 'graduate endowment' so that undergraduate tuition became 'free' for students from Scotland going to Scottish universities.[72] (Those living in the other countries of the UK paid fees at the same level as universities in England if they went to Scottish universities and when the UK was in the EU, under Treaty obligations, students from any EU country except England, Wales and Northern Ireland were entitled to free tuition in Scottish universities.) On 18 November 2018, which was Alex Salmond's penultimate day as first minister in the Scottish Parliament, he unveiled a commemorative stone at Heriot-Watt University inscribed with his March 2011 commitment to 'free' tuition at university: 'The rocks will melt with the sun before I allow tuition fees to be imposed on Scottish students.'[73] In 2020, a spokesperson for Heriot-Watt University said:

> Following consultation with the Heriot-Watt University Student Union, a decision has been taken to use the current location of the commemorative stone for an alternative public art work which will appeal to our international student community. The stone will be carefully looked after until an alternative location is found for it in future.[74]

The annual cost of free tuition in Scotland was estimated in 2019 to be over £800 million.[75]

What happened to school leavers' access to universities in England and Scotland? A 2019 study of access to higher education by Riddell et al compared Scotland with the other UK countries.[76] In 2010, Scotland had the lowest percentage of 18-year-olds going to university of all the UK's constituent countries (24 per cent compared with 30 per cent in England) and was only the only country where the numbers had fallen (by 2 per cent in 2013), compared with a 2 per cent increase in England. Riddell et al concluded that Scotland's policy of abolishing tuition fees had resulted in a lower proportion of Scottish students from the lower social classes going to universities compared with their English counterparts.[77] A 2019 study of England by Murphy et al found that in England the percentages of students enrolling in universities from the most disadvantaged quintile of wards increased from 10 per cent in 2004 to 20 per cent in 2016, and that there was little change for the proportion of students coming from most advantaged quintile of wards.[78]

Germany also experimented with introducing university fees. In 2005, its Federal Constitutional Court decided that the federal law that banned tuition fees for undergraduate education was unconstitutional. In 2006 and 2007, seven of Germany's 17 regional governments (*Laender*) introduced annual tuition fees of about €1,000 a year, with a comprehensive and generous loans programme that exempted many students (for example, 30 per cent in Bavaria). But, by 2014, all seven *Laender* had abolished tuition fees, on the grounds that they deterred high school graduates from applying to universities. A careful econometric study, by Kerstin Bruckmeier and Berthold Wigger, concluded, however, that the alleged deterrent effect of tuition fees had 'no solid empirical basis'.[79]

Conclusions

In Chile, the voucher system for schools delivered extremes of social segregation – by design. In England, the introduction of the quasi-market with additional funding for disadvantaged children was intended to remedy the selection by house price, which followed from the implementation of comprehensive schools in England and Wales in the 1960s. For the quasi-market information is generated on school performance, in England, from OFSTED reports and league tables of exam results. But the real value of this information is not so much to enable children to travel to better schools, but rather to create a system of 'Tiebout choice' in which the benefits of good local schools are capitalised on with increased house prices and local rents in their catchment areas.

The 2022 examination of inequalities in education in the England by the Institute for Fiscal Studies (IFS) reports this truly dispiriting finding:

> In virtually all OECD countries, literacy and numeracy skills are substantially higher among young people aged 16–24 than among the older generation (aged 55–65). England is the exception to the rule: while its 55- to 65-year-olds perform relatively well, especially in literacy, young people in England have not improved on these skills at all. That has left England ranked 25th out of 32 countries in terms of the literacy skills of its young people.[80]

In the UK's financialised housing market, good schools have become more accessible to affluent parents who are closely involved in the schooling of their children. Parents who are poor tend to have access to poorly performing schools with higher concentrations of problem students, lower parental support, and poor local environments. The 'natural experiment' from the government in Wales abandoning publication of league tables of exam results shows the power of reputation effects in generating non-market incentives to improve the performance of public services and is explored further in the Afterword to this book.

England's marketised system of competing universities financed by income-contingent loans aimed to optimise the size and quality of the sector, encourage innovation, be fiscally neutral and enable equity of access by ability. The outcomes have been disappointing. There are too many universities of low quality charging high fees that are not repaid by their graduates. There has been a lack of innovation. The projected debt of over £500 billion by 2050 entails annual interest payments of around £15 billion, which could be better spent on helping disadvantaged children. Scotland's system of 'free' tuition costs around £800 million, which imposes a similar per capita tax burden to England's on their populations.

Introducing competition between publicly funded providers of school and university education has proved to be far from the simple matter that Shleifer and other neoliberals foresaw. Yet, if the difficulties with realising neoliberal and 'new public management' ideas in education seem considerable, they look to be minor flaws when compared with the devastating impact of markets in healthcare – considered in the next chapter.

Endnotes

[1] Shleifer, Andrei (1998) 'State versus private ownership', *Journal of Economic Perspectives*, vol.12, no. 4, pp.133–150. https://doi.org/10.1257/jep.12.4.133

[2] Friedman, Milton and Friedman, Rose (1990) *Free to choose: A personal statement*, UK: Secker and Warburg, p.162.

[3] Friedman, Milton and Friedman, Rose, *Free to choose*, p.153.

[4] Friedman, Milton and Friedman, Rose, *Free to choose*.

[5] Armytage, Walter (1970) 'The 1870 Education Act', *British Journal of Educational Studies*, vol. 18, no. 2, pp.121–33. https://doi.org/10.1080/00071005.1970.9973277

[6] Beveridge, William (1942) *Social insurance and allied services*, UK: HMSO, p.170. https://archive.org/details/in.ernet.dli.2015.275849/page/n7/mode/2up

[7] Mayhew, Ken; Deer, Cécile; and Dua, Mehak (2004) 'The move to mass higher education in the UK: many questions and some answers', *Oxford Review of Education*, vol. 30, no. 1, p.66. https://doi.org/10.1080/0305498042000190069

[8] Devine, Jack (2014) 'What really happened in Chile: The CIA, the coup against Allende, and the rise of Pinochet', *Foreign Affairs*, vol. 93, no. 4, pp.26–35. https://www.jstor.org/stable/24483554

[9] Goldberg, Peter (1975) 'The politics of the Allende overthrow in Chile', *Political Science Quarterly*, vol. 90, no. 1, pp.93–116. https://doi.org/10.2307/2148700

[10] Fischer, Karin (2009) 'The influence of neoliberals in Chile before, during, and after Pinochet', in Mirowski, Philip and Plehwe, Dieter (eds) (2015) *The road from Mont Pèlerin: The making of the neoliberal thought collective, with a new preface*, UK: Harvard University Press, pp.305–46.

[11] *Encyclopaedia Britannica* (n.d) 'Augusto Pinochet' https://perma.cc/8QZF-ZWRD

[12] Forder, James (2019) 'Friedman in Chile' and 'Friedman and Thatcher'. In *Milton Friedman*, UK: Palgrave Macmillan, pp.42–50 and 61–64.

[13] Hirschman, Albert (1970) *Exit, voice, and loyalty: Responses to decline in firms, organizations, and states*, UK: Harvard University Press.

[14] Bellei, Cristian and Cabalin, Cristian (2013) 'Chilean student movements: Sustained struggle to transform a market-oriented educational system', *Current Issues in Comparative Education*, vol. 15, no. 2, pp.108–23. https://files.eric.ed.gov/fulltext/EJ1016193.pdf

[15] Hart, Julian (1971) 'The inverse care law', *The Lancet*, vol. 297, no. 7696, pp.405–12. https://doi.org/10.1016/S0140-6736(71)92410-X

[16] Le Grand, Julian (2007) 'School education', Chapter 3. In *The other invisible hand: Delivering public services through choice and competition*, UK: Princeton University Press, pp.63–93. https://muse.jhu.edu/pub/267/book/30044

[17] Chitty, Clyde (2004) *Education policy in Britain*, UK: Palgrave, pp.45–54.

[18] Chitty, Clyde, *Education policy in Britain*, pp.50–54.

[19] UCAS, Webpage, BTec Diplomas. https://perma.cc/726L-LD3M

[20] Wilson, Deborah and Piebalga, Anete (2008) 'Performance measures, ranking and parental choice: An analysis of the English school league tables', *International Public Management Journal*, vol. 11, no. 3, pp.344–66. https://doi.org/10.1080/10967490802301336

[21] Department of Education (2022) *The national funding formulae for schools and high needs. 2023–24*, UK: Department of Education. https://assets.publishing.service.gov.uk/government/uploads/system/uploads/attachment_data/file/1091988/2023-24_NFF_Policy_Document_.pdf; Department of Education (2021) 'How does school funding work and how does the Budget affect it?' https://perma.cc/KRN8-ASJU

[22] Department of Education (2022) *The national funding formulae for schools and high needs, 2023–24*.

[23] Bevan, Gwyn (2009) 'The search for a proportionate care law by formula funding in the English NHS', *Financial Accountability & Management*, vol. 25, no. 4, pp.391–410. https://doi.org/10.1111/j.1468-0408.2009.00484.x

[24] Farquharson, Christine; McNally, Sandra; and Tahir, Imran (2022) *Education inequalities*, UK: IFS Deaton Review of Inequalities, p.42. https://ifs.org.uk/inequality/wp-content/uploads/2022/08/Education-inequalities.pdf

[25] Hoxby, Carolyn (2006) *School choice: The three essential elements and several policy options*, Education Forum and New Zealand Association of Economists. Cited by Sibieta, Luke; Chowdry, Haroon; and Muriel, Alastair (2008) *Level playing field? The implications of school funding*, UK: CfBT Education Trust. https://ifs.org.uk/docs/level_playing.pdf

[26] Hoxby, Carolyn, *School choice*.

[27] Hanley, Lynsey (2016) 'Respectable in the nineties', Chapter 4 in *Respectable: The experience of class*, UK: Penguin, pp. 88–121.

[28] Hirsch, Fred (2005) *Social limits to growth*, UK: Routledge, pp. 47–51. https://doi.org/10.4159/harvard.9780674497900

29 West, Anne and Hind, Audrey (2016) *Secondary school admissions in London 2001 to 2015: compliance, complexity and control.* http://eprints.lse.ac.uk/66368/7/West%252C%2520A_Secondary%2520 school%2520admissions%2520in%2520London%25202001%2520to%2520 2015_West_Secondary_school_admissions.pdf

30 Farquharson, Christine et al, *Education inequalities*, pp.81–82.

31 Burgess, Simon; Greaves, Ellen; and Vignoles, Anna (2020) *School places: A fair choice? School choice, inequality and options for reform of school admissions in England*, UK: Sutton Trust, p.8. https://dera.ioe.ac.uk/35131/1/School-Places.pdf

32 Le Grand, Julian, *The other invisible hand: Delivering public services through choice and competition*, p.76.

33 Burgess, Simon et al, *School places*, pp.9–10.

34 Tiebout, Charles (1956) 'A pure theory of local expenditures', *Journal of Political Economy*, vol. 64, no. 5, p.422. https://www.jstor.org/stable/1826343

35 Burgess, Simon et al, *School places*, pp.12–14.

36 Ferreyra, María; Avitabile, Ciro; and Paz, Francisco (2017) *At a crossroads: higher education in Latin America and the Caribbean*, US: World Bank Publications, p.1. https://perma.cc/YX6R-YMDL

37 Timmins, Nicholas (2017) *The five giants: A biography of the welfare state* (3rd edition), UK: HarperCollins, p.600; Barr, Nicholas (2004) 'Higher education funding', *Oxford Review of Economic Policy*, vol. 20, no. 2, p.279. https://doi.org/10.1093/oxrep/grh015

38 This currently numbers 24, with one in Wales, one in Northern Ireland and two in Scotland: University of Birmingham, University of Bristol, University of Cambridge, Cardiff University, Durham University, University of Edinburgh, University of Exeter, University of Glasgow, Imperial College London, King's College London, University of Leeds, University of Liverpool, LSE (London School of Economics and Political Science), University of Manchester, Newcastle University, University of Nottingham, University of Oxford, Queen Mary University of London, Queen's University Belfast, University of Sheffield, University of Southampton, UCL (University College London), University of Warwick, University of York.

39 Oxford was 5th, Cambridge 6th, LSE 11th, Imperial College London 14th, UCL 34th, University of Manchester Institute of Science and Technology 43rd, and Edinburgh 48th. https://perma.cc/3WAE-J8LT

40 Holmes, Richard (2010) 'The THE-QS world university rankings, 2004–2009', *Asian Journal of University Education*, vol. 6, no. 1, pp.1–24. https://perma.cc/8TLV-U6UQ

[41] Barr, Nicholas (2004) 'Higher education funding', *Oxford Review of Economic Policy*, vol. 20, no. 2, pp.264–83. https://doi.org/10.1093/oxrep/grh015

[42] Barr, Nicholas, 'Higher education funding'.

[43] Timmins, Nicholas, *The five giants*, p.630.

[44] Liberal Democrats (2010) 'Liberal Democrat Manifesto 2010'. https://general-election-2010.co.uk/2010-general-election-manifestos /Liberal-Democrat-Party-Manifesto-2010.pdf

[45] Cutts, David and Russell, Andrew (2015) 'From coalition to catastrophe: the electoral meltdown of the Liberal Democrats', *Parliamentary Affairs* vol. 68, no. suppl_1, pp.70–87. https://doi.org/10.1093/pa/gsv028

[46] Paul, Kari (2022) 'Nick Clegg promoted to top Facebook role', *The Guardian*, 16 February. https://perma.cc/C6D3-H9WF

[47] Oxford was 2nd, Cambridge 3rd, Imperial College London 7th, UCL 8th, Edinburgh 16th, University of Manchester 27th, King's College London 35th, and LSE 49th. https://perma.cc/74LZ-LBHU

[48] Muellbauer, John and Soskice, David (2022) *The Thatcher legacy. Lessons for the future of the UK economy*, UK: The Resolution Foundation, p.25. https://perma.cc/7G84-87LN.

[49] Farquharson, Christine et al, *Education inequalities* p.42.

[50] University of Bolton (2023) Webpage. https://perma.cc/M47D-46QJ; London School of Economics and Political Science (2023) Webpage. https://perma.cc/TY9T-9XAL

[51] Sellgren, Katherine (2019) '"Conditional unconditional" offers on the rise', *BBC News*, 17 December. https://perma.cc/DA4Z-MRVV

[52] The Office for Students (2021) *English higher education 2021*. The Office for Students annual review, p.32. https://perma.cc/R7Q3-AKAM

[53] *Higher Education Student Statistics: UK, 2018/19 – Qualifications achieved*. https://perma.cc/L7CR-3T3A

[54] Office for Students (2018) *Analysis of degree classifications over time*. https://perma.cc/JG2Q-TL5Y

[55] Bolton, Paul (2021) *Student loan statistics*, UK: House of Commons Library. https://commonslibrary.parliament.uk/research-briefings/sn01079/

[56] Bank of England (2023) 'Interest rates and Bank Rate'. https://perma.cc/MD4N-T3H7

[57] HM Treasury (2022) 'Table 6.4 Central government own expenditure on services by sub-function, 2017-18 to 2024-25', in *Public Expenditure Statistical Analyses 2022*, p.94.

https://assets.publishing.service.gov.uk/government/uploads/system/uploads/attachment_data/file/1091951/E02754802_PESA_2022_elay.pdf

58 Barr, Nicholas (2012) 'The Higher Education White Paper: The good, the bad, the unspeakable–and the next White Paper', *Social Policy & Administration*, vol. 46, no. 5, pp.483–508. https://doi.org/10.1111/j.1467-9515.2012.00852.x

59 Chowdry, Haroon; Crawford, Claire; Dearden, Lorraine; Goodman, Alissa; and Vignoles, Anna (2010) *Widening participation in higher education: Analysis using linked administrative data*, IFS Working Paper W10/04, http://www.ifs.org.uk/publications/4951; Crawford, Claire; Dearden, Lorraine; Micklewright, John; and Vignoles, Anna (2017) *Family background and university success: Differences in higher education access and outcomes in England*, UK: Oxford University Press. https://doi.org/10.1093/acprof:oso/9780199689132.001.0001. Farquharson, Christine et al, *Education inequalities*, pp.89–90.

60 Barr, Nicholas, 'The Higher Education White Paper'.

61 Bolton, Paul (2011) *Education Maintenance Allowance (EMA) Statistics*, UK: House of Commons Library. https://dera.ioe.ac.uk/22792/1/SN05778.pdf

62 Doyle, Michael and Griffin, Martyn (2012) 'Raised aspirations and attainment? A review of the impact of Aimhigher (2004–2011) on widening participation in higher education in England', *London Review of Education*, vol. 10, no. 1, pp.75–88. http://dx.doi.org/10.1080/14748460.2012.659060

63 Bate, Alex and Foster, David (2017) *Sure Start (England)*, UK: House of Commons Library, Briefing Paper Number 7257. https://commonslibrary.parliament.uk/research-briefings/cbp-7257/

64 *The Guardian* (2001) 'Publication of league tables to be scrapped in Wales', 20 July. https://perma.cc/Y85F-QEFK

65 Burgess, Simon; Wilson, Deborah; and Worth, Jack (2013) 'A natural experiment in school accountability: The impact of school performance information on pupil progress', *Journal of Public Economics*, vol. 106, pp.57–67. https://doi.org/10.1016/j.jpubeco.2013.06.005

66 Sizmur, Juliet; Ager, Robert; Bradshaw, Jenny; Classick, Rachel; Galvis, Maria; Packer, Joanna; Thomas, David; and Wheater, Rebecca (2019) *Achievement of 15-year-olds in England: PISA 2018 results*, UK: Department of Education, pp.17–18. https://perma.cc/EH4X-LF6P

67 Burgess et al, 'A natural experiment in school accountability: The impact of school performance information on pupil progress', p.66.

68 Office for National Statistics (2009) *Regional trends online tables*. https://www.data.gov.uk/dataset/f41ac1bf-1612-4a55-ace1-b0cff2def937/regional-trends-online-tables

69 Burgess et al, 'A natural experiment in school accountability: The impact of school performance information on pupil progress', p.63.

70 Cardim-Dias, Joana and Sibieta, Luke (2022) *Inequalities in GCSE results across England and Wales*, UK: Education Policy Institute. https://epi.org.uk/wp-content/uploads/2022/07/Inequalities-in-Wales -and-England.pdf

71 Masetti, Francesca (2019) *Devolution in Scotland and the case study of the Scottish higher education system*, European Diversity & Autonomy Papers, EDAP 01/2019. https://bia.unibz.it/esploro/outputs/journalArticle/Devolution-in -Scotland-and-the-Case/991005772704701241

72 *BBC News* (2008) 'MSPs vote to scrap endowment fee', 28 February. https://perma.cc/5L2P-ZJXZ

73 Havergal, Chris (2014) 'Salmond unveils 'free tuition' monument at Heriot-Watt', *Times Higher Education Supplement*, 18 November. https://perma.cc/L2KA-6M2L

74 Hutcheon, Paul (2020) 'Heriot Watt University to remove stone unveiled by Alex Salmond', *Daily Record*, 20 May. https://perma.cc/U6E9-K2TX

75 Scottish Parliament Information Centre (2019) *The price of free tuition in Scotland*. https://perma.cc/RYB4-ZRJG

76 Riddell, Sheila; Blackburn, Lucy; and Minty, Sarah (2013) *Widening access to higher education: Scotland in UK comparative perspective*, UK: University of Edinburgh. http://www.docs.hss.ed.ac.uk/education/creid/NewsEvents/52_v_CoWA _Paper.pdf

77 Riddell, Sheila et al, 'Widening access to higher education', p.18. (These classes are: 4, Small employers and own account workers; 5, Lower supervisory and technical occupations; 6, Semi-routine occupations; and 7, Routine occupations.)

78 Murphy, Richard; Scott-Clayton, Judith; and Wyness, Gill (2019) 'The end of free college in England: Implications for enrolments, equity, and quality', *Economics of Education Review*, vol. 71, pp.7–22. https://doi.org/10.1016/j.econedurev.2018.11.007

79 Bruckmeier, Kerstin and Wigger, Berthold (2014) 'The effects of tuition fees on transition from high school to university in Germany', *Economics of Education Review*, vol. 41, pp.14–23. https://doi.org/10.1016/j.econedurev.2014.03.009

80 Farquharson, Christine et al, *Education inequalities*, p.2.

8. Healthcare: to marketise or not to marketise?

Selfishness beats altruism within groups. Altruistic groups beat selfish groups. The rest is commentary.

David Wilson[1]

Kenneth Arrow won the Nobel Prize in Economics in 1951 for his development of a theory of how effective markets work.[2] A decade later, he set out the root causes of why markets would fail for healthcare in a famous 1963 paper: uncertainty in the incidence of diseases and efficacy of treatments; and doctors (suppliers) not patients ('consumers') frame the demand for care.[3] In that paper he also made the penetrating observation that, although a system like that of the British National Health Service (NHS) looks to be based on altruism and redistribution, it can also be seen as a highly beneficial insurance arrangement that pools risk over generations. This is a working example of John Rawls's social contract. Rawls's theory of *justice as fairness* used the device of a 'veil of ignorance' as a fair and consensual way of agreeing distributional questions in a social contract for a fair society.[4] Behind that 'veil of ignorance', we would not know, for example, what job we might have – an investment banker? A nurse? – in deciding how much we think different jobs should be paid we should choose without knowing which slot would be ours.

For most of us, for most of our lives, we live with no certain knowledge of what our future needs for healthcare might be. Behind that 'veil of ignorance', the NHS makes sense as a social contract that is financed by ability to pay, and gives free access according to health need. The private sector can successfully pool and price idiosyncratic risk for cars and houses, but not the systemic risk of ageing populations and pandemics.[5] Aneurin Bevan recognised the great boon from government organising risk pooling across generations:

Society becomes more wholesome, more serene and spiritually healthier if it knows that its citizens have at the back of their

How to cite this book chapter:

Bevan, Gwyn (2023) *How Did Britain Come to This? A century of systemic failures of governance*, London: LSE Press, pp. 197–219. https://doi.org/10.31389/lsepress.hdb.h License: CC BY-NC consciousness the knowledge that not only themselves, but all their fellows, have access, when ill to the best that medical care can provide.[6]

No country has an optimal system of healthcare that satisfies the three objectives that make up its 'iron triangle': cost control, equity of access according to need, and high performance.[7] The first section of this chapter looks at a 'natural experiment' of Canada and the US. That experiment shows the advantages of the way the NHS is financed for effective cost control *and* equity. The abiding weakness of the NHS is the lack of systems that deliver high performance. That is why, paradoxically, the Thatcher government looked at lessons from the United States in trying to marketise the NHS. The second section examines the transaction costs of the model of an NHS internal market (that is, with no change to the way it is financed), which has been tried by Conservative, Labour and coalition governments. This examination shows that the internal market model is designed to fail, which poses the question: if we abandon markets, how do we generate incentives to improve performance? The third section gives evidence of how that can be done by designing systems of public reporting that impact on the reputations of those who deliver healthcare. As there is no prospect of substantial increases in the NHS funding over the next decade, the final section is about how it can manage by developing systems to improve the way we allocate its resources.

8.1 Equity and cost control in Canada but not the US

In 1961, Ronald Reagan raised the alarm about the US abandoning its reliance on private markets to finance healthcare.[8] The target of his criticism was what became, from 1965, the federal programme of Medicare in the US for insuring the elderly (and disabled). Reagan saw this as leading to the hell of 'socialised medicine', and communism. His belief in constraining health demands on government by making people face up to the costs of healthcare was shared by the finance director of a not-for-profit hospital in Greensborough, North Carolina. When I met him, in the summer of 1983, he had to take an urgent phone call. It involved negotiations with a couple over what they would be required to pay, every month, for the rest of their lives, for their baby to be given life-saving care in his hospital's neonatal intensive care unit.

The US's system was designed to produce hardship for the couple and deficits for the neonatal intensive care unit. This was because so many of the babies needing that care were from poor families without health insurance. When, in 2009, President Obama proposed legislation to reduce the number of uninsured Americans he received a citizen's letter that read: 'I don't want government-run healthcare. I don't want socialized medicine. And don't touch my Medicare.'[9]

Canada used to have similar systems to the US's for insurance and delivery of healthcare. Coverage was incomplete and entailed high user charges. Hospitals and doctors were independent of government and paid according to the services they supplied. From 1971, the Canadian federal government instead became the single payer in a universal system of insurance for hospitals and doctors that was free at the point of delivery, but made no changes to the organisation of the delivery of care. Figure 8.1 shows how the two health systems in the US and Canada operated before and after 1971. In the US system, only 80 per cent of people were insured and they faced high user charges, so conventional (demand and supply) economic analysis would predict that its future costs would be lower than Canada's. However, Figure 8.2

Figure 8.1: Healthcare systems in the United States and Canada

Aspect	**US**	**Canada before 1971**	**Canada after 1971**
Hospitals	Private (funded by charges for all care)		
Doctors	Fee for service		
Insurers	Multiple		Monopoly
Coverage	Incomplete		Universal
Patients	User charges		'Free'

Figure 8.2: Healthcare expenditure as a percentage (%) of GDP in Canada and the US, 1965 to 2021

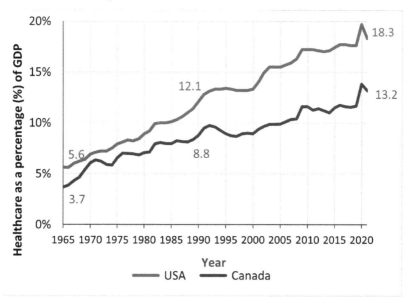

Source: Centers for Medicare & Medicaid Services (US); Canadian Institute for Health Information, Government of Canada, and CountryEconomy.com (Canada).[10]

shows the outcomes of this 'natural experiment': the costs of the system in the US increasingly escalated well past those of Canada.

Robert Evans (professor of economics at the University of British Columbia) developed an economic explanation of why Canada, by implementing an equitable system, had discovered that it had also implemented a highly effective system of cost control.[11] Health insurance covers the risk of needing healthcare when you are healthy: once you have cancer or a chronic disease and continue to need healthcare, it ceases to be insurance. The US system of multiple health insurers and incomplete coverage is designed to generate incentives for each insurer to shift costs on to another payer, and direct their efforts to risk detection and selection. In any population, the most costly 5 per cent of people typically account for more than 50 per cent of the total annual costs of care.[12] The way that multiple insurers resolved their weakness in negotiations with suppliers of healthcare was by increasing premiums. In Canada, as there was universal coverage, the government avoided the deadweight loss from spending effort on risk selection. And, as a single payer, it had to confront total costs and was empowered to do so. Evans emphasises that, in healthcare, effective cost control is directed at providers. He laments that:

> economic analysis has been largely incapable of grasping this process [and] encouraged a fruitless concern with the prices faced by patients, while ignoring the overwhelming significance of the structure and objectives of the insurer.[13]

In 1971, in the US, the RAND organisation began a quite remarkable experiment to evaluate the impacts of user charges on costs and health outcomes under traditional indemnity insurance.[14] Families were randomly allocated to four levels of medical costs that they would have to pay in the RAND roulette wheel of (mostly) misfortune: only a lucky minority had 'free' care; others had to pay 25, 50 and 95 per cent of their medical costs. (Would that experiment be deemed to be ethical now?) That study found that high user charges did (as expected) deter people from seeking care *and reduced their use of effective acute care by about a third.* User charges as a policy instrument suffer the same conflicts of income-contingent loans for undergraduate university education (detailed in Chapter 7): charges are required to both deter and not deter people from seeking care when they are ill.

The RAND experiment also compared different levels of user charges (under traditional indemnity insurance) with the radically different model of the health maintenance organisation (HMO). That model integrated the roles of insurer and provider of secondary, primary and preventive healthcare. HMOs are financed by capitation: families enrolled with an HMO pay a monthly rate (regardless of services used). They have free access to a primary care physician (equivalent to a general practitioner), who acts as gatekeeper to specialised services and restricts their choices. Although integration has potential to be an optimal form of organising care, to achieve that requires satisfying a demanding set of conditions.[15] Integration of healthcare is now being developed in less ambitious ways in the US in accountable care organisations.[16] RAND found that the per capita expenditure on health services of those enrolled with the HMO Group Health Cooperative of Puget Sound was 40 per cent lower than free care under traditional indemnity insurance, which was the same as those required to pay 95 per cent of their medical cost. The HMO, however, achieved these cost savings without reducing use of effective care. That is why the RAND study suggested that the NHS arrangement of free access to a GP who acts as a gatekeeper is more appropriate than high user charges as a way of organising access to healthcare.

In 2001, Uwe Reinhardt (professor of political economy at Princeton University) argued that, since the publication of Arrow's 1963 paper, health economics and health policy in the US had been fuelled by the vain hope that:

> with the aid of better information technology … the efficient allocation of health care resources could be entrusted to the 'invisible hand' of a price-competitive marketplace, which economists are uniquely qualified to understand.[17]

The outcomes of this market failure have been appalling outcomes on all three vertices of the 'iron triangle':

- Inequity: the US is one of the three OECD countries (with Mexico and Poland) with the lowest percentage of population coverage for core health services.
- Poor performance: the US is the only OECD country to report a fall in life expectancy between 2012 and 2017.
- Failure to control costs: the US has the highest spend on healthcare (nearly 17 per cent in 2018, compared with 9.8 per cent for the UK).[18]

The 2021 report from the Commonwealth Fund found that, compared to 10 other countries, 'Americans of all incomes have the hardest time affording the healthcare they need' and the system 'ranks at the bottom on health care outcomes'.[19] The US's system of employer-based health insurance is a tax on jobs: in 2019, the annual cost for insuring an employee's family would be about $21,000.[20] As Anne Case and Angus Deaton argued, this stymies attempts to develop new opportunities for employment in the areas that have experienced deindustrialisation.[21]

8.2 An internal market for hospitals: a concept lost in translation?

In 1985, Alain Enthoven (a Stanford professor who had worked for RAND) described England's NHS as suffering from 'gridlock'.[22] For the US, he had been a strong advocate of the competing HMO model as a means of developing universal coverage.[23] He proposed for the NHS that the government implemented two changes.[24] First, it should transform the existing 200 local district health authorities (districts) into the HMO model (as described above), but without competition and defined geographically (Figure 8.3a). In the NHS in 1985, districts were responsible for secondary, community and preventive healthcare but primary care was delivered by independent contractors. Enthoven argued strongly for making districts responsible for integrating primary and secondary care. Second, he recommended creating an 'internal market', in which each district could threaten those suppliers (hospitals or GPs) providing poor services with loss of jobs by outsourcing to other providers.

One reason why the US spends so much on healthcare is that it has such a high rate of pay for doctors and nurses. OECD estimated that, in 2017, hospital prices in the US were nearly twice those of the UK.[25] After making prices comparable, Richard Feachem et al found in 2002 that a Californian HMO, Kaiser Permanente, achieved:

> better performance at roughly the same cost as the NHS because of integration throughout the system, efficient management of hospital use, the benefits of competition, and greater investment in information technology.[26]

A year later, Ham et al reported that the use of hospital beds in the NHS for 11 leading causes of admission was three and a half times that of Kaiser's standardised rate. They highlighted the reasons for Kaiser's superior performance were the integration of all elements along care pathways of prevention, diagnosis and treatment in primary, inpatient and outpatient care.[27]

Under the influence of neoliberal and 'new public management' thinking, the Thatcher government implemented an 'internal market' based on a 'purchaser/provider' split. Districts were the principal purchasers; providers were local hospitals and community service units that became self-governing providers. Districts as 'purchasers' were to assess the needs of their local populations and meet them by contracting selectively with providers that were to compete on price and quality. The governments of Margaret Thatcher in 1989, Tony Blair in 2002, and the coalition in 2010 tried to develop hospital competition under different arrangements in which GPs were on the purchaser side of the split.[28] The failures of the Thatcher and Blair internal markets were described in Chapter 1. The third attempt by the coalition in legislation

Figure 8.3: The NHS as a hierarchy (in 1980) and its 'internal market' form (in 2012)

(a) Pre-reform (1980) structure

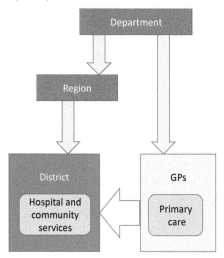

(b) Post-2012 reform structure

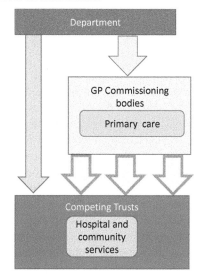

Source: Author.

was described as 'Dr Lansley's monster' (Andrew Lansley was the minister responsible).[29] In the Lansley model, which was implemented in 2012, funding went primarily to the grouping of GP practices. They ran primary care directly and 'commissioned' hospital care and community services from competing NHS and independent providers (Figure 8.3b). It was so controversial that it was subjected to an unprecedented 'pause', whilst the proposals were reviewed, and subjected to 2,000 amendments.[30] It was criticised by an unprecedented joint editorial condemning the bill in the leading journals for the medical profession (*British Medical Journal*), managers (*Health Service Journal*) and nurses (*Nursing Times*), for resulting in upheaval that 'has been unnecessary, poorly conceived, badly communicated, and a dangerous distraction at a time when the NHS is required to make unprecedented savings'.[31] Thus, Enthoven's 1985 proposals for care integration on HMO lines were completely lost in translation by the Thatcher government in 1989 and subsequent 'reforms'.[32] Such integration is particularly important for the effective management of chronic diseases in an ageing population. Dr Lansley's monster was abandoned because it obstructed the integration needed in caring for an ageing population.[33]

Figures 8.4 and 8.5 apply my translation of Williamson's framework to examine the model of local districts or GP commissioners contracting selectively with hospitals for the care of their populations. They show that asking NHS purchasers to contract with hospitals raises a red flag on all six of Williamson's criteria. Districts and GP commissioners alike have faced profound uncertainty over the future complex needs of their populations – as shown so vividly by the changing impacts of the global pandemic of Covid-19 on admissions to hospitals and intensive care units (ICUs) (see Chapter 9). Hence contracts were necessarily incomplete. The asymmetry of information was so difficult to overcome because 'purchasers' depended on hospitals to determine the need for patients' care once they were referred or admitted as an emergency and lacked data on the quality of most of the care provided. There was little supply-side flexibility. The assets of a hospital are highly specific and for most services (emergency and chronic care) they need to be local. That created problems even in closing hospital departments, and ruled out letting 'failing' hospitals exit the market. Although hospital care is provided frequently, Chapter 1 gave examples showing that this did not enable 'purchasers' to become more skilled in contracting and monitoring. Reviews consistently found systemic weaknesses in commissioning or contracting where this has been tried in several country cases.[34] It was one of those sad cases where contracting over 10 years is one year's experience 10 times over.

The 'atmosphere' in which patients are treated is crucial. Timothy Besley and Maitreesh Ghatak argue that high performance of public services follows from matching their missions to the motivation of those who deliver them.[35] So, for example, teachers who derive intense satisfaction from educating the

Figure 8.4: Causes of high transaction costs in contracting with hospitals

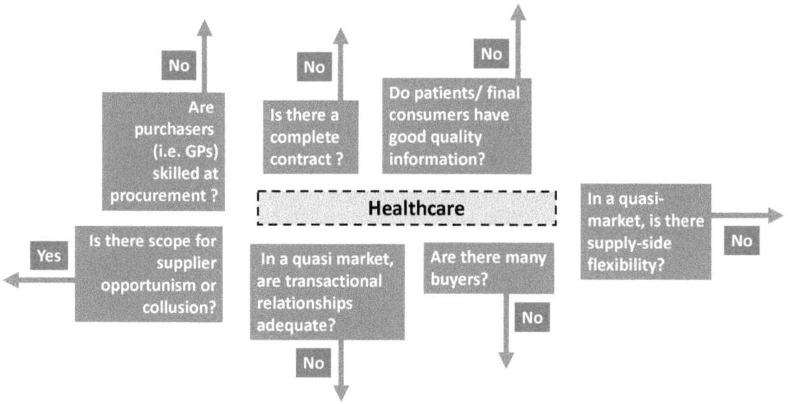

Source: Author.

Figure 8.5: Describing the high transaction costs of contracting with hospitals

Question	High transaction costs in using a market
1. Can a complete contract be specified?	No. The 'purchaser' is uncertain over when and at what scale a service will be needed and the service needed is too complex to be specified in advance.
2. Is the buyer able to assess the adequacy of the quality and costs of what is supplied?	No. Hospitals can supply services that a well-informed purchaser would not want to pay for, and 'quality shade' services in ways that purchasers would find very hard to detect.
3. Is there supply-side flexibility?	No. There are few accessible local hospitals, those that fail do not exit the market, and the dominant suppliers are not challenged by new entrants.
4. Are there many buyers?	No. Hospitals have had to invest in assets (equipment and staff) that are specific to the 'purchaser'.
5. Is the transactional relationship between buyer and supplier adequate to cover all aspects?	No. The quality of service supplied is impaired by a transactional relationship – 'atmosphere' matters.
6. Is there scope for suppliers to behave with opportunism?	Yes: the 'purchaser' is vulnerable to being exploited by being overcharged for an excessive or inadequate volume of services of poor quality.
7. Is the buyer a skilled purchaser?	No. The service is so complex and uncertain that there is no 'learning by doing' from contracting over time.

young will not seek large financial rewards. Much of modern medical professionalism stress how vital it is that healthcare is delivered by committed staff who continuously put patients' interests first. The scandal described in Chapter 1 at Mid Staffordshire hospital showed the appalling consequences of running a hospital that had lost sight of Florence Nightingale's first principle, to do the sick no harm. So, in the NHS, the contracts between purchasers and hospitals can only work if they are not transactional but relational and built on trust. But a hospital will only enter into a relational contract without the threat of competition.

8.3 Designing public reporting systems to improve performance

Most people want good local public services – for them, having choice is of secondary importance. Those who advocate choice in markets argue that is the key means to the end of providing good local public services. The choice mechanism would improve the quality of hospital care if those needing care were well-informed about differences in the quality of different hospitals, and could exercise choice and go to those with high quality of care.[36] But systematic reviews of public reporting of hospital performance in the US found that it had no impact on choice of hospitals by patients; and, after hospitals had been publicly reported as performing poorly, sometimes they improved quality and sometimes they did not.[37]

Judith Hibbard's explanation of this puzzle was that public reporting could generate powerful incentives for a poorly performing hospital to improve if it were designed to inflict damage on its reputation. She cites her study of a controlled experiment in Wisconsin, which specified four requirements for public reporting to drive improvements through its impacts on reputations:

- performance needs to be ranked;
- the ranking has to be designed to make clear where performance is good or poor;
- the information has to be published in forms that are easily and widely accessible for all to see; and
- performance information must be produced regularly.[38]

In healthcare, three different systems of public reporting that satisfied those criteria have given strong evidence of the power of reputation, even though each system was initially designed to drive change through market mechanisms.

The first system is the Cardiac Surgery Reporting System (CSRS) of estimating risk-adjusted mortality rates (RAMRs) by surgeon and hospital, which began in 1989 in New York State. Those who benefit most from cardiac surgery are at highest risk of dying from the operation. So, the skilled surgeons who operate on difficult cases tend to have the highest mortality rates. That was why Mark Chassin, who was then the commissioner for health in New York State, developed a good method of risk adjustment for public reporting. Over the next three years, New York State's risk-adjusted mortality fell by 41 per cent.[39] It 'had the lowest risk-adjusted mortality rate of any state in the nation and the most rapid rate of decline of any state with below-average mortality'.[40] Chassin emphasised that market forces played no role in driving that improvement. Patients did not switch from hospitals that were statistical outliers with high mortality, nor to those with low mortality. Nor did HMOs switch their contracts for their insured populations.[41] The CSRS was designed to inflict reputational damage on hospitals that were statistical outliers with high mortality. And Chassin found that it was those hospitals that made efforts to improve their quality of care.[42]

The second system is the regime of 'star ratings' that was implemented in the NHS in England from 2000 to 2005 (as mentioned in Chapter 1). Figure 1.1 showed the scale at which the Blair government threw money at the NHS from 2000 onwards, which applied to England, Scotland, Wales and Northern Ireland.[43] After the election of the Blair government in 1997, under governance by 'trust and altruism' (see Chapter 1), hospitals that failed to meet targets for reducing waiting times received extra funding. This system of perverse incentives rewarded failure, and continued, after 2000, in the devolved governments in Scotland, Wales and Northern Ireland.[44] Only in England, however, did the government require fundamental change in its implicit contract with the NHS to transform its performance. *The NHS Plan* of 2000 set out demanding targets for reducing hospital waiting times in England as set by the Prime Minister's Delivery Unit. The Department of Health changed the rules of the game to ensure these targets were met. Under England's 'star rating' regime, those who worked in hospitals that missed the targets were no longer rewarded with more money but punished instead.[45] In the 'star rating' regime, NHS trusts that 'failed' were zero-rated, and 'high-performing' NHS trusts were awarded three stars. The chief executives of 'failing' trusts were at high risk of being sacked, as happened to six of the 12 failing hospitals ('the dirty dozen') in the first set of 'star ratings'. This threat was initially seen to be the key driver to deliver the required transformation in NHS performance. I was involved in the development of 'star ratings' when I worked at the Commission for Health Improvement. In the meetings I had with those running acute hospitals, I came to understand the power of the reputational impacts of publishing 'star ratings'. One chief executive told me that what she most feared about her hospital being demoted from a three-star to a two-star trust was how that would be the lead story in her local newspaper at the weekend.

At the CHI, we were responsible for reviewing the implementation of clinical governance in England and Wales (see Chapter 1). I was stunned by the decision of the government in Wales not to develop any comparable system of public reporting of performance. I was told by an official that, having abandoned school league tables (see Chapter 7), it was inconceivable that the government in Wales would introduce an analogous system into its NHS. In 2005 the Auditor General for Wales issued three damning reports on the dreadful performance of NHS in Wales as compared with England.[46] In 2005, the sum of the two waiting time targets to be referred to a specialist *and* admitted for an operation was nine months in England and three years in Wales (see Figure 8.6). Furthermore, hospitals hit their targets in England and missed them in Wales. In Wales in 2005 there was no commitment to match the transformation in the performance in England, where (by 2008) hospitals were hitting the target waiting time of 18 weeks from referral by a GP to admission for an elective operation. And, in 2005, ambulances met 75 per cent of life-threatening emergency calls within the target response time of eight minutes in England, whereas this was only 55 per cent in Wales.

The third system is the Tuscan Performance Evaluation System (PES) in Italy's national health service, which is modelled on the UK's NHS. The Italian

Figure 8.6: Waiting time targets (in weeks) in England and Wales

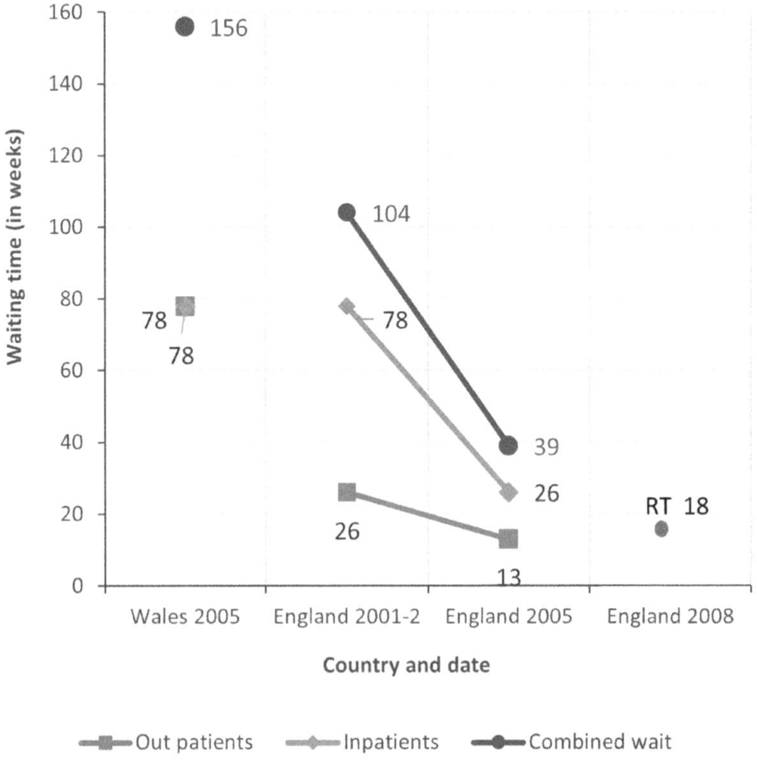

Sources: Auditor General for Wales and Department of Health.[47]

health service is devolved to 21 regions (five are autonomous provinces) that are similar in some respects to the devolved nations of the UK. They are funded centrally but have autonomy over the structure and governance of their health services. Italy's national outcome evaluation programme (NOEP) measures and publicly reports the performance of each region against minimum standards for essential levels of care (Livelli Essenziali di Assistenza or LEAs). They are held to account by central government in a system similar to that of the NHS 'star rating' regime: failure to eliminate financial deficits or to achieve a minimum grid score on its LEAs can result in the sacking of the region's president and the chief executive officers of local providers.

The Tuscan PES began, in 2006, as an initiative by Tuscany's elected regional councillor for health. He funded a research unit, MeSLab, led by Sabina Nuti at the elite Scuola Sant'Anna in Pisa, to develop what became the Tuscan PES. The regional councillor aimed to drive improvement by using that PES in deciding performance-related pay for the chief executives in its 12 local health authorities. They were responsible for planning and running healthcare for their populations.

By 2012, 12 'regions' had voluntarily chosen to use the Tuscan PES in the network of the Inter-Regional Performance Evaluation System (IRPES). Each region processed its own data and used the same set of indicators for benchmarking. The results were shown by region and by health authorities.[48] Figure 8.7 shows how the Tuscan dartboard displayed 160 indicators across eight dimensions (population health, efficiency, user and staff satisfaction, meeting strategic goals, types of care, and governance) for the two regions of Marche and Tuscany. The dots represent the performance of the composite indicators and are organised into segments for each dimension of performance. Indicators with excellent performance are in the green zones near the centre of the dartboard; those with poor performance are in the red zone on the outer circle. The health of the population is reported above the dartboard to highlight that it represents the ultimate goal towards of every health district.

Comparing two regions, Figure 8.7 clearly shows that, on most indicators, Tuscany had better performance than Marche. The dartboard ranks performance but avoids the crudity of systems that aggregate performance across multiple indicators to give a single rank (as in star rating and the annual health check). Such crude rankings cast an unjustified shadow on those delivering a high-quality service in an organisation with a poor ranking in aggregate and vice-versa.

In the Tuscany region, MeSLab presented results to six-monthly stock-take meetings of the senior managers and clinicians, and heads of departments of the districts and region. Managers and clinicians in Tuscany were closely involved in the development of the indicators and were trained by the Sant'Anna School of Advanced Studies in the use of this information. Those whose service performed poorly on an indicator could learn from those who performed well.

Figure 8.7: The Tuscan system dartboards displaying the health performance of two regions, Tuscany and Marche, in 2015

(a) Tuscany

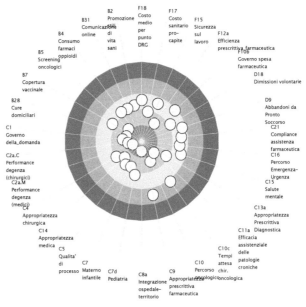

One evaluation of Italy's 'natural experiment' with different systems of governance in its 21 'regions' compared performance across 14 indicators in 2007 and how that had changed over the next five years.[49] This showed that all five 'regions' that published rankings improved their performance. The performance of Lombardy deteriorated markedly. This is the only region in Italy that has persisted with trying to make hospital competition work.[50] Tuscany had good performance in 2007 and improved to be the best in 2012. In 2015 the regional councillor for health decided to end its system of performance-related pay for chief executives in making savings in response to a financial crisis. However, this change had no effect because its performance evaluation system was still used to hold them to account for performance and had become embedded in a social process of collegial benchmark competition.

(b) Marche

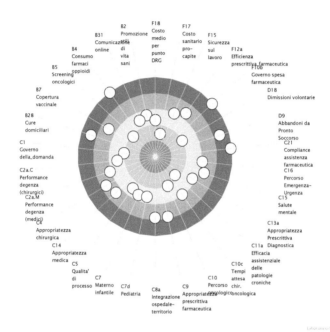

Marche

Valutazione dello stato di salute della popolazione. Anni 2011-2013

A10 Stili di vita (PASSI) A4 Mortalita' per suicidi A2 Mortalita' per tumori A3 Mortalita' per malattie circolatorie A1 Mortalita' infantile

Bersaglio 2015

Source: Nuti and Vola, MeSLab.[51]

Notes: Each 'dartboard' shows performance in that region on a wide range of different performance indicators, specific to each area of health system operations. The white dot shows how close to the central target aspiration performance got, across five ratings from very good (green) to poor (red). In this figure, Tuscany (with almost outcomes within the green and yellow zones) clearly performs better than Marche (where few results are in green zones, and others spread out more into the orange and red zones).

8.4 Managing the commons

Like all healthcare systems, the NHS struggles with competing demands on its common pool of resources. The nature of that collective action problem was vividly captured by the English economist William Forster Lloyd. In his 1833 pamphlet, he used the analogy of shepherds sharing the commons for grazing their sheep. Each shepherd gains if he can increase his sheep over his allotted number but, if they all do, that results in the unrestrained overgrazing of the commons and all shepherds then lose any grazing at all. Lloyd's pamphlet was developed by Garrett Hardin into the economic theory of the 'Tragedy of the Commons', which was published in *Science* in 1968. He argued that the only way to resolve the tragedy was by assigning property rights, even though that would result in injustice, because that outcome 'is preferable to total ruin'.[52] Since then, however, Elinor Ostrom's substantial body of empirical research showed that groups of small to moderate size could manage common-pool resources without assigning property rights.[53] The principles of how to do that for healthcare have been developed by Ronald Dworkin, Norman Daniels and James Sabin, and they offer different approaches at the national and local levels.

We generate our common pool of resources for healthcare when we are able to work by paying for others who are too sick, too young or too old to do so. For Ronald Dworkin, that frames our willingness to pay for insurance for healthcare over a lifetime:

> Most young people on reflection would not think it prudent to buy insurance that could keep them alive by expensive medical intervention, for four or five months at the most, if they had already lived into old age. They would think it wiser to spend what that insurance would cost on better health care earlier, or on education, or training or investment that would, provide greater benefit or more important security.[54]

Norman Daniels has argued that we ought to give priority to services directed at the young because that helps them survive into old age and they have greater potential life years to gain from treatment. This is a key way to achieve greater equity in life expectancy.[55] A tension in the NHS constitution is that it aims to be available irrespective of age and 'to promote equality through … particular attention to groups or sections of society where improvements in health and life expectancy are not keeping pace with the rest of the population'.[56]

The systems of resource allocation in the NHS aim to allocate resources to local populations according to need. But the way those resources are used shows dramatic unwarranted variations in patterns of expenditures and rates of treatment for different types of care.[57] The local systems that deliver healthcare have evolved over time in different ways. They were not designed to make optimal use of our limited resources. To do that we need to reorganise our local healthcare systems (prevention, primary and hospital care, and rehabilitation) for different conditions.

Daniels and Sabin proposed a process for doing this in their 'Accountability for Reasonableness' framework.[58] This requires the development of a rationale, based on relevant evidence, reasons and principles, for making decisions in a process that is publicly accessible and that allows scope for revisions and appeals, and regulation to ensure these conditions are met. A start on doing this was made in the NHS in meetings with stakeholders (including patients, carers, doctors, nurses, managers, treasurers) to compare the value for money of different interventions along the care pathway for the same condition (for example, stroke, low back pain). These analyses typically show that most resources are consumed by hospital admissions that produce little value. As a result, only limited resources are available for undertaking the early interventions that are high value and can prevent the worsening of people's condition and need for hospitalisation. Hence there is considerable scope to increase the value produced by the NHS by reallocating how we as a society use our resources.[59]

Conclusions

As Arrow explained in 1963, markets will fail for healthcare. There is strong evidence that:

- User charges as a means of cost control belong in the firmament of zombie economics.
- Providing information for insurers and users on the performance of hospitals has little impacts on their market shares.
- Purchasers fail to contract selectively with providers of healthcare.

But there are working examples of effective to alternatives to markets in healthcare. The UK and Canada developed effective systems of cost control based on universal coverage, financed by taxation, free at the point of delivery. These are obviously more equitable than the patchwork of arrangements of incomplete coverage in the US, characterised by high user charges, spending the highest share of GDP across the OECD, and exceptionally having falling life expectancy. We can improve performance of providers of healthcare by developing well-designed systems of public reporting that can lead to improvements. These systems generate high-powered incentives from their impacts on the reputations of those who provide services. (This is also what was found to be the main impact from publishing information on school performance in exams in England and Wales, as described in Chapter 7.)

Looking back to the various radical policies of the coalition government from 2010 to 2015, it is difficult to decide which did most harm: cuts in funding for local government and social care?[60] Universal credit?[61] Finance of undergraduate university education?[62] Abolition of schemes to enable children from poor families to benefit from education?[63] But it seems that, out of this rich cornucopia, the prime minister, David Cameron, believed that it was Dr Lansley's 'monster' reorganisation, which subjected the English NHS to unnecessary and misconceived radical reform (and relegated adult social care to malign neglect). Thankfully, that third abortive attempt to make an internal market work in the NHS has been abandoned. But Lansley's monster also had the collateral damage of fatally undermining England's public health capability to respond to a global pandemic – the subject of the next chapter.

Endnotes

[1] Wilson, David (2015) *Does altruism exist? Culture, genes, and the welfare of others*, UK: Yale University Press. https://doi.org/10.12987/9780300206753

[2] Nobel Prize (2023) 'Kenneth J. Arrow – Facts'. https://perma.cc/6Z39-KK3T

[3] Arrow, Kenneth (1963) 'Uncertainty and the welfare economics of medical care', *American Economic Review*, vol. 53, no. 1–2, pp.941–73. https://www.jstor.org/stable/1816184

[4] Rawls, John (1973) *A theory of justice*, UK: Oxford University Press, pp.17–22, 118–83.

[5] I am grateful to Jonathan Lane for making this point.

[6] Bevan, Aneurin (1978) *In place of fear*, UK: Quartet Books, p.100.

[7] Bevan, Gwyn; Helderman, Jan-Kees; and Wilsford, David (2010) 'Changing choices in health care: Implications for equity, efficiency and cost', *Health Economics, Policy and Law*, vol. 5, no. 3, pp.251–67.

[8] fusion07mp4 (2010) 'Ronald Reagan – Medicare will bring a socialist dictatorship'. [Video]. *YouTube*, 14 December. https://www.youtube.com/watch?v=Bejdhs3jGyw

[9] Cesca, Bob (2017) 'Keep your goddamn government hands off my Medicare!' *Huffpost*, 5 September. https://perma.cc/XQ6F-FV6J

[10] Centers for Medicare and Medicaid Services (2022) *Historical* [National Health Expenditure Accounts]. https://www.cms.gov/Research-Statistics-Data-and-Systems/Statistics-Trends-and-Reports/NationalHealth ExpendData/NationalHealthAccountsHistorical; Canadian Institute for Health Information (2022) *National health expenditure trends*. https://www.cihi.ca/en/national-health-expenditure-trends#data-tables; Government of Canada (1992) *Public finance historical data 1965/66– 1991/92*. https://publications.gc.ca/collections/collection_2016/statcan /CS68-512-1992.pdf; CountryEconomy.com (2022) *Canada GDP – gross domestic product*. https://perma.cc/XE8K-LRPZ

[11] Evans, Robert G. (1987) 'Public health insurance: The collective purchase of individual care', *Health Policy*, vol. 7, no. 2, pp.115–34. https://doi.org/10.1016/0168-8510(87)90026-1

[12] Berk, Marc and Monheit, Alan (2001) 'The concentration of health care expenditures, revisited', *Health Affairs*, vol. 20, no. 2, pp.9–18. https://doi.org/10.1377/hlthaff.20.2.9

[13] Evans, Robert, 'Public health insurance: the collective purchase of individual care'.

[14] Brook, Robert; Lohr, Kathleen; and Keeler, Emmett (2006) *The health insurance experiment: A classic RAND study speaks to the current health care reform debate*, US: RAND Corporation. https://perma.cc/FD68-LPDA

[15] Bevan, Gwyn and Janus, Katharina (2011) 'Why hasn't integrated health care developed widely in the United States and not at all in England?' *Journal of Health Politics, Policy and Law*, vol. 36, no. 1, pp.141–64. https://doi.org/10.1215/03616878-1191135

[16] Alderwick, Hugh; Shortell, Stephen; Briggs, Adam; and Fisher, Elliott (2018) 'Can accountable care organisations really improve the English NHS? Lessons from the United States', *BMJ*, vol. 360, k921. https://doi.org/10.1136/bmj.k921

[17] Reinhardt, Uwe (2001) 'Can efficiency in health care be left to the market?' *Journal of Health Politics, Policy and Law*, vol. 26, no. 5, pp.967–92. https://muse.jhu.edu/article/15621

[18] OECD (2019) *Health at a glance 2019*. France: OECD. https://www.oecd.org/health/health-systems/health-at-a-glance-19991312 .htm

[19] Commonwealth Fund (2021) *New international study: U.S. health system ranks last among 11 countries; many Americans struggle to afford care as income inequality widens*. https://perma.cc/MLP5-HSKA; Schneider, Eric; Shah, Arnav; Doty, Michelle; Tikkanen, Roosa; Fields, Katharine; and Williams II, Reginald (2021) *Mirror, mirror 2021. Reflecting poorly: health care in the U.S. compared to other high-income countries*, US: Commonwealth Fund. https://perma.cc/PNU2-3BFM

[20] Himber, Vaughn (2022) 'How much is the cheapest small business health insurance?', *eHealth*, 28 October. https://perma.cc/MWG2-EFNE

[21] Case, Anne and Deaton, Angus (2021) *Deaths of despair and the future of capitalism*, UK: Princeton University Press. https://doi.org/10.1515/9780691199955

[22] Enthoven, Alain (1985) *Reflections on the management of the NHS*, UK: Nuffield Provincial Hospitals Trust, p.9. https://perma.cc/5S95-8ZFF

[23] Enthoven, Alain (1978) 'Consumer-choice health plan (second of two parts). A national-health-insurance proposal based on regulated competition in the private sector', *The New England Journal of Medicine*, vol. 298, no. 13, pp.709–20. https://doi.org/10.1056/nejm197803302981304

[24] Enthoven, Alain (1985) 'An internal market model for the NHS', Chapter 10 in *Reflections on the management of the NHS*, UK: Nuffield Trust, pp.38–42.

[25] OECD (2020) *Health care prices*. France: OECD. https://perma.cc/K264-RB7Y

[26] Feachem, Richard; Dixon, Jennifer; Berwick, Donald; Enthoven, Alain; Sekhri, Neelam; and White, Karen (2002) 'Getting more for their dollar: A comparison of the NHS with California's Kaiser Permanente', *BMJ*, vol. 324, pp.135–43. https://doi.org/10.1136/bmj.324.7330.135

[27] Ham, Chris; York, Nick; Sutch, Steve; and Shaw, Rob (2003) 'Hospital bed utilisation in the NHS, Kaiser Permanente and the US Medicare programme: Analysis of routine data', *BMJ*, vol. 327, 1275. https://doi.org/10.1136/bmj.327.7426.1257

[28] Secretaries of State for Health, Wales, Northern Ireland and Scotland (1989) 'Funding hospital services', in *Working for Patients*. Cm 555, UK: The Stationery Office; Secretary of State for Health (2002) *Delivering the NHS Plan*. Cm 5503, UK: The Stationery Office. https://perma.cc /TFQ8-9DRC; Secretary of State for Health (2010) *Equity and excellence: Liberating the NHS*. Cm 7881, UK: Department of Health. https://assets .publishing.service.gov.uk/government/uploads/system/uploads/attach ment_data/file/213823/dh_117794.pdf; Bevan, Gwyn and Janus, Katharina, 'Why hasn't integrated health care developed'.

[29] Delamothe, Tony and Godlee, Fiona (2011) 'Dr Lansley's monster', *BMJ*, vol. 342, d408. https://doi.org/10.1136/bmj.d408

[30] Timmins, Nicholas (2012) *Never again?: The story of the Health and Social Care Act 2012: A study in coalition government and policy making*, UK: Institute for Government & The King's Fund. https://www.kingsfund.org.uk/sites/default/files/field/field_publication _file/never-again-story-health-social-care-nicholas-timmins-jul12.pdf

[31] McLellan, Alastair; Middleton, Jenni; and Godlee, Fiona (2012) 'Lansley's NHS "reforms"', *BMJ*, vol. 34, e709. https://doi.org/10.1136/bmj.e709.

[32] Secretaries of State for Health, Wales, Northern Ireland and Scotland (1989) 'Funding hospital services', Chapter 4 in *Working for patients*. Cm 555, UK: The Stationery Office, pp.30–38.

[33] NHS England (2019) *The NHS long term plan*, UK: NHS England. https://perma.cc/5VD3-WV5A; Alderwick, Hugh; Dunn, Phoebe; Gard- ner, Tim; Mays, Nicholas; and Dixon, Jennifer (2021) 'Will a new NHS structure in England help recovery from the pandemic?' *BMJ*, vol. 372, n248. https://doi.org/10.1136/bmj.n248; Health and Care Act 2022, c31. https://www.legislation.gov.uk/ukpga/2022/31/contents/enacted

[34] Ham, Christopher (2008) 'World class commissioning: A health policy chimera?' *Journal of Health Services Research & Policy*, vol. 13, no. 2, pp.116–21. https://doi.org/10.1258/jhsrp.2008.007177; Smith, Judith and Curry, Natasha (2011) 'Commissioning', in Dixon, Anna; Mays, Nicholas;

and Jones, Lorelei (eds) *Understanding New Labour's market reforms of the English NHS*, UK: King's Fund, pp.30–51. https://www.kingsfund.org.uk/sites/default/files/New-Labours-market-reforms-Chapter-3-Commissioning-Judith-Smith-Natasha-Curry-September-2011.pdf; Maarse, Hans; Jeurissen, Patrick; and Ruwaard, Dirk (2016) 'Results of the market-oriented reform in the Netherlands: A review', *Health Economics, Policy and Law*, vol. 11, no. 2, pp.161–78. https://doi.org/10.1017/S1744133115000353

[35] Besley, Timothy and Ghatak, Maitreesh (2001) 'Government versus private ownership of public goods', *The Quarterly Journal of Economics*, vol. 116, no. 4, pp.1343–72. https://doi.org/10.1162/003355301753265598

[36] Berwick, Donald; James, Brent; and Coye, Molly (2003) 'Connections between quality measurement and improvement', *Medical Care*, vol, 41, no. 1, pp.I-30–I-38. https://www.jstor.org/stable/3767726

[37] Marshall, Martin; Shekelle, Paul; Leatherman, Sheila; and Brook, Robert (2000) 'The public release of performance data: What do we expect to gain? A review of the evidence', *JAMA*, vol. 283, no. 14, pp.1866–74. https://doi.org/10.1001/jama.283.14.1866; Fung, Constance H.; Lim, Yee-Wei; Mattke, Soeren; Damberg, Cheryl; and Shekelle, Paul (2008) 'Systematic review: The evidence that publishing patient care performance data improves quality of care', *Annals of Internal Medicine*, vol. 148, no. 2, pp.111–23. https://doi.org/10.7326/0003-4819-148-2 -200801150-00006; Hibbard, Judith (2008) 'What can we say about the impact of public reporting? Inconsistent execution yields variable results', *Annals of Internal Medicine*, vol. 148, no. 2, pp.160–61. https://doi.org/10.7326/0003-4819-148-2-200801150-00011

[38] Hibbard, Judith; Stockard, Jean; and Tusler, Martin (2003) 'Does publicizing hospital performance stimulate quality improvement efforts?' *Health Affairs*, vol. 22, no. 2, pp.84–94. https://doi.org/10.1377 /hlthaff.22.2.84; Hibbard, Judith; Stockard, Jean; and Tusler, Martin (2005), 'Hospital performance reports: impact on quality, market share, and reputation', *Health Affairs*, vol. 24, no. 4, pp.1150–60. https://doi.org/10.1377/hlthaff.24.4.1150

[39] Chassin, Mark (2002) 'Achieving and sustaining improved quality: lessons from New York State and cardiac surgery', *Health Affairs*, vol. 21, no. 4, pp.40–51. https://doi.org/10.1377/hlthaff.21.4.40

[40] Chassin, Mark, 'Achieving and sustaining improved quality', p.45.

[41] Chassin, Mark, 'Achieving and sustaining improved quality', p.46.

[42] Chassin, Mark, 'Achieving and sustaining improved quality', p.48.

[43] 'Figure 4.3: NHS expenditure per capita in England, Scotland, Wales and Northern Ireland (1996, 2002 and 2006)', in Connolly, Sheelah and Mays, Nicholas (2014) *The four health systems of the United Kingdom: How do*

they compare? UK: Health Foundation, p.39. https://www.health.org.uk
/publications/the-four-health-systems-of-the-united-kingdom-how-do
-they-compare

44 Bevan, Gwyn; Karanikolos, Marina; Exley, Josephine; Nolte, Ellen;
Connolly, Sheelah; and Mays, Nicholas (2014) *The four health systems of
the United Kingdom: How do they compare?*, UK: Health Foundation.
https://www.health.org.uk/publications/the-four-health-systems-of-the
-united-kingdom-how-do-they-compare

45 Secretary of State for Health (2000) *The NHS Plan.* Cm 4818-I, UK: The
Stationery Office, p.28.

46 Auditor General for Wales (2005) *NHS waiting times in Wales, vol. 1,
The scale of the problem*, UK: The Stationery Office. https://senedd.wales
/media/hnxidjjp/bus-guide-n00000000000000000000000000027636
-english.pdf; Auditor General for Wales (2005) *NHS waiting times in
Wales, vol. 2, Tackling the problem*, UK: The Stationery Office.
https://senedd.wales/media/ccgpbi3s/bus-guide-n000000000000000000
0000000027392-english.pdf; Auditor General for Wales (2006) *Ambulance services in Wales*, UK: The Stationery Office.

47 Auditor General for Wales, *NHS waiting Times in Wales, vol. 1*, p.16;
Department of Health (2002) *NHS performance ratings. Acute trusts,
ambulance trusts, mental health trusts*, UK: Department of Health, p.2.

48 Bevan, Gwyn; Evans, Alice; and Nuti, Sabina (2019) 'Reputations count:
Why benchmarking performance is improving health care across the
world', *Health Economics, Policy and Law*, vol. 14, no. 2, pp.141–61.
https://doi.org/10.1017/S1744133117000561

49 Nuti, Sabina; Vola, Federico; Bonini, Anna; and Vainieri, Milena (2016)
'Making governance work in the health care sector: Evidence from a
"natural experiment" in Italy', *Health Economics, Policy and Law*, vol. 11,
no. 1, pp.17–38. https://doi.org/10.1017/S1744133115000067

50 Lisi, Domenico; Moscone, Francesco; Tosetti, Elisa; and Vinciotti, Veronica (2021) 'Hospital quality interdependence in a competitive institutional environment: Evidence from Italy', *Regional Science and Urban
Economics*, vol. 89, 103696.
https://doi.org/10.1016/j.regsciurbeco.2021.103696

51 Nuti, Sabina and Vola, Federico (2015) *Il sistema di valutazione della
performance dei sistemi sanitari regionali. Report 2015*, pp.94, 118.
https://www.iris.sssup.it/handle/11382/509893

52 Hardin, Garrett (1968) 'The tragedy of the commons: The population
problem has no technical solution; it requires a fundamental extension in
morality'. *Science*, vol. 162, no. 3859, pp.1243–48.
https://doi.org/10.1126/science.162.3859.12

53 Ostrom, Elinor (1990) *Governing the commons: The evolution of institutions for collective action*, UK: Cambridge University Press. https://doi.org/10.1017/CBO9781316423936

54 Dworkin, Ronald (2000) *Sovereign virtue: The theory and practice of equality*, UK: Harvard University Press, pp.340–46.

55 Daniels, Norman (1990) 'Am I my parents' keeper', Chapter 5 in *Just Health Care*, UK: Cambridge University Press, pp.86–113. https://doi.org/10.1017/CBO9780511624971

56 Department of Health and Social Care (2021) *The NHS Constitution for England*. https://www.gov.uk/government/publications/the-nhs-constitution -for-england/the-nhs-constitution-for-england

57 NHS Atlas series. https://perma.cc/BC6Q-NDW5

58 Daniels, Norman and Sabin, James (2008) 'Accountability for reasonableness: An update', *BMJ*, vol. 337. https://doi.org/10.1136/bmj.a1850

59 The Health Foundation (2012) *Looking for value in hard times*. https://www.health.org.uk/publications/looking-for-value-in-hard-times

60 Crewe, Tom (2016) 'The strange death of municipal England', *London Review of Books*, vol. 38, no. 24, pp.6–10. https://perma.cc/PX5X-L63K

61 Timmins, Nicholas (2016) *Universal Credit: From disaster to recovery?* UK: Institute for Government. https://perma.cc/H963-EQZV

62 Barr, Nicholas (2012) 'The Higher Education White Paper: The good, the bad, the unspeakable–and the next White Paper', *Social Policy & Administration*, vol. 46, no. 5, pp.483–508. https://doi.org/10.1111/j.1467-9515.2012.00852.x

63 Barr, Nicholas, 'The Higher Education White Paper'.

9. Playing the opening and middle games against Covid-19

There is no doubt that the Prime Minister [Johnson] made some very bad misjudgements and got some very serious things wrong. It is also the case that there is no doubt that he was extremely badly let down by the whole system. It was a system failure.

> Dominic Cummings, chief adviser to PM Boris Johnson (July 2019 to mid-November 2020), giving evidence to a House of Commons committee on 26 May 2021.[1]

Ingmar Bergman's classic film *The Seventh Seal* was set during the worst global pandemic in human history, the Black Death. It centres on the story of a Swedish knight, who, on his return home from the Crusades, plays a chess match for his life against Death. Inevitably he loses. Chess offers an analogy for the 'game' against Covid-19: the opening game took place in 2020, before effective vaccines had been developed. The middle game occurred after these vaccines were available. And the end game has unfolded in countries after mass vaccinations, where Covid-19 has become like regular flu. Both in chess and in battling a pandemic, having an effective strategy is absolutely vital in the 'opening game', because mistakes in the initial moves have fatal consequences. The first section of this chapter charts the UK government's chaotic start at the onset of Covid-19 in 2020, when the government played the initial moves against Covid-19 like a beginner at chess, who knows how the pieces move but blunders in the absence of a strategy. The following sections consider later changes in UK policymaking, when the PM and ministers switched strategy, reluctantly (and slowly) accepting the need for repeated lockdowns of the economy – to keep the Covid-19 burdens on the National Health Service within the bounds that the NHS could cope with. The last section of this chapter considers the 'middle game', beginning in 2021, when the UK government performed superbly in speedily procuring, licensing and deploying anti-Covid vaccines.

How to cite this book chapter:

Bevan, Gwyn (2023) *How Did Britain Come to This? A century of systemic failures of governance*, London: LSE Press, pp. 221–261.
https://doi.org/10.31389/lsepress.hdb.i License: CC BY-NC

9.1 The opening game

On 12 December 2019, Boris Johnson led the Conservative Party to a landslide victory in the UK general election with the promise 'to get Brexit done'. On 24 January 2020, his government recognised the threat Covid-19 posed to the UK by convening the first meeting of its committee for responding to emergencies in the Cabinet Office Briefing Room A (COBRA). However, the prime minister himself did not attend.[2] On 29 January, the first recorded cases of Covid-19 were confirmed in Britain.[3] On 30 January, the director-general of the World Health Organization (WHO) declared that the Covid-19 outbreak constituted a public health emergency of international concern.[4] The same day the Italian government proclaimed a national health emergency for six months, and suspended flights to and from China.[5]

For Boris Johnson, however, 31 January was: 'the moment when the dawn breaks and the curtain goes up on a new act in our great national drama … potentially a moment of real national renewal and change': that was the day that the UK formally left the EU.[6] And four days later he made clear that, for his government, the real threat from Covid-19 was overreaction:

> When barriers are going up, and when there is a risk that new diseases such as coronavirus will trigger a panic and a desire for market segregation that go beyond what is medically rational to the point of doing real and unnecessary economic damage, then at that moment humanity needs some government somewhere that is willing at least to make the case powerfully for freedom of exchange, some country ready to take off its Clark Kent spectacles and leap into the phone booth and emerge with its cloak flowing as the supercharged champion, of the right of the populations of the earth to buy and sell freely among each other. And here in Greenwich in the first week of February 2020, I can tell you in all humility that the UK is ready for that role.[7]

A month later, on 2 March 2020, Boris Johnson finally attended a COBRA meeting on the pandemic for the first time (its sixth).[8] David Caleb's letter to *The Guardian* on 11 January 2022 pointedly asked: 'Is it my imagination that during the pandemic Boris Johnson has attended more unlawful gatherings [i.e. parties in 10 Downing Street that broke lockdown regulations] than he has Cobra meetings?'[9] The chaotic way that decisions were made by the Johnson government in 2020 is described by Jonathan Calvert and George Arbuthnott, investigative journalists for the *Sunday Times*, in their book *Failures of State*,[10] and by Dominic Cummings, in his oral evidence to a joint meeting of the Science and Technology Committee and the Health and Social Care Committee of the House of Commons, on 26 May 2021 (Figure 9.5).[11] All three criticised the Johnson government for its deadly delayed decision on the first lockdown, made only on 23 March, and are righteously indignant about that delay later being repeated for the second and third times in November 2020 and January 2021.

One interpretation of these delays is that Johnson's role model was the mayor of Amity in Stephen Spielberg's film *Jaws*, who gives priority to the town's prosperity, in ordering the beach to remain open, despite overwhelming evidence of the presence of its massive man-eating shark.[12] *Jaws* was an updated exploration of that theme in Henrik Ibsen's play, of 1882, in which a Norwegian town's medical officer, Dr Stockman, proposed closing its new municipal baths after he discovered its water supply was toxic and posed 'the gravest possible danger to the public health'. The town mayor won public support for keeping the baths open and Stockman became Ibsen's *Enemy of the People*.[13] Johnson was determined to avoid that fate.[14] Dominic Cummings reported that, after April 2020, Johnson's view was that the first 'Lockdown was all a terrible mistake. I should have been the mayor in "Jaws". We should never have done lockdown 1.'[15]

For many British people, every step we take by the 500-metre-long Covid Memorial Wall in London (Figure 9.1) makes us wish that, back in February 2020, we had had a prime minister with a different view. Yet at least Johnson

Figure 9.1: The National Covid-19 Memorial Wall in London

Source: Kelly Foster. Available under a Creative Commons Attribution-Share Alike licence (CC BY-SA 4.0).[16]

was not Donald J. Trump, the 45th president of the US. On 27 February 2020 he made clear that his view of Covid-19 was that 'one day, it's like a miracle, it will disappear'.[17] That was the first of 38 such predictions. On 24 April 2020, he proposed, on a live nationwide broadcast, 'interesting' treatments that official scientists might test (in randomised controlled trials?):

> So, supposing we hit the body with a tremendous – whether it's ultraviolet or just very powerful light … supposing you brought the light inside of the body, which you can do either through the skin or in some other way … And then I see the disinfectant where it knocks it out in a minute. One minute. And is there a way we can do something like that, by injection inside or almost a cleaning?[18]

Imagine what it would feel like if you were there as Deborah Birx, the coronavirus response coordinator in the White House, who sat in silence. Later, in March 2021, she said that she thought every day about what she ought to have done.[19]

9.2 'Following the science'

A strategic response in the opening game against Covid-19 required a model because of our incapability in making sense of its complex interactions of feedback and delay:

- between a new case being infected and infecting others (with Covid-19 whilst asymptomatic) and experiencing symptoms, being diagnosed, possibly requiring admission to hospital or an intensive care unit (ICU), and (eventually) death or recovery;
- in the reporting of data on observable outcomes (infections, admissions to hospitals and ICUs, and deaths);
- in the effects of actions taken to stop the spread of the disease on observable outcomes.

We learn quickly when feedback is instant, but not when it is delayed, as in using a shower for the first time. Peter Senge illustrates our failure in 'learning by doing' within a system with multiple components that give delayed feedback using a famous example – the MIT 'beer game'.[20] There are three players: a retailer, a wholesaler and a microbrewery. The wholesaler responds with a lag to a change in the order from the retailer, and the microbrewery responds to the wholesaler also with a lag. In the game, the retailer knows customer demand, the wholesaler knows demand from the retailer, and the microbrewery demand from the wholesaler. The game begins with a stable weekly demand on the retailer for four cases a week. When that is increased to a new stable weekly demand of eight cases a week, the retailer is initially under-supplied and so keeps on increasing his weekly demand until it is met. By this time the microbrewery is on a schedule of ramping up its production to meet ever-increasing demands. Chaos ensues. Senge's book *The Fifth Discipline* is about the need to develop models to designed for such systems to understand what is going on and how to intervene.

For a government to formulate a strategy for a pandemic it needs a model of that complex system. But the initial moves against Covid-19 had to be made with neither good understanding of nor good data on the progress of the disease. That created what John Kay and Mervyn King describe as radical uncertainty.[21] The mantra of the UK government in its initial moves of the opening game against Covid-19 was that it was 'following the science'. But the 'science' it chose to follow proved to be inadequate for the radical uncertainty that undermined our capability to model how the disease would spread. The 'science' government needed was what Michael Lewis describes as 'redneck epidemiology': developing a simple model that could use the limited data that were available; and not starting with a complex model and waiting for the data that it required to become available. In *January 2020*, Carter Melcher (one of Lewis's 'redneck epidemiologists') used the available data from Wuhan and estimated that the range of expected deaths from taking no government action in the US could range from 900,000 to 1.8 million.[22] In April 2023, the total number of deaths attributed to Covid-19 in the US was over 1.1 million.[23] For the UK, the comparable range would have been from 180,000 to 360,000, and actual Covid-19 deaths were over 210,000. In March 2020, however, 'a senior health official said the UK would do well if it managed to keep the coronavirus death toll below 20,000 people'[24] – that number was exceeded by 19 April 2020.[25]

The players in the beer game were unable to make sense of a step change in demand. Pandemics are frightening when the rate of infections increase, not in step changes but exponentially. That means the larger the number, the greater is the rate of increase. 'Exponential growth bias' describes the common belief that the future will always increase at a steady rate. (It is well known in the world of finance, where people typically underestimate the benefit of compounding interest in savings.) The nature of exponential growth is the subject of the fairy tale about Sissa ibn Dahir, an impoverished mathematician, who invented the game of chess in mediaeval India. When his king, Shihram, insisted on offering him a reward, Sissa asked for one grain of rice for the first square of the board and the number to be doubled on each successive square (from 2 to 4 to 8 to 16 and so on). The king was disabused of his belief that such a reward was quite inadequate when he learnt that, before the 30th square was reached, his whole kingdom's supply of rice was exhausted. (The pay-off from the 64th square has been estimated to be enough rice to cover the entire country of India with a layer a metre high.[26])

What determined whether the increase in the number of cases with Covid-19 was exponential was the rightly famous R number: the average number of people infected by one infected individual. The number of cases increases exponentially if R is greater than one, stays at a constant rate if R equals one, and decreases if R is less than one. When the R number in England was greater than one, ministers seemed as bewildered as King Shihram. They would say things like: 'No one could imagine that two weeks ago this is where we would be today.' Prior to the UK's first lockdown, on 23 March 2020, cases were doubling every three days and peaked, on 10 April, at 70 cases per million. If that exponential growth had continued unchecked, then 45 days later everyone in England would have been infected and 'herd immunity' would have been achieved – with devastating consequences in deaths and illness.

The beer game is played for low stakes without the players being exposed to media coverage as they blunder along. The Covid-19 'game' was played for the highest of stakes, and its key players were subjected to intense unrelenting pressure from all kinds of media. They faced the systemic combination of feedback and delay, radical uncertainty and exponential growth. That meant that waiting until there was strong evidence that Covid-19 posed a serious threat would be acting too late.[27] Given the high drama of a president and prime minister in denial about the pandemic's arrival and seriousness, the US and the UK each needed a public health organisation with the expertise, authority and independence 'to speak truth to power', like Germany's Robert Koch Institute (RKI).

In 2005, the German government developed its first National Pandemic Plan and, in 2008, it decided to develop the RKI into a modern public health institute for the control of infectious diseases.[28] The RKI employed 700 scientists and was headed by experts in microbiology and infectious disease epidemiology.[29] It had been founded, in 1891, as the Royal Prussian Institute for Infectious Diseases, and later led by Robert Koch (who won the Nobel Prize in Medicine in 1905 for his discovery of the tuberculosis pathogen). The RKI revised Germany's National Pandemic Plan based on experience of the 2009 outbreak of swine flu.[30] That meant that the country was 'meticulously prepared for a pandemic'.[31] The RKI recognised the urgency and importance of scaling up testing and tracing for Covid-19:

> Once it became clear that the spread of the virus was serious, a reporting system involving the RKI and all public health offices came into play. Plus, a detailed 'epidemic strategy' lying in the drawer for years outlined payment structures for laboratories for diagnostic tests. There were no questions, nor any disputes, about costs and accounting.[32]

In response to the 2020 emergence of Covid-19, the RKI published risk assessments, strategy documents, response plans, daily surveillance reports on the disease, and technical guidelines, and worked with national and international public health authorities as channels for distributing communication.[33] The RKI followed 'the South Korean model of widespread testing and isolation that helped flatten the curve of new infections in Germany'.[34] South Korea had learnt from following the SARS and MERS epidemics of 2002/03 and 2015[35] and it had a lower number of deaths than would be expected until October 2020.[36]

In January 2020, one of the first diagnostic tests for Covid-19 was developed in Charité University Hospital in Berlin (where Robert Koch had worked).[37] The RKI then developed a highly effective system of testing, tracking and tracing.[38] The institute:

- urgently scaled up testing, tracking and tracing (its testing capacity was 50,000 people per day by mid-March 2020);
- developed a smartwatch app by 7 April that ensured privacy with a decentralised, anonymous approach to contact warning, which asked individuals to report their positive test status via the app, and Bluetooth connections between phones would trigger alerts to people who had come into contact with someone who tested positive;
- hired and trained 'containment scouts' to support understaffed local authorities; and
- from April 2020 implemented gathering data by monitoring its spread in local communities and nationally through representative screening.

The RKI's National Pandemic Plan enabled the German federal government to take timely action to restrict the spread of the Covid-19 infections:[39]

- from 28 February, all travellers entering country from high-risk areas (for example, China or Italy) were required to provide information on previous exposure and contact details;
- from 10 March, mass meetings of over 1,000 people were prohibited;
- from 18 March all non-EU citizens were barred from entering the European Union for 30 days; and
- from 10 April all travellers to Germany were required to quarantine for 14 days.[40]
- The RKI's national guidelines required hospital patient cases discharged to care homes to have tested negative or undergone quarantine at an isolation area for 14 days.

9.3 Making astrology look good

The concern over delays in the global response to Ebola in 2014:

> prompted calls for measurement and transparent reporting of countries' public health capacities [and] a need to better understand and measure—on a transparent, global, and recurring basis—the state of international capability for preventing, detecting, and rapidly responding to epidemic and pandemic threats.[41]

To meet that concern, experts produced a ranking of 195 countries, in October 2019, of how well each was prepared for the next global pandemic. The Global Health Security (GHS) Index categorised countries into three divisions. The governments in the US and the UK were sitting pretty as winner and runner up in the first division, hence they could relax. Germany languished in the second division and was ranked 14th. When compared with countries' subsequent performance, these pre-Covid judgements of health systems' preparedness made astrology look good (like economic forecasting – see Chapter 3).

So how did the UK and the US compare with Germany? The reliability of data on cases diagnosed with, or confirmed deaths from, Covid-19 can vary over time and location. Figure 9.2 gives estimates of confirmed deaths from Covid-19 per 100,000 in 2020 from Mathieu et al for the US, Germany and the UK.[42] Figure 9.2 also gives five sets of estimated rates of excess deaths (over what would be expected from past data for normal periods) for the US, Germany, and either the UK as a whole or separately for England and Wales or Scotland, by the WHO, *The Economist*, Islam et al, Parildar et al and Kontis et al.[43] These estimates aim to avoid variations in the reliability of diagnosing Covid-19.[44] Figure 9.2 shows that the WHO estimate for Germany, which was published on 5 May 2022, was an upper outlier, and it was later found to be wrong.[45] This error was acknowledged by the WHO in 2023.[46] The WHO rate for 2020 is higher than the estimate by Kontis et al, which was from mid-February 2020 to mid-February 2021.[47] The other three studies give estimates for 2020.[48] Their lowest estimate of the number who would have survived in the UK, or England and Wales, with Germany's mortality rate from Covid-19, was 40,000. That is equivalent to two jumbo jets crashing each week from March to December in 2020. (Tragically, even though we have reached the end game against Covid-19 in the UK, systemic failings in access to the NHS mean that scale of loss continued into 2022. Analysis by *The Times* found that that there were 50,000 excess deaths in 2022, the highest number since 1951, except for 2020.[49])

9.4 Hindsight bias and fighting the last war

In 2020, Boris Johnson framed his government's policy choice on Covid-19 like the town mayors in Amity and Norway: acting to either 'save lives' or protect the economy. The German government correctly framed the decision as one between either acting expeditiously or with a delay – which would result in greater loss of lives and suffering, longer more draconian lockdowns, and consequent damage to the economy. Germany had a 5 per cent loss in GDP in 2020 compared with 2019, which was about half that of the UK.[50] But the governments that acted expeditiously in the face of radical uncertainty could have been proved wrong, and been judged later with the bias of hindsight, as described by Daniel Kahneman:

Figure 9.2: Estimated excess deaths and confirmed deaths from Covid-19 in 2020

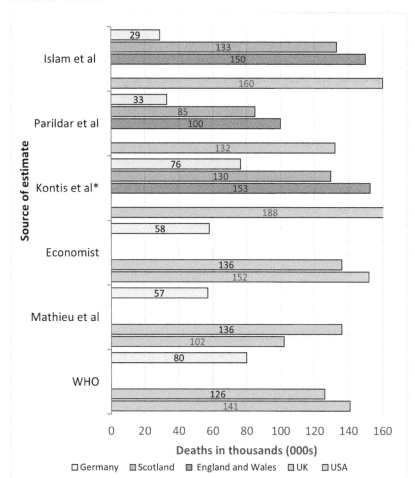

Sources: Islam et al (2021); Parildar et al (2021); Kontis et al (2021); Economist (2021); WHO (2023); Mathieu et al (2020).[51]
Notes: Excess deaths are estimated by comparing the actual with expected numbers from past data for normal periods. For Kontis et al (2021), the period covered is February 2020 to February 2021.

Hindsight is especially unkind to decision-makers who act as agents for others – physicians, financial advisers, third-base coaches, CEOs, social workers, diplomats, politicians. We are prone to blame decision makers for good decisions that worked out badly and to give them too little credit for successful outcomes that appear obvious only after the fact. … When the outcomes are bad, the clients often blame their agents for not seeing the handwriting on the wall

– forgetting that it was written in invisible ink that became logical only afterward. Actions that were deemed prudent in foresight can look irresponsibly negligent in hindsight.[52]

Hindsight brings an unforgiving glare when the counterfactual – that is, what would have happened otherwise – is obvious. Decisions over lockdowns are still contested. The delays over their imposition in England did not seem to 'cut through' with the public at large. (What did were the 14 parties held during lockdowns in 10 Downing Street investigated by Sue Gray.[53]) The counterfactual would have been obvious if the government had imposed a lockdown and, as Trump predicted, like a miracle Covid-19 had disappeared. So, what happened to lead institutions of public health that recommended preventive actions against swine flu epidemics that failed to materialise, in 1976 in the US, and in 2009 in the UK and Germany?

During a local outbreak of swine flu at an army base (Fort Dix in New Jersey), in 1976, Dr David Sencer, the director of the US's Centers for Disease Control (CDC), convinced the federal government to implement a policy of mass vaccination. Some people were paralysed and died from side effects of the vaccine. Mark Moore featured that as a case study of how *not* to create public value. His list of its downsides included: setting a precedent for exposing the government to damage claims, weakening trust in immunisation, damaging the credibility of the CDC, and tarnishing the reputations of Sencer and President Ford.[54] Mark Moore argued that, in 1976, Sencer ought to have recommended stockpiling vaccines, so that the country would have been prepared for rapid mass vaccination against swine flu, if that were to prove necessary.[55]

Michael Lewis explains that one consequence of the swine flu mistake was that federal governments undermined the independence of the director of the CDC, who ceased to be a tenured civil servant chosen from within the agency itself. Instead, he or she became a presidential appointee who (much later on) could be sacked in a tweet by Donald J. Trump in 2020.[56] In 2020 the CDC began its pandemic policies with restricted testing for patients who had been in China and were already in intensive care. There was hence a lack of evidence of its domestic transmission within the US, and the CDC downplayed the threat of the virus.[57] Lewis argues that:

> The American institutions built to manage risk and respond to a virus had been engaged in a weird simulation of a crisis response that did not involve actually trying to stop the virus.[58]

He concludes that CDC was 'stuck in an infinite loop of first realizing it was in need of courage, and then remembering that courage didn't pay'.[59] Charity Dean, the heroine of Michael Lewis's book, was the youngest person ever to be appointed as chief health officer of a county in California (Santa Barbara).[60] She demonstrated the professional courage needed to recommend the timely preventive actions, which was so lacking in the leadership of CDC and in public health at the state level in California. She despaired at what she saw as CDC's aim, which had been to convince the world that containment was not possible.[61] In June 2020, she was driven to resign, wondering: '*Why doesn't the United States have the institutions it needs to save itself?*' [emphasis in original].[62]

On 10 June 2009, WHO raised its alert level about swine flu becoming a global pandemic to the highest and warned countries to prepare for a second wave of cases. The director-general, Dr Margaret Chan, declared that 'The world is moving into the early days of its first influenza pandemic in the 21st century ... The virus is now unstoppable.'[63] The UK's response in 2009 was led by Liam Donaldson, the chief medical officer for England. The government implemented his recommendation to stockpile vaccines in case they were needed. Because of uncertainty over how this pandemic would develop, projections indicated the most likely outcome, and the best- and worst-case scenarios. The last features in the media that are in 'the bad news business'. That dominated the front-page news of the *Daily Mail* of Friday, 9 July 2009. Its banner headline was:

Swine flu: it's getting serious

The subheading was:

Medical Chief: 65,000 could die, one in three could be infected, and retired GPs are being recruited to fight pandemic

Six months later, however, after the worst case did not materialise, a January 2010 headline in the *Daily Mail* ran: 'After this awful fiasco over swine flu, we should never believe the State scare machine again.' The article went on to say:

So the Government, as the *Daily Mail* has revealed, is trying to get rid of £1 billion-worth of unwanted swine flu vaccine – because the deadly epidemic they were promising us all last year never materialised.[64]

(By comparison, the estimated costs of Covid-19 in 2020 were £250 billion to the UK economy and £370 billion to the public purse.[65]) In June 2010, the Conservative–Liberal Democrat coalition government published the White Paper for the NHS in England that laid out the third failed design to try to make competition work in the NHS ('Dr Lansley's monster' – see Chapter 8).[66] It also removed the regional and local infrastructure for public health in the NHS and so undermined England's institutional capability to respond to a pandemic.

In 2009 the federal government in Germany also stockpiled vaccines against swine flu on the advice of the RKI. There too a key newspaper, *Der Spiegel*, asked: 'When the next pandemic arrives, who will believe their assessments?'[67]

Figure 9.3: Organogram of pandemic preparedness and response structures in the UK and England – August 2019, UK Covid-19 Inquiry

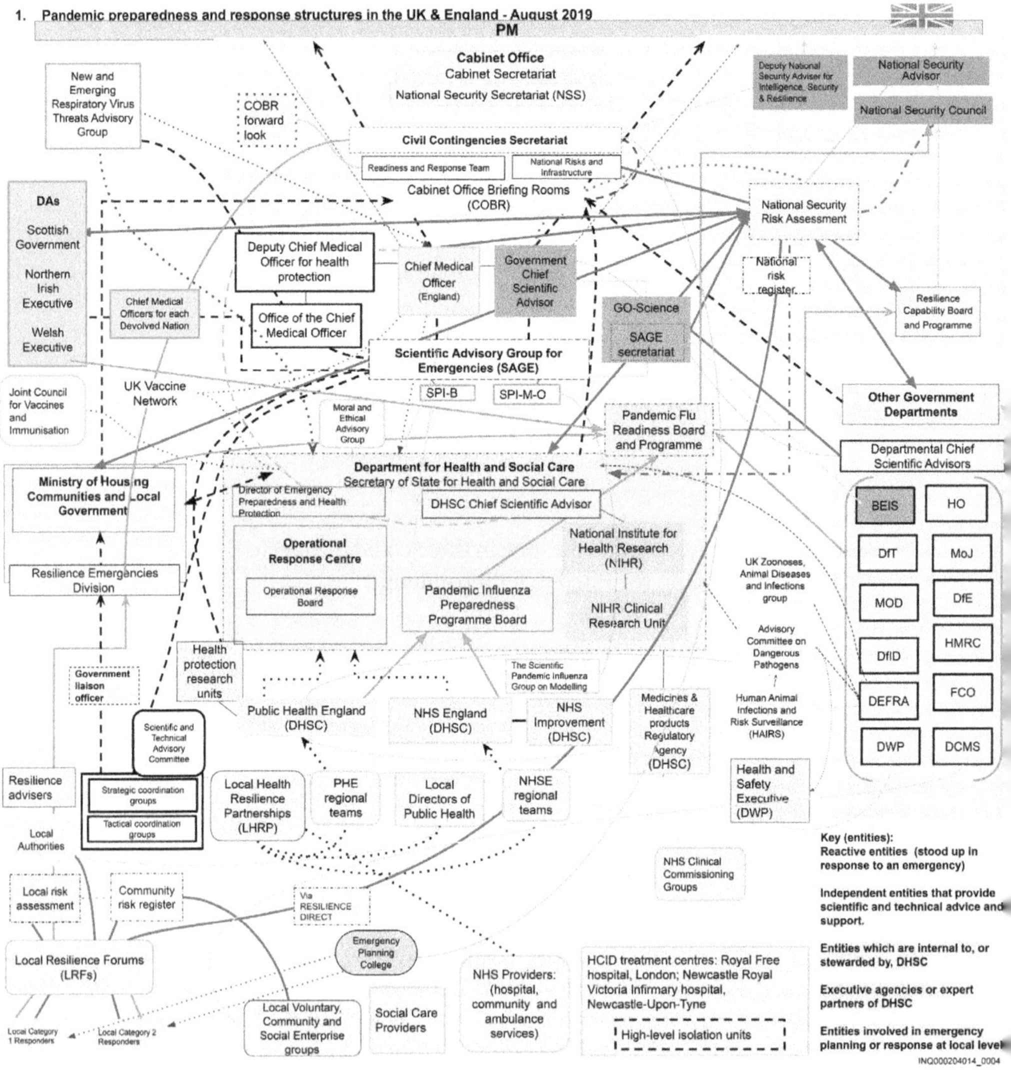

Source: UK Covid-19 Inquiry, 2023, Crown Copyright, published under the Open Government Licence.[68]

Yet the German government apparatus understood that pandemics are like a game of Russian roulette. Just because you have the good luck to survive one shot does not mean you will continue to be lucky on the next. The RKI remained intact and revised its pandemic plan.

'Dr Lansley's monster' established Public Health England (PHE) as a new national agency in England, at arm's length from, and subservient to, the Department of Health and Social Care.[69] PHE's chief executive was an experienced official from the Department of Health and Social Care, who joked on his appointment that his public health credentials could be fitted 'on a postage stamp'.[70] The chief medical officer, who remained in the department, played a central role in developing policies for Covid-19. The transfer of directors of public health and their teams from the NHS to local authorities often resulted in the function being stripped of resources and postholders experiencing a loss of power and influence.[71] Local directors of public health were accountable not to PHE but to their elected councillors, who were forced to make draconian cuts to staff and services under the government's austerity programme. They had to reduce their budgets by nearly 30 per cent for 2019–20 (from the 2010–11 funding levels).[72] England abandoned a hierarchy for public health but lacked Germany's integrated system of close federal–Laender (regional state) cooperation. Figure 9.3 is an organogram of the 'Pandemic preparedness and response structures in the UK and England – August 2019', which was painstakingly developed by legal counsel for the UK's Covid Inquiry.[73] In its bewildering complexity it is hard to understand the relationships between PHE, the chief medical officer and local directors of public health. Evidence to the Covid Inquiry, as reported in The Guardian, was that, for directors of public health, 'Communication from central government was so poor during parts of the Covid pandemic that [they] relied on TV and newspapers to find out about key decisions'.[74]

Although Scotland's mortality rates have consistently been 20 per cent higher than England,[75] Scotland's excess mortality in 2020 was at least 10 per cent lower than England and Wales (in each estimate of Figure 9.2). Britain's devolved governments were spared the Lansley redisorganisation of public health. So, did devolution save lives in Scotland from Covid-19?

9.5 Herd immunity by default in England

In January 2020, like their colleagues in Germany, UK scientists developed one of the first diagnostic tests for Covid-19.[76] In October 2021, the joint report from the Health and Social Care and the Science and Technology Committees was published. It was heavily critical that the UK's leading position in diagnostics was squandered (unlike in Germany). The consequence was that the UK moved into a state of permanent crisis.[77] The report criticised PHE for not learning from South Korea: quickly expanding testing capacity, developing effective systems to track and trace those with the disease, and imposing travel restrictions and social distancing.[78]

In 2016, PHE had organised a simulation exercise about how to handle the onset of a pandemic. Called Project Cygnus, it showed that the UK was alarmingly vulnerable *after* a pandemic had become rampant. In 2017 it resulted in a long slate of recommended steps to reduce the vulnerability of England and the UK. The subsequent lack of action was in part because the government was preoccupied by the real and present danger from a no-deal Brexit.[79] And Brexit continued to dominate the agenda for ministers and officials, as Camilla Cavendish lamented in 2019.[80] Project Cygnus was *not* designed to test the capability of the UK to prevent a pandemic becoming rampant.[81]

PHE was restructured (again) in the midst of the pandemic. In 2020, commenting on its demise, Gabriel Scally pointed out that the agency 'was never intended to be a mass provider of microbiological testing services to the population'.[82] On 21 February 2020, PHE's chief executive posted a blog claiming that, because of its robust systems of infection control, diagnosis and testing, there had been no positive cases that week in the UK. In fact, it has been estimated that there were then about 1,600 cases, and Covid-19 was already spiralling out of control.[83] As the pandemic spread across England, PHE rapidly found that it was unable to control the spread of infections and ran out of testing capacity. These shortfalls meant that:

- On 12 March PHE was forced to abandon all community testing and contact tracing, a major reason why 'herd immunity' became the UK government's policy by default.[84]
- The subsequent black-out on Covid-19's spread then contributed to 'the delay in the critical decision to instigate a nationwide lockdown'.[85]
- PHE mounted only inadequate testing of people arriving in Britain from abroad, which resulted in an underestimate of the number of cases being imported.[86]

In later public statements, the government denied that it was following 'herd immunity' policies: that letting things rip early on was the best way to generate quickly natural protections from reinfection.[87] 'Herd immunity' had three main political attractions.[88] First, a lockdown was the last thing that Prime Minister Boris Johnson wanted to do. Second, 'herd immunity' was initially favoured by some advisers and civil servants in Whitehall because it would also bring the peak of Covid-19 infections forward to the spring/summer of 2020, and so it would not occur during the regular winter crisis in the NHS, which lasts from December to February.[89] Third, Conservative ministers and some advisers believed that 'behavioural fatigue' would set in and that the British public would not accept a lockdown for a significant period. That belief had no basis in behavioural science and was later proved to have been wrong, except for those in 10 Downing Street.[90]

The meaning of the government's endlessly repeated mantra that it was 'following the science' was explained on 11 March 2020 in a 'fireside chat'. It took

Figure 9.4: The fireside chat between PM Boris Johnson and Dr Jenny Harries

Boris Johnson ✔
@BorisJohnson

Dr Jenny Harries, Deputy Chief Medical Officer, came into Downing Street to answer some of the most commonly asked questions on coronavirus.

People tend to leave them on, they contaminate the face mask and then wipe it over something.

2:52 / 4:51

3:23 PM · Mar 11, 2020

Source: Boris Johnson/UK Government.[91]

place in the study of 10 Downing Street, between Boris Johnson and Dr Jenny Harries (then deputy chief medical officer), and it was broadcast on Twitter (Figure 9.4).[92]

Johnson: Tell us the value of wearing face masks, you see face masks all around the place. Is there any point to that?

Harries: If a health professional has not advised you to wear a face mask, it's usually quite a bad idea. People tend to leave them on, they contaminate the face mask and then wipe it over something. So, really it's not a good idea and doesn't help…

Johnson: And it's noticeable that there are some countries where they have banned big sporting events and they've stopped mass gatherings of one kind or another. Tell us why, so far, the medical advice in this country is not to do that.

Harries: In this country we have expert modellers looking at what we think will happen with the virus. We've looked at what sorts of interventions might help manage this as we go forward and push the peak of the epidemic forward. And in general, those sorts of events and big gatherings are not seen to be something which is going to have a big effect. So, we don't want to disrupt people's lives unduly.

Johnson: Right, there's obviously people under a lot of pressure, politicians and governments, so they may do things that are not necessarily dictated by the science.

Harries: So, as a professional, I am absolutely delighted that we are following the science and the evidence. There are other things we can do in this country and the timing of that is really important…

Johnson: And the timing is very important isn't it?

Harries: Critical. Absolutely critical. If we put it in too early we will just pop up with another epidemic peak later on. If we leave it too late we will have missed the boat. Because we have such brilliant modellers we are pretty confident we will know the right point. We have got very clear advice about when we should intervene and that's exactly what I think we should do, which is what we're advising you as a government.

The Johnson government used its Scientific Advisory Group for Emergencies (SAGE) as a key part of its claim to be 'following the science'. SAGE's terms of reference were 'coordinating and peer reviewing, as far as possible, scientific and technical advice to inform decision-making'.[93] As the Institute for Government pointed out, 'in the initial months, ministers put too much weight on SAGE, relying on it to fill the gap in government strategy and decision making that it was not its role to fill'.[94] In early 2020 the experts on SAGE lacked the data they required to develop models that would give a sound basis to challenge the policy of 'herd immunity', which was favoured by a prime minister whose hero was the mayor of Amity.[95] The *unanimous* view at the meeting of SAGE on 13 March was that 'measures seeking to completely suppress the spread of Covid-19 will cause a second peak'.[96] The Institute for Government observed that: 'At times the prime minister and ministers waited until the scientific evidence was overwhelming rather than using it alongside other inputs to make their own judgements.'[97]

9.6 Lockdowns – a later part of the opening game

For Dominic Cummings, Tim Gowers made the vital contribution of 'redneck epidemiology'. Gowers is a brilliant professor of mathematics at Cambridge – winner of the Fields Medal (the mathematics equivalent of a Nobel Prize). His analysis showed that 'we can't infect 60 per cent of the population in a matter of months without overwhelming the hospitals and having to let a very large number of people die untreated'.[98] According to the *Financial Times*, in three days Dominic Cummings drove SAGE to reverse its recommendation for 'herd immunity'. And that volte-face was still opposed by some scientists because they feared this would lead to a second peak.[99] Michael Lewis describes the frustration of Charity Dean in her lowly position within the state of California. The implication is that, with better access to the governor, things might have played out differently there.[100] Jeremy Hunt rightly described Dominic Cummings (in March 2020) as 'the most powerful person in Downing Street after the Prime Minister'[101] and asked why, given Cummings's doubts about the policy of 'herd immunity', he did not advise Boris Johnson 'to cancel the Cheltenham Gold Cup (held on 10 March, that attracted 250,000), or the Champions League [European football] matches, or to lock down the borders—the things that could have prevented a lockdown'.[102] Cummings explained what it felt like then to challenge 'the science' of 'herd immunity' and the courage this required as a lone individual:

> I was incredibly frightened – I guess is the word – about the consequences of me kind of pulling a massive emergency string and saying, 'The official plan is wrong, and it is going to kill everyone, and you've got to change path', because what if I'm wrong? What if I persuade him [the PM] to change tack and that is a disaster? Everyone is telling me that if we go down this alternative path, it is going to be five times worse in the winter, and what if that is the consequence?[103]

The issues that consumed the bandwidth of the prime minister's office on 12 March 2020 were vividly captured by Cummings' testimony:

> [It] started off, with us thinking, 'Okay, today is going to be all about covid and whether or not we are going to announce the household quarantine' … Suddenly the national security people came in and said, 'Trump wants us to join a bombing campaign in the middle east tonight and we need to start having meetings about that through the day with Cobra as well.' … Then, to add to that day – it sounds so surreal it couldn't possibly be true – *The Times* had run a huge story about the Prime Minister and his girlfriend and their dog, and the Prime minister's girlfriend was going completely crackers about this story and demanding that the press office dealt with that.[104]

Figure 9.5: Dominic Cummings (Boris Johnson's former chief of staff) giving evidence to the joint session of Health and Social Care Committee and Science and Technology Committee on 26 May 2021

Source: Parliament Live, available under the Open Parliament Licence.[105]

In the week starting 16 March, an expert team from Imperial College led by Neil Ferguson (a key member of SAGE) had produced a compelling report warning that the NHS would soon be overwhelmed by demand for intensive care beds.[106] The disease was then spreading exponentially, which meant that every week counted. Ferguson told the Science and Technology Committee that if the national lockdown had been instituted even a week earlier 'we would have reduced the final death toll by at least a half'.[107] The joint report of the two select committees observes:

> It seems astonishing looking back that—despite the documented experiences of other countries; despite the then Secretary of State [of Health] referring to data with a Reasonable Worst Case Scenario of 820,000 deaths; despite the raw mathematics of a virus which, if it affected two-thirds of the adult population and if one percent of people contracting it died would lead to 400,000 deaths—it was not until 16 March that SAGE advised the Government to embark on a full lockdown … and not until 23 March that the Government announced it.[108]

In early 2020 the blunders made by the UK government, compared with Germany, included:

- *Excess deaths in care homes.* The UK government, having delayed lockdown for fear that NHS hospitals would be overwhelmed, issued guidance on 19 March 2020 that they must discharge patients who did not satisfy a specific set of requirements. On 2 April 2020 the shortage of testing resulted in the Department of Health clarification that 'negative [coronavirus] tests are not required prior to transfers/admissions into the care home'.[109] Discharges of patients to care homes with Covid-19 imperilled both other residents and the staff who worked there, and clearly caused many premature deaths. In the first Covid-19 wave, excess deaths in care homes were 16,600 in the UK and 3,500 in Germany (which has 40 per cent more people aged over 65 than the UK).[110]

- *The failure of the NHS app for contact tracing.* On 10 April 2020, Google and Apple announced that they were going to develop decentralised apps, where the matching between infected people and their list of contacts happened between their phones (as in Germany). Two days later, Matt Hancock, then secretary of state for health and social care, announced the development of an NHS app, which was designed to use a central database, owned by a health authority, to do the matching and storing the sensitive data. It was abandoned in June 2020 and so became yet another yet another government IT disaster.[111] (In that highly competitive field, Anthony King and Ivor Crewe awarded the Titanic Prize to another failed NHS system: the NHS National Programme for IT, which was estimated to have cost over £30 billion in the 2000s.[112])
- *No border controls.* In May 2020 a global map showed the UK to be the only country without controls on international arrivals.[113] Dominic Cummings later explained that this was based on advice to Johnson that before April 2020 it would have no effect, and afterwards because it would destroy the travel industry.[114]

The judgement of the joint select committees was that 'it is clear the first lockdown was called too late, it is not however possible to make such a clear-cut judgement about the second lockdown' (on 31 October 2020).[115] This is because it was only in December 2020 that it was definitely known that the alpha variant of the virus was significantly more transmissible than the initial strain of Covid-19. But Dominic Cummings was frustrated over the delay of the second lockdown:

> I think the same thing happened in the autumn as happened in January: it was bad policy and bad decisions. … the Prime Minister made some terrible decisions and got things wrong, and then constantly U-turned on everything.[116]

Calvert and Arbuthnott point out: 'By allowing the virus to proliferate for over a year, the government had significantly increased the risk it would mutate into something more dangerous.'[117] They are heavily critical of delays in the second lockdown[118] and of the shambolic handling of the third lockdown, which was introduced in a rush on 4 January 2021 after a brief non-lockdown period over Christmas sparked a surge of cases from festive get-togethers.[119]

Figure 9.6 gives the cumulative number of deaths from Covid-19 from March 2020 to March 2023 and the periods of the three lockdowns. Without taking account of the systemic lags in data reporting for cases and deaths reporting, Figure 9.6 might be taken as suggesting that the lockdowns in the UK and England *caused* the numbers of cases to peak. The explanation is that lockdowns were delayed until it was clear surges were occurring and that failing to act would overwhelm the NHS and result in large numbers of deaths.

Figure 9.7 compares the numbers of cases and deaths for the UK and Germany in the opening and middle games against Covid-19. It shows that in January 2021 the number of cases of Covid-19 in the UK peaked (at 880 cases per million people), exactly during the normal 'winter crisis' of the NHS. It also shows that in Germany the number of cases fell so much more quickly after the lower initial peak in March 2020, and that in the UK the high case fatality rate in the first wave explains why there were so many more deaths.

Figure 9.6: The cumulative numbers of people in England who died with Covid-19 from March 2020 to April 2023

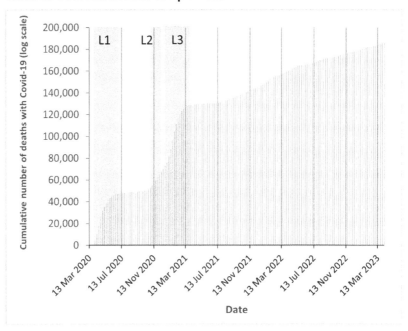

Source: UK Health Security Agency (for deaths numbers) and Institute for Government (for lockdown dates).[120]
Notes: The approximate periods for the three lockdowns (L1, L2 and L3) are shown shaded orange.

Figure 9.7: Daily new Covid-19 cases and deaths per million population in the UK and Germany, March 2020 to June 2021

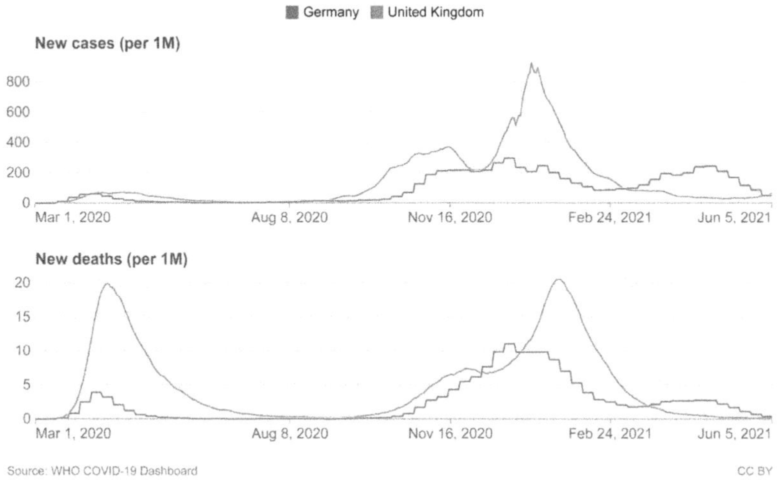

Source: Our World in Data Dashboard, published under a CC-BY license.[121]
Notes: Seven-day rolling average.

9.7 Failures of outsourcing

In 2009, the government stockpiled personal protective equipment (PPE) to respond to that year's swine flu threat. In 2016, Project Cygnus (see Section 9.5) had highlighted the importance of PPE for any time when a pandemic became rampant. Lackadaisical handling of the PPE stockpile, and the export of 279,000 items to China in February 2020, meant that, when the UK urgently needed PPE, it was in global competition for just-in-time contracts with existing suppliers.[122] So the Department of Health and Social Care looked to procure from potential suppliers who had never produced PPE before. Chapter 6 described the inadequacy of England's institutional arrangements for outsourcing. In November 2020 the National Audit Office report was heavily critical of the department for its many inadequacies in procuring PPE: much equipment arrived too late to help or proved to be unusable or unsuitable.[123] Dominic Cummings described the department as a 'smoking ruin'.[124] Members of Parliament and the public expressed concerns to the NAO about the quality of the PPE delivered through contracts awarded to suppliers through the VIP lane (or 'high-priority lane'), which were suggested by government officials, ministers' offices, Conservative Members of Parliament, senior NHS staff and other health professionals. In March 2022, the National Audit Office reported that 46 of the 115 contracts awarded before May 2020 to VIP lane suppliers did not go through the eight-stage due-diligence process.[125] And

'53 per cent of VIP lane suppliers provided some PPE items that are classified as not currently suitable for front-line services'.[126] Scandals around this episode have rumbled on, with the Department of Health and Social Care taking legal action for breach of a government deal awarded in June 2020.[127]

For Nick Macpherson, permanent secretary to the Treasury from 2005 to 2016, however, NHS Test and Trace 'wins the prize for the most wasteful and inept public spending programme of all time'.[128] On 20 May 2020, after the

Figure 9.8: The high transaction costs of outsourcing Test and Trace

Question	High transaction costs in using a market
1. Could a complete contract have been specified?	No. The task was highly complex and the future was radically uncertain. For the first three months call handlers (e.g. students or staff previously at travel centres) were on fixed contracts.[129] In June and August 2020 they were idle for 99 per cent of their time.[130] In September 2020 it had far too many call handlers supposed to arrange tests or track carriers with nothing to do,[131] yet at the same time it faced an acute shortage of lab testing capacity (with long turnaround times and potential users told to go to test sites hundreds of miles away from where they were[132]).
2. Was the buyer able to assess the adequacy of the quality and costs of what was supplied?	No. And it would have been costly to try to find out if the supplier were overcharging for the volume and quality of services supplied.
3. Was there supply-side flexibility?	No. There was the 'fundamental transformation' to one supplier after the contract had been let.
4. Were there many buyers?	No. The supplier had to invest in equipment and staff that were specific to the buyer.
5. Was a transactional relationship between buyer and supplier adequate to cover all aspects?	No. The buyer had to trust the supplier.
6. Was there scope for suppliers to behave with opportunism?	Yes. The buyer was vulnerable to being overcharged for an excessive or inadequate volume of services of poor quality.
7. Was the buyer a skilled purchaser?	No. The contract was one-off. The service was complex and uncertain. The MIT beer game (Section 9.2) illustrates that you do not learn how to handle complex systems of feedback and delay by 'learning by doing'. The select committees pointed out that Test and Trace lacked the modelling capability it needed.[133]

intense phase of the first lockdown, Boris Johnson told the nation that 'we have growing confidence that we will have a test, track and trace operation that will be world-beating and, yes, it will be in place by June 1st'.[134] The government decided to boldly go where no other government had gone before: to outsource what was misleadingly called 'NHS Test and Trace'.[135] That brand-new and extemporised organisation aimed to develop a centralised national system from scratch both for administering tests, and for tracing people exposed to contact with Covid-19 carriers.[136]

Test and Trace did not involve the public health departments in local authorities. It was outsourced to key firms of management consultants; some were paid more than £6,000 a day to bring in 'skills' lacking in government.[137] They designed and recruited staff for call handling. Private labs and some university labs delivered the testing components. Chapter 6 developed a framework based on Oliver Williamson's analysis of where high transaction costs make contracting problematic. Figure 9.8 applies that framework to outsourcing Test and Trace. The answers to each of the seven questions entail high transaction costs, and explain why Test and Trace failed extravagantly, at a cost of £13.5 billion in 2020–21.[138] And the assessment of the joint report by two select committees was: 'Were it not for the success of the Vaccine Taskforce and the NHS vaccination programme, it is likely that further lockdown restrictions would have been needed in Summer 2021'.[139]

9.8 Vaccines – the middle game against Covid-19

Blunders in the opening game of chess would be expected to offer dismal prospects for even making it to the middle game. But the 'middle game' against Covid-19 offered a fresh start in which the UK/England was an exemplar of inspired decisive leadership. A quite different set of strategies needed to be developed and implemented around an anti-Covid-19 vaccine for its procurement, regulation and roll-out. In contrast, the slower-moving EU decisions (which included Germany) blundered on all three aspects. Figure 9.7 also shows that the number of Covid-19 cases in the UK fell below those in Germany in February 2021. That is because in the middle game against Covid-19 the UK did so much better than Germany.

Unlike lockdowns, successes in these elements of the strategy for the middle game appealed to Boris Johnson because they promised a quicker route back to economic recovery. In May 2020, Kate Bingham, a life sciences venture capitalist, was asked to lead the UK's Vaccine Task Force (VTF). She initially refused because she knew that a successful Covid-19 vaccine was 'the longest of long shots'.[140] Thankfully she changed her mind. She later made clear that Sir Patrick Vallance, the government's overall chief scientific officer (located in the Department of Business and Industry), was a key figure in developing the institutional arrangements that enabled England's successes in procurement by the VTF, and rapid approval of the vaccine for use on patients by the Medicines and Healthcare Products Regulatory Agency (MHRA). Bingham oversaw delivery of the VTF's overriding objective, as set in May 2020, which was to secure the quantity of vaccines needed 'to vaccinate the appropriate UK population against Covid-19 *as soon as possible*'.[141] Her experience gave her direct access to vaccine companies and she was empowered to have direct access to the key senior ministers with the authority to make decisions quickly. She brought inspired leadership to an extraordinary team of talented and dedicated staff who were stunningly successful. By March 2021, the UK had secured early access to 457 million doses of eight of the world's most promising vaccines.[142]

We expect decisions on procurement of vaccines to be informed by their estimated costs and benefits.[143] Kate Bingham could make a strong case in two short sentences.[144] If a vaccine were to bring an end to further lockdowns (without an increase in the number of infections), that would save weekly costs of about £5 billion to the UK economy and £7 billion to the public purse.[145] Hence, given high confidence in vaccine safety in the UK, it was worth paying a high price to procure an ample supply of vaccines. But the VTF was required to produce a 100-page justification of the strategic economic, commercial, financial and management cases (but not the scientific case); give monetary estimates of the impact of vaccines on British economy; and reconcile differences in the value of life as assessed by the Department of Transport (£2 million) and Department of Health and Social Care (£0.5 million).[146] Bingham was later obstructed in trying to promote to the public the merits of being vaccinated and subjected to hostile briefing against her, much of which she discovered came from advisers inside 10 Downing Street.[147] As her husband, Jesse Norman MP, rightly pointed out, 'she has earned nothing, and does not expect to earn anything from her work as chair of the Vaccine Task Force'.[148]

Brexit helped the UK in the middle game compared with Germany, because Germany's procurement and regulation of vaccines were done at the EU level, which aimed to ensure fairness across its member states.[149] Coordination across governments made the process of procurement cumbersome. There was an intrinsic conflict between procuring quickly and agreeing with the manufacturers the degree of liability that they would accept if anything went wrong.[150] The benefits of vaccines to the different governments also depended on what percentages of their citizens thought that vaccines were generally safe. Figure 9.9 shows that just before Covid-19 arrived this proportion ranged from a high 80 per cent in Portugal to a low 40 per cent in Bulgaria.

By procuring jointly at scale across multiple countries, the EU did succeed in agreeing lower prices with vaccine suppliers than had the UK and the US for most vaccines. The costs per dose for each vaccine for Pfizer/BioNTech were £12 in the EU, £15 in the UK and £16 in the US. For AstraZeneca, the costs per

Figure 9.9: The percentage of opinion poll respondents in 2018 who said that the vaccines in use were safe across European Union countries

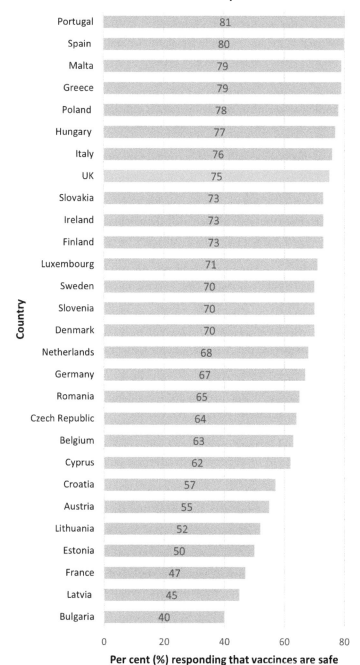

Source: Wellcome Global Monitor (2018).[151]

shot were £1.56 for the EU, £2.17 in the UK and £2.89 in the US.[152] But Chris Bickerton, writing in the *New York Times* in May 2021, observed that:

> When vaccine producers hit problems, Europe quickly found itself at the back of the line — while Israel, the United States and Britain, which had spent much more per capita on vaccines, enjoyed successful rollouts.[153]

The approval of a vaccine by regulators entails difficult judgements over when there is sufficient evidence from randomised controlled trials (RCTs) to justify its approval, while trading off the risks to patients from Covid-19 and from the vaccine's side effects, especially for subgroups of the population. Kate Bingham gave high praise to Dr June Raine, chief executive of the UK's MHRA, for recognising the urgency of approval. Raine pioneered a close partnership with the producers of the vaccines by organising rolling reviews and encouraging the sharing of data from the trials immediately they were generated.[154] The UK was the first country in world to authorise with due rigour both the Pfizer/BioN-Tech and AstraZeneca (AZ) vaccines for all people aged over 18, on 2 and 30 December 2020.[155] The European Medicines Agency (EMA) had to be much more conscious of public anxieties over vaccine safety and authorised Pfizer/BioNTech and AZ vaccines for people aged over 18 on 21 December 2020 (19 days later) and 29 January 2021 (30 days later). The EU Commission president, Ursula von der Leyen, observed, 'We were late in granting authorisation.'[156]

Kate Bingham singled out AstraZeneca for high praise. By the end of 2021, it had supplied two billion doses of its cheap vaccine, sold on a non-profit basis to 178 countries around the world. It is likely to have saved more lives than any other vaccine.[157] But, in early 2021, regulators and government committees faced two difficulties with the AZ vaccine.

First, although there was compelling evidence that the risk of dying from Covid-19 increased dramatically in the older age groups, early evidence showed the vaccine to be of proven effectiveness only in people aged under 55.[158] (At that stage, people aged 65–74 and 75–84 were eight and 20 times greater to die from Covid-19, respectively, than those aged 40–49.[159]) President Macron of France publicly suggested that the AZ vaccine would not work in the elderly.[160]

Second, when the AZ vaccine was rolled out, rigorous monitoring for possible side effects showed a low but troubling rate of blood clots, some of which were serious and resulted in deaths. Chancellor Merkel of Germany was reported to have decided not to take it.[161] Both the MHRA and EMA emphasised, however, that the risks from blood clots from the AZ vaccine had to be compared with the higher risks of not being vaccinated.[162] The EMA concluded that:

> the benefits of the AstraZeneca COVID vaccine, with the latest data suggesting an 85 per cent reduction in hospitalisation and death from COVID disease, far outweigh any possible risks of the vaccine.[163]

What is perplexing is why the governments in Germany and other European countries wrongly framed key decisions, in early 2021, as who ought to receive the AZ vaccine. Germany began by restricting the AZ vaccine to those under 65,[164] then paused its use altogether,[165] and then later restricted its use only to those over 60.[166] The UK's Joint Committee on Vaccination and Immunisation (JCVI) broadly followed the recommendations of the MRHA. The AZ vaccine was prescribed and indeed targeted and prioritised for those aged 65 and over from the start. Later, when evidence of risks of blood clots became available, the JCVI recommended vaccination by Pfizer/BioNTech instead if that were available, but still recognised that the risk from the AZ vaccine was less than from Covid-19.

The national roll-out of England's vaccination programme by PHE, the NHS and general practitioners was a triumph. It was directed at those at high risk without the tergiversations over the AZ vaccine that occurred in Germany. The first persons in the world received the Pfizer/BioNTech on 8 December and the AZ vaccine on 4 January. The UK hit its target of offering a vaccine to everyone in its top four priority groups by mid-February 2021, with more than 20 million people having had their first jab.[167]

Conclusions

There were multiple systemic failings by the UK government in the 'opening game' against Covid-19. Careful leadership and courage were conspicuously lacking, albeit with one noble exception. Dominic Cummings could see that 'herd immunity' would lead to a catastrophe, and had the courage to act as a lone voice to challenge its acceptance. Money was wasted scandalously on unusable PPE and the extravagant calamity of the outsourced 'NHS' Test and Trace. By contrast, in the 'middle game', the VTF led by Kate Bingham showed how an expert dedicated team could deliver in 'the longest of long shots'. And, in their rapid and rigorous approval of vaccines, the MHRA led by June Raine showed the urgency that was so lacking by PHE in early 2020. The UK was the first in the successful roll-out of vaccines, which was accomplished smoothly through PHE, the NHS and primary care. But those successes also prompt troubling thoughts. Thankfully, Patrick Vallance, the chief scientific officer, recognised how inadequate the existing machinery of government would have been in procuring vaccines. Bingham identified the biggest threat to the success of the VTF to have been 'Large parts of Whitehall' and felt at times like Alice in Wonderland acting scenes out of *Monty Python*.[168] She did not demur from Dominic Cummings's description of the Department of Health and Social Care as a 'smoking ruin'.[169]

In August 2020, between the first and second lockdown, the government announced that a new UK Health Security Agency (UKHSA) would be established. This is responsible for the health protection functions of former PHE, 'NHS' Test and Trace, and the Joint Biosecurity Centre. It took more than a year for UKHSA to become fully (?) operational (in October 2021). Dr Jenny

Harries (the official who explained how the UK was 'following the science' in March 2020 in a fireside chat with PM Johnson) is its first chief executive. This was a surprising appointment because, as the report of the Public Accounts Committee of June 2023 points out: 'despite her expertise in the science of public health (she) did not have experience in the other elements of running a complex organisation'.[170] She faced four challenges: first, 'creating a FTSE 50 sized company through a merger of three entities, with different systems and cultures, in six months'; second, 'decreasing its workforce from 18,000 to 6,700 full-time equivalents'; third, its creation was so rushed that it lacked appropriate arrangements for governance; and, fourth, the Department of Health and Social Care supported the UKHSA in 'a very light-touch way'; that is, the department's 'Audit and Risk Committee had discussions on two occasions about the risks facing UKHSA in its establishment'. The systems of governance of UKHSA are so inadequate that the Comptroller and Auditor General:

> was unable to give an opinion on whether the accounts were 'true and fair' or on whether the transactions recorded in the accounts were applied to the purposes intended by Parliament.[171]

We can see why Boris Johnson was keen to ensure the public inquiry into Covid-19 would not report until after the next general election. In June 2023, the UK Covid-19 Inquiry began its investigation into the first of its four modules, resilience and preparedness.[172] Chapter 1 of this book cited the Report of the Public Inquiry (the Kennedy Report) into the scandal at the Bristol Royal Infirmary (BRI), which diagnosed the systemic failings in the NHS that allowed that scandal to continue in the 1980s and 1990s.[173] It described my recurrent thought experiment, when I was working for the Commission for Health Improvement, in 2001: If we had reviewed the BRI's systems for clinical governance, would we have discovered the failings there in paediatric cardiac surgery? The Kennedy Report published in 2002 did not consider that question. The inquiry into Covid-19 must quickly make recommendations for better institutional arrangements than those displayed in Figure 9.3, which look to be even worse with the rushed creation of the UKHSA. Since 2000, there have been outbreaks of SARS-CoV in 2002, swine flu in 2009, MERS-CoV in 2012, Ebola in 2014 and 2018, and Covid-19 in 2020.[174] The government needs to act decisively to transform the UK's resilience and preparedness for the next pandemic.

I end this chapter with two striking contrasts that powerfully make the case of a country that has lost its way.

In June 2023, the Public Accounts Committee reported that:

> Three years after the start of the COVID-19 pandemic, the Department of Health and Social Care (the Department) has spent £14.9 billion of public money overpaying and over ordering significant

volumes of Personal Protective Equipment (PPE), COVID-19 medicines and vaccines. The Department will never use a significant
proportion of the PPE purchased, which will end up being burnt at
a significant cost to the taxpayer.[175]

In June 2021, to enable schools to help their pupils make up for lost learning
from school closures during lockdowns, the education recovery tsar, Sir Kevan
Collins, was reported to have proposed that they be allocated £15 billion. Only
£1.4 billion was allocated by ministers – about £50 extra per pupil per year.[176]

In June 2022, Lord Agnew, the minister responsible for Whitehall efficiency
and responsible for efforts to counter fraud, resigned in the House of Lords
'given the lamentable track record that we have demonstrated since I took up
this post nearly two years ago'.[177] In contrast, the Post Office was able, between
2000 and 2014, on evidence from a faulty Post Office IT system, to prosecute
'736 subpostmasters and postmistresses … for theft, fraud and false accounting in their branches'.[178] That miscarriage of justice is the subject of another
ongoing public inquiry.[179]

What follows is a short Afterword that argues that we need a new political
settlement.

Endnotes

[1] House of Commons, Health and Social Care Committee and Science
    and Technology Committee (2021) *Oral evidence: Coronavirus: Lessons
    learnt*. HC 95, Wednesday 26 May. Q. 1054.
    https://committees.parliament.uk/event/4435/formal-meeting-oral
    -evidence-session/

[2] Calvert, Jonathan and Arbuthnott, George (2021) *Failures of state: The
    inside story of Britain's battle with coronavirus*, UK: HarperCollins, p.55.

[3] Calvert, Jonathan and Arbuthnott, George, *Failures of state*, p.84.

[4] World Health Organization (2020) *COVID-19 public health emergency
    of international concern (PHEIC) Global Research and Innovation Forum*,
    World Health Organization, 12 February.
    https://www.who.int/publications/m/item/covid-19-public-health
    -emergency-of-international-concern-(pheic)-global-research-and
    -innovation-forum

[5] Anonymous (2020) 'Timeline of the COVID-19 pandemic in Italy',
    Wikipedia. https://perma.cc/26FK-66K4

[6] Johnson, Boris (2020) *PM address to the nation: 31 January 2020*. Crown
    Copyright.
    https://www.gov.uk/government/speeches/pm-address-to-the-nation-31
    -january-2020

7   Johnson, Boris (2020) 'PM speech in Greenwich: 3 February 2020'. Prime Minister's Office, 10 Downing Street. https://www.gov.uk/government/speeches/pm-speech-in-greenwich-3 -february-2020

8   Calvert, Jonathan and Arbuthnott, George, *Failures of State*, p.76.

9   Caleb, David (2022) 'Letters: The party's over. Now Boris Johnson's career should be too', *The Guardian*, 11 January. https://perma.cc/Z5LK-XW2S

10 Calvert, Jonathan and Arbuthnott, George, *Failures of State*.

11 House of Commons, *Oral evidence: Coronavirus: Lessons learnt.*

12 Heritage, Stuart (2020) 'Boris Johnson's hero is the mayor who kept the beaches open in Jaws. That's fine by me'. *The Guardian*, 13 March. https://perma.cc/NX6F-7RUD; *Oral evidence: Coronavirus: Lessons learnt*, Q. 1091.

13 Ibsen, Henrik (1882) *Enemy of the People*. https://www.fulltextarchive.com/pdfs/An-Enemy-of-the-People.pdf

14 House of Commons, *Oral evidence: Coronavirus: Lessons learnt*, Q. 1091.

15 House of Commons, *Oral evidence: Coronavirus: Lessons learnt*, Q. 1091.

16 Foster, Kelly (2021) *The National Covid Memorial Wall, London*, 16 April 2021, published under a Creative Commons (CC BY-SA 4.0) licence. https://commons.wikimedia.org/wiki/File:The_National_Covid _Memorial_Wall,_London,_2021-04-16_04.jpg

17 Dale, Daniel and Wolfe, Daniel (2020) '"It's going to disappear": A timeline of Trump's claims that Covid-19 will vanish', *CNN*, 31 October. https://perma.cc/4UQA-ZEFS

18 *The Telegraph* (2020) 'President Trump claims injecting people with disinfectant could treat coronavirus' [Video]. YouTube, 24 April. https://www.youtube.com/watch?v=33QdTOyXz3w

19 Gittleson, Ben (2021) 'Birx on Trump's disinfectant "injection" moment: "I still think about it every day"' [Video]. *abcNews*, 15 March. https://abcnews.go.com/Politics/birx-trumps-disinfectant-injection -moment-day/story?id=76474960

20 Senge, Peter (2006) *The fifth discipline: The art and practice of the learning organization*, UK: Currency.

21 Kay, John and King, Mervyn (2020) *Radical uncertainty. Decision-making beyond the numbers*, UK: Bridge Street Press.

22 Lewis, Michael (2022) *The premonition*, UK: Penguin, p.176.

23 Mathieu, Edouard; Ritchie, Hannah; Rodés-Guirao, Lucas; Appel, Cameron; Gavrilov, Daniel; Giattino, Charlie; Hasell, Joe; Macdonald,

Bobbie et al (2023) *Coronavirus (COVID-19) deaths, Our World in Data.* https://ourworldindata.org/covid-deaths

[24] Taylor, Matthew (2022) 'The NHS was left ill-prepared for Covid', *Financial Times*, 8 January. https://perma.cc/H58F-YQTT

[25] Mathieu, Edouard; Ritchie, Hannah; Rodés-Guirao, Lucas; Appel, Cameron; Gavrilov, Daniel; Giattino, Charlie; Hasell, Joe et al (2023) *Cumulative confirmed COVID-19 deaths. Coronavirus Pandemic (COVID-19), Our World in Data.* https://ourworldindata.org/covid-deaths#citation

[26] David (2022) 'Rice on a chessboard – exponential numbers'. *Owlcation*, 24 June. https://perma.cc/5CXN-U4FN

[27] Lewis, Michael, *The premonition*, p.41.

[28] Robert Koch-Institut (2023) 'Informative film about the Robert Koch Institute'. [Video]. YouTube. https://www.youtube.com/watch?v=lNGLOp-oFYg

[29] Robert Koch Institut (2023) *What we do – Departments and units at the Robert Koch Institute.* https://perma.cc/WGV8-Y4P9

[30] Robert Koch Institut (2020) *Ergänzung zum Nationalen Pandemieplan – COVID-19 – neuartige Coronaviruserkrankung* [Supplement to the National Pandemic Plan – COVID-19 – Novel Coronavirus Disease]. Germany: Robert Koch Institute. https://www.rki.de/DE/Content/InfAZ/N/Neuartiges_Coronavirus /Ergaenzung_Pandemieplan_Covid.html

[31] Eckner, Constantin (2020) 'How Germany has managed to perform so many Covid-19 tests'. *The Spectator*, 6 April. https://perma.cc/BZH9-WFS3

[32] Eckner, Constantin, 'How Germany has managed to perform so many Covid-19 tests'.

[33] Wieler, Lothar; Rexroth, Ute; and Gottschalk, René (2020) *Emerging COVID-19 success story: Germany's strong enabling environment*, Our World in Data. https://ourworldindata.org/covid-exemplar-germany-2020

[34] Eckner, Constantin, 'How Germany has managed to perform so many Covid-19 tests'.

[35] House of Commons, Health and Social Care Committee and Science and Technology Committee (2021) *Coronavirus: lessons learned to date.* HC 92, p.61. https://committees.parliament.uk/work/657/coronavirus-lessons-learnt/

[36] Mathieu, Edouard; Ritchie, Hannah; Rodés-Guirao, Lucas; Appel, Cameron; Gavrilov, Daniel; Giattino, Charlie; Hasell, Joe et al (2020) *Estimated cumulative excess deaths per 100,000 people during COVID-19'. Coronavirus Pandemic (COVID-19), Our World in Data.*

https://ourworldindata.org/explorers/coronavirus-data-explorer?zoomTo
Selection=true&time=2020-03-01..2020-10-29&country=PRK~KOR
&pickerSort=asc&pickerMetric=location&Metric=Excess+mortality
+%28estimates%29&Interval=Cumulative&Relative+to+Population
=true&Color+by+test+positivity=false

[37] Charité and the DZIF (2020) 'Researchers develop first diagnostic test for
novel coronavirus in China'. Press release, *Charité – Universitätsmedizin*,
16 January. https://perma.cc/KAZ7-LKTC

[38] Wieler, Lothar et al, 'Emerging COVID-19 success story'.

[39] Wieler, Lothar et al, 'Emerging COVID-19 success story'.

[40] Imanuel, Marcus (2020) 'Chronology 2020: Germany and the Corona
Pandemic', *Berlin Spectator*. 20 December, https://perma.cc/RQT4-BYWJ;
Wieler, Lothar et al, *Emerging COVID-19 success story*

[41] Cameron, Elizabeth; Nuzzo, Jennifer; and Bell, Jessica (2019) *Global
Health Security Index*, p.7. https://perma.cc/3GXW-K5KF

[42] Mathieu, Edouard et al (n.d.) *Coronavirus (COVID-19) Deaths: Cumulative confirmed deaths per million people. Coronavirus Pandemic (COVID-
19), Our World in Data.* https://ourworldindata.org/covid-deaths

[43] World Health Organization (WHO) (2022) *Global excess deaths
associated with COVID-19* (modelled estimates). https://www.who.int
/data/sets/global-excess-deaths-associated-with-covid-19-modelled
-estimates and https://ourworldindata.org/excess-mortality-covid#
citation; *The Economist* and Solstad, Sondre. (2021) 'The pandemic's true
death toll', *The Economist.* https://www.economist.com/graphic-detail
/coronavirus-excess-deaths-estimates and https://ourworldindata.org
/excess-mortality-covid#citation; Islam, Nazrul; Shkolnikov, Vladimir;
Acosta, Rolando; Klimkin, Ilya; Kawachi, Ichiro; Irizarry, Rafael; Alicandro, Gianfranco et al (2021) 'Excess deaths associated with covid-19
pandemic in 2020: age and sex disaggregated time series analysis in 29
high income countries', *BMJ*, vol. 373, n1137. https://doi.org/10.1136
/bmj.n1137; Parildar, Ufuk; Perara, Rafael; and Ok, Jason (2021) *Excess
mortality across countries in 2020.* https://www.cebm.net/covid-19
/excess-mortality-across-countries-in-2020/; Kontis, Vasilis; Bennett,
James; Parks, Robbie; Rashid, Theo; Pearson-Stuttard, Jonathan; Asaria,
Perviz; Zhou, Bin et al (2022) 'Lessons learned and lessons missed: Impact
of the coronavirus disease 2019 (Covid-19) pandemic on all-cause mortality in 40 industrialised countries and US states prior to mass vaccination',
Wellcome Open Res, vol. 6, p.279.
https://doi.org/10.12688/wellcomeopenres.17253.2

[44] Mathieu, Edouard et al (n.d.) *What is 'excess mortality'? Coronavirus
pandemic (COVID-19)*, Our World in Data.
https://ourworldindata.org/excess-mortality-covid

45 Van Noorden, Richard (2022) 'COVID death tolls: Scientists acknowledge errors in WHO estimates', *Nature*, vol. 606, no. 7913, pp.242–44. https://www.nature.com/articles/d41586-022-01526-0

46 WHO, *Global excess deaths associated with COVID-19*; Karlinsky, Ariel; Knutson, Victoria; Aleshin-Guendel, Serge; Chatterji, Somnath; and Wakefield, Jon (2023) 'The WHO estimates of excess mortality associated with the COVID-19 pandemic', *Nature*, vol. 613, no. 7942, pp.130–37. https://doi.org/10.1038/s41586-022-05522-2.

47 Kontis, Vasilis et al, 'Lessons learned and lessons missed'.

48 *The Economist* and Solstad, 'The pandemic's true death toll'; Islam, Nazrul et al, 'Excess deaths associated with Covid-19 pandemic in 2020'; Parildar, Ufuk et al, *Excess mortality across countries in 2020*.

49 Smyth, Chris; Saunders, Thomas; and Lay, Kat (2022) '1,000 excess deaths each week as the NHS buckles', *The Times*, 10 January. https://perma.cc/TK47-XB3D

50 Partington, Richard (2021) 'German economy shrank by just 5% in 2020 amid Covid-19', *The Guardian*, 14 January. https://perma.cc/7645-6QHT; *BBC News* (2021) 'UK economy suffered record annual slump in 2020', 12 February 2021. https://perma.cc/B2VK-6Z6D

51 Islam, Nazrul et al, 'Excess deaths associated with Covid-19 pandemic in 2020'; Parildar, Ufuk et al, *Excess mortality across countries in 2020*; Kontis, Vasilis et al, 'Lessons learned and lessons missed'; *The Economist* and Solstad, 'The pandemic's true death toll'; World Health Organization, 'Global excess deaths associated with COVID-19'; Mathieu, Edouard et al, 'Cumulative confirmed COVID-19 deaths'.

52 Kahneman, Daniel (2011) *Thinking, fast and slow*, US: Farrar, Straus and Giroux, p.203.

53 Gray, Sue (2022) *Findings of second permanent secretary's investigation into alleged gatherings on government premises during Covid restrictions*, UK: Cabinet Office. https://assets.publishing.service.gov.uk/government/uploads/system/uploads/attachment_data/file/1078404/2022-05-25_FINAL_FINDINGS _OF_SECOND_PERMANENT_SECRETARY_INTO_ALLEGED _GATHERINGS.pdf

54 Moore, Mark (1995) *Creating public value: Strategic management in government*, US: Harvard University Press, p.145.

55 Moore, Mark, *Creating public value*, p.147.

56 Lewis, Michael, *The premonition*, p.290.

57 Lewis, Michael, *The premonition*, p.210.

58 Lewis, Michael, *The premonition*, p.274.

[59] Lewis, Michael, *The premonition*, p.226.

[60] Lewis, Michael, *The premonition*, p.224.

[61] Lewis, Michael, *The premonition*, p.274.

[62] Lewis, Michael, *The premonition*, p.280.

[63] Meikle, James and Carrell, Severin (2009) 'WHO declares swine flu pandemic', *The Guardian*, 11 June. https://perma.cc/5X2J-T3CH

[64] Booker, Christopher (2010) 'After this awful fiasco over swine flu, we should never believe State scare machine again', *Daily Mail*, 12 January https://perma.cc/T9AR-WB33

[65] Elliott, Larry (2021) 'A year of Covid lockdowns has cost the UK economy £251bn, study says', *The Guardian*, 22 March. https://perma.cc/R3WC-39RF; Lilly, Alice; Tetlow, Gemma; Davies, Oliver; and Pope, Thomas (2020) *The cost of Covid-19. The impact of coronavirus on the UK's public finances*, UK: Institute for Government. https://perma.cc/V3VG-4UDR

[66] Secretary of State for Health (2010) *Equity and excellence: Liberating the NHS*. Cm 7881, UK: The Stationery Office. https://assets.publishing.service.gov.uk/government/uploads/system /uploads/attachment_data/file/213823/dh_117794.pdf

[67] Spiegel staff (2010) 'The Swine Flu Panic of 2009', *Spiegel International*, 10 March. https://perma.cc/CF55-QSJ4

[68] UK Covid-19 Inquiry (2023) *Organogram of pandemic preparedness and response structures in the UK and England – August 2019*. https://covid19.public-inquiry.uk/documents/inq000204014_0004 -pandemic-preparedness-organograms-covering-2009-2020-2

[69] Scally, Gabriel (2020) 'The demise of Public Health England', *BMJ*, vol. 370: m3263, p.1.http://dx.doi.org/10.1136/bmj.m3263

[70] Calvert, Jonathan and Arbuthnott, George, *Failures of state*, p.131.

[71] Scally, Gabriel, 'The demise of Public Health England', p.1.

[72] National Audit Office (NAO) (2020) *Initial learning from the government's response to the COVID-19 pandemic*. https://www.nao.org.uk/wp-content/uploads/2021/05/Initial-learning -from-the-governments-response-to-the-COVID-19-pandemic.pdf

[73] UK Covid-19 Inquiry (2023) 'INQ000204014_0004 – Extract of Pandemic Preparedness Organograms covering 2009-2020, Evidence, 21 June'. https://covid19.public-inquiry.uk/documents/inq000204014_0004 -pandemic-preparedness-organograms-covering-2009-2020-2/

74 Booth, Robert (2023) 'UK Covid inquiry: public health bosses relied on media for information', *The Guardian*, 5 July, https://perma.cc/EEN7-WNQ5

75 Bevan, Gwyn; Karanikolos, Marina; Exley, Josephine; Nolte, Ellen; Connolly, Sheelah; and Mays, Nicholas (2014) *The four health systems of the United Kingdom: How do they compare?* UK: The Health Foundation and Nuffield Trust, pp.83–84.
https://www.health.org.uk/publications/the-four-health-systems-of-the
-united-kingdom-how-do-they-compare

76 House of Commons, *Coronavirus: Lessons learned to date*, p.61.

77 House of Commons, *Coronavirus: Lessons learned to date*, pp.61, 62.

78 House of Commons, *Coronavirus: Lessons learned to date*, p.61;
Graham-Harrison, Emma (2020) 'Experience of SARS a key factor in countries' response to coronavirus', *The Guardian*, 15 March.
https://perma.cc/TP23-4PFE

79 Calvert, Jonathan and Arbuthnott, George, *Failures of State*, pp.88–90.

80 Cavendish, Camilla (2019) 'Brexit is absorbing the oxygen needed to solve other problems', *Financial Times*, 5 April.
https://perma.cc/W5Y7-FRGV

81 House of Commons, *Oral evidence: Coronavirus: Lessons learnt*, p.18.

82 Scally, Gabriel, 'The demise of Public Health England', p.1.

83 Calvert, Jonathan and Arbuthnott, George, *Failures of state*, p.131.

84 House of Commons, *Coronavirus: Lessons learned to date*, pp.62, 63.

85 House of Commons, *Coronavirus: Lessons learned to date*, p.64.

86 House of Commons, *Coronavirus: Lessons learned to date*, p.63.

87 House of Commons, *Oral evidence: Coronavirus: Lessons learnt*, Q. 992 and Q. 993.

88 House of Commons, *Coronavirus: Lessons learned to date*, pp.33–34.

89 House of Commons, *Coronavirus: Lessons learned to date*, p.63.

90 Parker, George; Cookson, Clive; Neville, Sarah; Payne, Sebastian; Hodgson, Camilla; Gross, Anna; and Hughes, Laura (2020) 'Inside Westminster's coronavirus blame game', *Financial Times*, 16 July.
https://perma.cc/E8CS-3KVZ

91 Johnson, Boris [@BorisJohnson] (2020) 'Dr Jenny Harries, Deputy Chief Medical Officer, came into Downing Street to answer some of the most commonly asked questions on coronavirus', Twitter, 11 March.
https://twitter.com/BorisJohnson/status/1237760976482598913. Archived at

https://web.archive.org/web/20200312035546/https://twitter.com
/BorisJohnson/status/1237760976482598913

[92] Johnson, Boris [@BorisJohnson] (2020, 11March) 'Dr Jenny Harris'.

[93] Cabinet Office and Scientific Advisory Group for Emergencies (2012) 'Scientific Advisory Group for Emergencies (SAGE): A strategic framework'.
https://www.gov.uk/government/publications/scientific-advisory
-group-for-emergencies-sage

[94] Sasse, Tom; Haddon, Catherine; and Nice, Alex (2020) *Science advice in a
crisis*. London: Institute for Government, p.5. https://perma.cc/62Q3-ZB2H

[95] House of Commons, *Coronavirus: Lessons learned to date*, pp.40, 63.

[96] Health and Social Care Committee and Science and Technology
Committee, *Coronavirus: Lessons learned to date*, p.34.

[97] Sasse, Tom et al, *Science advice in a crisis*, p.5.

[98] Quinn, Ben (2021) 'A look at Prof Gowers' herd immunity document
sent to Dominic Cummings', *The Guardian*, 28 May.
https://perma.cc/S748-S8M8

[99] Parker, George et al, 'Inside Westminster's coronavirus blame game'.

[100] Lewis, Michael, *The premonition*, p.231.

[101] House of Commons, *Oral evidence: Coronavirus: Lessons learnt*, Q. 1008.

[102] House of Commons, *Oral evidence: Coronavirus: Lessons learnt*, Q. 1008.

[103] House of Commons, *Oral evidence: Coronavirus: Lessons learnt*, Q. 1008.

[104] House of Commons, *Oral evidence: Coronavirus: Lessons learnt*, Q. 1003.

[105] House of Commons, Science and Technology Committee and Health and
Social Care Committee (2021) *Subject: Coronavirus: lessons learnt*, p.30.
https://www.parliamentlive.tv/Event/Index/d919fbc9-72ca-42de-9b44
-c0bf53a7360b

[106] Parker, George et al, 'Inside Westminster's coronavirus blame game'.

[107] House of Commons, *Coronavirus: lessons learned to date*, p.32.

[108] House of Commons, *Coronavirus: lessons learned to date*, p.39.

[109] HM Government (2020) *COVID-19 hospital discharge service requirements*, pp.30, 10; Reality Check Team (2023) 'Covid: What happened to
care homes early in the pandemic?, *BBC News*,
https://perma.cc/5KMS-367C

[110] Ioannidis, John; Axfors, Cathrine; and Contopoulos-Ioannidis, Despina
(2021) 'Second versus first wave of COVID-19 deaths: Shifts in age
distribution and in nursing home fatalities', *Environmental Research*,
vol. 195, 110856. https://doi.org/10.1016/j.envres.2021.110856

[111] Cellan-Jones, Rory (2020) 'Coronavirus: What went wrong with the UK's contact tracing app?' *BBC News*, 20 June. https://perma.cc/MP7D-SMKN

[112] King, Anthony and Crewe, Ivor (2013) 'IT – technology and pathology', Chapter 13 in *The blunders of our governments*, UK: Oneworld.

[113] Brown, Faye (2020) 'UK only country in world not doing airport health checks or closing border', *Metro*, 7 May. https://metro.co.uk/2020/05/07/uk-country-world-not-airport-health -checks-closing-border-12669125/

[114] House of Commons, *Oral evidence: Coronavirus: Lessons learnt*, Q. 1091.

[115] House of Commons, *Coronavirus: Lessons learned to date*, p.52.

[116] House of Commons, *Oral evidence: Coronavirus: Lessons learnt*, Q. 1110.

[117] Calvert, Jonathan and Arbuthnott, George, *Failures of state*, p.390.

[118] Calvert, Jonathan and Arbuthnott, George, *Failures of state*, pp.352–80.

[119] Calvert, Jonathan and Arbuthnott, George, *Failures of state*, pp.383–405.

[120] UK Health Security Agency (2023) *Daily deaths with COVID-19 on the death certificate by date of death*, updated 20 April. https://coronavirus.data.gov.uk/details/deaths?areaType=nation&areaN ame=England;

Institute for Government (2022) *Timeline of UK government coronavirus lockdowns and restrictions*. https://www.instituteforgovernment.org.uk/data-visualisation/timeline -coronavirus-lockdowns

[121] Our World in Data (2023) *Daily new confirmed COVID-19 cases & deaths per million people*. https://ourworldindata.org/explorers/coronavirus-data-explorer?zoom ToSelection=true&time=2020-03-01..2021-06-05&uniformYAxis= 0&country=GBR~DEU&pickerSort=asc&pickerMetric=location& Metric=Cases+and+deaths&Interval=7-day+rolling+average&Relative +to+Population=true&Color+by+test+positivity=false

[122] Calvert, Jonathan and Arbuthnott, George, 'Sleepwalk', Chapter 4 in *Failures of state*, pp.81–106.

[123] National Audit Office (2020) *The supply of personal protective equipment (PPE) during the COVID-19 pandemic*. https://www.nao.org.uk/wp -content/uploads/2020/11/The-supply-of-personal-protective-equipment -PPE-during-the-COVID-19-pandemic.pdf, p.9.

[124] Health and Social Care Committee and Science and Technology Committee, *Oral evidence: Coronavirus: Lessons learnt*, Q. 1015.

[125] National Audit Office (2022) *Investigation into the management of PPE contracts*, p.8.

https://www.nao.org.uk/reports/investigation-into-the-management
-of-ppe-contracts/

126 National Audit Office, *Investigation into the management of PPE
contracts*, p.10.

127 Cameron-Chileshe, Jasmine; Gross, Anna; and Croft, Jane (2022)
'UK government to sue PPE supplier over pandemic contracts
linked to Tory peer', *Financial Times*, 19 December.
https://perma.cc/N9SA-KQTU

128 Macpherson, Nick [@nickmacpherson2] (2021) 'The wins the prize for
the most wasteful and inept public spending programme of all time. The
extraordinary thing is that nobody in the government seems surprised or
shocked. No matter: the BoE will just print more money. #soundmoney'
[Tweet]. *Twitter*, 10 March.
https://twitter.com/nickmacpherson2/status/1369554007472082944

129 NAO, *The government's approach to Test and Trace in England – interim
report*, p.13.

130 NAO, *The government's approach to Test and Trace in England – interim
report*, p.69.

131 NAO, *The government's approach to Test and Trace in England – interim
report*, p.69.

132 NAO, *The government's approach to Test and Trace in England – interim
report*, p.10.

133 House of Commons, *Coronavirus: lessons learned to date*, p.70.

134 Marsh, Sarah (2020) 'England Test and Trace: What senior ministers
promised and when', *The Guardian*, 4 June. https://perma.cc/G2S8-7S7G

135 National Audit Office (NAO) (2020) *The government's approach to Test
and Trace in England – interim report*, p.8.
https://www.nao.org.uk/report/the-governments-approach-to-test-and
-trace-in-england-interim-report/

136 NAO, *The government's approach to Test and Trace in England – interim
report*, pp.7–8.

137 Andersson, Jasmine (2020) 'Test and Trace: NHS contact tracing consultants paid up to £7,000 a day', *i News*, 15 October.
https://inews.co.uk/news/uk/test-and-trace-nhs-contract-tracing
-consultants-uk-paid-721126

138 National Audit Office (2021) *Test and Trace in England – progress update*, p.5.
https://www.nao.org.uk/report/test-and-trace-in-england-progress-update/

139 House of Commons, *Coronavirus: Lessons learned to date*, p.81.

[140] Bingham, Kate and Hames, Tim (2022) *The long shot: The inside story of the race to vaccinate Britain*, UK: Oneworld, p.6.

[141] May Dean's Dialogue (2021) Professor Velasco in conversation with Kate Bingham to discuss *Inside the Race to Develop a COVID-19 Vaccine*. LSE, 25 May.

[142] Update on the Vaccine Taskforce: 1 March 2021. https://www.gov.uk/government/news/update-on-the-vaccine-taskforce-1-march-2021

[143] Appleby, John (2020) 'Will Covid-19 vaccines be cost effective—and does it matter?' *BMJ*, vol. 371, m4491. https://doi.org/10.1136/bmj.m4491

[144] Bingham, Kate and Hames, Tim, *The long shot*, p.117.

[145] Elliott, Larry (2021) 'A year of Covid lockdowns'; Lilly, Alice et al, *The cost of Covid-19*.

[146] Bingham, Kate and Hames, Tim, *The long shot*, pp.112–13.

[147] Bingham, Kate and Hames, Tim, *The long shot*, pp.309–27.

[148] Bingham, Kate and Hames, Tim, *The long shot*, p.127.

[149] Fleming, Sam and Peel, Michael (2021) 'Ursula von der Leyen acknowledges errors in EU's Covid vaccines strategy', *Financial Times*, 10 February. https://perma.cc/XEL9-HC5A

[150] Kaufman, Sylvie (2021) 'Europe's vaccine rollout has descended into chaos', *The New York Times*, 4 February. https://perma.cc/6QXL-5WEW

[151] Wellcome (2018) *Wellcome Global Monitor 2018, Appendix C: Country-level data*. https://wellcome.org/reports/wellcome-global-monitor/2018/appendix-country-level-data

[152] The Week staff (2021) 'What Covid vaccines cost – and the countries paying over the odds', *The Week*, 30 March. https://perma.cc/UB6L-VAJT; Birnbaum, Michael; Rowland, Christopher; and Ariès, Quentin (2020) 'Europe is paying less than U.S. for many coronavirus vaccines', *Washington Post*, 18 December. https://perma.cc/2UC8-6Y7J

[153] Bickerton, Chris (2021) 'Europe failed miserably with vaccines. Of course it did', *New York Times*, 17 May. https://perma.cc/SMJ4-TPFQ

[154] Neville, Sarah and Kuchler, Hannah (2023) '"No 3am moments": MHRA chief June Raine on race for Covid vaccine', *Financial Times*, 2 April. https://perma.cc/N5JS-8VAJ

[155] https://www.gov.uk/government/news/oxford-universityastrazeneca-covid-19-vaccine-approved

156 Hyde, Rob (2021) 'von der Leyen admits to COVID-19 vaccine failures', *Lancet*, vol. 397, no. 10275, p.655. https://doi.org/10.1016/S0140-6736(21)00428-1

157 Bingham, Kate and Hames, Tim, *The long shot*, p.289.

158 European Medicines Agency (EMA) (2021) 'EMA recommends COVID-19 Vaccine AstraZeneca for authorisation in the EU' https://perma.cc/RUZ5-FEUM

159 National Center for Immunization and Respiratory Diseases (NCIRD), Division of Viral Diseases (2023) *Risk for COVID-19 infection, hospitalization, and death by age group*, Centers for Disease Control and Prevention. https://perma.cc/3M53-T93R

160 Bingham, Kate and Hames, Tim, *The long shot*, p.160.

161 Bingham, Kate and Hames, Tim, *The long shot*, p.160.

162 EMA (2021) *COVID-19 Vaccine AstraZeneca: benefits still outweigh the risks despite possible link to rare blood clots with low blood platelets*, EMA, 18 March. https://perma.cc/Y5RF-B9AX; MHRA (2021) *MHRA issues new advice, concluding a possible link between COVID-19 Vaccine Astra-Zeneca and extremely rare, unlikely to occur blood clots*, 7 April. https://www.gov.uk/government/news/mhra-issues-new-advice -concluding-a-possible-link-between-covid-19-vaccine-astrazeneca-and -extremely-rare-unlikely-to-occur-blood-clots

163 EMA (2021) *Signal assessment report on embolic and thrombotic events (SMQ) with COVID-19 vaccine*. EMA, https://perma.cc/92LW-NRD3

164 Hall, Ben; Peel, Michael; and Chazan, Guy (2021) 'EU vaccine woes shift from supply squeeze to rollout', *The Financial Times*, 25 February. https://perma.cc/98U6-X5ZK

165 Khan, Mehreen; Peel, Michael; and Hindley, David (2021) 'EU countries halt vaccine drives as AstraZeneca angst deepens', *Financial Times*, 16 March. https://perma.cc/KG8L-NLSL

166 Dombey, Daniel and Mancini, Donato (2021) 'Spain and Italy to restrict AstraZeneca's Covid jab to over-60s', *Financial Times* 8 April. https://perma.cc/BMB9-98HU

167 Update on the Vaccine Taskforce: 1 March 2021. https://www.gov.uk/government/news/update-on-the-vaccine-taskforce -1-march-2021

168 Bingham, Kate and Hames, Tim, *The long shot*, pp.125, 118.

169 Bingham, Kate and Hames, Tim, *The long shot*, p.6.

170 PAC, *Department of Health and Social Care annual report and accounts 2021–22*, p.11.

[171] PAC, *Department of Health and Social Care annual report and accounts 2021–22*, p.263.

[172] UK Covid-19 Inquiry (2023) *Update: UK Covid–19 Inquiry to begin hearing evidence in June for its first investigation.* https://covid19.public-inquiry.uk/news/update-uk-covid-19-inquiry-to -begin-hearing-evidence-in-june-for-its-first-investigation/

[173] Secretary of State for Health (2001) *Learning from Bristol – Report of the public inquiry into children's heart surgery at the Bristol Royal Infirmary* (The Kennedy Report). CM 5207(1), UK: The Stationery Office.

[174] https://www.cfr.org/timeline/major-epidemics-modern-era

[175] Public Accounts Committee (PAC) (2023) *Department of Health and Social Care annual report and accounts 2021–22*, Sixty-Second Report of Session 2022–23. HC 997 UK: HMSO, p.3. https://committees.parliament.uk/publications/40738/documents /198470/default

[176] Coughlan, Sean (2021) 'Boris Johnson promises more school catch-up cash in "damp squib" row', *BBC News*, 2 June. https://perma.cc/GLA6-KPPU

[177] Payne, Sebastian and Thomas, Daniel (2022) 'UK anti-fraud minister quits over "lamentable" Covid loan oversight', *Financial Times*, 24 January. https://perma.cc/VZ4N-LLWW

[178] Hyde, Marina (2023) 'Hundreds of lives ruined. Not a single person held to account. And still: silence on the Post Office scandal', *The Guardian*, 2 May. https://perma.cc/KA7M-8JWU

[179] Post Office Horizon IT Inquiry. For more, see: https://www.postofficehorizoninquiry.org.uk

10. Afterword: re-engaging with public governance

Political writers have established it as a maxim, that in contriving any system of government, and fixing the several checks and controls of the constitution, every man ought to be supposed a knave and to have no other end, in all his actions, than private interest. By this interest, we must govern him and, by means of it, notwithstanding his insatiable avarice and ambition, co-operate to the public good.[1]

David Hume (1777)

10.1 Pathologies of neoliberalism

Ronald Reagan began his 1981 presidential address by remarking on how, in the US,

The orderly transfer of authority as called for in the Constitution routinely takes place, as it has for almost two centuries, and few of us stop to think how unique we really are. In the eyes of many in the world, this every-four-year ceremony we accept as normal is nothing less than a miracle.

That address is remembered, however, for setting out the case for neoliberalism in one sentence: 'In our current crisis, government is not the solution to our problems: government is the problem.'[2] In 1989, towards the end of Reagan's second term, he drafted an executive order to establish a new government agency. It was to act on the findings of the secret Project Socrates, led by Michael Sekora, which had diagnosed the underlying cause of America's declining competitiveness. That project found that the falling competitiveness

How to cite this book chapter:

Bevan, Gwyn (2023) *How Did Britain Come to This? A century of systemic failures of governance*, London: LSE Press, pp. 263–277.
https://doi.org/10.31389/lsepress.hdb.j License: CC BY-NC

of the US was the consequence of its institutions shifting their focus from technological innovation to 'increasingly sophisticated economic *shell games* to maximize profits' (emphasis in original).[3] That was the outcome of taking seriously Friedman's 1970 doctrine that:

> there is one and only one social responsibility of business – to use its resources and engage in activities designed to increase its profits so long as it stays within the rules of the game, which is to say, engages in open and free competition without deception [or] fraud.[4]

Reagan's term of office ended before his executive order could be signed.[5] His successor, President George Bush, abolished Project Socrates. In the 2000s and 2010s, increasingly sophisticated economic shell games continued to be played in the financialisation of the economies of the US and UK, with four pathological consequences.

The primary pathology is the corrosive impact of financialisation on what used to be great companies in the real economy (see Chapter 5). The mission of maximising shareholder value overturned almost all other arguments about what was needed to build great corporations – by making money the core mission and sole rationale of the organisation and those who work for it. In the 1990s, Boeing was the world's most commercially successful aircraft company, thanks to the success of its 747 aircraft, which was designed and developed by people who 'eat breathe and sleep the world of aeronautics'.[6] After its takeover by McDonnell Douglas 20 years ago, Boeing's core mission became 'improving the company's financial profile'.[7] In 1976, Fred Hirsch wrote:

> In principle, individual maximisation can be held to its social purpose – making the best of opportunities for all – so long as it operates on the basis of properly designed and implemented rules; yet individual maximisation means manipulating these rules too.[8]

In 2018, in Indonesia, Boeing's 737 Max 8 airline, 'which was practically new, crashed minutes after takeoff, killing all 189 people on board'.[9] In 2019, in Ethiopia, another Boeing 737 Max 8 crashed, again killing all 346 people on board.[10] On 22 September 2022, the *New York Times* reported that:[11]

> Boeing reached a $200 million settlement with U.S. securities regulators on Thursday to resolve an investigation into claims that the aircraft manufacturer and a former chief executive had deceived investors about problems with its 737 Max plane … The aircraft manufacturer last year reached a $2.5 billion settlement with federal prosecutors as part of a deferred prosecution agreement … Last year, a group of Boeing directors agreed to a $237.5 million settlement

with shareholders who accused them of failing to adequately oversee the company, allowing the lapses that led to the crashes.

The secondary pathology is the consequences of major shocks to the body politic in the US and the UK as a consequence of the 2008 Global Financial Crisis. Everyone could see that the rules of the game in the institutions of financialisation were privatising gains and socialising losses and that undermined trust in our institutions. Fiona Hill was brought up as the daughter of an unemployed miner and midwife in Bishop Auckland and went 'From coal house to White House', becoming an adviser on foreign affairs to US Presidents George W. Bush, Barack Obama and Donald Trump. She saw the same pathologies led to those in the deindustrialised areas, which had been left behind, to vote for new political settlements: in 2016, for Brexit in the UK, with its promise to 'take back control', and Donald Trump in the US, as the 45th president, with his promise to Make America Great Again (MAGA).[12] Brexit now makes the British economy look like a team of athletes who used to struggle to compete in the Olympics and have decided to go on a fast-food diet: they can still run but not compete effectively.[13] Trump's refusal to accept his defeat in the presidential election of 2020 resulted in that infamous day of 6 January 2021, when five people died in the Capitol in Washington. That ceased to be Reagan's miracle of 'orderly transfer of authority'.[14]

The third pathology is a set of direct malign consequences from the growth of the UK financial sector and its lobbying power. John Muellbauer and David Soskice highlight the following:

- lax regulation and generous tax treatment of capital gains and hedge funds;
- a seamy underbelly of the UK financial and property service sector, abetted by the UK's overseas territories, making international tax evasion easier;
- credit-fuelled property booms, and high property prices; and
- diminished productivity growth.[15]

The fourth pathology is, perhaps, the most troubling of all: the low productivity of the UK as compared with other countries in Europe, and the UK's rate of increase in productivity over the decade to 2018, which was the lowest in the last 250 years.[16] The UK's stagnating economy is why there have been historically high levels of taxation and failing services (for example, nearly 26,000 waiting more than one year for treatment in the NHS).[17] Those struggling to deliver front-line services are trapped in a vicious circle of being underpaid and overworked, which creates problems of retention and recruitment, and so staff leave. The government's plans to tackle staff shortages in emergency care were deemed to have been misdirected for 'a demoralised and burnt-out workforce seeing high rates of people leaving, and a social care system devastated by years of squeezed budgets and bad pay'.[18]

10.2 Second thoughts on markets and quasi-markets

The quintessential neoliberal philosopher Robert Nozick, in 1974, argued that the market ought to be allowed free rein. He carefully chose what then seemed to be an innocuous example: the willingness of baseball fans to pay to watch one of the sport's greatest players, Wilt Chamberlain.[19] In his book *What Money Can't Buy: The Moral Limits of Markets*, Michael Sandel offers troubling examples of what the rich can now buy: access to an elite university, shooting endangered black rhinos, and the right to immigrate into the US.[20] He still has the ticket from when he was 12 years old and went, with his father, to watch their baseball team, the Minnesota Twins, play in the World Series. They lost and he was devastated. There was then little difference in the prices of admission for the two types of seats, box seats and stand seats. The market for sport is now financialised. In 2012, a box seat to see the New York Yankees costs $260.[21] I remember, when I was 18 and at school, paying out of my pocket money to watch George Best play for Manchester United at Old Trafford. Those who now pay up to £239 to watch a game at Manchester United are buying not only hospitality but also exclusivity.[22] Sandel's argument is that these changes have undermined how watching sport used to develop a strong sense of belonging to the same local community.

Timothy Besley responds to Sandel's book by showing that economists have recognised the problems he illustrates when only money matters.[23] I noted above that Julian Le Grand's quasi-market theory is that this encourages those who are 'knights', who are altruistic, and discourages 'knaves', who are driven by self-interest, because the former are rewarded and the latter penalised by changes in market shares and funding. Timothy Besley and Maitreesh Ghatak question the efficacy of seeking to generate incentives from financial gains and losses for those who have chosen to work in *not-for-profit* organisations.[24] They argue that high performance of public services follows from matching their missions to the motivation of those who deliver them. For example, teachers who derive intense satisfaction from educating the young are committed to their calling as professionals and do not seek large financial rewards.[25] This approach stands in radical contrast to the mission of maximising shareholder value and financialisation by re-emphasising the core mission of the organisation and those who work for it. Chapter 8 showed that healthcare is an exemplar for where markets fail and where effective alternatives have been implemented.

We would expect a quasi-market for schools to work best in cities. But it failed in London, which is why the Blair government launched the London Challenge. This combined 'experimentation on the ground, [and] rapid feedback and learning by advisers and officials, with strong project management across different strands of the policy'. It ran from 2003 to 2011 and improved the performance of secondary schools in inner London local authorities from being 'the worst performing to the best performing nationally'.[26] It has had an abiding impact. In 2019, Farquharson, McNally and Tahir showed that more than three-quarters of local authorities where at least 70 per cent of primary school leavers met the expected level in reading, writing and maths were in London.[27] They also found that the impacts of poverty, as indicated by eligibility for free school meals (see Chapter 7) on attainment at GCSE in London schools was around half of that in the rest of the country. They emphasise that this was 'entirely driven by better performance among disadvantaged pupils, meaning that lower educational inequality in the capital is a result of "levelling up" rather than levelling down'.[28]

Although Julian Le Grand and Samuel Bowles start from David Hume's maxim, with which this chapter began, they argue for, and against, the use of market mechanisms as a system of governance of public services. Le Grand was aware of the risk that introducing quasi-markets could crowd out altruism by turning 'knights' into 'knaves'.[29] Samuel Bowles argues in *The Moral Economy* that this is what quasi-markets are designed to do, because individuals are motivated either by altruism or by market mechanisms, but not both.[30] And, as these processes cannot be separated (as is required for quasi-markets to work), market mechanisms undermine, rather than reinforce, 'knightly' behaviour. Market mechanisms also typically fail to provide sanctions for 'knaves' because it is so problematic for a failing provider (school, university or hospital) to exit the market. What happens instead to failing providers in a quasi-market is that they continue to provide a poor service with inadequate funding. That is what happened to the comprehensive school of Chelmsley Wood council estate, and was found by the Institute for Fiscal Studies for schools in England (see Chapter 4).

Hume observes that 'it appears somewhat strange' that his political maxim 'that *every man must be supposed a knave* ... should be true in politics which is false in fact'.[31] Indeed, it is reasonable to assume that most who choose to deliver a public service start out aiming to be 'knights'. So, we require a more discriminating system of governance than treating all as if they were 'knaves'. Ian Ayres and John Braithwaite lay out the principles of regulatory discrimination of a strategy of tit-for-tat based on the conduct of those providing services: being punitive for 'knavish' and persuasive for 'knightly' conduct.[32] Adam Oliver proposes a system of governance by reciprocal altruism, which offers an alternative to a market mechanism. Reciprocal altruism has two different systems of negative reciprocity, which sanctions unacceptably poor performance by 'knaves', and positive reciprocity, which encourages excellence from 'knights'.[33] Diagnoses of, and remedies to, the pathologies of neoliberalism have been developed by those known as 'behavioural economists'. That raises an obvious question: isn't all economics about human behaviour? To which the answer is: not when it is based on mathematical models abstracted from institutions and human behaviour.

David Hume's close friend Adam Smith has a strong claim to be the first 'behavioural economist'.[34] His *Theory of Moral Sentiments* emphasised the importance of sympathy, that we feel loss more acutely than a gain of similar magnitude, and introduced the concepts of positive and negative reciprocity.[35] Scholars of Smith's work have sought to reclaim the breadth of his vision of society from its misrepresentation by neoliberal economists (including Ludwig von Mises, Friedrich von Hayek and Milton Friedman). Glory Liu reviews the scholarly literature on what is known as 'Das Adam Smith Problem', namely the cognitive dissonance between the *Theory of Moral Sentiments* and the Chicago School's version of Smith as 'an economist who believes in the social productiveness of self-interest alone, and whose metaphor of "the invisible hand" illustrates how free markets – not government – protect and promote individual freedom'.[36] Jesse Norman's book on Smith lucidly sets out how 'In Friedmanite fashion [the discipline of economics] has long been overly preoccupied with its own models rather than the real-world phenomena they are supposed to represent'. [37] In 1976, Milton Friedman won the Nobel Prize in Economics and celebrated the 200th anniversary of the publication of *The Wealth of Nations* in his paper 'Adam Smith's Relevance for today'.[38] Jesse Norman describes that paper as a 'master class in adjusting the facts to fit one's own theory': Friedman was being economical with the truth in his account of Smith's position on Britain being overgoverned, the efficacy of free markets, and the importance of the 'invisible hand'.[39] Scholars of Smith's work have sought to reclaim the breadth of his vision of society from its misrepresentation by neoliberal economists (including Ludwig von Mises, Friedrich von Hayek and Milton Friedman). Jacob Soll argues that they failed to understand that Smith's thought was grounded in Cicero's economic vision in which 'good morals … drove a healthy market'.[40] Glory Liu points out that Barack Obama cited Smith:

> They who feed, clothe and lodge the whole body of the people should have such a share of the produce of their own labour to be themselves tolerably well fed, clothed and lodged.

Obama translated that to mean 'if you work hard [you] should make a decent living [and] be able to support a family'.[41] The failings of neoliberalism to deliver a promised land after 40 years of trying can be understood as a consequence of a fundamental misreading of Adam Smith. In economic behaviour, what matters is not only, or even primarily, money.

10.3 Governing by reciprocal altruism

In the UK, teachers, doctors and nurses, who provide vital public services, were three of the top four most trusted professions in 2020 (the other was engineers).[42] The reputational damage from 'naming and shaming' members of these professions for unacceptably poor performance brings a loss of esteem that undermines their core identity – like being unfrocked in public. The regime of 'star ratings' is an exemplar of how that sanction of negative reciprocity tackled unacceptably poor performance in the English NHS. If 'naming and shaming' does not work, then negative reciprocity requires dismissal – as applied in the 'star rating' regime (see Chapter 8).

Negative reciprocity is, however, limited in scope: it can be effective only when performance is unacceptably poor, for example if waiting time at a hospital for a hip operation were three years (and the target were 18 months) but not if it were 19 weeks (and the target were 18 weeks). Positive reciprocity encourages high performance through collegial benchmarking with recognition for high achievement by peers and the public. Timothy Besley and Maitreesh Ghatak describe that kind of competition as sustaining and supporting the mission of excellence to deliver outcomes that benefit citizens.[43] Positive reciprocity is encouraged through recognition of excellence by awards in a process of 'naming and faming', for example from winning a Nobel Prize.[44] In the US, the Sammies are annual awards of medals that highlight excellence in the federal workforce.[45] Our honours system does not do the same for our public servants. Positive reciprocity is most effective in concert with negative reciprocity. For example, it would have been futile to try to develop collegial competition for developing care of high quality at Mid Staffordshire hospital between 2006 and 2010 (see Chapter 1).

Oliver argues against trying to use the same system for both positive and negative reciprocity.[46] But that is what we do for public services in England with, for example, NHS star ratings, school league tables, and inspections by the Care Quality Commission and OFSTED. Christopher Hood argues that it is easier to implement punitive policies, such as negative reciprocity, in big countries because of the substantial *relational distance* between the government and those who deliver public services.[47] This may explain why the devolved government in Wales stopped publication of school league tables, and did not follow England in implementing a regime similar to 'star ratings' in its NHS, with consequent worse outcomes in Wales than in England.[48] Oliver argues that positive reciprocity of learning through collegial competition against benchmarks needs to operate at a regional scale. Regions need to be large enough that there are enough producers of public services to learn from each other but small enough that the key players in each organisation can meet in the same room at the same time to learn from those delivering exceptional performance, as in the London Challenge. As so often in the case in the UK, that was a localised one-off exercise.[49] We need to institutionalise that capacity to learn as integral to our running of devolved public services, as in the network of the Interregional Performance Evaluation System across and within Italian regions (see Chapter 8). Veneto, which is part of that network, showed more resilience when Covid-19 hit Italy than did Lombardy, which is the only region in Italy that persisted with trying to make hospital competition work. At the end of March 2020, Pisano et al reported that the mortality rates per 100,000 were six in Veneto and 50 in Lombardy.[50]

George Akerlof and Rachel Kranton developed the economics of identity, which explains the power of negative and positive reciprocity for public services as compared with financial incentives.[51] Negative reciprocity defines what is, and is not, acceptable behaviour. They describe the initial rite of passage for new cadets at the United States Military Academy at West Point ('R day'). They are stripped to their underwear, have a severe haircut, are put into uniform and required to salute and address an older cadet 'until they get it exactly right, while being reprimanded for even the smallest mistake'.[52] The mission of West Point is:

> to educate, train, and inspire the Corps of Cadets so that each graduate is a commissioned leader of character committed to the values of Duty, Honor, Country and prepared for a career of professional excellence and service to the Nation as an officer in the United States Army.[53]

West Point has developed processes to develop a cadre for whom reciprocity (not self-interest) is fundamental. Akerlof and Kranton highlight the profound sense of identity imbued within that cadre. For example, a soldier would rather risk his life than let down his peers and, after leaving military service, will experience acute disappointment on being offered jobs by potential future employers who assume that only money matters.[54]

If we look to developing governance based on reciprocal altruism, the UK's current constitutional arrangements look like one hand clapping. England has the scale for negative reciprocity but lacks a regional organisation for positive reciprocity. The devolved countries are at the scale for positive reciprocity but lack the relational distance for negative reciprocity. Devolution in England remains problematic because, as I found, officials in Whitehall devolve power as willingly as a leech gives up sucking blood (see Chapter 1). A review of devolution in Manchester pointed out that devolution in England has resulted in 'very little local autonomy, major areas not devolved and hardly any tax raising powers'.[55] But the evidence from more than 20 years of fuller devolution to national governments within the UK has shown them to be more vulnerable to producer capture, which is why their schools and hospitals have tended to perform worse than in England.[56] Devolution to Scotland, Wales and Northern Ireland is necessarily asymmetric because the scale of England dwarfs that of the other countries. That means that it makes no sense to have a Parliament for England.[57] That does not, however, justify our two deficiencies compared with proper federal arrangements.[58]

First, our public services are funded by taxes on a UK-wide basis without a constitutional basis for agreeing what should be the UK-wide elements of policy: for example, charging for medicines and other prescriptions (which continues in England only) or not charging tuition fees for undergraduate education (which continues in Scotland only). Second, one promise of federal arrangements is that they offer a laboratory to experiment with different kinds of governance so enable learning about which works. We have experiments across the UK but lack the capability to learn from them, partly because we lack a federal institution to negotiate arrangements for reporting performance across our countries. Over time it has become increasingly difficult to compare public services' performance across the four countries of the UK – a blind spot that reduces the scope for citizens to put pressure on their governments to remedy their shortcomings.[59] Requiring each government to collect basic data, following common definitions, so that performance can be compared and lessons learnt, does not constrain the different parts of the UK from having different priorities or pursuing different policies. This was recognised in the Concordat on Statistics of October 2021 in which the UK government and devolved administrations agreed on the objective of producing 'coherent/comparable statistics at the UK and disaggregated levels'.[60] But, in August 2023, it was reported that the UK statistics authority had problems in being supplied with comparable NHS data.[61]

The development of performance monitoring at the national and regional levels in Italy offers a good model for a new constitutional settlement for the UK in which there is full devolution to regions within England combined with effective scrutiny of their use of public money and by the devolved countries of the UK. An example is the performance agreements linked to funding for government departments as implemented by the Treasury under Gordon Brown in the Blair government in the early 2000s.[62] In a new constitutional settlement, the Treasury would report to the public on how effectively their taxes are being used by the devolved countries and English regions. And these bodies would develop their own systems of comparing performance of local providers of public services by developing collegial competition between them. These services would include healthcare, and all education except for an elite set of internationally competitive research-intensive universities. Regions would also look to develop means of better use of our resources for healthcare along the pathways of care and education over a lifetime.

10.4 A new political settlement

In 2022, Peter Hennessy, writing in *A Duty of Care*, hoped Covid-19 would be followed by a new political settlement, as after the 1942 Beveridge Report (see Chapter 3).[63] William Beveridge set the agenda for the Attlee government with his five giant evils: *Want, Idleness, Disease, Ignorance* and *Squalor* (see Chapter 3). This is a game you can play. My take on our current five giant evils is as follows:

- *Want* (or poverty and lack of means) was caused by the economics of less eligibility for the unemployed. Beveridge showed that the UK could have afforded to abolish it in the 1930, and how that could be done in the 1940s, in a system of social security. In modern Britain, *Want* has re-emerged as a giant everywhere. The high cost of housing in a financialised market is a primary cause of poverty. And, contrary to Adam Smith's view of a well-ordered society, all too often having a job offers no escape. In-work poverty means too many have to trade off heating and eating, or childcare versus employment.

- *Idleness* was a consequence of market failure that sustained armies of unemployed people over a decade. Now regulatory failures of complex markets generate *Insecurity* in our future supplies of privatised water and energy, from toxic social media (the murders of Jo Cox and David Ames give menace to the anonymous death threats our MPs receive every week), in our financial institutions, and from the existential threat of climate change and developments of artificial intelligence (AI).
- *Disease* was prevalent from lack of access to healthcare. Now we have *Ill-health* from overall policy systems so designed that many people 'freely' choose ways of living that have resulted in 'epidemics' of obesity and diabetes.[64]
- *Ignorance* was caused by lack of access to secondary education. Now we have *Miseducation*, with degrees awarded by our bloated university sector, from which only 25 per cent of graduates earn enough to pay back their student loans in full. Uniquely across the OECD, our younger generations of people in the UK are no more numerate or literate than those born four decades earlier.[65]
- *Squalor* was caused by the mismatch between where people lived and opportunities for employment, leading to very poor living environments. While some problems here have been ameliorated by post-war economic growth, rundown areas remain on almost the same scale, leaving people living in them vulnerable to *Despair*, where those on benefits or with gloomy jobs see no escape for themselves (or their children) from a life of drudgery, low pay and low status. In the US, despair is a leading cause of deaths from drugs and suicide.[66]

Beveridge's 400-page report was focused on tackling *Want*. (His recommendation for the governing principles of what became our NHS was because this would tackle *Want* – and, of course, *Disease*.) He described the five giant evils in two short paragraphs. It is beyond the scope of this book, and my knowledge, to suggest how we tackle what I have suggested are our five giant evils. Indeed, the purpose of this book is to inform debate over their causes, so others more expert than I can debate how we ought to tackle them. I conclude with the following observations on our systems of governance.

- We are still living in the Thatcher settlement based on neoliberalism as if there were no alternative. Indeed, Colin Crouch, in 2011, described what failed to follow the Global Financial Crisis as *The Strange Non-death of Neo-liberalism*.[67]
- For neoliberalism to die, we need a new political settlement: the enabling state, which recognises that now *market failures are the problem of government*. As Chapter 5 argued, it would be a mistake to go back to the Attlee settlement based on the state 'rowing'. This new settlement

is where the state steers different systems of governance: regulating markets where they can work effectively (not just for shareholders and senior executives) and developing alternatives where they do not.

- Effective devolution is vital to developing an enabling state in the UK, with consequent radical changes in the skills, staffing and attitudes of those working in Whitehall and Westminster.

Endnotes

1   Hume, David and Miller, Eugene (1994) *Essays: Moral, political, and literary*, US: Liberty Fund, p.42.

2   Reagan, Ronald (1981) *Inaugural Address.* https://perma.cc/E2SP-RNER

3   Sekora, Michael (2010) *An unfinished legacy: President Reagan and the Socrates Project.* https://perma.cc/G7CS-QDCK

4   Friedman, Milton (1970) 'The first and core principle is that "the social responsibility of business is to increase its profits"', *New York Times.* https://perma.cc/5Y9J-VQRQ

5   Sekora, Michael, *An unfinished legacy.*

6   Kay, John (2011) *Obliquity: Why our goals are best achieved indirectly*, UK: Profile, p.21.

7   Kay, John, *Obliquity*, pp.21–22; Bushey, Claire and Edgecliffe-Johnson, Andrew (2020) 'Damning emails threaten Boeing's reputation with the flying public', *Financial Times*, 10 January. https://perma.cc/Z2SY-AWBW

8   Hirsch, Fred (2005) *Social limits to growth*, UK: Routledge, p.131. https://doi.org/10.4159/harvard.9780674497900

9   Specia, Megan (2018) 'What we know about the Lion Air Flight 610 crash', *New York Times*, 9 November. https://perma.cc/X3WC-VW45

10 Ahmed, Hadra; Onishi, Norimitsu; Searcey, Dionne; and Beech, Hannah (2019) 'Ethiopian Airlines plane is the 2nd Boeing Max 8 to crash in months', *New York Times*, 10 March. https://perma.cc/T97T-PANJ

11 Goldstein, Matthew and Chokshi, Niraj (2022) 'Boeing reaches $200 million settlement with regulators over its 737 Max', *New York Times*, 22 September. https://perma.cc/QUT2-J866

12 Hill, Fiona (2021) *There Is Nothing for You Here. Finding Opportunity in the Twenty-First Century*, US: Harper Collins.

13 Wolf, Martin (2022) 'The UK government should stop doing stupid stuff', *Financial Times*, 27 November. https://perma.cc/524D-G4FQ; Giles, Chris (2022) 'Brexit and the economy: The hit has been "substantially

negative"', *Financial Times*, 30 November. https://perma.cc/ZQ48-X73E; Foster, Peter (2023) 'UK manufacturers warn Brexit is undermining their place in EU', *Financial Times*, 28 June. https://perma.cc/SY6X-UQS6

14 Farley, Robert (2021) 'How many died as a result of Capitol riot?' FactCheck.org, 1 November. https://perma.cc/N3NA-SDVS

15 Muellbauer, John and Soskice, David (2022) *The Thatcher legacy. Lessons for the future of the UK economy*, UK: The Resolution Foundation, p.13. https://perma.cc/7G84-87LN

16 Crafts, Nicholas and Mills, Terence (2020) 'Is the UK productivity slowdown unprecedented?' *National Institute Economic Review*, vol. 251, pp.R47–R53. https://doi.org/10.1017/nie.2020.6

17 Johnson, Paul (2023) 'Opening remarks', *Spring Budget 2023*, UK: Institute for Fiscal Studies. https://ifs.org.uk/spring-budget-2023; Warner, Max and Zaranko, Ben (2023) *One year on from the backlog recovery plan: What next for NHS waiting lists?* UK: Institute for Fiscal Studies. https://ifs.org.uk/sites/default/files/2023-02/IFS-Report-R241-One-year -on-from-the-backlog-recovery-plan-what-next-for-NHS-waiting-lists -final.pdf

18 Neville, Sarah and Cameron-Chileshe, Jasmine (2023) 'Doctors warn NHS must tackle staff shortages to fix emergency care crisis', *Financial Times*, 30 January. https://perma.cc/S2B6-6Q6M

19 Nozick, Robert (1974) *Anarchy, state, and utopia*, UK: Blackwell, pp.160–64.

20 Sandel, Michael (2012) *What money can't buy: The moral limits of markets*, UK: Macmillan, pp.3–4.

21 Sandel, Michael, *What money can't buy*, p.164.

22 Manchester United Football Club (n.d.) 'Hospitality'. https://tickets.manutd.com/hospitality

23 Besley, Timothy (2013) 'What's the good of the market? An essay on Michael Sandel's What Money Can't Buy', *Journal of Economic Literature*, vol. 51, no. 2, pp.478–95. https://doi.org/10.1257/jel.51.2.478

24 Besley, Timothy and Ghatak, Maitreesh (2001) 'Incentives, choice, and accountability in the provision of public services', *Oxford Review of Economic Policy*, vol. 19, no. 2, pp.235–49. https://doi.org/10.1093/oxrep/19.2.235

25 Besley, Timothy and Ghatak, Maitreesh (2001) 'Government versus private ownership of public goods', *The Quarterly Journal of Economics*, vol. 116, no. 4, pp.1343–72. https://doi.org/10.1162/003355301753265598

26 Kidson, Marc and Norris, Emma (2014) *Implementing the London Challenge*, UK: Joseph Rowntree Foundation, p.2.

https://camdenlearning.org.uk/wp-content/uploads/2019/06
/Implementing-the-London-Challenge.pdf

27 Farquharson, Christine; McNally, Sandra; and Tahir, Imran (2022)
    Education inequalities, UK: IFS Deaton Review of Inequalities, p.59.
    https://ifs.org.uk/inequality/wp-content/uploads/2022/08/Education
    -inequalities.pdf.

28 Farquharson, Christine et al, *Education inequalities*, p.66.

29 Le Grand, Julian (2003) *Motivation, agency, and public policy: Of knights
    and knaves, pawns and queens*, UK: Oxford University Press, p.58.
    https://doi.org/10.1093/0199266999.001.0001

30 Bowles, Samuel (2016) *The moral economy: Why good incentives are no
    substitute for good citizens*, UK: Yale University Press.

31 Hume, David and Miller, Eugene, *Essays: Moral, political, and literary*,
    pp.42–43.

32 Ayres, Ian and Braithwaite, John (1995) 'The benign big gun', Chapter 2
    in *Responsive regulation: Transcending the deregulation debate*, UK:
    Oxford University Press, pp.19–53.

33 Oliver, Adam (2018) 'Do unto others: On the importance of reciprocity
    in public administration', *The American Review of Public Administration*,
    vol. 48, no. 4, pp.279–90. https://doi.org/10.1177/0275074016686826;
    Oliver, Adam (2019) *Reciprocity and the art of behavioural public
    policy*, UK: Cambridge University Press.
    https://doi.org/10.1017/9781108647755

34 Norman, Jesse (2018) *Adam Smith: What he thought, and why it matters*,
    UK: Penguin; Oliver, Adam (2017) *The origins of behavioural public
    policy*, UK: Cambridge University Press.
    https://doi.org/10.1017/9781108225120

35 Smith, Adam (2002) *Theory of Moral Sentiments* (ed. Haakonssen,
    Knud), UK: Cambridge University Press.
    https://assets.cambridge.org/97805215/91508/sample/9780521591508ws
    .pdf

36 Liu, Glory (2022) *Adam Smith's America: How a Scottish philosopher
    became an icon of American capitalism*, US: Princeton University Press,
    p.193. https://doi.org/10.1515/9780691240879

37 Norman, Jesse, *Adam Smith: What he thought, and why it matters*, p.292.

38 Friedman, Milton (1976) *Adam Smith's relevance for 1976*, US: Gradu-
    ate School of Business, University of Chicago (Selected Papers No. 50).
    https://perma.cc/VCZ9-26ME

39 Norman, Jesse, *Adam Smith: What he thought, and why it matters*, p.xiv.

[40] Soll, Jacob (2022) *Free market: The history of an idea*, US: Basic, p.25.

[41] Cited in Liu, Glory, *Adam Smith's America*, p.299.

[42] Clemence, Michael (2020) *Ipsos Veracity Index 2020*. Ipsos. https://www.ipsos.com/ipsos-mori/en-uk/ipsos-mori-veracity-index -2020-trust-in-professions

[43] Besley, Timothy and Ghatak, Maitreesh, 'Incentives, choice, and account-ability'.

[44] Frey, Bruno (2013) 'How should people be rewarded for their work?' in A. Oliver (ed.) *Behavioural public policy*, UK: Cambridge University Press, pp.165–83.

[45] Service to America Medals (n.d.) 'About Sammies'. *Partnership for Public Service*. https://perma.cc/HFZ5-KYSA

[46] Oliver, Adam, 'Do unto others'.

[47] Hood, Christopher (2007) 'Public service management by numbers: Why does it vary? Where has it come from? What are the gaps and the puzzles?' *Public Money and Management*, vol. 27, no. 2, pp.95–102. https://doi.org/10.1111/j.1467-9302.2007.00564.x

[48] Bevan, Gwyn and Wilson, Deborah (2013) 'Does "naming and shaming" work for schools and hospitals? Lessons from natural experiments following devolution in England and Wales', *Public Money and Management*, vol. 33, no. 4, pp.245–52. https://doi.org/10.1080/09540962.2013.799801

[49] Hunt, Tristram (2013) 'The London Challenge is a lesson in how to turn around poor pupils' lives', *The Guardian*, 9 December. https://perma.cc/HLV7-59ZW

[50] Pisano, Gary; Sadun, Raffaella; and Zanini, Michele (2020) 'Lessons from Italy's response to coronavirus', *Harvard Business Review*. https://perma.cc/C4RG-2UQW

[51] Akerlof, George and Kranton, Rachel (2010) *Identity economics*, UK: Princeton University Press, p.72.

[52] Akerlof, George and Kranton, Rachel, *Identity economics*, p.39.

[53] West Point (n.d.) 'About West Point'. https://perma.cc/8L82-PREJ

[54] Akerlof, George and Kranton, Rachel, *Identity economics*, pp.46–47.

[55] Lupton, Ruth; Hughes, Ceri; Peake-Jones, Sian; and Cooper, Kerris (2018) *City-region devolution in England*. SPDO Research Paper 2, p.10. https://www.nuffieldfoundation.org/wp-content/uploads/2020/01 /SPDO-Research-Paper-2-min.pdf

[56] Atkins, Graham; Dalton, Grant; Phillips, Andrew; and Stojanovic, Alex (2021) *Devolved public services. The NHS, schools and social care in the*

four nations, UK: Institute for Government.
https://www.instituteforgovernment.org.uk/publications/devolved
-public-services

[57] Bogdanor, Vernon (2001) *Devolution in the United Kingdom*, UK: Oxford University Press.

[58] Bevan, G. (2014) *The impacts of asymmetric devolution on health care in the four countries of the UK*. London: Health Foundation.
https://www.health.org.uk/sites/default/files/TheImpactsOfAsymmetric
DevolutionOnHealthCareInFourCountriesUK.pdf

[59] Bevan, G. *The impacts of asymmetric devolution.*

[60] Cabinet Office, Department of Finance (Northern Ireland), Scottish Government, UK Statistics Authority, Welsh Government (2021) *Concordat on Statistics.*
https://uksa.statisticsauthority.gov.uk/publication/concordat-on-statistics/

[61] Beckford, Martin (2023) 'Keir Starmer's chief of staff Sue Gray is accused of helping to cover up the failures of the Labour-run NHS in Wales' *Daily Mail*, 14 August. https://perma.cc/Q9FJ-9XEQ

[62] James, Oliver (2004) 'The UK core executive's use of public service agreements as a tool of governance', *Public Administration*, vol. 82, no. 2, pp.397–419. https://doi.org/10.1111/j.0033-3298.2004.00400.x

[63] Hennessy, Peter (2022) *A duty of care*, UK: Penguin.

[64] Janssen, Fanny; Bardoutsos, Anastasios; and Vidra, Nikoletta (2020) 'Obesity prevalence in the long-term future in 18 European countries and in the USA', *Obesity facts*, vol. 13, no. 5, pp.514–27. https://doi
.org/10.1093/advances/nmy055; Bevan, Gwyn; De Poli, Chiara; Keng, Mi Jun; and Raine, Rosalind (2020) 'How valid are projections of the future prevalence of diabetes? Rapid reviews of prevalence-based and Markov chain models and comparisons of different models' projections for England', *BMJ open*, vol. 10, no. 3: e033483.
http://dx.doi.org/10.1136/bmjopen-2019-033483

[65] Farquharson, Christine et al, *Education inequalities*, p.18.

[66] Case, Anne and Deaton, Angus (2021) *Deaths of despair and the future of capitalism*, UK: Princeton University Press.

[67] Crouch, Colin (2011) *The strange non-death of neo-liberalism*, UK: Polity.

Selected bibliography

Abbasi, Kamran (1998) 'Butchers and gropers'. *BMJ*, vol. 317, no. 7172, p.1599. https://doi.org/10.1136/bmj.317.7172.1599b

Abel-Smith, Brian (1964) *The hospitals 1800–1948*, UK: Heinemann.

Acemoglu, Daron and Robinson, James (2012) *Why nations fail: The origins of power, prosperity and poverty*, UK: Profile.

Addison, Paul (1975) *The road to 1945: British politics and the Second World War* (revised edition), UK: Jonathan Cape.

Adonis, Andrew and Pollard, Stephen (1997) *A class act: the myth of Britain's classless society*, UK: Hamish Hamilton.

Akerlof, George and Kranton, Rachel (2010) *Identity economics*, UK: Princeton University Press. https://doi.org/10.1515/9781400834181

Alderwick, Hugh; Dunn, Phoebe; Gardner, Tim; Mays, Nicholas; and Dixon, Jennifer (2021) 'Will a new NHS structure in England help recovery from the pandemic?' *BMJ*, vol. 372, n248. https://doi.org/10.1136/bmj.n248;

Alderwick, Hugh; Shortell, Stephen; Briggs, Adam; and Fisher, Elliott (2018) 'Can accountable care organisations really improve the English NHS? Lessons from the United States', *BMJ*, vol. 360, k921. https://doi.org/10.1136/bmj.k921

Alt, James (1987) 'Crude politics: Oil and the political economy of unemployment in Britain and Norway, 1970–85', *British Journal of Political Science*, vol. 17, no. 2, pp.149–99. https://doi.org/10.1017/S0007123400004695

Appleby, John (2020) 'Will Covid-19 vaccines be cost effective—and does it matter?' *BMJ*, vol. 371, m4491. https://doi.org/10.1136/bmj.m4491

Archer, Tom and Cole, Ian (2021) 'The financialisation of housing production: Exploring capital flows and value extraction among major housebuilders in the UK', *Journal of Housing and the Built Environment*, vol.36, p.1376. https://doi.org/10.1007/s10901-021-09822-3

Armytage, Walter (1970) 'The 1870 Education Act', *British Journal of Educational Studies*, vol. 18, no. 2, pp.121–33. https://doi.org/10.1080/00071005.1970.9973277

Arrow, Kenneth (1963) 'Uncertainty and the welfare economics of medical care', *American Economic Review*, vol. 53, no. 1/2, pp.941–73. https://www.jstor.org/stable/1816184

Atkins, Graham; Dalton, Grant; Phillips, Andrew; and Stojanovic, Alex (2021) *Devolved public services. The NHS, schools and social care in the four nations*, UK: Institute for Government. https://www.instituteforgovernment.org.uk/publications/devolved -public-services

Atteridge, Aaron and Strambo, Claudia (2021) *Decline of the United Kingdom's steel industry*, Sweden: Stockholm Environment Institute. https://euagenda.eu/upload/publications/decline-of-the-steel-industry -in-the-uk.pdf

Auditor General for Wales (2005) *NHS waiting times in Wales, vol. 1, the scale of the problem*, UK: The Stationery Office. https://senedd.wales/media/hnxidjjp/bus-guide-n0000000000000000000 000000027636-english.pdf

Auditor General for Wales (2005) *NHS waiting times in Wales, vol. 2, tackling the problem*, UK: The Stationery Office. https://senedd.wales/media/ccgpbi3s/bus-guide-n0000000000000000000 000000027392-english.pdf

Auditor General for Wales (2006). *Ambulance services in Wales*, UK: The Stationery Office.

Ayres, Ian and Braithwaite, John (1995) *Responsive regulation: Transcending the deregulation debate*, UK: Oxford University Press.

Bank of England (n.d.) *A millennium of macroeconomic data*. https://www.bankofengland.co.uk/statistics/research-datasets

Barber, Michael (2008) *Instruction to deliver: Fighting to transform Britain's public services*, UK: Politicos.

Barber, Michael (2015) *How to run a government so that citizens benefit and taxpayers don't go crazy*, UK: Penguin.

Barber, Michael (2020) *Ten characters who shaped a school system. 1870 – 2020: 150 Years of universal education in England*, UK: Foundation for Education Development. https://perma.cc/45KF-BDEK

Barr, Nicholas (2004) 'Higher education funding', *Oxford Review of Economic Policy*, vol. 20, no. 2, p.279. https://doi.org/10.1093/oxrep/grh015

Barr, Nicholas (2012) 'The Higher Education White Paper: The good, the bad, the unspeakable – and the next White Paper', *Social Policy & Administration*, vol. 46, no. 5, pp.483–508. https://doi.org/10.1111/j.1467-9515.2012.00852.x

Bate, Alex and Foster, David (2017) *Sure Start (England)*, UK: House of Commons Library, Briefing Paper Number 7257. https://commonslibrary.parliament.uk/research-briefings/cbp-7257/

Bell, Derek and Gray, Tim (2002) 'The ambiguous role of the environment agency in England and Wales', *Environmental Politics*, vol. 11, no. 3, pp.76–98. https://doi.org/10.1080/714000630

Bell, Trudy and Esch, Karl (1987) 'The fatal flaw in flight 51-1', *IEEE Spectrum*, vol. 24, no. 2, pp.36–37. https://doi.org/10.1109/MSPEC.1987.6448023

Bellei, Cristian; and Cabalin, Cristian (2013) 'Chilean student movements: Sustained struggle to transform a market-oriented educational system', *Current Issues in Comparative Education*, vol. 15, no. 2, pp.108–23. https://files.eric.ed.gov/fulltext/EJ1016193.pdf

Berk, Marc and Monheit, Alan (2001) 'The concentration of health care expenditures, revisited', *Health Affairs*, vol. 20, no. 2, pp.9–18. https://doi.org/10.1377/hlthaff.20.2.9

Berliner, Joseph (1988) *Soviet industry from Stalin to Gorbachev: Essays on management and innovation*, UK: Edward Elgar.

Berwick, Donald; James, Brent; and Coye, Molly (2003) 'Connections between quality measurement and improvement', *Medical Care*, vol, 41, no. 1, pp.I30–I38. https://www.jstor.org/stable/3767726

Besley, Timothy (2013) 'What's the good of the market? An essay on Michael Sandel's *What Money Can't Buy*', *Journal of Economic Literature*, vol. 51, no. 2, pp.478–95. https://doi.org/10.1257/jel.51.2.478

Besley, Timothy and Ghatak, Maitreesh (2001) 'Government versus private ownership of public goods', *The Quarterly Journal of Economics*, vol. 116, no. 4, pp.1343–72. https://doi.org/10.1162/003355301753265598

Besley, Timothy and Ghatak, Maitreesh (2001) 'Incentives, choice, and accountability in the provision of public services', *Oxford Review of Economic Policy*, vol. 19, no. 2, pp.235–49. https://doi.org/10.1093/oxrep/19.2.235

Bevan, Aneurin (1978) *In place of fear*, UK: Quartet Books.

Bevan, Gwyn (1980) 'Cash limits', *Fiscal Studies*, vol. 1, no 4, pp.26–43. https://doi.org/10.1111/j.1475-5890.1980.tb00450.x

Bevan, Gwyn (2009) 'The search for a proportionate care law by formula funding in the English NHS', *Financial Accountability & Management*, vol. 25, no. 4, pp.391–410. https://doi.org/10.1111/j.1468-0408.2009.00484.x

Bevan, Gwyn (2014) *The impacts of asymmetric devolution on health care in the four countries of the UK*, UK: Health Foundation.

https://www.health.org.uk/sites/default/files/TheImpactsOfAsymmetric
DevolutionOnHealthCareInFourCountriesUK.pdf

Bevan, Gwyn and Cornwell, Jocelyn (2006) 'Structure and logic of regulation and governance of quality of health care: Was OFSTED a model for the Commission for Health Improvement?' *Health Economics, Policy and Law*, vol, 1, no. 4, p.357. https://doi.org/10.1017/S1744133106005020

Bevan, Gwyn; De Poli, Chiara; Keng, Mi Jun; and Raine, Rosalind (2020) 'How valid are projections of the future prevalence of diabetes? Rapid reviews of prevalence-based and Markov chain models and comparisons of different models' projections for England', *BMJ Open*, vol. 10, no. 3, e033483. http://dx.doi.org/10.1136/bmjopen-2019-033483

Bevan, Gwyn; Evans, Alice; and Nuti, Sabina (2019) 'Reputations count: Why benchmarking performance is improving health care across the world', *Health Economics, Policy and Law*, vol. 14, no. 2, pp.141–61. https://doi.org/10.1017/S1744133117000561

Bevan, Gwyn and Hamblin, Richard (2009) 'Hitting and missing targets by ambulance services for emergency calls: effects of different systems of performance measurement within the UK', *Journal of the Royal Statistical Society: Series A (Statistics in Society)*, vol. 172, no. 1, pp.161–90. https://doi.org/10.1111/j.1467-985X.2008.00557.x

Bevan, Gwyn; Helderman, Jan-Kees; and Wilsford, David (2010) 'Changing choices in health care: Implications for equity, efficiency and cost', *Health Economics, Policy and Law*, vol. 5, no. 3, pp.251–67. https://doi.org/10.1017/S1744133110000022

Bevan, Gwyn and Hood, Christopher (2006) 'What's measured is what matters: Targets and gaming in the English public health care system', *Public Administration*, vol. 84, no. 3, pp.517–38. https://doi.org/10.1111/j.1467-9299.2006.00600.x

Bevan, Gwyn; Karanikolos, Marina; Exley, Josephine; Nolte, Ellen; Connolly, Sheelah; and Mays, Nicholas (2014) *The four health systems of the United Kingdom: How do they compare?* UK: Health Foundation. https://www.health.org.uk/publications/the-four-health-systems-of-the -united-kingdom-how-do-they-compare

Bevan, Gwyn and Janus, Katharina (2011) 'Why hasn't integrated health care developed widely in the United States and not at all in England?' *Journal of Health Politics, Policy and Law*, vol. 36, no. 1, pp.141–64. https://doi.org/10.1215/03616878-1191135

Bevan, Gwyn and Wilson, Deborah (2013) 'Does "naming and shaming" work for schools and hospitals? Lessons from natural experiments following devolution in England and Wales', *Public Money and*

Management, vol. 33, no. 4, pp.245–52.
https://doi.org/10.1080/09540962.2013.799801

Beveridge, William (1942) *Social insurance and allied services* ('The
Beveridge Report'), UK: HMSO.
https://archive.org/details/in.ernet.dli.2015.275849/page/n7/mode/2up

Beveridge, William (1943) *Pillars of security and other war-time essays and
addresses*, UK: George Allen & Unwin.

Bingham, Kate and Hames, Tim (2022) *The long shot: The inside story of the
race to vaccinate Britain*, UK: Oneworld.

Bjørnland, Hilde (1998) 'The economic effects of North Sea oil on the
manufacturing sector', *Scottish Journal of Political Economy*, vol. 45, no. 5,
p.582. https://doi.org/10.1111/1467-9485.00112

Black, Fischer and Scholes, Myron (1973) 'The pricing of options and corporate liabilities', *Journal of Political Economy*, vol. 81, no. 3, pp.637–54.
https://www.jstor.org/stable/1831029

Board of Education (1926) *Report of the Consultative Committee on the
Education of the Adolescent* (The Hadow Report), UK: HMSO.
http://www.educationengland.org.uk/documents/hadow1926
/hadow1926.html#02

Board of Education (1938) *Report of the Consultative Committee on Secondary Education with Special Reference to Grammar Schools and Technical
High Schools* (The Spens Report), UK: HMSO.
http://www.educationengland.org.uk/documents/spens/spens1938.html

Bogdanor, Vernon (2001) *Devolution in the United Kingdom*, UK: Oxford
University Press.

Bolton, Paul (2011) *Education Maintenance Allowance (EMA) statistics*, UK:
House of Commons Library. https://dera.ioe.ac.uk/22792/1/SN05778.pdf

Bowles, Samuel (2008) 'Policies designed for self-interested citizens may
undermine "the moral sentiments": Evidence from economic experiments', *Science*, vol. 320, no. 5883, pp.1605–09.
https://doi.org/10.1126/science.1152110

Bowles, Samuel (2016) *The moral economy: Why good incentives are no
substitute for good citizens*, UK: Yale University Press.

Bowley, Marion (1937) *Nassau Senior and classical economics*, UK: George
Allen & Unwin.

Brook, Robert; Lohr, Kathleen; and Keeler, Emmett (2006) *The health insurance experiment: A classic RAND study speaks to the current health care
reform debate*, US: RAND Corporation. https://perma.cc/FD68-LPDA

Brown, Archie (2010) *The rise and fall of communism*, UK: Vintage.

Bruckmeier, Kerstin and Wigger, Berthold (2014) 'The effects of tuition fees on transition from high school to university in Germany', *Economics of Education Review*, vol. 41, pp.14–23. https://doi.org/10.1016/j.econedurev.2014.03.009

Bullough, Oliver (2018) *Moneyland: Why thieves and crooks now rule the world and how to take it back*, UK: Profile.

Burgess, Simon; Greaves, Ellen; and Vignoles, Anna (2020) *School places: A fair choice? School choice, inequality and options for reform of school admissions in England*, UK: Sutton Trust. https://dera.ioe.ac.uk/35131/1/School-Places.pdf

Burgess, Simon; Wilson, Deborah; and Worth, Jack (2013) 'A natural experiment in school accountability: The impact of school performance information on pupil progress', *Journal of Public Economics*, vol. 106, pp.57–67. https://doi.org/10.1016/j.jpubeco.2013.06.005

Burkhead, Jesse (1954) 'The balanced budget', *The Quarterly Journal of Economics*, vol. 68, no. 2, pp.191–216. https://doi.org/10.2307/1884446

Business, Energy and Industrial Strategy and Work and Pensions Committees [House of Commons] (2018) *Carillion: Second joint report from the Business, Energy and Industrial Strategy and Work and Pensions Committee*, Session 2017–19 HC 769, UK: The Stationery Office. https://publications.parliament.uk/pa/cm201719/cmselect/cmworpen/769/76903.htm

Butler, Richard (1944) Education Act 1944, UK: HMSO. https://www.legislation.gov.uk/ukpga/Geo6/7-8/31/contents/enacted

Butler, Richard (1973) *The art of the possible*, UK: Harmondsworth.

Byatt, Ian (2019) *A regulator's sign off: Changing the taps in Britain*, UK: Short Run Press.

Cabinet Office and Scientific Advisory Group for Emergencies (2012) 'Scientific Advisory Group for Emergencies (SAGE): A strategic framework'. https://www.gov.uk/government/publications/scientific-advisory-group-for-emergencies-sage

Calvert, Jonathan and Arbuthnott, George (2021) *Failures of state: The inside story of Britain's battle with coronavirus*, UK: HarperCollins.

Campbell, John (1997) *Nye Bevan: A biography*, UK: Richard Cohen Books.

Cardim-Dias, Joana and Sibieta, Luke (2022) *Inequalities in GCSE results across England and Wales*, UK: Education Policy Institute. https://epi.org.uk/wp-content/uploads/2022/07/Inequalities-in-Wales-and-England.pdf

Carter, Zachary (2021) *The price of peace: money, democracy, and the life of John Maynard Keynes*, US: Penguin.

Case, Anne and Deaton, Angus (2021) *Deaths of despair and the future of capitalism*, UK: Princeton University Press. https://doi.org/10.1515/9780691199955

Chandler Jr, Alfred D. (1977) *The visible hand*, US: Harvard University Press. http://library.mpib-berlin.mpg.de/toc/z2010_942.pdf

Chassin, Mark (2002) 'Achieving and sustaining improved quality: Lessons from New York State and cardiac surgery', *Health Affairs*, vol. 21, no. 4, pp.40–51. https://doi.org/10.1377/hlthaff.21.4.40

Chitty, Clyde (2004) *Education policy in Britain*, UK: Palgrave.

Chowdry, Haroon; Crawford, Claire; Dearden, Lorraine; Goodman, Alissa; and Vignoles, Anna (2010) *Widening participation in higher education: Analysis using linked administrative data*, UK: IFS Working Paper W10/04. http://www.ifs.org.uk/publications/4951

Chrystal, K. Alec (1984) 'Dutch disease or monetarist medicine? The British economy under Mrs. Thatcher', *Federal Reserve Bank of St. Louis Review*, vol. 66, no. 5, pp.27–37. https://perma.cc/Y3KG-BLZH

Clarendon, Lord (1864) *Report of Her Majesty's Commissioners appointed to inquire into the revenues and management of certain colleges and schools and the studies pursued and the instruction given therein* (The Clarendon Report), UK: George Edward Eyre and William Spottiswoode. https://books.google.com/books?id=rYNLAAAAcAAJ&pg=PR1& source=gbs_selected_pages&cad=2#v=onepage&q&f=false

Coase, Ronald (1937) 'The nature of the firm', *Economica*, vol. 4, no. 16, pp.386–405. https://doi.org/10.1111/j.1468-0335.1937.tb00002.x

Coase, Ronald (1964) 'Papers and proceedings of the Seventy-Sixth Annual Meeting of the American Economic Association', *The American Economic Review*, vol. 54, no. 3, pp.194–95. https://www.jstor.org/stable/1818503.

Coase, Ronald (1988) '1. The nature of the firm: Origin', *The Journal of Law, Economics, and Organization*, vol. 4, no. 1, pp.3–17. https://doi.org/10.1093/oxfordjournals.jleo.a036946.

Coase, Ronald (1988) '3. The nature of the firm: Influence', *The Journal of Law, Economics, and Organization*, vol. 4, no. 1, pp.33–47. https://doi.org/10.1093/oxfordjournals.jleo.a036947

Colin Thomé, David (2009) *Mid Staffordshire NHS Foundation Trust: A review of lessons learnt for commissioners and performance managers following the Healthcare Commission investigation*, UK: Department of Health. https://www.londoncouncils.gov.uk/node/7595

Commission for Health Improvement (2002) *Report of a clinical governance review at Mid Staffordshire General NHS Trust*, UK: The Stationery Office.

Commission for Health Improvement (2003) *NHS performance ratings, acute trusts, specialist trusts, ambulance trusts*, UK: Commission for Health Improvement.

The Community Cohesion Review Team (Chair Ted Cantle) (2001) *Community cohesion: A report of the Independent Review Team*, UK: Home Office, p.10. https://tedcantle.co.uk/pdf/communitycohesion%20cantlereport.pdf

Comptroller and Auditor General (2019) *Help to Buy: Equity Loan scheme – progress review* (HC 2216), UK: National Audit Office. https://www.nao.org.uk/reports/help-to-buy-equity-loan-scheme -progress-review/

Comptroller and Auditor General (2020) *Investigation into the rescue of Carillion's PFI hospital contracts*, Session 2019–20, HC23. https://www.nao.org.uk/reports/investigation-into-the-rescue-of -carillions-pfi-hospital-contracts/1

Connolly, Sheelah; Bevan, Gwyn; and Mays, Nicholas (2010) *Funding and performance of healthcare systems in the four countries of the UK before and after devolution*, UK: The Nuffield Trust. https://researchonline.lshtm.ac.uk/id/eprint/3827/1/funding_and _performance_of_healthcare_systems_in_the_four_countries_report _full.pdf.

Consultative Council on Medical and Allied Services (Ministry of Health, Great Britain) (1920/1950) *The Dawson report on the future provision of medical and allied services 1920: An interim report to the Minister of Health*, UK: King Edward's Hospital Fund for London. https://archive.kingsfund.org.uk/concern/published_works/000018795?l ocale=en#?cv=10&xywh=-2827,-269,7228,2289

Conway, Earl and Batalden, Paul (2015) 'Like Magic? ("Every system is perfectly designed…")', *Institute for Healthcare Improvement*, blogpost. 21 August. http://www.ihi.org/communities/blogs/origin-of-every-system-is -perfectly-designed-quote

Cooper, Luke and Cooper, Christabel (2020) '"Get Brexit done": The new political divides of England and Wales at the 2019 election', *The Political Quarterly*, vol. 91, no. 4, pp.751–61. https://doi.org/10.1111/1467-923X.12918

Cornford, F.M. (1908) *Microcosmographia Academica*, UK: Bowes and Bowes. https://www.maths.ed.ac.uk/~v1ranick/baked/micro.pdf

Coutts, Ken; Tarling, Roger; Ward, Terry; and Wilkinson, Frank (1981) 'The economic consequences of Mrs Thatcher', *Cambridge Journal of Economics*, vol. 5, no. 1, pp.81–93. https://www.jstor.org/stable/23596658

Crafts, Nicholas and Mills, Terence (2020) 'Is the UK productivity slowdown unprecedented?' *National Institute Economic Review*, vol. 251, pp.R47–R53. https://doi.org/10.1017/nie.2020.6

Crawford, Claire; Dearden, Lorraine; Micklewright, John; and Vignoles, Anna (2017) *Family background and university success: Differences in higher education access and outcomes in England*, UK: Oxford University Press. https://doi.org/10.1093/acprof:oso/9780199689132.001.0001

Crewe, Tom (2016) 'The strange death of municipal England'. *London Review of Books*, vol. 38, no. 24, pp.6–10. https://perma.cc/PX5X-L63K

Crosland, Anthony (1967) *The future of socialism*, US: Schocken.

Crossman, Richard (1975) *The diaries of a cabinet minister, vol. 1, minister of housing 1964–66*, UK: Hamish Hamilton and Jonathan Cape.

Crouch, Colin (2011) *The strange non-death of neo-liberalism*, UK: Polity.

Dahrendorf, Ralf (1995) *LSE. A history of the London School of Economics and Political Science*, UK: Oxford University Press. https://doi.org/10.1093/acprof:oso/9780198202400.001.0001

Daniels, Norman (1990) *Just health care*, UK: Cambridge University Press. https://doi.org/10.1017/CBO9780511624971

Daniels, Norman and Sabin, James (2008) 'Accountability for reasonableness: an update', *BMJ*, vol. 337. https://doi.org/10.1136/bmj.a1850

Davies, Aled (2013) '"Right to buy": The development of a Conservative housing policy, 1945–1980', *Contemporary British History*, vol. 27, no. 3, pp.421–44. https://doi.org/10.1080/13619462.2013.824660

Davis, John (2002) 'The Inner London Education Authority and the William Tyndale Junior School affair', *Oxford Review of Education*, vol. 28, no 2–3, pp.275–98. https://doi.org/10.1080/03054980220143423

Delamothe, Tony and Godlee, Fiona (2011) 'Dr Lansley's monster', *BMJ*, vol. 342, d408. https://doi.org/10.1136/bmj.d408

Department of Education (2021) 'How does school funding work and how does the budget affect it?' https://perma.cc/KRN8-ASJU

Department of Education (2022) *The national funding formulae for schools and high needs. 2023–24*, UK: Department of Education. https://assets.publishing.service.gov.uk/government/uploads/system/uploads/attachment_data/file/1091988/2023-24_NFF_Policy_Document_.pdf

Department of Health (2002) *NHS performance ratings. Acute trusts, ambulance trusts, mental health trusts*, UK: Department of Health.

Devine, Jack (2014) 'What really happened in Chile: The CIA, the coup against Allende, and the rise of Pinochet', *Foreign Affairs*, vol. 93, no. 4, pp.26–35. https://www.jstor.org/stable/24483554

Dixon, Huw (1996) 'Deindustrialisation and Britain's industrial performance since 1960', *The Economic Journal*, vol. 106, no. 434, pp.170–71. https://doi.org/10.2307/2234940

Dobb, Maurice (1970) *Socialist planning: Some problems*. London: Lawrence and Wishart.

Dobson, R.B. (ed.) (1970) *The peasants' revolt of 1381*, UK: Macmillan.

Doyle, Michael and Griffin, Martyn (2012) 'Raised aspirations and attainment? A review of the impact of Aimhigher (2004–2011) on widening participation in higher education in England'. *London Review of Education*, vol. 10, no. 1, pp.75–88. http://dx.doi.org/10.1080/14748460.2012.659060

Dunleavy, Patrick (1978) *The politics of high rise housing in Britain: Local communities tackle mass housing*, UK: University of Oxford. http://eprints.lse.ac.uk/82066/

Dunleavy, Patrick and Hood, Christopher (1994) 'From old public administration to new public management', *Public Money & Management*, vol. 14, no. 3, pp.9–16. https://doi.org/10.1080/09540969409387823

Dworkin, Ronald (2000) *Sovereign virtue: The theory and practice of equality*, UK: Harvard University Press.

Eckstein, Harry (1958) *The English Health Service*, US: Harvard University Press.

Eckstein, Harry (1963) 'The genesis of the National Health Service', *Current History*, vol. 45, no. 263, pp.6–51. https://www.jstor.org/stable/45310948

The Economist and Solstad, Sondre (2021) 'The pandemic's true death toll', *The Economist*. https://www.economist.com/graphic-detail/coronavirus-excess-deaths-estimates

Eichengreen, Barry (1996) 'Explaining Britain's economic performance: A critical note', *Economic Journal*, vol. 106, no. 434, p.213. https://doi.org/10.2307/2234944

Elliott, Martin (2015) *The Bristol scandal and its consequences: Politics, rationalisation and the use and abuse of information*. Gresham Lecture, 18 February.

https://www.gresham.ac.uk/lectures-and-events/the-bristol-scandal
-and-its-consequences-politics-rationalisation-and-the-use

Enthoven, Alain (1978) 'Consumer-choice health plan (second of two parts). A national-health-insurance proposal based on regulated competition in the private sector', *The New England Journal of Medicine*, vol. 298, no. 13, pp.709–20. https://doi.org/10.1056/nejm197803302981304

Enthoven, Alain (1985) *Reflections on the management of the NHS*, UK: Nuffield Provincial Hospitals Trust. https://perma.cc/5S95-8ZFF

Environment Agency (2022) *Water and sewerage companies in England: Environmental performance report 2021*.
https://www.gov.uk/government/publications/water-and-sewerage
-companies-in-england-environmental-performance-report-2021
/water-and-sewerage-companies-in-england-environmental
-performance-report-2021

European Commission (2019) 'Regional GDP per capita ranged from 31 per cent to 626 per cent of the EU average in 2017'. *Eurostat News Release 34/2019*, 26 February.
https://ec.europa.eu/eurostat/documents/portlet_file_entry/2995521/1
-26022019-AP-EN.pdf/f765d183-c3d2-4e2f-9256-cc6665909c80#:~:
text=In%20all%20Member%20States%20where%20there%20are%20
more,in%20these%2020%20regions%20is%2022.9%20million%20persons

Evans, Robert (1987) 'Public health insurance: The collective purchase of individual care', *Health Policy*, vol. 7, no. 2, pp.115–34.
https://doi.org/10.1016/0168-8510(87)90026-1

Expenditure Committee (1973–74) *Public expenditure to 1977–78 (Cmnd 5519), Public Expenditure and the Balance of Resources*, UK: HMSO.

Farquharson, Christine; McNally, Sandra; and Tahir, Imran (2022) *Education inequalities*, UK: IFS Deaton Review of Inequalities.
https://ifs.org.uk/inequality/wp-content/uploads/2022/08/Education-in
equalities.pdf

Feachem, Richard; Dixon, Jennifer; Berwick, Donald; Enthoven, Alain; Sekhri, Neelam; and White, Karen (2002) 'Getting more for their dollar: A comparison of the NHS with California's Kaiser Permanente', *BMJ*, vol. 324, pp.135–43. https://doi.org/10.1136/bmj.324.7330.135

Ferguson, Niall (2021) *Doom: The politics of catastrophe*, UK: Penguin.

Ferreyra, María; Avitabile, Ciro; and Paz, Francisco (2017) *At a crossroads: Higher education in Latin America and the Caribbean*, US: World Bank Publications. https://perma.cc/YX6R-YMDL

Feynman, Richard (1989) *What do you care what other people think?* UK: Bantam.

Foot, Michael (1962) *Aneurin Bevan: A Biography; Volume One: 1897–1945*, UK: MacGibbon & Kee.

Foot, Michael (1975) *Aneurin Bevan: Volume two: 1945–1960*, UK: Paladin.

Forder, James (2019) *Milton Friedman*, UK: Palgrave Macmillan.

Foroohar, Rana (2016) *Makers and takers. How Wall Street destroyed Main Street*, US: Currency.

Frey, Bruno (2013) 'How should people be rewarded for their work?' in Oliver, Adam (ed.) *Behavioural public policy*, UK: Cambridge University Press, pp.165–83. https://doi.org/10.1017/CBO9781107337190

Friedman, Milton (1970) 'The first and core principle is that "the social responsibility of business is to increase its profits"', *New York Times*. https://perma.cc/7MMB-67DY

Friedman, Milton (1976) *Adam Smith's relevance for 1976*, US: Graduate School of Business, The University of Chicago (Selected Papers No. 50). https://perma.cc/VCZ9-26ME

Friedman, Milton and Friedman, Rose (1990) *Free to choose: A personal statement*, UK: Secker and Warburg.

Friedman, Milton and Schwartz, Anna (2008) *A monetary history of the United States, 1867–1960*, US: Princeton University Press. https://muse.jhu.edu/pub/267/monograph/book/36656

Fung, Constance; Lim, Yee-Wei; Mattke, Soeren; Damberg, Cheryl; and Shekelle, Paul (2008) 'Systematic review: The evidence that publishing patient care performance data improves quality of care', *Annals of Internal Medicine*, vol. 148, no. 2, pp.111–23. https://doi.org/10.7326/0003-4819-148-2-200801150-00006

Gerstle, Gary (2022) *The rise and fall of the neoliberal order: America and the world in the free market era*, UK: Oxford University Press. https://doi.org/10.1093/oso/9780197519646.001.0001

Goldberg, Peter (1975) 'The politics of the Allende overthrow in Chile', *Political Science Quarterly*, vol. 90, no. 1, pp.93–116. https://doi.org/10.2307/2148700

Goodhart, Charles (1964) 'A monetary history of the United States, 1867–1960', *Economica*, New Series, vol. 31, no. 123, p.314. https://www.jstor.org/stable/2550627

Goodhart, Charles (1984) *Problems of monetary management: The UK experience*, UK: Macmillan Education.

Goodhart, Charles (1997) 'Whither now?' *PSL Quarterly Review*, vol. 50, no. 203. https://rosa.uniroma1.it/rosa04/psl_quarterly_review/article/view/10583

Goodman, Geoffrey (2003) *From Bevan to Blair: Fifty years' reporting from the political front line*, UK: Pluto Press.

Gorlizki, Yoram and Khlevniuk, Oleg (2020) *Substate dictatorship: Networks, loyalty, and institutional change in the Soviet Union*, US: Yale University Press. https://www.jstor.org/stable/j.ctv14rmq50.11

Gray, Sue (2022) *Findings of second permanent secretary's investigation into alleged gatherings on government premises during Covid restrictions*, UK: Cabinet Office. https://assets.publishing.service.gov.uk/government/uploads/system /uploads/attachment_data/file/1078404/2022-05 25_FINAL_FIND INGS_OF_SECOND_PERMANENT_SECRETARY_INTO_ALLEGED _GATHERINGS.pdf

Hajikazemi, Sara; Aaltonen, Kirsi; Ahola, Tuomas; Aarseth, Wenche; and Andersen, Bjorn (2020) 'Normalising deviance in construction project organizations: A case study on the collapse of Carillion', *Construction Management and Economics*, vol. 38, no. 12, p.1128. https://doi.org/10.1080/01446193.2020.1804069

Ham, Christopher (2008) 'World class commissioning: A health policy chimera?' *Journal of Health Services Research & Policy*, vol. 13, no. 2, pp.116–121. https://doi.org/10.1258/jhsrp.2008.007177

Ham, Chris; York, Nick; Sutch, Steve; and Shaw, Rob (2003) 'Hospital bed utilisation in the NHS, Kaiser Permanente and the US Medicare programme: Analysis of routine data', *BMJ*, vol. 327, no. 1275. https://doi.org/10.1136/bmj.327.7426.1257

Hanley, Lynsey (2016) *Respectable: The experience of class*, UK: Penguin.

Hanley, Lynsey (2017) *Estates an intimate history*, UK: Granta.

Hardin, Garrett (1968) 'The tragedy of the commons: The population problem has no technical solution; it requires a fundamental extension in morality', *Science*, vol. 162, no. 3859, pp.1243–48. https://doi.org/10.1126/science.162.3859.12

Harris, Jose (1997) *William Beveridge: A biography*, UK: Oxford University. https://doi.org/10.1093/acprof:oso/9780198206859.001.0001

Harris, Jose (2009) 'The Webbs and Beveridge', in *From the workhouse to welfare*, UK: Fabian Society. https://fabians.org.uk/publication/from-workhouse-to-welfare/

Harris, Kenneth (1984) *Attlee*, UK: Weidenfeld and Nicolson.

Hart, Julian Tudor (1971) 'The inverse care law', *The Lancet*, vol. 297, no. 7696, pp.405–12. https://doi.org/10.1016/S0140-6736(71)92410-X

Hart, Oliver (2008) 'Economica Coase lecture: Reference points and the theory of the firm', *Economica*, vol. 75, no. 299, pp.404–11. https://doi.org/10.1111/j.1468-0335.2007.00659.x

Hatcher, John (1994) 'England in the aftermath of the Black Death', *Past & Present*, vol. 144. https://doi.org/10.1093/past/144.1.3

Hayek, Friedrich von (1944) *The road to serfdom*, UK: Routledge.

Hayek, Friedrich von (1999) *The condensed version of The Road to Serfdom by F. A. Hayek as it appeared in the April 1945 edition of Reader's Digest*, UK: The Institute of Economic Affairs. https://iea.org.uk/publications/the-road-to-serfdom/

Hayek, Friedrich von (1945) 'The use of knowledge in society', *The American Economic Review*, vol. 35, no. 4, pp.518–30. https://www.jstor.org/stable/1809376

Healey, Denis (1979) 'Oil, money and recession', *Foreign Affairs*, vol. 58, no. 2, pp.217–30. https://doi.org/10.2307/20040412

Health and Social Care Committee and Science and Technology Committee [House of Commons] (2021) *Oral evidence: Coronavirus: Lessons learnt*, HC 95, Wednesday, 26 May https://committees.parliament.uk/event/4435/formal-meeting-oral -evidence-session/

House of Commons, Health and Social Care Committee and Science and Technology Committee [House of Commons] (2021) *Coronavirus: Lessons learned to date*, HC 92. https://committees.parliament.uk/work/657/coronavirus-lessons-learnt/

Healthcare Commission (2009) *Investigation into Mid Staffordshire NHS Foundation Trust*, UK: Healthcare Commission. https://www.bl.uk/collection-items/investigation-into-mid-stafford-shire-nhs-foundation-trust

The Health Foundation (2012) *Looking for value in hard times*, https://www.health.org.uk/publications/looking-for-value-in-hard-times

Hennessy, Peter (1993) *Never again: Britain 1945–51*, UK: Vintage.

Hennessy, Peter (2022) *A duty of care*, UK: Penguin.

Her Majesty's Stationery Office (1963) *Report of the Committee appointed by the prime minister under the chairmanship of Lord Robbins*, UK: HMSO. http://www.educationengland.org.uk/documents/robbins/robbins1963 .html

Herkert, Joseph (1991) 'Management's hat trick: Misuse of "engineering judgment" in the Challenger incident', *Journal of Business Ethics*, vol.10, pp.617–20. https://www.jstor.org/stable/25072193

Hewes, Amy (1926) 'The task of the English Coal Commission', *Journal of Political Economy*, vol. 34, no. 1, pp.1–12. https://doi.org/10.1086/253735

Hibbard, Judith (2008) 'What can we say about the impact of public reporting? Inconsistent execution yields variable results', *Annals of Internal Medicine*, vol. 148, no. 2, pp.160–61. https://doi.org/10.7326/0003-4819-148-2-200801150-00011

Hibbard, Judith; Stockard, Jean; and Tusler, Martin (2005) 'Hospital performance reports: Impact on quality, market share, and reputation', *Health Affairs*, vol. 24, no. 4, pp.1150–60. https://doi.org/10.1377/hlthaff.24.4.1150

Hibbard, Judith; Stockard, Jean; and Tusler, Martin (2003) 'Does publicizing hospital performance stimulate quality improvement efforts?' *Health Affairs*, vol. 22, no. 2, pp.84–94. https://doi.org/10.1377/hlthaff.22.2.84

Hicks, John (1969) *A theory of economic history*, UK: Oxford University Press.

Hill, Fiona (2021) *There Is Nothing for You Here. Finding Opportunity in the Twenty-First Century*, US: Harper Collins.

Hillman, Nicholas (2010) 'The Public Schools Commission: "Impractical, expensive and harmful to children"?' *Contemporary British History*, vol. 24, no. 4, pp.511–31. https://doi.org/10.1080/13619462.2010.518413

Hirsch, Fred (2005) *Social limits to growth*, UK: Routledge. https://doi.org/10.4159/harvard.9780674497900

Hirschman, Albert (1970) *Exit, voice, and loyalty: Responses to decline in firms, organizations, and states*, UK: Harvard University Press.

Hitchens, Peter (2022) *A revolution betrayed: How egalitarians wrecked the British education system*, UK: Bloomsbury.

Hodge, Margaret (2017) *Called to account: How corporate bad behaviour and government waste combine*, UK: Little, Brown.

Honigsbaum, Frank (1979) *The division in British medicine: A history of the separation of general practice from hospital care, 1911–1968*, US: St Martin's Press.

Hood, Christopher (1995) 'The "new public management" in the 1980s: Variations on a theme', *Accounting, Organizations and Society*, vol. 20, no 2–3, pp.93–109. https://doi.org/10.1016/0361-3682(93)E0001-W

Hood, Christopher (2007) 'Public service management by numbers: Why does it vary? Where has it come from? What are the gaps and the puzzles?' *Public Money and Management*, vol. 27, no. 2, pp.95–102. https://doi.org/10.1111/j.1467-9302.2007.00564.x

Hood, Christopher; Emmerson, Carl; and Dixon, Ruth (2009) *Public spending in hard times*, ESRC Public Services Programme. https://perma.cc/K4FE-3J8Q

Hood, Christopher; James, Oliver; Jones, George; Scott, Colin; and Travers, Tony (1999) *Regulation inside government: Waste watchers, quality police, and sleazebusters*, UK: Oxford University Press. https://doi.org/10.1093/0198280998.001.0001

House of Lords Industry and Regulators Committee (HLIRC) (2023) *The affluent and the effluent: Cleaning up failures in water and sewage regulation*, HL Paper 166. https://committees.parliament.uk/committee/517/industry-and -regulators-committee/HoL

Hume, David and Miller, Eugene (1994) *Essays: Moral, political, and literary*, US: Liberty Fund. https://apps.thelemistas.org/PDF/Hume_D-Essays.pdf

Ibsen, Henrik (1882) *Enemy of the people*. https://www.fulltextarchive.com/pdfs/An-Enemy-of-the-People.pdf

Industrial Strategy Council (2021) *Annual report*, UK: Industrial Strategy Council. https://industrialstrategycouncil.org/sites/default/files/attachments /ISC%20Annual%20Report%202021.pdf

Intriligator, Michael; Wedel, Janine; and Lee, Catherine (2006) 'What Russia can learn from China in its transition to a market economy', Chapter 5 in Verweij, Marco and Thompson, Michael (eds) *Clumsy solutions for a complex world*, UK: Palgrave Macmillan, pp.105–31. https://link.springer.com/content/pdf/10.1057/9780230624887_5. pdf?pdf=inline%20link

Ioannidis, John; Axfors, Cathrine; and Contopoulos-Ioannidis, Despina (2021) 'Second versus first wave of COVID-19 deaths: Shifts in age distribution and in nursing home fatalities', *Environmental Research*, vol. 195, 110856. https://doi.org/10.1016/j.envres.2021.110856

Islam, Nazrul; Shkolnikov, Vladimir; Acosta, Rolando; Klimkin, Ilya; Kawachi, Ichiro; Irizarry, Rafael; Alicandro, Gianfranco; Khunti, Kamlesh, et al (2021) 'Excess deaths associated with Covid-19 pandemic in 2020: Age and sex disaggregated time series analysis in 29 high income countries', *BMJ*, 373, n1137. https://doi.org/10.1136/bmj.n1137

James, Oliver (2004) 'The UK core executive's use of public service agreements as a tool of governance', *Public Administration*, vol. 82, no. 2, pp.397–419. https://doi.org/10.1111/j.0033-3298.2004.00400.x

Janssen, Fanny; Bardoutsos, Anastasios; and Vidra, Nikoletta (2020) 'Obesity prevalence in the long-term future in 18 European countries and in the USA'. *Obesity facts*, vol. 13, no. 5, pp.514–27. https://doi.org/10.1093/advances/nmy055

Jensen, Michael and Meckling, William (1976) 'Theory of the firm: Managerial behavior, agency costs and ownership structure', *Journal of*

Financial Economics, vol. 3, no. 4, pp.305–60.
https://doi.org/10.1016/0304-405X(76)90026-X

Johnson, Boris [@BorisJohnson] (2020, 11 March). *Dr Jenny Harries, Deputy Chief Medical Officer, came into Downing Street to answer some of the most commonly asked questions on coronavirus* [Tweet]. Twitter, https://twitter.com/BorisJohnson/status/1237760976482598913. Archived at https://web.archive.org/web/20200312035546/https://twitter.com/BorisJohnson/status/1237760976482598913

Johnson, Michael (1992) 'Evaluating the privatisation of the English and Welsh water industry', *The Economic and Labour Relations Review*, vol. 3, no. 2, pp.72–97. https://doi.org/10.1177/103530469200300204

Johnson, Paul (2019) *Doubling of the Housing Benefit bill is a sign of something deeply wrong*, UK: Institute for Fiscal Studies. https://ifs.org.uk/publications/13940

Jowett, Benjamin (Translator) (1970) *The dialogues of Plato. Volume 4 The republic*, UK: Sphere Books, p.186.

Kahneman, Daniel (2011) *Thinking, fast and slow*, US: Farrar, Strauss and Giroux.

Kampfner, John (2020) Why the Germans do it better: Notes from a grown-up country, UK: Atlantic.

Karlinsky, Ariel; Knutson, Victoria; Aleshin-Guendel, Serge; Chatterji, Somnath; and Wakefield, Jon (2023) 'The WHO estimates of excess mortality associated with the COVID-19 pandemic', *Nature*, vol. 613, no. 7942, pp.130–37. https://doi.org/10.1038/s41586-022-05522-2.

Kay, John (2011) *Obliquity: Why our goals are best achieved indirectly*, UK: Profile.

Kay, John (2015) *Other people's money*, UK: Profile.

Kay, John and King, Mervyn (2020) *Radical uncertainty. Decision-making beyond the numbers*, UK: The Bridge Street Press.

Kelly, Gavin; and Pearce, Nick (2021) 'Beveridge at eighty: Learning the right lessons', *The Political Quarterly*, https://doi.org/10.1111/1467-923X.13227

Keynes, John Maynard (1919/2017) *The economic consequences of the peace*, UK: Routledge. https://www.econlib.org/library/YPDBooks/Keynes/kynsCP.html

Keynes, John Maynard (1925) *The economic consequences of Mr. Churchill*, UK: Hogarth Press. https://books.google.co.uk/books?hl=en&lr=&id=euArAAAAMAAJ&oi=fnd&pg=PA5&dq=the+economic+consequences+of+mr+churchill&ots=sI_VzFewmP&sig=wPMI3MQKrgBA--qJrgLupztlOy0#v=onepage&q=the%20economic%20consequences%20of%20mr%20churchill&f=false

Keynes, John Maynard (1936/1973) *The general theory of interest, employment and money*, UK: Macmillan. https://www.files.ethz.ch/isn/125515/1366_keynestheoryofemployment.pdf

Kidson, Marc and Norris, Emma (2014) *Implementing the London Challenge*, UK: Joseph Rowntree Foundation. https://camdenlearning.org.uk/wp-content/uploads/2019/06/Implementing-the-London-Challenge.pdf

King, Anthony and Crewe, Ivor (2013) *The blunders of our governments*, UK: Oneworld.

Knight, Frank (1921) *Risk, uncertainty and profit*, US: Houghton Mifflin. https://fraser.stlouisfed.org/files/docs/publications/books/risk/riskuncertaintyprofit.pdf

Kogan, Maurice (2006) 'Anthony Crosland: Intellectual and politician', *Oxford Review of Education*, vol. 32, no. 1, p.78. https://doi.org/10.1080/03054980500496452

Kontis, Vasilis; Bennett, James; Parks, Robbie; Rashid, Theo; Pearson-Stuttard, Jonathan; Asaria, Perviz; Zhou, Bin et al (2022) 'Lessons learned and lessons missed: Impact of the coronavirus disease 2019 (Covid-19) pandemic on all-cause mortality in 40 industrialised countries and US states prior to mass vaccination', *Wellcome Open Research*, vol. 6, p.279. https://doi.org/10.12688/wellcomeopenres.17253.2

Kornai, Janos (1959) *Overcentralization in economic administration: A critical analysis based on experience in Hungarian light industry*, UK: Oxford University Press.

Krugman, Paul (1994) *Peddling prosperity: Economic sense and nonsense in the age of diminished expectations*, UK: WW Norton & Company.

Kuper, Simon (2022) *Chums: How a tiny caste of Oxford Tories took over the UK*, UK: Profile.

Labour Research Department (1926) *The coal crisis: Facts from the Samuel Commission*, UK: Labour Research Department. https://books.google.com/books?id=oN4wAAAAIAAJ&printsec=frontcover&source=gbs_ViewAPI#v=onepage&q&f=false

Laverty, Anthony; Smith, Peter; Pape, Utz; Mears, Alex; Wachter, Robert; and Millett, Christopher (2012) 'High-profile investigations into hospital safety problems in England did not prompt patients to switch providers', *Health Affairs*, vol. 31, no. 3, pp.593–601. https://doi.org/10.1377/hlthaff.2011.0810

Le Grand, Julian (2003) *Motivation, agency and public policy: Of knights and knaves, pawns and queens*, UK: Oxford University Press. https://doi.org/10.1093/0199266999.001.0001

Le Grand, Julian (2007) *The other invisible hand: Delivering public services through choice and competition*, UK: Princeton University Press. https://muse.jhu.edu/pub/267/book/30044

Lee, Simon (2009) *Boom and bust: The politics and legacy of Gordon Brown*, UK: Oneworld.

Lewis, Arthur (1949) *The principles of economic planning*, UK: George Allen & Unwin.

Lewis, Michael (2022) *The premonition*, UK: Penguin.

Lilly, Alice; Tetlow, Gemma; Davies, Oliver; and Pope, Thomas (2020) *The cost of Covid-19. The impact of coronavirus on the UK's public finances*, UK: Institute for Government. https://www.instituteforgovernment.org.uk/sites/default/files/publications/cost-of-covid19.pdf

Lisi, Domenico; Moscone, Francesco; Tosetti, Elisa; and Vinciotti. Veronica (2021) 'Hospital quality interdependence in a competitive institutional environment: Evidence from Italy', *Regional Science and Urban Economics*, vol. 89, 103696. https://doi.org/10.1016/j.regsciurbeco.2021.103696

Liu, Glory (2022) *Adam Smith's America: How a Scottish philosopher became an icon of American capitalism*, US: Princeton University Press. https://doi.org/10.1515/9780691240879

Lupton, Ruth; Hughes, Ceri; Peake-Jones, Sian; and Cooper, Kerris (2018) *City-region devolution in England*, SPDO Research Paper 2. https://www.nuffieldfoundation.org/wp-content/uploads/2020/01/SPDO-Research-Paper-2-min.pdf

Maarse, Hans; Jeurissen, Patrick; and Ruwaard, Dirk (2016) 'Results of the market-oriented reform in the Netherlands: A review', *Health Economics, Policy and Law*, vol. 11, no. 2, pp.161–78. https://doi.org/10.1017/S1744133115000353

MacGregor, Neil (2014) *Germany: Memories of a nation*, UK: Penguin.

Maddison, Angus (2006) *The World Economy*, France: Organisation for Economic Co-operation and Development (OECD), p.178. http://dx.doi.org/10.1787/486663055853

Malpass, Peter (2003) 'The wobbly pillar? Housing and the British postwar welfare state', *Journal of Social Policy*, vol. 32, no. 4, pp.589–606. https://doi.org/10.1017/S0047279403007177

Markovits, Daniel (2019) *The meritocracy trap*, UK: Penguin. [This is summarised in the STICERD Morishima Lecture at the London School of Economics, 8 May 2019 at https://www.lse.ac.uk/Events/Events-Assets/PDF/2019/02-ST/20190508-The-Meritocracy-Trap.pdf]

Marmot, Alexi (1981) 'The legacy of Le Corbusier and high-rise housing', *Built Environment*, vol. 7, no. 2, pp.82–95. https://www.jstor.org/stable/23288674

Marsh, Sue (2011) '1930s means test', *Diary of a Benefit Scrounger*, https://perma.cc/2A4U-WV9F

Marshall, Martin; Shekelle, Paul; Leatherman, Sheila; and Brook, Robert (2000) 'The public release of performance data: What do we expect to gain? A review of the evidence', *JAMA*, vol. 283, no. 14, pp.1866–74. https://doi.org/10.1001/jama.283.14.1866

Martin, Wolf (2023) *The crisis of democratic capitalism*, UK: Penguin.

Marx, Karl (1867/2004) 'The transformation of surplus value into capital', in *Capital* (Volume 1), translated by Ben Fowkes, UK: Penguin. [The 1887 edition edited by Friedrich Engels is available at https://www.marxists.org/archive/marx/works/download/pdf/Capital-Volume-I.pdf]

Masetti, Francesca (2019) 'Devolution in Scotland and the case study of the Scottish higher education system', *European Diversity & Autonomy Papers*, EDAP 01/2019. https://bia.unibz.it/esploro/outputs/journalArticle/Devolution-in-Scotland-and-the-Case/991005772704701241

Mattinson, Deborah (2020) *Beyond the red wall: Why Labour lost, How the Conservatives won and what will happen next?*, UK: Biteback.

Mayhew, Ken; Deer, Cécile; and Dua, Mehak (2004) 'The move to mass higher education in the UK: Many questions and some answers', *Oxford Review of Education*, vol. 30, no. 1, p.66. https://doi.org/10.1080/0305498042000190069

Mazzucato, Mariana (2018) *The value of everything: Making and taking in the global economy*, UK: Hachette.

McCulloch, Gary (2006) 'Cyril Norwood and the English tradition of education', *Oxford Review of Education*, vol. 32, no. 1, p.61. https://doi.org/10.1080/03054980500496460

McKibbin, Ross (1975) 'The economic policy of the second Labour government 1929–1931', *Past & Present*, vol. 68, no. 1, pp.95–123. https://doi.org/10.1093/past/68.1.95

McLellan, Alastair; Middleton, Jenni; and Godlee, Fiona (2012) 'Lansley's NHS "reforms"', *BMJ*, vol. 34, e709. https://doi.org/10.1136/bmj.e709

Meade, James (1948) *Planning and the price mechanism: The liberal socialist solution*, UK: George Allen & Unwin Ltd.

The Minority Report of the Poor Law Commission (1909).
https://wellcomecollection.org/works/qyhjfw7n

Minton, Anna (2022) 'From gentrification to sterilization? Building on big capital', *Architecture and Culture*, pp.1–21.
https:/doi.org/10.1080/20507828.2022.2105573

Mirowski, Philip and Plehwe, Dieter (eds) (2015) *The road from Mont Pèlerin: The making of the neoliberal thought collective, with a new preface*, UK: Harvard University Press. https://doi.org/10.4159/9780674495111

Moore, Mark (1995) *Creating public value: Strategic management in government*, US: Harvard University Press.

Moran, Michael (2003) *The British regulatory state: High modernism and hyper-innovation*, UK: Oxford University Press.
https://epdf.pub/the-british-regulatory-state-high-modernism-and -hyper-innovation.html

Muellbauer, John and Soskice, David (2022) *The Thatcher legacy. Lessons for the future of the UK economy*, UK: The Resolution Foundation.
https://perma.cc/7G84-87LN

Murphy, Richard; Scott-Clayton, Judith; and Wyness, Gill (2019) 'The end of free college in England: Implications for enrolments, equity, and quality', *Economics of Education Review*, vol. 71, pp.7–22.
https://doi.org/10.1016/j.econedurev.2018.11.007

National Audit Office (NAO) (2020) *The supply of personal protective equipment (PPE) during the COVID-19 pandemic.*
https://www.nao.org.uk/wp-content/uploads/2020/11/The-supply-of-per sonal-protective-equipment-PPE-during-the-COVID-19-pandemic.pdf

NAO (2022) *Investigation into the management of PPE contracts.*
https://www.nao.org.uk/reports/investigation-into-the-management-of -ppe-contracts/

NAO (2020) *The government's approach to test and trace in England –interim report.*
https://www.nao.org.uk/report/the-governments-approach-to-test-and -trace-in-england-interim-report/

NAO (2021) *Test and trace in England – progress update.*
https://www.nao.org.uk/report/test-and-trace-in-england-progress-update/

NHS England (2019) *The NHS long term plan*, UK: NHS England.
https://perma.cc/5VD3-WV5A

Nightingale, Florence (1863) *Notes of hospitals* (3rd edition), UK: Longman.
https://archive.org/details/notesonhospital01nighgoog/page/n10 /mode/2up

Norman, Jesse (2018) *Adam Smith: What he thought, and why it matters*, UK: Penguin.

North, Douglass (1990) *Institutions, institutional change and economic performance*, UK: Cambridge University Press. https://doi.org/10.1017/CBO9780511808678

Norwood, Sir Cyril (Chair) (1943) *Report of the Committee of the Secondary School Examinations Council appointed by the president of the Board of Education in 1941*, UK: HMSO. http://www.educationengland.org.uk/documents/norwood/norwood 1943.html

Nove, Alec (1972) *An economic history of the USSR*, UK: Penguin.

Nove, Alec (1961) *The Soviet economy*, UK: George Allen and Unwin.

Nozick, Robert (1974) *Anarchy, state, and utopia*, UK: Blackwell.

Nuti, Sabina, Federico Vola, Anna Bonini, and Milena Vainieri (2016) 'Making governance work in the health care sector: Evidence from a "natural experiment" in Italy', *Health Economics, Policy and Law*, vol. 11, no, 1, pp.17–38. https://doi.org/10.1017/S1744133115000067

Oliver, Adam (2017) *The origins of behavioural public policy*, UK: Cambridge University Press. https://doi.org/10.1017/9781108225120

Oliver, Adam (2018) 'Do unto others: On the importance of reciprocity in public administration', *The American Review of Public Administration*, vol. 48, no. 4, pp.279–90. https://doi.org/10.1177/0275074016686826

Oliver, Adam (2019) *Reciprocity and the art of behavioural public policy*, UK: Cambridge University Press. https://doi.org/10.1017/9781108647755

Oppenheimer, Melanie and Deakin, Nicholas (eds) (2011) *Beveridge and voluntary action in Britain and the wider British world*, UK: Manchester University Press. https://hdl.handle.net/1959.11/9277

Ostrom, Elinor (1990) *Governing the commons: The evolution of institutions for collective action*, UK: Cambridge University Press. https://doi.org/10.1017/CBO9781316423936

Parildar, Ufuk; Perara, Rafael; and Ok, Jason (2021) *Excess mortality across countries in 2020*. https://www.cebm.net/covid-19/excess-mortality-across-countries-in -2020/

Parker, George; Cookson, Clive; Neville, Sarah; Payne, Sebastian; Hodgson, Camilla; Gross, Anna and Hughes, Laura (2020) 'Inside Westminster's coronavirus blame game'. *Financial Times*, 16 July. https://perma.cc/E8CS-3KVZ

Paxman, Jeremy (2021) *Black gold: The history of how coal made Britain*, UK: HarperCollins.

Peden, George (1993) 'The road to and from Gairloch: Lloyd George, unemployment, inflation, and the "Treasury View" in 1921', *Twentieth Century British History*, vol. 4, no. 3, pp.224–49. https://doi.org/10.1093/tcbh/4.3.224

Peden, George (2003) 'British Treasury responses to the Keynesian revolution, 1925–1939', *Annals of the Society for the History of Economic Thought*, vol. 44, pp.31–44. https://doi.org/10.11498/jshet1963.44.31

Piketty, Thomas (2020) *Capital and ideology*, US: Harvard University Press. https://doi.org/10.4159/9780674245075

Pisano, Gary; Sadun, Raffaella; and Zanini, Michele (2020) 'Lessons from Italy's response to coronavirus', *Harvard Business Review*. https://perma.cc/C4RG-2UQW

Pistor, Katharina (2019) *The code of capital. How the law creates wealth and inequality*, US: Princeton University Press. https://muse.jhu.edu/pub/267/monograph/book/64439

Powell, Christopher (1974) 'Fifty years of progress', *Built Environment*, vol. 3, no. 10, pp.532–35. https://www.jstor.org/stable/44398033

Power, Anne (2012) 'Social inequality, disadvantaged neighbourhoods and transport deprivation: An assessment of the historical influence of housing policies', *Journal of Transport Geography*, vol. 21, p.42. https://doi.org/10.1016/j.jtrangeo.2012.01.016

Propper, Carol (1989) 'An econometric analysis of the demand for private health insurance in England and Wales', *Applied Economics*, vol. 21, no. 6, pp.777–92. https://doi.org/10.1080/758520273

Public Accounts Committee (House of Commons) (2023) *Department of Health and Social Care annual report and accounts 2021–22*, Sixty-Second Report of Session 2022–23. HC 997 UK: HMSO, p.3. https://committees.parliament.uk/publications/40738/documents/198470/default/

Putnam, Robert; Leonardi, Robert; and Nanetti, Rafaella (1992) *Making democracy work: Civic traditions in modern Italy*, US: Princeton University Press. https://doi.org/10.1515/9781400820740

Raikes, Luke (2022) *Levelling up? Lessons from Germany*, UK: Fabian Society. https://fabians.org.uk/publication/levelling-up/

Rajan, Raghuram (2005) *Has financial development made the world riskier?* NBER Working Paper Series, no. 11728, US: National Bureau of Economic Research. https://www.nber.org/papers/w11728.pdf

Rajan, Raghuram (2011) *Fault lines*, US: Princeton University Press. https://doi.org/10.1515/9781400839803

Ramsay, J.H. Rolland (1994) 'A king, a doctor, and a convenient death', *BMJ*, vol. 308, p.1445 https://doi.org/10.1136/bmj.308.6941.1445

Rawls, John (1973) *A Theory of Justice*, UK: Oxford University Press.

Reeves, Aaron; Friedman, Sam; Rahal, Charles; and Flemmen, Magne (2017) 'The decline and persistence of the old boy: Private schools and elite recruitment 1897 to 2016', *American Sociological Review*, vol. 82, no. 6, pp.1139–66. https://doi.org/10.1177/0003122417735742

Reinhardt, Uwe (2001) 'Can efficiency in health care be left to the market?' *Journal of Health Politics, Policy and Law*, vol. 26, no, 5, pp.967–92. https://muse.jhu.edu/article/15621

Riddell, Sheila; Blackburn, Lucy; and Minty Sarah (2013) *Widening access to higher education: Scotland in UK comparative perspective*, UK: University of Edinburgh. http://www.docs.hss.ed.ac.uk/education/creid/NewsEvents/52_v_CoWA_Paper.pdf

Rimfeld, Kaili; Malanchini, Margherita; Krapohl, Eva; Hannigan, Laurie; Dale, Philip; and Plomin, Robert (2018) 'The stability of educational achievement across school years is largely explained by genetic factors', *NPJ Science of Learning*, vol. 3, no. 1, pp.1–10. https://doi.org/10.1038/s41539-018-0030-0

Robbins, Lionel (1971) *Autobiography of an economist*, London: Macmillan.

Rogers, William (Chair) (1986) *Report to the president by the Presidential Commission on the Space Shuttle Challenger Accident* (Report of the Rogers Commission). https://sma.nasa.gov/SignificantIncidents/assets/rogers_commission_report.pdf

Romaniuk, Anna; Osborne, Catherine; Rainsford, Emily; and Taylor, Abigail (2020) *Understanding the policy-making processes behind local growth strategies in England*, UK: Industrial Strategy Council, pp.6–7. https://industrialstrategycouncil.org/understanding-policy-making-processes-behind-local-growth-strategiesengland

Rothschild, Emma (1994) 'Adam Smith and the invisible hand', *The American Economic Review*, vol. 84, no. 2, pp.319–22. https://www.jstor.org/stable/2117851

Rothstein, Bo (2015) *The Quality of Government Institute. Report for the first ten years of a research programme at University of Gothenburg.* https://www.gu.se/en/research/the-quality-of-government-institute

Rothstein, Bo (2021) *Controlling corruption: The social contract approach*, US: Oxford University Press. https://doi.org/10.1093/oso/9780192894908.001.0001

Sandel, Michael (2012) *What money can't buy: The moral limits of markets*, UK: Macmillan.

Sasse, Tom; Haddon, Catherine; and Nice, Alex (2020) *Science advice in a crisis*, UK: Institute for Government. https://www.instituteforgovernment.org.uk/publications/science -advice-crisis

Saviano, Roberto (2006) *Gomorrah*, UK: Pan Macmillan.

Saviano, Roberto (2016) *Zero Zero Zero*, UK: Penguin.

Scally, Gabriel (2020) 'The demise of Public Health England', *BMJ*, vol. 370: m3263, p.1. http://dx.doi.org/10.1136/bmj.m3263

Schneider, Eric; Shah, Arnav; Doty, Michelle; Tikkanen, Roosa; Fields, Katharine; and Williams II, Reginald (2021) *Mirror, mirror 2021. Reflecting poorly: Health care in the U.S. compared to other high-income countries*, US: Commonwealth Fund. https://perma.cc/PNU2-3BFM

Secretaries of State for Health, Wales, Northern Ireland and Scotland (1989) *Working for patients*, Cm 555, UK: The Stationery Office.

Secretary of State for Health (SSH) (2000) *The NHS plan*. Cm 4818-I, UK: The Stationery Office.

SSH (2010) *Equity and excellence: Liberating the NHS*, Cm 7881, UK: The Stationery Office. https://assets.publishing.service.gov.uk/government/uploads/system /uploads/attachment_data/file/213823/dh_117794.pdf

SSH (2001) *Learning from Bristol – Report of the public inquiry into children's heart surgery at the Bristol Royal Infirmary* (The Kennedy Report), CM 5207(1), UK: The Stationery Office. https://webarchive.nationalarchives.gov.uk/ukgwa/20090811143758 /http://www.bristol-inquiry.org.uk/index.htm

SSH (2002) *Delivering the NHS plan*, Cm 5503. UK: The Stationery Office. https://www.nuffieldtrust.org.uk/sites/default/files/2019-11/delivering thenhsplan.pdf

SSH (2010) *Independent inquiry into care provided by Mid Staffordshire NHS Foundation Trust January 2005–March 2009*, volume I (Chaired by Robert Francis QC). https://assets.publishing.service.gov.uk/government/uploads/system /uploads/attachment_data/file/279109/0375_i.pdf,

SSH (2013) *Report of the Mid Staffordshire NHS Foundation Trust Public Inquiry*, UK: The Stationery Office. https://assets.publishing.service.gov.uk/government/uploads/system /uploads/attachment_data/file/279124/0947.pdf

Secretary of State for Levelling Up, Housing and Communities (2022) *Levelling up the United Kingdom*, CP 604, UK: HMSO. https://www.gov.uk/government/publications/levelling-up-the-united -kingdom

Sekora, Michael (2010) *An unfinished legacy: President Reagan and the Socrates Project*, https://perma.cc/G7CS-QDCK

Senge, Peter (2006) *The fifth discipline: The art and practice of the learning organization*, UK: Currency.

Sharp, Thomas (1940) *Town planning*, UK: Pelican.

Shleifer, Andrei (1998) 'State versus private ownership', *Journal of Economic Perspectives*, vol. 12, no. 4, pp.133–50. https://doi.org/10.1257/jep.12.4.133

Sibieta, Luke; Chowdry, Haroon; Muriel. Alastair (2008) *Level playing field? The implications of school funding*, UK: CfBT Education Trust. https://ifs.org.uk/docs/level_playing.pdf

Simons, Henry (1934) *Economic policy for a free society*, US: University Press of Chicago.

Simons, Richard (1953) 'The British Coal Industry-A Failure of Private Enterprise', *The Historian*, vol. 16, no. 1, p.15. https://doi.org/10.1111/j.1540-6563.1953.tb00150.x

Skidelsky, Robert (1992) *John Maynard Keynes: The economist as saviour, 1920–1937*, vol. 2, UK: Macmillan.

Skidelsky, Robert (2001) *John Maynard Keynes: Fighting for Britain, 1937–46*, vol. 3, US: Viking.

Smee, Clive (2005) *Speaking truth to power: Two decades of analysis in the Department of Health*, UK: Radcliffe Press.

Smith, Adam (1776/1976) *The wealth of nations*, US: University of Chicago Press. (An edition published by Ryerson University Toronto is available at https://openlibrary-repo.ecampusontario.ca/jspui/bitstream/123456789 /1181/5/An-Inquiry-Into-the-Nature-and-Causes-of-the-Wealth-of -Nations-1645639496.pdf)

Smith, Judith and Curry, Natasha (2011) 'Commissioning', Chapter 3 in Mays, Nicholas; Dixon Anna; and Jones, Lorelei (eds) *Understanding New Labour's market reforms of the English NHS*, UK: King's Fund, pp.30–51. https://www.kingsfund.org.uk/sites/default/files/New-Labours-market

-reforms-Chapter-3-Commissioning-Judith-Smith-Natasha-Curry
-September-2011.pdf

Soll, Jacob (2022) *Free market: The history of an idea*, US: Basic Books.

Stansbury, Anna; Turner, Daniel; and Balls, Ed (2023) *Tackling the UK's regional economic inequality: Binding constraints and avenues for policy intervention*, M-RCBG Associate Working Paper Series, US: Harvard University's DASH repository.
https://nrs.harvard.edu/URN-3:HUL.INSTREPOS:37374470

Stevens, Rosemary (2009) *Medical practice in modern England: the impact of specialization and state medicine*, US: Transaction.

Taleb, Nassim (2007) *The black swan: The impact of the highly improbable*, UK: Penguin.

Tawney, Richard (1920) 'The British coal industry and the question of nationalization', *The Quarterly Journal of Economics*, vol. 35, no. 1, p.65.
https://doi.org/10.2307/1883570

Tawney, Richard (1952) *Equality*, UK: George Allen and Unwin.
https://archive.org/details/in.ernet.dli.2015.275419/page/n3/mode/2up

Tiebout, Charles (1956) 'A pure theory of local expenditures', *Journal of Political Economy*, vol. 64, no. 5, p.422.
http://links.jstor.org/sici?sici=0022-3808%28195610%2964%3A5%3C416%3AAPTOLE%3E2.0.CO%3B2-P

Timmins, Nicholas (2012) *Never again? The story of the Health and Social Care Act 2012: A study in coalition government and policy making*, UK: Institute for Government & The King's Fund.
https://www.kingsfund.org.uk/sites/default/files/field/field_publication_file/never-again-story-health-social-care-nicholas-timmins-jul12.pdf

Timmins, Nicholas (2016) *Universal Credit: From disaster to recovery?* UK: Institute for Government.
https://www.instituteforgovernment.org.uk/publication/report/universal-credit-disaster-recovery

Timmins, Nicholas (2017) *The five giants: A biography of the welfare state* (3rd paperback edition), UK: HarperCollins.

Tookey, Mark (2000) *The Labour Party and nationalisation from Attlee to Wilson, 1945–1968: Beyond the commanding heights*, UK: Durham theses, Durham University. http://etheses.dur.ac.uk/4522/

Tooze, Adam (2018) *Crashed: How a decade of financial crises changed the world*, UK: Penguin.

Travaglino, Giovanni; Abrams, Dominic; and De Moura, Georgina (2016) 'Men of honor don't talk: The relationship between masculine honor and social activism against criminal organizations in Italy', *Political Psychology*, vol. 37, no. 2, pp.183–99. https://doi.org/10.1111/pops.12226

Tuohy, Carolyn (1999) *Accidental logics: The dynamics of change in the health care arena in the United States, Britain, and Canada*, UK: Oxford University Press.

Turner, Alwyn (2010) *Rejoice! Rejoice! Britain in the 1980s*, UK: Aurum Press.

UK Covid-19 Inquiry (2023) *Update: UK Covid-19 Inquiry to begin hearing evidence in June for its first investigation*. https://covid19.public-inquiry.uk/news/update-uk-covid-19-inquiry-to -begin-hearing-evidence-in-june-for-its-first-investigation/

Van Noorden, Richard (2022) 'COVID death tolls: scientists acknowledge errors in WHO estimates', *Nature*, vol. 606, no. 7913, pp.242–44. https://www.nature.com/articles/d41586-022-01526-0

Vaughan, Diane (1990) 'Autonomy, interdependence, and social control: NASA and the space shuttle Challenger', *Administrative Science Quarterly*, vol. 35, no. 2, p.247. https://doi.org/10.2307/2393390

Vaughan, Diane (1996) *The Challenger launch decision. Risky technology, culture, and deviance at NASA*, US: University of Chicago Press.

Wapshott, Nicholas (2011) *Keynes Hayek: The clash that defined modern economics*, UK: WW Norton & Company.

Ward, Stephanie (2008) 'The means test and the unemployed in South Wales and the north-east of England, 1931–1939', *Labour History Review*, vol. 73, no. 1, p.114. https://doi.org/10.1179/174581808X279136

Warwick-Ching, Anthony (2020) *Stolen heritage: The strange death of industrial England*, UK: Troubador.

Watkin, Brian (1975) *Documents on health and social services. 1834 to the present day*, UK: Methuen.

Webster, Charles (1991) *Bevan on the NHS*, UK: Wellcome Unit for the History of Medicine.

Webster, Charles (1998) *The National Health Service: A political history*, UK: Oxford University Press.

Wieler, Lothar; Rexroth, Ute; and Gottschalk, René (2020) 'Emerging COVID-19 success story: Germany's strong enabling environment', *Our World in Data*. https://ourworldindata.org/covid-exemplar-germany-2020

Wellings, Richard (2014) 'The privatisation of the UK railway industry: An experiment in railway structure', *Economic Affairs*, vol. 34, no. 2, pp.255–66. https://doi.org/10.1111/ecaf.12083

West, Anne and Hind, Audrey (2016) *Secondary school admissions in London 2001 to 2015: Compliance, complexity and control.* http://eprints.lse.ac.uk/66368/

Williamson, Oliver (1975) *Markets and hierarchies: Analysis and antitrust implications,* UK: The Free Press.

Williamson, Oliver (1985) *The economic institutions of capitalism. Firms, markets, relational contracting,* UK: The Free Press.

Wilson, David (2015) *Does altruism exist? Culture, genes, and the welfare of others,* UK: Yale University Press. https://doi.org/10.12987/9780300206753

Wilson, Deborah; and Piebalga, Anete (2008) 'Performance measures, ranking and parental choice: An analysis of the English school league tables', *International Public Management Journal,* vol. 11, no. 3, pp.344–66. https://doi.org/10.1080/10967490802301336

Wilson, Wendy and Barton, Cassie (2022) *What is affordable housing?* UK: House of Commons Briefing Paper. https://researchbriefings.files.parliament.uk/documents/CBP-7747/CBP -7747.pdf

Witmer, Helen Leland (1931) 'Some effects of the English Unemployment Insurance Acts on the number of unemployed relieved under the Poor Law', *The Quarterly Journal of Economics,* vol. 45, no. 2, pp.262–88. https://doi.org/10.2307/1885475

Wolf, Martin (2023) *The crisis of democratic capitalism,* UK: Penguin.

Wolmar, Christian (2022) *British Rail: A new history,* UK: Michael Joseph.

World Health Organization (WHO) (2022) *Global excess deaths associated with COVID-19* (modelled estimates). https://www.who.int/data/sets/global-excess-deaths-associated-with -covid-19-modelled-estimates